Recommended Books in Spanish for Children and Young Adults

2004–2008

OTHER SCARECROW TITLES BY ISABEL SCHON

Basic Collection of Children's Books in Spanish
The Best of the Latino Heritage
The Best of the Latino Heritage, 1996–2002
A Bicultural Heritage
Books in Spanish for Children and Young Adults
Books in Spanish for Children and Young Adults, Series II
Books in Spanish for Children and Young Adults, Series III
Books in Spanish for Children and Young Adults, Series IV
Books in Spanish for Children and Young Adults, Series V
Books in Spanish for Children and Young Adults, Series VI
A Hispanic Heritage
A Hispanic Heritage, Series II
A Hispanic Heritage, Series III
A Hispanic Heritage, Series IV
A Latino Heritage, Series V
Recommended Books in Spanish for Children and Young Adults,
    1991–1995
Recommended Books in Spanish for Children and Young Adults,
    1996 through 1999
Recommended Books in Spanish for Children and Young Adults,
    2000 through 2004

Recommended Books in Spanish for Children and Young Adults

2004–2008

Isabel Schon

The Scarecrow Press, Inc.
Lanham, Maryland • Toronto • Plymouth, UK
2009

SCARECROW PRESS, INC.

Published in the United States of America
by Scarecrow Press, Inc.
A wholly owned subsidiary of
The Rowman & Littlefield Publishing Group, Inc.
4501 Forbes Boulevard, Suite 200, Lanham, Maryland 20706
www.scarecrowpress.com

Estover Road
Plymouth PL6 7PY
United Kingdom

Ref
Z
1037.7
.S387
2009

British Library Cataloguing in Publication Information Available

Library of Congress Cataloging-in-Publication Data

Schon, Isabel.
  Recommended books in Spanish for children and young adults, 2004–2008 /
Isabel Schon.
      p. cm.
  Includes bibliographical references and index.
  ISBN-13: 978-0-8108-6386-6 (cloth : alk. paper)
  ISBN-10: 0-8108-6386-3 (cloth : alk. paper)
  ISBN-13: 978-0-8108-6387-3 (ebook)
  ISBN-10: 0-8108-6387-1 (ebook)
1. Children's literature, Spanish—Bibliography. 2. Children's literature, Spanish
American—Bibliography. 3. Young adult literature, Spanish—Bibliography.
4. Young adult literature, Spanish American—Bibliography. 5. Children's
literature—Translations into Spanish—Bibliography. 6. Young adult literature—
Translations into Spanish—Bibliography. 7. Children's libraries—Book lists.
8. Children—Books and reading. I. Title.
  Z1037.7.S387 2009
  [PN1009.A1]
  011.62—dc22   2008033390

∞™ The paper used in this publication meets the minimum requirements of
American National Statndard for Information Sciences—Permanence of Paper
for Printed Library Materials, ANSI/NISO Z39.48-1992.
Manufactured in the United States of America.

To Dr. Fernando Arizmendi, muchas gracias.

To Eric and Alex Pitrofsky, con mucho cariño.

To my husband, Ricardo, siempre.

Contents

Introduction

Recommended Books in Spanish for Children and Young Adults: 2004–2008, whether used for the development and support of an existing library collection or for the creation of a new library serving Spanish-speaking young readers, includes 1231 books in print that deserve to be read by Spanish-speaking children and young adults (or those who wish to learn Spanish). These books have been selected because of their quality of art and writing, presentation of material and appeal to the intended audience, and support the informational, educational, recreational, and personal needs of Spanish speakers from preschool through the twelfth grade.

This book is arranged in the following sections: Reference Books; Nonfiction Books, which includes Philosophy, Psychology, Religion, Social Science, Folklore, Language, Science, Technology, Health and Medicine, The Arts, Recreation and Sports, Literature, Poetry, Geography, History and Biography; Publishers' Series; and Fiction Books, which includes Easy Books, General Fiction and Graphic Novels. Completing the volume is an appendix of dealers of books in Spanish, followed by author, title, and subject indexes. Each book is listed under its main entry, which is usually the author. For some books, however, the main entry is under the title or series title.

To assist the non-Spanish-speaking selector, I have translated each title into English and provided an extensive annotation. Also, I have indicated a tentative grade level for each book, but the individual student's Spanish reading ability, interest, taste and purpose should be the main criteria for determining the true level of each book. In addition, I have provided a price for each book. It is important to note, however, that prices of books in Spanish definitely will vary with dealer and time of purchase.

All of the books reviewed were still in print as of June 2008. Unfortunately, as any experienced teacher or librarian knows, it is impossible to determine with any degree of certainty the availability of books in Spanish. Selectors are encouraged to check with various dealers (in the United States and abroad) before assuming that a book is out of print.

The selector will note that most of the books were published in the United States, Spain, Mexico, Venezuela, and Argentina. These countries are now publishing the best books in Spanish for children and young adults.

Selectors will undoubtedly discover some gaps in this recommended collection of books in Spanish for children and young adults. Omission of some important topics is due to unavailability, nonexistence at the time of compilation, or by my own lack of awareness.

I wish to express my appreciation for their invaluable assistance and marvelous cooperation to Karen Irwin, María Zulma Cardona, Pauline Robbins, Pamela Castillo, Walter Evans, Yoko Kakimoto, Miguel Padilla, Joan Bannister, Christina Douglas, Natalie Diamond, and Professor David Foster.

Reference

Atlases

Atlas enciclopédico infantil. (The Children's Visual World Atlas) Translated by Alberto Jiménez Rioja. León: Everest, 2005. 176p. ISBN: 84-241-1255-5. $31.99. Gr. 3–6.

Basic information about the Earth and the continents and countries of the world are presented through 100 easy-to-read maps and more than 1500 color drawings, charts, and photographs. Originally published by Weldon Owen, Australia, this large-format publication includes numerous sidebars with such facts as population, history at a glance, natural resources and important people and events.

Dalby, Elizabeth. *Mi primer atlas. (My First Atlas)* Translated by Pilar Dunster. Tulsa: EDC Publishing, 2004. 64p. ISBN: 0-7460-6392-X. $12.95. Gr. 3–5.

Full color maps, drawings and photographs and a brief text, clear captions, and informative sidebars introduce readers to the geography of the world and to unique customs and traditions worldwide. From a Mayan temple, to an Inuit hunter from Canada, to the Amazonian forest, to the Himalaya Mountains in Asia, to the Sahara desert in Africa, this is an enticing primer to maps and the world. Cyber-enthusiasts will appreciate the publisher's numerous Web links with supplemental information and games that complement this book.

Disney Atlas. (Disney Atlas) León: Everest, 2005. 96p. ISBN: 968-893-104-7. $14.99. Gr. 2–3.

1

With simple and most understandable explanations, this basic atlas introduces the young to the universe, the solar system, the Earth, the continents and highlights important facts about selected countries—e.g., diamonds in *Botsuana* (Botswana), bananas in Honduras, oil in *Arabia Saudí* (Saudi Arabia), the Alps in Switzerland. Despite the cutesy and at times even corny Disney characters, the uncluttered maps, colorful illustrations and comprehensive index make this a useful primer.

Dictionaries

Barron's Spanish-English Dictionary/Diccionario Español-Inglés. Hauppauge, NY: Barron's, 2006. 1309p. ISBN: 978-0-7641-3329-9. pap. $16.99. Gr. 8–adult.

This is indeed a most practical bilingual dictionary with more than 100,000 entries of current vocabulary in English and Spanish including excellent examples of words used in context to illustrate idiomatic usage. In addition, it provides pronunciation in both languages with Spanish-American pronunciation given first, followed by *ceceo*, generally associated with Spain. Also, users will appreciate the numerous culture notes, grammar guides and verb conjugation lists. Spanish learners will welcome the inclusion of such Mexicanisms as *ándale*, expressions such as *¡vete a freír churros!* and the use of *vosear* and *vosotros* in Latin America; English learners will note the inclusion of such expressions as "f-word," "yucky" and "zap." With a plasticized cover, this paperback dictionary includes an e-ticket for a free downloadable electronic dictionary.

Bosque, Ignacio. *Redes: Diccionario combinatorio del español contemporáneo. (Webs: Integrative Dictionary of Contemporary Spanish)* Madrid: SM, 2004. 1839p. ISBN: 84-675-0276-2. $29.95. Gr. 9–adult.

The purpose of this dictionary is not to define words nor to offer a selection of synonyms; rather to explain how words are combined in Spanish and the context in which they are used. Serious students of the language will appreciate numerous examples of current unusual and idiosyncratic words and phrases and how these are combined to determine meaning.

Collins Spanish Concise Dictionary. New York: HarperCollins, 2006. 1193p. ISBN: 978-0-06-057578-6. pap. $15.00. Gr. 6–adult.

In an easy-to-read, two-color format, this concise bilingual paperback dictionary includes more than 190,000 entries and translations as well as a clear 315-page guide to Spanish grammar with simple examples and idiomatic usage. Although this gives priority to everyday contemporary language and expressions, its emphasis is on British English and Peninsular Spanish. Users should note that the pronunciation given is for Castilian Spanish and that entries highlight aspects of life and culture in Britain, e.g., the United Kingdom's "by-election," "colour," and "High Court" and from Spain *comunidad autónoma, estanco,* and *selectividad,* rather than from the United States or Latin America.

Collins Spanish Dictionary. New York: HarperCollins, 484p. ISBN: 978-0-06-113102-8. pap. $5.99. Gr. 6–adult.

Revised with American English and Latin-American Spanish usages, this pocket size paperback is just right for those seeking a portable, compact bilingual dictionary. With more than 40,000 entries and 70,000 translations, it includes informative culture notes, about the United States and Mexico, such as "Pledge of Allegiance" and *maquiladora.* Especially noteworthy are the notes on English and Spanish words that are commonly confused, such as a framed note following "exit" stating "[!]Be careful not to translate exit by the Spanish word *éxito.*" And "[!]*No confundir 'gentil' con la palabra inglesa 'gentle'.*" (Do not confuse *gentil* with the English word "gentle.")

Diccionario de sinónimos y antónimos. (Dictionary of Synonyms and Antonyms) Madrid: Espasa, 2005. 1225p. ISBN: 84-239-2170-0. $47.95. Gr. 8–adult.

With more than 30,000 entries and 200,000 synonyms and antonyms in an easy-to-use A-to-Z dictionary format, this thesaurus of the Spanish language provides fast access to numerous word choices including current terms and idiomatic expressions.

Diccionario general de la lengua española. (General Dictionary of the Spanish Language) Barcelona: Edebé, 2005. 1455p. ISBN: 84-236-71348. $22.95. Gr. 8–adult.

With more than 30,000 entries and a clear, easy-to-read format and design, this is a good basic Spanish-language dictionary. Contemporary speakers will appreciate the inclusion of current neologisms such as chat, e-mail, *móvil, videoteléfono,* as well as colloquial expressions.

Also useful are the grammar notes and sidebars as well as the informative appendices that include such topics as common language errors and the use of computer spell checkers. One caveat: most examples consider only Peninsular Spanish usage.

Diccionario enciclopédico 2004. (Encyclopedic Dictionary 2004) México: Larousse, 2003. 1826p. ISBN: 970-22-0920-X. $38.00. Gr. 7–adult.

Divided in two parts—dictionary of the Spanish language and biographical/geographic entries—this one-volume encyclopedic dictionary with more than 90,000 entries and 5,000 color illustrations, charts, and maps will be most useful to those that can afford only one reference source in Spanish. With information up to 2003 and just as attractively designed as its predecessors (including the same limitations—e.g., four pages devoted to Spain, two to the United States), users will appreciate the wide coverage, neologisms and Latin Americanisms. Although some readers may object to the small size font, most will appreciate its conciseness.

Diccionario escolar de la lengua española. (Student Dictionary of the Spanish Language) León: Everest, 2005. 1183p. ISBN: 84-241-1107-9. pap. $30.99. Gr. 5–9.

Especially designed for students, this easy-to-use, plastic-covered dictionary with more than 25,000 entries includes synonyms, antonyms, simple definitions and illustrative examples. Spanish-language learners will appreciate the verb conjugation and other special topic charts such as *Atmósfera* (Atmosphere) and *Los edificios más altos* (The Tallest Buildings), as well as the grammatical and literary appendices. Includes a CD-ROM.

Diccionario lengua española. (Spanish Language Dictionary) Barcelona: Edebé, 2006. 937p. ISBN: 84-236-6807-X. pap. $16.99. Gr. 3–7.

Especially designed for elementary students, this clearly labeled, easy-to-use Spanish dictionary includes more than 25,000 definitions, 32 color charts, numerous grammatical sidebars with usage explanations about topics such as punctuation, part-of-speech labels, accents, prepositions, synonyms, antonyms, and prepositions, as well as always needed verb conjugation charts. Beginning dictionary users will appreciate the easy-to-understand introduction, clear notes and illustrative examples. An attractive plasticized cover adds appeal to this paperback dictionary. One caveat: It is obvious that most words and expressions considered offensive, vulgar or off-color have been excluded. What a shame!

Diccionario práctico: Sinónimos, antónimos y parónimos. (Practical Dictionary: Synonyms, Antonyms and Paronyms) León: Everest, 2005. 624p. ISBN: 84-241-1218-0. pap. $12.99. Gr. 7–adult.

With more than 8,000 entries and 70,000 synonyms, antonyms and paronyms, this easy-to-use paperback thesaurus is designed especially for students and teachers. It also includes part-of-speech labels in an easy-to-read design.

Dragoni, Giorgio, and others. *Quién es quién en la ciencia. (Who is Who in the Sciences)* Translated by Juan Vivanco and others. Madrid: Acento, 2004. 2 vols. ISBN: 84-483-0781-X (Vol. 1); 84-483-0780-1 (Vol. II). $49.99. Gr. 9–adult.

Originally published in Italy, this dictionary includes biographical entries of outstanding world scientists and a description of their principal achievements. From one-paragraph entries—Abbe, Ernst (1840–1905)—to six pages devoted to Einstein, Albert (1879–1955), to the Austrian chemist Zsigmondy, Richard Adolf (1865–1929), this is a panoramic view of recognized scientists and their theories or contributions. The lack of illustrations, of any kind, limits its use to serious students.

Ferrera Cuesta, Carlos. *Diccionario de historia de España. (Dictionary of Spanish History)* 552p. ISBN: 84-206-5898-7. $8.99.

Gómez Espelosín, Francisco Javier. *Diccionario de términos del mundo antiguo. (Dictionary of Terms of the Ancient World)* 226p. ISBN: 84-206-5900-2. Ea. vol.: (Biblioteca de Consulta) Madrid: Alianza, 2005. pap. $10.99. Gr. 9–adult.

Designed as practical aids, not as exhaustive reference tools, these handy paperback publications will assist history students in the understanding of basic terminology and facts through brief easy-to-understand entries in alphabetical order. More than 1300 events, institutions, concepts and biographical reviews, such as *franquismo, leyenda negra* (Black legend) and *Carlos I* (Charles I), are included in *Diccionario de historia de España.* References to the political, cultural, religious and social life of the Greek, Roman, Mesopotamian and Egyptian ancient worlds, such as *civitas, doreai, Hibernia,* and *sine nobilitate*, are concisely explained in *Diccionario de términos del mundo antiguo.*

Gran diccionario inglés/español, español/inglés: Larousse. (Great Dictionary English/Spanish, Spanish/English: Larousse) Barcelona: Larousse, 2006. 1668p. ISBN: 84-8332-668-X. $56.95. Gr. 8–adult.

With a wide range of idiomatic uses and expressions, this bilingual dictionary includes more than 400,000 translations and more than 250,000 words. Although it also includes American English and Latin-American Spanish words and expressions, users will note an emphasis on British English and Peninsular Spanish words and cultural notes. For example, it describes "A levels" (United Kingdom exams), *colour* followed by "color," "football," (first definition "soccer," second "American football"), *ONCE* (Spanish Association for the Blind) and "computer" (first *ordenador* (Spain), second *computadora* (Latin America). Students of both languages will appreciate the tables of irregular English verbs, Spanish verbs, and English and Spanish pronunciation guides as well as the clear labels and design.

Nuevo Espasa ilustrado. (New Illustrated Espasa) Madrid: Espasa, 2005. 1400p. ISBN: 84-670-1664-7. $29.95. Gr. 6–adult.

With more than 90,000 entries and 3,500 color illustrations, charts and maps, this is a basic attractive encyclopedic dictionary. It includes up-to-date biographical and geographical entries and, especially useful to Spanish learners, tables with the inflected forms of irregular verbs.

Nuevo Océano Uno: Diccionario enciclopédico color. (New Océano One: Encyclopedic Color Dictionary) Barcelona: Océano, 2006. 1784p. ISBN: 84-494-3063-1. $70.00. Gr. 8–12.

More than 82,000 entries and 8000 color illustrations, maps and charts make this updated encyclopedic dictionary a most useful addition to schools and libraries serving Spanish speakers. Especially noteworthy are the numerous contemporary scientific and technological entries as well as the lexical and encyclopedic information about Hispanic America. Users will also appreciate the good-quality paper, thematic acetate overlays and informative appendices. A CD-ROM is included.

El pequeño Larousse ilustrado. (The Small Illustrated Larousse) Barcelona: Larousse, 2006. 1824p. ISBN: 84-8332-858-5. $41.95. Gr. 7–adult.

Like its well-known predecessors, this updated encyclopedic dictionary with more than 90,000 entries, 5000 color photographs, drawings and charts and 320 maps is the long-time favorite of those who can't afford a Spanish encyclopedia. Especially noteworthy are the current scientific and technical terms and the numerous neologisms, lexical and encyclopedic entries from both sides of the Atlantic, as well as the clear (albeit small) typography, color photos and drawings. The first part includes the dictionary, followed by the encyclopedic entries—biographic, geographic, scientific, historical and current events.

Pérez Martínez, Herón. *Refranero mexicano. (Mexican Proverbs)* Mexico: Fondo de Cultura Económica, 2004. 458p. ISBN: 968-16-7070-1. pap. $13.95. Gr. 9–adult.

Arranged in alphabetical order, this scholarly compendium of proverbs that originated in Mexico or came from other countries but are now in widespread use in Mexico is a dream come true for students of proverbs. From short sayings that express basic truths such as *lo caído, caído,* to practical precepts such as *negocioplaticado, negocio no arreglado* students will find thoughtful explanations, well-organized themes, including variants and grammatical structures that clarify meaning.

Real Academia Española/Asociación de Academias de la Lengua Española. *Diccionario panhispánico de dudas. (Panhispanic Dictionary of Doubts)* Bogotá: Santillana/Real Academia Española, 2005. 848p. ISBN: 958-704-368-5. $29.95. Gr. 9–adult.

This long-awaited dictionary of doubts provides expert usage guidance based on up-to-date recommendations from the twenty-two *Academias* from the Spanish-speaking world, the universally accepted arbiters of the lexicon and semantics of the Spanish language. It guides users through the most common doubts, including regional variants, regarding proper usage with clear and precise definitions and examples. In addition to grammatical issues, students of the language will especially appreciate the emphasis on the current linguistic concerns of speakers from all the Spanish-speaking regions of the world. For example, it provides valuable cross-references from such unnecessary Anglicisms as *accesar* to the proper Spanish verb *acceder* and clarifies that the verb *chequear* is now an accepted term, although it reminds users of Spanish equivalents: *control, examen, inspección, comprobación y reconocimiento (médico),* or *revisión (médica).*

¿Sabes quién? (Do You Know Who?) 3 vols. Barcelona: Océano, 2005.
  872p. ISBN: 84-494-1931-X. $67.00 Gr. 3–6.

    Profusely illustrated with color photographs, drawings and charts,
this three-volume biographical dictionary highlights the achievements
of more than 400 distinguished men (and a few women) throughout
world history. Volume I includes notables in history and science; volume II, literature, architecture and sports; volume III, inventions, music
and art. The brevity of each entry—one or two pages—and informative
sidebars make this an appealing introduction to reluctant readers to various fields of learning. With such entry headings as *¿Sabes quién fue el
emperador austríaco de México?* (Do you know who was the Austrian
emperor of Mexico?) and *¿Sabes quién inventó el psicoanálisis?* (Do
you know who invented psychoanalysis?), these brief biographical
summaries will encourage curious browsers. Although each volume includes a table of contents in chronological order, the only alphabetical
index is included in volume III, which may confuse students in search
of a specific person.

Savaiano, Eugene, and Lynn W. Winget. *Spanish Idioms.* Hauppauge, N.Y.:
  Barron's, 2007. 396p. ISBN: 978-0-7641-3557-6. pap. $8.99. Gr.
  8–adult.

    Intended primarily for English speakers, this practical pocket-size
paperback includes approximately 2500 Spanish idioms, arranged under key works in alphabetical order followed by their English translations. Idiomatic expressions, especially in a second language, are never
easy to grasp, yet those included here, which come from contemporary
spoken Spanish from Latin America, are clearly accompanied by brief,
illustrative sentences to clarify meaning. Common English idioms, pronunciation guides and abbreviations are appended.

Toboso Sánchez, Pilar. *Diccionario de historia del mundo actual. (Dictionary of Current History of the World)* Madrid: Alianza, 2005. 607p.
  ISBN: 84-206-5976-2. pap. $12.95. Gr. 9–adult.

    With more than 1200 entries, this dictionary of current history
of the world provides brief and concise information about the international events, facts, processes, politicians, public figures and or-
ganizations that have influenced world events from 1945 up to 2005.
In alphabetical order and with numerous cross-references, it proffers
information regarding current geopolitical, social and economic
world issues in a handy paperback format. Librarians will not appre-

ciate the poor binding and narrow margins and some students will not like the generally cluttered design, but history buffs will welcome its succinctness.

Encyclopedias

Enciclopedia de la República Dominicana. (Encyclopedia of the Dominican Republic) Barcelona: Océano, 2005. 2 vols. 432p. ISBN: 84-494-2507-7. $60.00. Gr. 9–adult.

In an appealing, well-organized format, this two-volume encyclopedia provides detailed information about the Dominican Republic. Numerous color photographs and maps and informative sidebars add interest to the comprehensive text. Volume I includes the geography, climate, ecological problems, economy, tourism and society of the Dominican Republic. Volume II discusses its history, literature, arts, sports and customs. It also includes biographical sketches of noted people, a well-done chronology and an index.

Enciclopedia hispánica. (Hispanic Encyclopedia) 18 vols. Barcelona: Barsa Planeta, 2005/Distributed by World Book. ISBN: 1-56409-070-1. $1399.00. Gr. 8–adult.

Long considered one of the best general encyclopedias in the Spanish language, it includes a 14-volume Macropedia with more than 5000 generic and specific topics arranged in alphabetical order, a two-volume Micropedia with basic information on 34,000 entries, a Temapedia with 40 general essays that classify knowledge and a Datapedia that presents information in tables and charts. With 380 new articles, excellent color photos, charts, maps and drawings as well as updated information up to 2004, this is indeed a must-have Spanish-language encyclopedia.

Rogers, Kirsteen, and Clare Hickman. *Religiones del mundo. (World Religions)* Illus: Leonard Le Rolland. Translated by Sonia Tapia and others. London: Usborne, 2005. 128p. ISBN: 0-7460-5093-3. $22.95. Gr. 5–9.

This attractive, large-format encyclopedia describes the history, beliefs and customs of the great religions of the world as well as the rites and festivals of other local religions from Africa, Central and South America, and Australia. Profusely illustrated with color photographs, drawings and charts, it also includes a world map of religions, a chronology and an index.

Handbooks

García Ponce de León, Paz. *Breve historia de la pintura. (Brief History of Painting)* Madrid: Libsa, 2006. 256p. ISBN: 84-662-1251-5. $27.99. Gr. 9–adult.

The purpose of this attractive, large-format publication is to provide a systematic overview of the evolution of painting from prehistoric times up to Spanish painting in the 1980s. Divided into ten chapters and with more than 500 exquisite color reproductions, the author describes in a somewhat dry, academic tone the most important painting techniques, movements, styles and artists throughout time. An important limitation is that it only includes an index of illustrations. It does not have an artist or subject index, seriously reducing its usefulness.

El gran libro de la Navidad. (The Big Book of Christmas) Edited by Ana Garralón. Illus: Federico Delicado. Madrid: Grupo Anaya, 2003. 288p. ISBN: 84-667-2761-2. $33.95. Gr. 5–9.

More than 90 stories, poems, carols, recipes and brief essays about Christmas traditions and customs in the Spanish-speaking world are included in this attractive, large-format compendium. From exquisite Spanish renditions of short stories by classical authors—Hans Christian Andersen, Isaac Bashevis Singer, Gabriela Mistral—to traditional carols from Mexico, Spain, Puerto Rico and Argentina, to contemporary poems and interesting discussions of well-known customs (e.g., *Papá Noel, San Nicolás* and *Santa Claus),* this is indeed a joyous panorama to celebrate Christmas. Delicado's witty, black-ink and watercolor illustrations with an almost irreverent tone add a festive, contemporary touch.

Orozco Linares, Fernando. *Fechas históricas de México: Las efemérides más destacadas desde la época prehispánica hasta nuestros días. (Historical Dates of Mexico: The Most Significant Events from Pre-Columbian Times until the Present)* Mexico: Panorama, 2006. 264p. ISBN: 968-38-0295-8. pap. $12.95. Gr. 6–9.

Divided into six historical periods—*la época prehispánica* (Pre-Columbian), *el Virreinato* (the Viceroy Period), *la Independencia* (Independence), *la República* (the Republic), *la Revolución* (the Revolution), and *el México contemporáneo* (Contemporary Mexico)—this guide briefly describes, in strict chronological order, the most significant events in the history of Mexico. The author states that this is not a history text; rather, it is a supplement to the history of Mexico. Beginning in 1064 when the Toltecs founded Culhuacan, to such important dates as 1536, October 18, the arrival in Mexico of the first printing press in the Americas; 1849, March 9, the American troops land on the beaches of Veracruz; up to 1991, September 22, the signing of the first Trade Agreement in the Americas, students of Mexican history will appreciate this easy-to-use compendium. Unfortunately, it does not include an index.

Orozco Linares, Fernando. *Gobernantes de México: Desde la época pre-hispánica hasta nuestros días. (Rulers of Mexico: From Pre-Columbian Times until Today)* Illus: José Narro. Mexico: Panorama, 2005. 484p. ISBN: 968-38-0260-5. pap. $8.95. Gr. 6–12.

Neither engaging nor well-written, this is nonetheless a handy paperback that includes difficult-to-find, basic information about the rulers of Mexico from 1325 up to President Vicente Fox Quesada (2000–2006). Each entry, which includes a prosaic black-and-white drawing, varies in length from one paragraph—Huitzilíhuitl and Pedro Vélez—to twelve pages—Benito Juárez. Most disturbingly, it lacks an index, although persistent readers can resort to the table of contents. Despite its numerous limitations, students of Mexico's rulers do not have many options.

Nonfiction

Philosophy

Brenifier, Oscar. *El bien y el mal ¿qué es eso? (Evil and Goodness, What Is That?)* Illus: Clément Devaux. Translated by Luis E. Pérez Villanueva. ISBN: 970-37-0237-6.

——. *¿Qué es la vida? (What Is Life?)* Illus: Jérôme Ruillier. Translated by Una Pérez Ruiz. ISBN: 970-37-0236-8.

——. *¿Que son los sentimientos? (What Are Feelings?)* Illus: Serge Bloch. Translated by Una Pérez Ruiz, ISBN: 970-37-0238-4.

Ea. vol.: 90p. (Los libros de Filo y Sofía) Mexico/U.S.: Destino/Planeta, 2005. pap. $15.95. Gr. 3–5.

Spanish speakers from the Americas will especially appreciate this most ingenious introduction to basic philosophical questions about life, behavior, and personal feelings and values. Originally published in France and maintaining its carefree, beguiling style, this series invites children to examine important premises, principles and beliefs through simple questions, open-ended answers and numerous *Sí, pero . . .* (Yes, but . . .) queries. Each title includes witty, cartoonish, color illustrations that encourage readers to reflect further on each issue. Questions about good and evil, such as possible limits to obedience, freedom and generosity are included in *El bien y el mal ¿qué es eso?* Happiness, death, ambition and other life concerns are explored in *¿Qué es la vida?* Love, jealousy, friendship, and other feelings are analyzed in *¿Qué son los sentimientos?*

Psychology

Moore-Mallinos, Jennifer. *¿Tienes un secreto? (Do You Have a Secret?)* (¡Hablemos de Esto!) Illus: Marta Fábrega. Hauppage, NY: Barron's, 2005. 32p. ISBN: 0-7641-3171-0. pap. $6.95. Gr. Preschool–2.

By describing the difference between *secretos buenos* (good secrets)—such as a surprise birthday gift for *mamá* or a secret handshake with a good friend and *secretos malos* (bad secrets)—those that make you feel bad, children are encouraged to share the latter with their parents, or a trusted adult. The almost whimsical, pencil and watercolor illustrations add a sense of intimacy to the easy-to-understand text. A parent guide at the end gives parents advice as they talk to the young.

Other titles in this series are:
Los colores del arco iris (Colors of the Rainbow) ISBN: 978-0-7641-3278-0, *Cuando mis padres se olvidaron de ser amigos (When My Parents Forgot to Be Friends)* ISBN: 978-0-7641-3173-8, *Mis abuelitos son especiales (My Grandparents Are Special)* ISBN: 978-0-7641-3507-1, *Perdida y encontrada (Lost and Found)* ISBN: 978-0-7641-3511-8, *Yo recuerdo (I Remember)* ISBN: 978-0-7641-3276-6.

Religion

Rotner, Shelley, and Sheila M. Kelly. *De muchas maneras: Cómo las familias practican sus creencias y religiones. (Many Ways: How Families Practice Their Beliefs and Religions)* Photos by Shelley Rotner. Translated by translations.com. Minneapolis: Lerner, 2007. 32p. ISBN: 0-8225-6506-4. $15.95. Gr. K–2.

Simply and joyfully, this attractively illustrated book highlights the religious practices, symbols and places of worship of Buddhists, Christians, Hindus, Jews, Muslims, and Sikhs. Like the original English version, the pleasant Spanish rendition reinforces the message that all religions share the same values. It is unfortunate that the captions identifying each excellent color photo are included at the end of the book, rather than accompanying each photo. Sadly, only English titles are provided for further reading. Nonetheless, this is a wonderful invitation for the young to love one another and our beautiful earth.

Sollish, Ari. *Un toque de Pesaj. (A Touch of Passover)* Illus: Boruch Becker. New York: Merkos, 2004. 14p. ISBN: 0-8266-0022-0. $8.00. Ages 2–5.

This simple Spanish rendition describes the special food that is served during Passover, the springtime Jewish holiday that commemorates the exodus of the Jews from Egypt. Especially enticing is the "touch and feel" aspects whereby youngsters can see the shiny red wine and touch the sticky drops of wine, feel the leather of the *Hagadá* (Haggadah), the bumpy *matzá* (matzah), and the silky matzah bag. Despite the static, cartoonish illustrations, this well-constructed board book is a good introduction to this holiday for the very young.

Social Sciences

Ancona, George. *Mi barrio/My Neighborhood.* ISBN: 0-516-23689-X.
——. *Mi casa/My House.* ISBN: 0-516-23688-1.
——. *Mi escuela/My School.* ISBN: 0-516-23686-5.
——. *Mi familia/My Family.* ISBN: 0-516-23687-3.
——. *Mis amigos/My Friends.* ISBN: 0-516-23690-3.
——. *Mis bailes/My Dances.* ISBN: 0-516-23691-1

Ea. vol.: 32p. Photos by the author. (Somos Latinos/We Are Latinos) Chicago: Children's Press, 2004. $14.70. Gr. 1–3.

Through candid color photographs of Latino children in the United States and simple bilingual texts, readers are exposed to Latino people and culture. Marc Anthony, who lives in a Brooklyn barrio, tells about his life and his Puerto Rican background in *Mi barrio/My Neighborhood.* Araceli, whose parents came from Mexico, describes her life on a ranch in Oregon in *Mi casa/My House.* Christopher, whose parents came from Central America, narrates his life in an American school in *Mi escuela/My School.* Camila, whose Cuban grandparents went to Venezuela and later to Miami, tells about her family in *Mi familia/My Family.* Amelia, whose mother came from the Dominican Republic, narrates fun activities with her friends in *Mis amigos/My Friends.* Cuauhtémoc, whose parents came from Spain and Mexico, highlights Latino dances in *Mis bailes/My Dances.* Although each title includes a glossary, it is unfortunate that the Spanish nouns listed do not include the definite articles. How will Spanish learners know whether it is *"la"* or *"el" tradición; "la"* or *"el" arte; "la"* or *"el" pastel* and many others?

Ancona, George. *Mi música/My Music.* ISBN: 0-516-25295-X.
——. *Mis abuelos/My Grandparents.* ISBN: 0-516-25294-1.
——. *Mis comidas/My Foods.* ISBN: 0-516-25292-5.
——. *Mis fiestas/My Celebrations.* ISBN: 0-516-25290-9.
——. *Mis juegos/My Games.* ISBN: 0-516-25293-3.
——. *Mis quehaceres/My Chores.* ISBN: 0-516-25291-7.
   Ea. vol.: 32p. Photos by the author. (Somos Latinos) Chicago: Children's Press, 2005. $14.28. Gr. 1–3.
   Like the previous titles in this simple bilingual series, these include candid color photos of Latino children in the United States. Janira and her brother demonstrate flamenco music, Jovita sings Mexican *rancheras,* and Juan Julián plays Caribbean Salsa in *Mi música/My Music.* Sebastián and Helena describe life with their Colombian grandparents in *Mis abuelos/ My Grandparents.* Alex, whose parents came from Venezuela, enjoys *sancocho* and other Venezuelan dishes in *Mis comidas/My Foods.* José tells about Puerto Rican celebrations, Valeria dances during Bolivian Independence Day, Cristóbal celebrates the Day of the Dead and Zofía appreciates *Las Posadas* in *Mis fiestas/My Celebrations.* Basketball, *Lotería,* soccer, pick-a-stone and other games are enjoyed by Latino children in *Mis juegos/My Games.* Jazmine and Andrés tell about their chores at home and at school in *Mis quehaceres/My Chores.* Although each title includes a list of words in Spanish and their English equivalents, the Spanish nouns do not include definite articles.

Ángel, Varinia del, and Gabriela León. *El secreto de las plantas. (The Secret of Plants)* 48p. ISBN: 970-20-0832-8.
Cortés Hernández, Santiago. *El hombre que se convirtió en toro y otras historias de la Inquisición. (The Man Who Became a Bull and Other Stories about the Inquisition)* 60p. Illus: Edgar Clement. ISBN: 970-20-0831-X.
López, Oresta. *Hemos cambiado: Educación, conquistas y deseos de las niñas en el siglo XIX. (We Have Changed: Education, Conquests and Wishes of the Girls in the 19th Century)* 60p. Illus: Manuel Monroy. ISBN: 970-20-0834-4.
Montecino Aguirre, Sonia. *Lucila se llama Gabriela. (Lucila is Called Gabriela)* 60p. Illus: Luis San Vicente. ISBN: 970-20-0828-X.
Speckman Guerra, Elisa. *¿Quién es criminal? Un recorrido por el delito, la ley, la justicia y el castigo en México (desde el virreinato hasta el siglo XX). (Who Is a Criminal? An Overview of Crime, Law, Justice and*

Punishment in Mexico (from Colonial Times until the 20th Century)
84p. Illus: Alejandro Magallanes. ISBN: 970-20-0829-8.
Ea. vol.: (La Otra Escalera) Mexico: Castillo, 2006. pap. $10.95. Gr.
6–10.

Important aspects that relate to Mexican society and how these have affected individuals and Mexico today are examined in these cogently written, at times gripping, accounts of topics almost never discussed in books for teens. With excellent candid color photographs, engrossing interviews and well-written explanations, comments and anecdotes, *El secreto de las plantas* depicts the life of the people of Amatlán, Mexico, and their use of traditional medicine to prevent illness, heal diseases and increase feelings of well-being. It highlights the uses of medicinal plants from pre-Columbian times up to Mexico today where it coincides with modern medicine. The power of the Inquisition in the New Spain to control ideas and society is depicted through accounts of the inquisitorial process, stylistic cartoon illustrations, and a comparative chronology in *El hombre que se convirtió en toro y otras historias de la Inquisición*. Beginning with a description of life in Mexico in the 19th century, where women were denied all rights, *Hemos cambiado: Educación, conquistas y deseos de las niñas en el siglo XIX* offers a panorama of the challenges that girls and adolescents still confront today in Latin America and Africa. Despite the at times childish ink-and-watercolor illustrations, *Lucila se llamaba Gabriela* focuses on the life, and especially the time, the poet Gabriela Mistral spent in Mexico. Speckman Guerra's convincing and authoritative prose and Magallanes's dynamic and expressive two-tone and full color illustrations, in broad strokes, dabs, and thick black lines, portray how views on crime, law, justice and punishment have evolved in Mexico from Colonial times up to the 20th century in *¿Quién es criminal? Un recorrido por el delito, la ley, la justicia y el castigo en México (desde el virreinato hasta el siglo XX)*.

Canals, Anna. *Llegué de Etiopía. (I Came from Ethiopia)* ISBN: 84-246-0449-0.
Elfa, Albert. *Llegué de Rusia. (I Came from Russia)* ISBN: 84-246-0448-2.
Gibert, Miguel M. *Llegué de China. (I Came from China)* ISBN: 84-246-0447-4.
Ea. vol.: 32p. Illus: Luci Gutiérrez. (Cuéntame mi Historia) Barcelona: La Galera, 2005. pap. $9.95. Gr. 1–3.

In the first-person voice of a happy, adoptive (white) mother talking to her three-year-old adopted daughter, Medina, who was born in

Ethiopia, *Llegué de Etiopía* describes the parents' excitement, their trip to Ethiopia to pick her up, Medina's early shyness, and her life at her new home with new friends and a new language. Perhaps Medina's background and quick adjustment to her adoptive parents depict a much too rosy picture; nonetheless, this is a positive view of adoption that African-origin children will especially appreciate. An adoptive father tells his adopted son how he had to marry his wife so that they could adopt him in Russia and bring him back home to Spain in *Llegué de Rusia*. Despite a few Peninsular Spanish pronouns and conjugations (*supieseis, os pusisteis*), Russian-born children will enjoy. One-year-old Litang, who was born in China and lived in an orphanage, learns about her adoption, her country and her early life at her new home in *Llegué de China*. The bold, digital artwork in bright primary colors complements the positive tone of each title. In addition, each title includes a two-page afterword with information about the country of birth of each child as well as four pages with suggestions to adoptive parents to assist them in answering the concerns of their adopted children.

Carvalhas, María Lúcia. *Cuando crezca quiero ser . . . (When I Grow Up I Want To Be . . .)* Illus: Raquel Pinheiro. Translated by Broquela Traductores. León: Everest, 2005. 46p. ISBN: 84-241-8008-9. pap. Gr. 2–4.

    Children are introduced to various occupations—doctor, cook, dancer, soccer player, teacher, computer expert, artist, and police woman—through a humorous, rhyming text and witty watercolors.

Doumerc, Beatriz. *La línea. (The Line)* Illus: Ayax Barnes. Buenos Aires: Ediciones Del Eclipse, 2003. 78p. ISBN: 987-9011-58-9. pap. $9.95. Gr. 6–10.

    Winner of Cuba's Casa de las Américas Award in 1975 and originally published in Cuba, this ingenious depiction of a little man and a solid line that, among other things, can be stepped over, crawled under, skipped over, sat on, used to isolate, run around in circles as well as divide two men, put behind bars, attack, unite or use *donde viva el hombre nuevo* (as a place where the new man can live). A thick black line with no details against a flat white background depicts an ever-changing, simply drawn man as he deals with the blue line for ultimately positive effects—freedom and love. Reluctant readers will be enticed by the brief, easy-to-understand text (one line per page) and the cartoonish-type design; others will agree with the political message. (According to the publishers, this book was briefly banned in Cuba shortly after its publication.)

Falip, Ester and Joan Molet. *Llegué de Ucrania. (I Came from Ukraine)* ISBN: 84-246-2046-1.
Montoriol, Mònica. *Llegué de Colombia. (I Came from Colombia)* ISBN: 84-246-2044-5.
Raventós, Joan, and Queti Vinyals. *Llegué de Nepal. (I Came from Nepal)* ISBN: 84-246-2029-1.
Ea. vol.: 32p. Illus: Luci Gutiérrez. (Cuéntame mi Historia) Barcelona: La Galera, 2005. pap. $9.95. Gr. 1–3.

Like the previous titles in this series, these depict the feelings and thoughts of adoptive parents as they describe the countries of origin of their adopted children. Each title includes bold, digital artwork in bright primary colors, a two-page afterword with basic facts about the child's country of birth and four pages with simple suggestions to adoptive parents to talk to their adopted children. In a first-person point of view, a Spanish mother tells about the parents' trip to Ukraine after landing in Kiev with highlights about special dishes, *balalaika* and other local customs where they adopted Helena and Sergio in *Llegué de Ucrania.* Another mother tells about Carlos, who was born in Manizales, Colombia, a country of kind people, beautiful weather and delightful customs in *Llegué de Colombia.* A happy couple adopts their daughter, Ravina, in Nepal where they were received with flowers and visited colorful temples in *Llegué de Nepal.* Despite a few Peninsular Spanish pronouns and conjugations (*seríais, sois*) in *Llegué de Ucrania*, these titles present honest, positive situations about the process of adoption that young Spanish speakers from the Americas will understand.

Geis, Patricia. *Néstor Tellini. (Néstor Tellini)* ISBN: 84-7864-798-8.
———. *Paca Lamar. (Paca Lamar)* ISBN: 84-7864-797-X.
———. *Pascual Midón. (Pascual Midón)* ISBN: 84-7864-799-6.
———. *Pepa Pas. (Pepa Pas)* ISBN: 84-7864-796-1.
Ea. vol.: 24p. (Mi Ciudad) Barcelona: Combel, 2003. $6.95. Gr. K–2.

Through an easy-to-read, relaxed text—two to three sentences per page—and witty, computer-generated illustrations children are introduced to four town workers: *Néstor Tellini* features a cook's assistant who has the important duty of peeling potatoes and making sure that all the pots and pans sparkle; *Paca Lamar,* who assists her mother, the local fish vendor; *Pascual Midón,* who one morning is left in charge of his parents' dry cleaning shop; and *Pepa Pas,* who assists her parents, the vegetable vendors. These are not simple depictions of the work of town residents; rather they are debonair depictions of unexpected daily mishaps.

Geis, Patricia. *Pequeña Tamazigh. (Little Tamazigh)* ISBN: 84-7864-882-8.
———. *Pequeño Bouyei. (Little Bouyei)* ISBN: 84-7864-881-X.
Ea. vol.: 32p. (Niños y Niñas del Mundo) Barcelona: Combel, 2005. $11.95. Gr. 1–3.
Like the previous six titles of this appealing series that introduces children to the fauna, flora, geography and lifestyle of people from around the world, these include simple yet dignified ink-and-watercolor illustrations in rich earth tones and accessible, easy-to-understand texts. Through Pequeña Tamazigh, a girl from Morocco, readers are exposed to the lifestyle and beliefs of a Moroccan family as well as their beautiful hand-woven carpets and exquisitely sweet dates in *Pequeña Tamazigh.* Although Pequeño Bouyei, a boy from southern China, does not follow his parents' instructions, he outwits a dangerous leopard, thereby saving himself and the family's pigs in *Pequeño Bouyei.*

Gibert, José. *¿Quieres ser paleontólogo? (Do You Want to be a Paleontologist?)* Illus: Carlos García and María Lería. ISBN: 978-84-236-8223-2.
De la Rosa, Pedro. *¿Quieres ser piloto de Fórmula 1? (Do You Want to be a Fórmula 1 Driver?)* Illus: Carlos García. ISBN: 978-84-236-8224-9.
Ea. vol.: 63p. (¿Quieres Ser . . .) Barcelona: Edebé, 2007. $19.95. Gr. 4–7.
In a first-person point of view and through the personal experiences of successful practitioners, the *¿Quieres ser . . . ?* series describes the training and dedication required in several professions. José Gibert, a well-known Spanish paleontologist, tells why he is so devoted to the study of the forms of life existing in prehistoric and geologic times. He is especially passionate about the practical aspects of his work, that is, to find remnants or traces of organisms of a past geologic age, such as skeletons or leaf imprints embedded in the Earth's crust, to study them and to write about his findings. He provides a brief history of his profession, the reasons he enjoys his work, and states that paleontologists need to love nature and adventure and to always persevere. Numerous color photos and subheads add to the appealing design. A glossary and suggestions for further reading are also included. The life of Pedro de la Rosa, a Formula 1 Spanish racing car driver, tells about his personal

and professional life in *¿Quieres ser piloto de Fórmula 1?* and Luis
Miguel Domínguez writes *¿Quieres ser naturalista? (Do You Want to be
a Naturalist?)*.

Gnojewski, Carol. *Cinco de Mayo: Se celebra el orgullo. (Cinco de Mayo:
Celebrating Hispanic Pride)* Translated by Carolina Jusid. ISBN: 0-
7660-2616-7.
——. *El Día de los Muertos: Una celebración de la familia y la vida.
(Day of the Dead: A Latino Celebration of Family and Life)* Translated
by Romina C. Cinquemani. ISBN: 0-7660-2615-9.
——. *El Día de Martin Luther King, Jr.: Honramos a un hombre de paz.
(Martin Luther King Jr. Day: Honoring a Man of Peace)* Translated by
Carolina Jusid. ISBN: 0-7660-2617-5.
Landau, Elaine. *El Día de Acción de Gracias: Un momento para agrade-
cer. (Thanksgiving Day: A Time to be Thankful)* Translated by Romina
C. Cinquemani. ISBN: 0-7660-2618-3.
——. *El Día de Colón: Celebramos a un explorador famoso. (Columbus
Day: Celebrating a Famous Explorer)* Translated by Carolina Jusid.
ISBN: 0-7660-2619-1.
——. *El Día de San Valentín: Caramelos, amor y corazones. (Valentine's
Day: Candy, Love and Hearts)* Translated by Susana C. Schultz. ISBN:
0-7660-2613-2.
Robinson, Fay. *Halloween: Disfraces y golosinas en la Víspera de Todos
los Santos. (Halloween: Costumes and Treats on All Hallows' Eve)*
Translated by Romina C. Cinquemani. ISBN: 0-7660-2614-0.
Ea. vol.: 48p. (Días Festivos) Berkeley Heights, N.J.: Enslow, 2005.
$23.93. Gr. 3–5.

Following the attractive presentations of the English originals
with clear, color photos and art reproductions, large fonts and simple
sidebars, these serviceable Spanish renditions present historical and
cultural information about holidays for new readers. Unfortunately, incomplete and at times clumsy glossaries and a few awkward, stilted
translations mar this otherwise noteworthy series. The importance of
the battle on May 5, 1862 in which the Mexican army and people of the
city of Puebla fought the French army is lively recounted in *Cinco de
Mayo: Se celebra el orgullo.* Mexican beliefs about death, cemeteries
and celebrations on the Day of the Dead are explained in *El Día de los
Muertos: Una celebración de la familia y la vida.* Martin Luther King,
Jr.'s life and the National Civil Rights Museum are honored in *El Día
de Martin Luther King, Jr.: Honramos a un hombre de paz.* A brief his-

torical background of Thanksgiving Day in 1620 in Plymouth, Massachusetts as well as Chinese, Jewish and contemporary Thanksgiving celebrations in American cities are described in *El Día de Acción de Gracias: Un momento para agradecer*. The life of Christopher Columbus, the Italian explorer, who in 1492 in the service of Spain arrived in the New World, is retold in *El Día de Colón: Celebramos a un explorador famoso*. The origins and various ways of celebrating Valentine's Day around the world are discussed in *El Día de San Valentin: Caramelos, amor y corazones*. The beginnings, traditions, symbols and modern Halloween celebrations are explained in *Halloween: Disfraces y golosinas en la Víspera de Todos los Santos*.

Kalman, Bobbie. *Bomberos al rescate. (Firefighters to the Rescue)*. ISBN: 978-0-7787-8428-9.
———. *Los veterinarios cuidan la salud de los animales. (Veterinarians Help Keep Animals Healthy)*. ISBN: 978-0-7787-8429-6.
Ea. vol.: 32p. Translated by translations.com (Mi Comunidad y Quienes Contribuyen a Ella) New York: Crabtree, 2007. $18.90. Gr. 2–4.

Just as informative and appealing as the original English edition, this well-rendered and well-illustrated Spanish series introduces readers to the work of community helpers. Concluding with the heroic efforts of firefighters in New York City on 9/11/2001 and with easy-to-follow fire safety suggestions, *Bomberos al rescate* describes the work that firemen do and how they help keep the community safe. *Los veterinarios cuidan la salud de los animales* highlights the myriad ways that veterinarians work to keep animals healthy, including at the clinic, in shelters and on the farm. English-language Web sites about veterinarians are listed. Each title includes an index and a glossary, albeit without definite articles.

Kelley, Emily. *La Navidad alrededor del mundo. (Christmas Around the World)* Illus: Joni Oeltjenbruns. ISBN: 978-0-8225-3116-6.
Kessel, Joyce K. *Halloween. (Halloween)* Illus: Nancy Carlson. ISBN: 978-0-8225-7990-4.
———. *Squanto y el primer Día de Acción de Gracias. (Squanto and the First Thanksgiving)* Illus: Lisa Donze. ISBN: 978-0-8225-7792-8.
Knudsen, Shannon. *La Pascua en todo el mundo. (Easter Around the World)* Illus: David L. Erickson. ISBN: 978-0-8225-7791-1.
Lowery, Linda. *El Día de los Muertos. (Day of the Dead)*. Illus: Barbara Knutson. ISBN: 978-0-8225-3122-7.

Ea. vol.: 48p. Translated by translations.com. (Yo Solo: Festividades) Minneapolis: Lerner, 2006-2008. $18.95. Gr. 1–3.

In contrast to the first two Spanish titles—*El cinco de mayo* and *El día de los Veteranos*—of this holiday series published in 2005, these are lively, easy-to-understand Spanish renditions with engaging illustrations that certainly do justice to the original English editions. *La Navidad alrededor del mundo* features Christmastime celebrations in eight countries—Mexico, Germany, Australia, Ethiopia, China, Lebanon, Russia and Sweden. *Halloween* explains the origin of Halloween and such traditions as *calabazas iluminadas* (jack-o-lanterns), *fantasmas* (ghosts) and *pedir dulces* (trick-or-treating). *Squanto y el primer Día de Acción de Gracias* describes the challenges the Pilgrims faced in 1620 and how a Patuxet Indian, Squanto, taught them how to survive. *La Pascua en todo el mundo* relates Easter celebrations in Sweden, Ethiopia, Russia, Egypt, Mexico, Philippines, Colombia and Germany. Despite an awkward beginning in which people are described as preparing to *¡Celebran la muerte!* (Celebrate Death) and followed by *¿Te parece extraño?* (Does it sound strange?), *El Día de los Muertos* does convey the spirit of the enduring Day of the Dead Mexican celebration.

McLaren, Thando. *Así es mi día. (My Day My Way)* Illus: Olivia Villet. Translated by Paulino Rodríguez. Barcelona: La Galera, 2006. 10p. ISBN: 84-246-2145-X. Gr. Preschool–2.

Through lively watercolor illustrations and well-placed overlays, readers/viewers lift the flaps to find out about the everyday lives of four children from four continents—Juan from Spain, Keiko from Japan, Alí from Morocco and Bibi from Guyana. It describes their houses, foods, schools, recreational activities and bedtime practices. A concluding poster describes further the geographical location, housing, food and sports of these countries.

Randolph, Joanne. *Ambulances/Ambulancias.* 2008. ISBN: 978-1-4042-7670-3.

———. *Coast Guard Boats/Lanchas guardacostas.* 2008. ISBN: 978-1-4042-7671-0.

———. *Emergency Helicopters/Helicópteros de emergencia.* 2008. ISBN: 978-1-4042-7672-7.

———. *Fire Trucks/Camiones de bomberos.* 2008. ISBN: 978-1-4042-7673-4.

——. *Police Cars/Patrullas.* 2008. ISBN: 978-1-4042-7674-1.

——. *Tow Trucks/Grúas.* 2008. ISBN: 978-1-4042-7675-8.

Ea. vol.: 24 p. Translated by Eduardo Alamán. (To The Rescue) New York: Editorial Buenas Letras, 2008. $21.25. Gr. K–1.

In a most simple bilingual text (one sentence per page), young readers are exposed to the work of rescue services and workers—ambulances, coast guard boats, emergency helicopters, fire trucks, police cars and tow trucks. To avoid confusing English and Spanish learners, the fluid Spanish rendition follows the English in a lighter font. Each title includes *Words to Know/Palabras que debes saber.*

Thomas, William David. *¿Cómo elegimos a nuestros líderes? (How Do We Elect Our Leaders?)* ISBN: 978-0-8368-8870-6.

——. *¿Cuáles son las partes del gobierno? (What Are the Parts of Government?* ISBN: 978-0-8368-8872-0.

——. *¿Qué es una constitución? (What Is a Constitution?)* ISBN: 978-0-8368-8873-7.

Ea. vol.: 32p. Translated by Adriana Rosa Bonewitz. (Mi Gobierno de Estados Unidos) Pleasantville, NY: Gareth Stevens, 2008. $23.93. Gr. 3–6.

Beginning with an anecdote about then-candidate Ronald Reagan when he walked out of a coffee shop without paying for a cup of coffee, *¿Cómo elegimos a nuestros líderes?* provides a compelling introduction to the U.S. system of electing the president, members of Congress, state officials and the importance of voting. The fluid Spanish rendition, numerous clear sidebars that further explain the text, interesting captions and timely color photographs will be appreciated by Spanish speakers unfamiliar with the U.S. system of electing its leaders. To avoid the often-inflated approach of other books about government, this series is written in a conversational style that clarifies difficult topics, such as to explain reelection, the subhead states *Uno, dos (no tres) períodos, y adiós* (One, Two (never three) periods, and Goodbye); to explain the controversy about the Electoral College, it states *¿Se Queda o se Va?* (Does it Stay or Go?). Each title includes a glossary, albeit without definite articles, an index and English-language-only suggested readings and Web sites. *¿Cuáles son las partes del gobierno?* explains the executive, legislative and judicial branches of government as well as state governments. *¿Qué es una constitución?* discusses the importance and history of the U.S. Constitution, the Amendments, the Bill of Rights and state constitutions. Also in this series: *¿Cuáles son los derechos básicos de los ciudadanos?* (What Are Citizens' Basic Rights?)

Folklore

Ada, Alma Flor, and F. Isabel Campoy. *Merry Navidad!: Christmas Carols in Spanish and English/Merry Navidad: Villancicos en español e inglés.* Illus: Viví Escrivá. Translated into English by Rosalma Zubizarreta. New York: HarperCollins, 2007. 64p. ISBN: 978-0-06-058434-4. $16.99. Gr. 2–5.

Nineteen traditional Christmas carols from Latin America and Spain are included in this attractive bilingual publication. From Bethlehem to *Las Posadas* to *Nanas de Navidad*/Christmas Lullabies to *Los Tres Reyes Magos*/The Three Wise Kings, English and Spanish speakers will enjoy the songs and *fiestas* of the Christmas season. Straightforward English renditions follow the original Spanish versions. A few musical notations and Escrivá's festive watercolor illustrations add to the holiday spirit.

Adivina esta cosa niño: Adivinanzas mayas yucatecas. (Guess Child: Mayan Riddles from Yucatán) Compiled by Fidencio Briceño Chel. Illus.: Marcelo Jiménez Santos. México: Artes de México, 2002. 48p. ISBN: 970-683-072-3. pap. $11.95. Gr. 2–6.

As an introduction to the beauty and achievements of the Mayan people from Yucatán, México, this exquisite collection of eighteen brief riddles, presented in five languages—Spanish, Maya, English, Tzotzil and French—is difficult to surpass. Especially noteworthy are the full-page illustrations with pre-Columbian-style methods and techniques that meticulously depict Maya customs, flora and fauna. From a hungry bucket to flying fire crackers, these riddles served as pastimes for children and adults in wakes or agricultural ceremonies. The well-written introduction (in Spanish only) and the explanatory notes (in Spanish, English and French) add further to readers' understanding of the cultural and linguistic legacy of the Mayan people.

Adivinanzas mexicanas. (Mexican Riddles) Compiled by José Antonio Flores Farfán. Illus: Cleofas Ramírez Celestino. Translated by Refugio Nava Nava and others. Mexico: Artes de Mexico, 2005. 30p. ISBN: 970-683-094-4. pap. $13.95. Gr. 2–6.

This collection of traditional riddles from central Mexico and presented in four languages—Spanish, English, Tlaxcaltecan and Catalan—joyfully depicts the wordplay, parlance and activities of the inhabitants of the region. Especially appealing are the colorful, full-page illustrations rendered in *amate*, a special paper from the bark of a tree popular in the area with folklore-type motifs. Some adults may object to a few references to bodily functions, but children will enjoy the guesswork. An author's afterword, (in Spanish only) explains the traditions and languages spoken by almost two million people and which originated in Mexico.

Afanásiev, A.N. *La bruja Yagá y otros cuentos-I. (Baba Yaga, the Witch and Other Stories-I)* 276p. Illus: Violeta López. ISBN: 978-84-667-6497-1.
———. *El anillo mágico y otros cuentos-II. (The Magic Ring and Other Stories-II)* 270p. Illus: Nicolai Troshinsky. ISBN: 978-84-667-6498-8.
———. *La princesa hechizada y otros cuentos-III. (The Bewitched Princess and Other Stories-III)* 306p. Illus: Raquel Aparicio. ISBN: 978-84-667-6499-5.
———. *El vampiro y otros cuentos-IV. (The Vampire and Other Stories-IV)* 264p. Illus: Beatriz Martín Vidal. ISBN: 978-84-667-6500-8.
Ea. vol.: Translated by Isabel Vicente. (Cuentos Populares Rusos) Madrid: Anaya, 2008. $19.95. Gr. 5–8.

Two-hundred-and-fifty memorable Russian tales by the 19th-century Russian folklorist are included in four volumes with attractive color illustrations that depict traditional costumes and early Russian settings. Especially noteworthy are Vicente's lively Spanish renditions, full of action and vigor, and Rodríguez Almodóvar always-insightful introduction highlighting important aspects about the author's life and the tales. *La bruja Yagá y otros cuentos* includes tales about animals and magic such as stories about *la bruja Yagá* (Baba Yaga), the fearsome Russian witch with iron teeth, and *El lobo y la cabra* similar to Grimm's *The Seven Little Goats and the Wolf* but with a different ending. *El anillo mágico y otros cuentos* contains more tales of animals and magic as well as manners and customs. *La princesa hechizada y otros cuentos* combines mostly fairy tales about wise princesses, bewitched czars and Vasilisa, the beautiful. *El vampiro y otros cuentos* includes tales based on historical heroes and mysterious events. A well-done glossary complements each volume.

Andersen, Hans Christian. *La sirenita y otros cuentos. (Cuentos Completos I) (The Little Mermaid and Other Stories I)* 317p. Illus: Elena Odriozola. ISBN: 84-667-4090-0.

———. *La pequeña cerillera y otros cuentos. (Cuentos Completos II) (Little Match Girl and Other Stories II)* 347p. Illus: Javier Sáez Castán. ISBN: 84-667-4010-4.

———. *Chiquilladas y otros cuentos. (Cuentos Completos III) (Childish Pranks and Other Stories)* 310p. Illus: Carmen Segovia. ISBN: 84-667-4011-2.

Ea. vol.: Translated by Enrique Bernárdez. (Cuentos Completos) Madrid: Grupo Anaya, 2004. $15.95. Gr. 4–7.

Based on Andersen's original stories, first published in 1874, these smooth Spanish renditions contain informative introductions by well-known Spanish authors and one or two color illustrations per story. *La sirenita y otros cuentos* includes thirty popular favorites such as *El traje nuevo del emperador* (The Emperor's New Clothes) and *El patito feo* (The Ugly Duckling). *La pequeña cerillera y otros cuentos* includes fifty-five brief stories, some as well-known as *Los zapatos rojos* (The Red Shoes) and *La rosa más bella del mundo* (The World's Fairest Rose) and other lesser known stories. *Chiquilladas y otros cuentos* is a compilation of 33 stories, including such always-favored as *Anne Lisbeth* (Anne Lisbeth) and *El titiritero* (The Puppeteer). As an exhaustive compilation of Andersen's children's fiction, this series will be selected by the Danish author's numerous admirers in the Spanish-speaking world.

Bofill, Francesc. *Rapunzel/Rapunzel.* Illus: Joma. ISBN: 978-0-8118-5059-9.

Carrasco, Xavier. *Rumpelstiltskin/Rumpelstiltskin.* Illus: Francesc Infante. ISBN: 978-0-8118-5972-1.

Escardó i Bas, Mercé. *The Three Little Pigs/Los tres cerditos.* Illus: Pere Joan. ISBN: 978-0-8118-5063-6.

Ros, Roser. *Beauty and the Beast/La bella y la bestia.* Illus: Cristina Losantos. ISBN: 978-0-8118-5970-7.

Ea. vol.: 24p. Translated into English by Elizabeth Bell. San Francisco: Chronicle Books, 2006–2007. pap. $6.95. Gr. K–3.

Fortunately, these new bilingual titles of these classic stories are as simple and appealing as those published in 2004–2006. Titles include straightforward English texts, followed by smooth Spanish renditions on the left side of the page, and face full-page color illustrations. Especially enticing are Joma's ink-and-watercolor illustrations of *Rapunzel/ Rapunzel*, which depict contemporary settings and characters in the traditional story of the beautiful girl with exceptionally long golden hair imprisoned in a lonely tower by a mean witch. Infante's stylized illustrations add a unique tone to the popular tale of the strange little man who helps the miller's daughter spin straw into gold in *Rumpelstiltskin*. Joan's animated computer graphic art shows the three little pigs as they seek their fortunes, encounter a threatening wolf, and ultimately live together in a sturdy brick house in the *The Three Pigs/Los tres cerditos*. Losantos's ink and watercolor illustrations blend humor with whimsy in this version of the kind and beautiful maid that releases a handsome prince from a spell in *Beauty and the Beast/La bella y la bestia*.

Caballero, Paola. *Los siete mejores cuentos escandinavos. (The Seven Best Scandinavian Tales)* Illus: Kal. ISBN: 958-04-8032-X.

———. *Los siete mejores cuentos mexicanos. (The Seven Best Mexican Tales)* Illus: Fabricio Vanden Broeck. ISBN: 958-04-8495-3.

Escobar, Melba. *Los siete mejores cuentos árabes. (The Seven Best Arab Tales)* Illus: Muyi Neira. ISBN: 958-04-7212-2.

———. *Los siete mejores cuentos egipcios. (The Seven Best Egyptian Tales)* Illus: Muyi Neira. ISBN: 958-04-8033-8.

Hoyos, Héctor. *Los siete mejores cuentos celtas. (The Seven Best Celt Tales)* Illus: David Niño and Rafaél Yockteng. ISBN: 958-04-8030-3.

———. *Los siete mejores cuentos indios. (The Seven Best Indian Tales)* Illus: Olga Cuéllar. ISBN: 958-04-7213-0.

Manosalva, Andrés. *Los siete mejores cuentos japoneses. (The Seven Best Japanese Tales)* Illus: Muyi Neira. ISBN: 958-04-7211-4.

Rocha Vivas, Miguel. *Los siete mejores cuentos peruanos. (The Seven Best Peruvian Tales)* Illus: Carmen García. ISBN: 958-04-8496-1.

Ea. vol.: 56p. (Los siete mejores cuentos) Bogotá: Grupo Editorial Norma, 2004–2006. $11.95. Gr. 5–8.

Maintaining the charm and magic of the original tales, these well-written and delightfully illustrated collections provide a most refreshing view of numerous cultures around the world. Of special interest to Spanish speakers are two that celebrate the Náhuatl (Mexico) and Quechua (Peru) cultures. *Los siete mejores cuentos mexicanos* includes seven well-known tales that depict life in pre-Columbian Uxmal in Yucatán; the end of Pancho the thief; the frailities of Clemente *un hombre perezoso, . . . haragán, . . . flojo . . . y, además, mentiroso* (a lazy man, . . . indolent, . . . careless . . . and, in addition, a liar); and other enigmatic personalities from the oral tradition of Mexico. Vanden Broeck's colorful full-page illustrations accompany each tale. *Los siete mejores cuentos peruanos* incorporates seven tales about wise animals, the brave Shipibo people, a devoted mother, exquisite musicians and other personages that bring the Quechua culture to life. In addition to García's full-page illustrations that joyously depict the fauna and flora of Peru, these tales include numerous words characteristic of Peruvian Spanish—*quinua, cuy, carachupa, picuro*—which highlight the special appeal of Peruvian customs and traditions. Others come from Scandinavia, Arabia, Egypt, the Celt people, India and Japan. Also in this series: *Los siete mejores cuentos centroamericanos. (The Seven Best Tales from Central America).*

Campoy, F. Isabel, and Alma Flor Ada. *Cuentos que contaban nuestras abuelas. (Tales Our Abuelitas Told: A Hispanic Folktale Collection)* Illus: Felipe Dávalos and others, New York: Atheneum, 2006. 118p. ISBN: 1-4169-1905-8. $19.95. Gr. 4–6.

An informative foreword to Hispanic culture and folklore introduces this joyful collection of twelve traditional tales with a few colorful illustrations. It includes well-known versions as well as lesser-known variants about a sly fox, a colorful bird, a clever turtle and a wise maiden. My favorites are *Juan Bobo*, the traditional scoundrel of the Spanish-speaking world; *La gaita alegre*, (The Joyful Bagpipes), which features the proverbial generous young brother and *La túnica del hombre feliz* (The Happy Man's Tunic), which highlights the meaning of true happiness. Personal and informal notes at the end of each tale add mirth to their tone and tempo.

Cañeque, Carlos. *El pequeño Borges imagina el Quijote. (Young Borges Imagines Don Quijote)* Illus: Ramón Moscardó. Barcelona: Sirpus, 2003. 30p. ISBN: 84-89902-57-7. $18.95. Gr. 4–7.

Intermingling reality with fiction, this story pretends to expose readers to great literature. Young Jorge Luis Borges, whose love of literature influenced his writing, imagines he is re-reading *El Quijote*. As he falls asleep, he dreams that he, his friend Luisito (representing Don Quijote), and Sancho Panza battle the windmills. Moscardó's strong, bold illustrations, full of energy and color, re-create some of the most popular characters of literature in Spanish. Despite the ponderous tone of this fantasy, devoted admirers of Borges and Cervantes will enjoy. Others, however, should only read the one-page introduction to the life and work of each author.

Cioulachtjean, Reine. *Cuentos y leyendas de Armenia (Tales and Legends from Armenia)*. Illus: Jordi Vila Delclòs. Translated by Ana

Conejo. Madrid: Anaya, 2005. 169p. ISBN: 84-667-4717-6. pap. $11.95. Gr. 5–9.

This delightful collection of eighteen brief tales from Armenia, a region and republic of Asia Minor south of Georgia, is full of the humor, irony and common sense of its people. From questioning men, to an infallible doctor, to the wisdom of an old man and the cleverness of a fool, this joyful Spanish rendition with a few black-and-white line illustrations is sure to appeal to reluctant readers. Serious readers will be interested in the appendix describing the current situation of these long-suffering people.

Darwiche, Jihad. *Sapiencia y artimañas de Nasredín, el loco que era sabio. (Wisdom and Trickery of Nasredín, the Crazy Fool)* 186p. Illus: David B. ISBN: 968-7381-76-0.

Favaro, Patrice. *Sapiencia y artimañas de Birbal, el Rajá. (Wisdom and Trickery of Birbal, the Rajah.)* 117p. Illus: Arnal Ballester. ISBN: 968-7381-75-2.

Ea. vol.: Translated by Arturo Vázquez Barrón and Roberto Rueda Monreal. Mexico: Tecolote, 2004. pap. $9.95. Gr. 3–5.

These small, unassuming paperback publications — 5½" × 6½" — present a joyous blend of wit, ingenuity and cultural authenticity through these collections of brief short stories that have appealed to generations of listeners in the Muslim world and India. Especially inviting because of the humorous, almost cartoonish, three-tone, ink and watercolor illustrations is *Sapiencia y artimañas de Nasredín,* which includes more than sixty brief tales set in the Muslim world that highlight universal truths such as greedy neighbors, arrogant misers, lazy fathers, amid couscous, *"lukums"* (a Middle Eastern dessert), and other Muslim celebrations. *Sapiencias y artimañas de Birbal*, set in 16th-century India, where Birbal, the closest adviser to the emperor Mogul Akbar is able to resolve disputes among treacherous folk through his wise and witty opinions. Unfortunately, the three-tone illustrations are mere decorations that do not add to the jocose tone of these reflections about tolerance, generosity and life. Originally published by Jeunesse, Paris, these are indeed delightful renditions.

Deedy, Carmen Agra. *Martina una cucarachita muy linda: Un cuento cubano. (Martina the Beautiful Cockroach: A Cuban Folktale)* Illus: Michael Austin. Translated by Cristina de la Torre. Atlanta: Peachtree, 2007. 30p. ISBN: 978-1-56145-425-9. $16.95. Gr. Preschool–2.

With the flair and tempo of a Cuban folktale, De la Torre's Spanish rendition is as perceptive as Cuban *abuelas* (grandmothers). Although Martina is skeptical of her Abuela's advice to use *la prueba del café* (the coffee test) to assess her suitors' tempers, she soon finds out she does not want the first three—a rooster, a pig and a lizard. Assuredly, gardener Pérez, a tiny brown mouse who also has a Cuban grandmother, knows exactly how to make her laugh. Austin's stylistic, double-page acrylic spreads in exaggerated and unusual perspectives present a charming view of *La Habana Vieja* (Old Havana).

Duerme, duerme, mi niño: Arrullos, nanas y juegos de falda. (Sleep, Sleep, My Child: Lullabies, Nursery Rhymes and Games) Selected by B. Oliva. Illus: Arcadio Lobato. Barcelona: Edebé, 2004. 60p. ISBN: 84-236-7249-2. $18.95. Ages 3–7.

This charming collection includes 57 traditional lullabies, rhymes and games from the Spanish-speaking world as well as children's poems by well-known authors such as Gloria Fuentes, Federico García Lorca and Rafael Alberti. Lobato's inviting double-spread watercolors with a strong Hispanic flavor make this a delightful experience for the young and their caregivers.

El libro de oro de las fábulas. (The Gold Book of Fables) Selected by Verónica Uribe. Illus: Constanza Bravo. Caracas: Ekaré, 2004. 126p. ISBN: 980-257-209-8. $13.95. Gr. 2–4.

Uribe selected and joyfully adapted twenty popular fables for this attractive collection, including fifteen commonly attributed to Aesop. From well-known favorites such as *Ratón de Campo y Ratón de Ciudad* (Country Mouse and City Mouse) to *La zorra y las uvas* (The Fox and the Grapes), these brief narratives with a single action followed by an obvious moral lesson are sure to please and perhaps instruct. Bravo's amusing ink and watercolor illustrations in rich earth tones add a lighthearted spirit and the author's afterword will be welcomed by parents and adults. The only caveat to this otherwise exquisite collection is the small size—4½" × 6½"—which will disappoint most readers.

Favret, Hafida, and Magdeleine Lerasle. *A la sombra del olivo. (By the Shade of the Olive Tree)* Illus: Nathalie Novi. ISBN: 84-88342-88-8. Includes a CD.

Soussana, Nathalie. *Cancioncillas del jardín del Edén.* *(Children's Songs from the Garden of Eden)* Illus: Beatrice Alemagna. ISBN: 84-88342-61-6. Includes a CD.
Ea. vol.: 57p. Translated by Miguel Ángel Mendo. Musical director: Paul Mindy. Madrid: Kókinos, 2005. $31.95. Gr. Preschool–3.

In an appealing large-format presentation, these collections of traditional Jewish and northwest African children's songs will delight children and serious students of these cultures. Each volume includes a musical CD and eye-catching full-page color illustrations highlighting the ambience and people of each culture. *A la sombra del olivo* contains 29 bilingual nursery rhymes, songs and games from the Maghreb region (Algeria, Tunisia, and Morocco) in their original language—Arabic or Berber—and in a Spanish rendition. Also included is a phonetic chart and appended explanations. This title received the 2005 Best Edited Award by the Spanish Ministry of Culture. *Cancioncillas del jardín del Edén* is a collection of 28 bilingual traditional Jewish children's songs in their original language—Hebrew, Judeo-Spanish (according to the author not to be confused with Ladino), Yiddish and Arabic—and in a Spanish rendition. An informative author's note on the different languages and an appendix highlighting cultural information about each song make this a joyous celebration of the diversity of Jewish traditions.

Fleischman, Sid. *La Gran Rata de Sumatra (The Giant Rat of Sumatra or Pirates Galore).* Illus: David Lara. Translated by Josefina Anaya. Mexico: Castillo, 2006. 175p. ISBN: 970-20-0855-7. pap. $11.95. Gr. 5–8.

Set in 1846 in San Diego amid the turbulence of the Mexican-American War, this fast-paced novel features *Náufrago*, a brave and resourceful American cabin boy, and his kind-hearted Mexican protector *capitán Cadalso.* Together they manage to survive narrow escapes at sea where pirates, bandits and precious jewels are part of their daily routine. Anaya's sprightly Spanish rendition maintains the humor, spirited prose and distinctive dialogue of the original. Unfortunately, Lara's pedestrian black-and-white illustrations are mere absurd distractions.

Fowles, Shelley. *El solterón y la alubia. (The Old Bachelor Who Lost a Bean)* Illus: the author. Translated by Miguel Ángel Mendo. Barcelona: Serres, 2004. 26p. ISBN: 84-8488-162-8. $14.95. Gr. Preschool–3.

Fowles's lively retelling of this Jewish folktale set in Morocco has maintained its humor and fast pace in this snappy Spanish rendition that is further enhanced with the original shimmering watercolor-and-ink illustrations. Although a nasty old lady repeatedly steals magic pots from the town's *viejo solterón* (old bachelor), he decides that with her bad temper she is just the right match for him. Of course, after the fabulous wedding, their quarrels could be heard *de un extremo de la ciudad al otro* (from one end of town to the other). Whether for read-alouds or individual enjoyment, Spanish speakers will appreciate the humor and the author's note explaining the term *alubias* (kidney beans) as they are known around the Spanish-speaking world.

Gardner, Sally. *Mis cuentos de princesas. (A Book of Princesses)* Illus: the author. Translated by Raquel Mancera. Barcelona: Serres, 2003. 93p. ISBN: 84-8488-114-8. $15.95. Gr. 2–5.

Five of the most popular tales about princesses—*La Cenicienta* (Cinderella), *El príncipe rana* (The Frog Prince), *La Bella Durmiente* (Sleeping Beauty), *La princesa y el guisante* (The Princess and the Pea) and *Blancanieves* (Snow White)—are included in this attractive publication, originally published by Orion, London. Dainty, black-line and pastel illustrations, full of wit and humor, and a fresh, carefree Spanish rendition add a contemporary tone that will entice young readers/listeners. It would be unfortunate if few Peninsular Spanish conjugations—e.g., *debisteis arrepentiréis*—discourage adult Spanish speakers from the Americas from sharing this book with the young.

Garralón, Ana, adapt. *Cuentos y leyendas hispanoamericanos. (Latin American Tales and Legends)* Illus: Javier Serrano and others. Madrid: Anaya, 2005. 251p. ISBN: 84-667-4700-1. $34.95. Gr. 4–7.

Divided into four sections—trickster, talking-beast, wonder and pourquoi tales—this engaging collection of sixty legends and tales from the oral tradition of Latin America maintains the tone, ingenuity and vernacular of the originals. It includes such well-known tales as *Sopa de piedras* (Stone Soup) to lesser-known legends and myths that tell why the ocean is salty and how winter began. The brevity of each narration—from two to five pages—and the brief, one-paragraph commentary that follows each tale and highlights its origin and significance, add to the readers' understanding and enjoyment. Also invaluable are the numerous useful footnotes included throughout that briefly and concisely explain the meaning of particular words, phrases or expressions used by different groups or countries in Latin America. The only caveat in this luxury, large-format publication is that most of the watercolor illustrations are either insipid embellishments or trite decorations.

Gerson, Mary-Joan. *Fiesta femenina: Celebrando a las mujeres a través de historias tradicionales mexicanas. (Fiesta Femenina: Celebrating Women in Mexican Folktales)* Illus.: Maya Christina Gonzalez. Translated by Una Pérez Ruiz. Mexico/U.S.: Destino/Planeta, 2003. 64p. ISBN: 970-690-684-3. $19.99. Gr. 4–8.

First published in English, this lively Spanish rendition is as engaging as the original. To celebrate the special talents and extraordinary aspects of Mexican women, Gerson selected eight popular tales from Mexico that feature powerful women. Especially appealing for younger children is *Por qué la Luna es libre*, which tells why la Luna (Moon) giggles with pleasure as she outwits the Sun. Older children, particularly from Mexico, will recognize two old-time favorites: *La Virgen de Guadalupe*, which re-creates the appearance of Our Lady of Guadalupe to Juan Diego, and *Malintzin de la Montaña*, which recounts the importance of this Aztec princess in the conquest of Mexico. Gonzalez's original lavish acrylics as well as a well-done introduction, source notes and glossary add to this joyous fiesta of Mexican folklore.

Grimm, Jacob, and Wilhelm Grimm. *Caperucita Roja y otros cuentos I. (Little Red Riding Hood and Other Stories I)* 236p. Illus: Jordi Vila Delclòs. ISBN: 84-667-5383-4.
———. *La Bella Durmiente y otros cuentos II. (Sleeping Beauty and Other Stories II.)* 262p. Illus: Jesús Gabán. ISBN: 84-667-5384-2.
———. *Piel de Oso y otros cuentos III. (Bearskin and Other Stories III)* 272p. Illus: Pablo Auladell. ISBN: 84-667-5385-0.
———. *La llave de oro y otros cuentos IV. (The Golden Key and Other Stories IV)* 208p. Illus: Gabriel Pacheco. ISBN: 84-667-5386-9.
Ea. vol.: Translated by María Antonia Seijo Castroviejo. (Cuentos Completos) Madrid: Anaya, 2006. $21.95. Gr. 2–6.

This four-volume series is an excellent Spanish rendition of the complete collection of stories by Jacob and Wilhelm Grimm, *Kinderund Hausmärchen*, first published in Berlin, 1812–1817. With a few full-page and numerous smaller illustrations, these stories resonate with the beloved characters, exciting plots and satisfying endings that generations of children around the world know and enjoy. Varying in length from a few paragraphs to seven pages, each volume includes a most insightful and informative prologue about the stories and their authors that serious readers should not miss. *Caperucita Roja y otros cuentos I*, with 39 stories includes such favorites as *La Cenicienta* (Cinderella), *El sastrecillo valiente* (The Brave Little Tailor), and *Los músicos de Bremen* (The Musicians of Bremen). *La Bella Durmiente y otros cuentos II*, 51 stories, is comprised of more cherished tales, such as *Blancanieves* (Snow White) and *El Enano Saltarín* (Rumpelstiltskin), and lesser known, such as *El clavel* (The Carnation). *Piel de Oso y otros cuentos III*, 63 stories, contains a few popular stories such as *Fernando fiel y Fernando infiel* (Faithful Ferdinand and Faithless Ferdinand) and *Los cuatro hermanos habilidosos* (The Four Clever Brothers) as well as other tales. *La llave de oro y otros cuentos IV*, is a collection of 59 of lesser known Grimm stories that still vibrate with the freshness and grace of the more noted tales.

Grimm, Wilhelm, and Jacob Grimm. *Hansel y Gretel.* (*Hansel and Gretel*) Illus: Anthony Browne. Translated by Miriam Martínez. Mexico: Fondo de Cultura Económica, 2004. 32p. ISBN: 968-16-7062-0. $10.95. Gr. 2–4.

Browne adds a contemporary ambience with his always-commanding, bold, flat illustrations in dark tones to the somber tale of a brother and sister abandoned in the woods by their parents and nearly eaten by a horrible witch. In contrast to more traditional illustrations, these are modern-looking Hansel and Gretel, a sophisticated mean stepmother and a poor woodcutter.

Gudule. *Cuentos de Las mil y una noches. (Tales from The Thousand Nights and a Night)* Illus: Jordi Vila Delclòs. Translated by Isabel Conejo. Madrid: Anaya, 2005. 141p. ISBN: 84-667-4716-8. pap. $11.95. Gr. 5–10.

This is indeed a wonderful selection/adaptation of 12 tales from *The Thousand Nights and a Night*, supposedly told by Scheherezade to King Shahryar of Baghdad in her effort to keep from being beheaded. Originally published by Èditions Nathan, Paris, Conejo's spirited Spanish rendition radiates with the magic of the original Arab tales in which powerful viziers, mighty sultans and mysterious women live, play and compete. The brevity of each account—from four to twelve pages each—the exquisitely entertaining Spanish rendition, and the informative footnotes make these tales a joyous experience for reluctant Spanish-speaking readers—or Spanish learners. A few black-and-white line illustrations depicting the distinctive flavor and ambiance of the Arab world are also included.

Hume, Lotta Carswell. *Cuentos de China y Tíbet. (Stories from China and Tibet)* Illus: Lo Koon-chiu. Translated by Patricia Torres Londoño. Bogotá: Norma, 2004. 113p. ISBN: 958-04-7837-6. pap. $9.95. Gr. 2–5.

Ten traditional stories from China and Tibet are included in this modest paperback publication. In a sprightly Spanish rendition with simple black-and-white illustrations, they tell about animals that speak and play tricks on each other, how the rooster acquired his crown and the ever-popular *La cenicienta China* (The Chinese Cinderella).

Jaffe, Nina. *La flor de oro: Un mito taíno de Puerto Rico. (The Golden Flower: A Taino Myth from Puerto Rico)* Illus: Enrique O. Sánchez. Translated by Gabriela Baeza Ventura. Houston: Arte Público, 2006. 30p. ISBN: 1-55885-463-0. $14.95. Gr. K–3.

The simple retelling of the popular Taíno myth that explains the origin of the sea, the forest and the beautiful island of Boriquén (Puerto Rico) is now available in this straightforward Spanish rendition. Sánchez's glowing, stylized full-color illustrations dramatically convey the pre-Columbian ambiance and mood, which *Así fue como, dicen los taínos, que entre el sol y el brillante mar azul nació su isla, su hogar— Boriquén* (as the Taíno say, between the sun and the sparkling blue sea, their island home—Boriquén—came to be).

Le thanh, Taï-Marc. *Babayaga. (Babayaga)* Illus: Rébecca Dautremer. Translated by P. Rozarena. Zaragoza: Edelvives, 2004. 32p. ISBN: 84-263-5505-6. $21.95. Gr. 2–4.

In this retelling of the Russian folktale, Babayaga is a one-toothed, lonely girl, rejected by all her classmates. Because the townspeople always make fun of her, *Babayaga se volvió mala.* (Babayaga became mean.) As an old lady, she is despised even more and she becomes *todavía más MALA muy REQUETE MALA* (even more MEAN, VERY, VERY MEAN). Although Babayaga and her sister, Cacayaga, make elaborate plans to get rid of beautiful Miguita, sweet Miguita, assisted by a grateful toad, finds a way to escape and return to her father. Babayaga remains hungry and angry. Originally published by Hachette Livre, this almost colloquial Spanish rendition maintains the gore and terrifying scenes, which are even more striking in the full-page illustrations, with exaggerated perspectives, further accentuated with deep-shaded reds and dark shadows. Fans of Russian folklore will find lots of babushkas and a few matrioshkas too.

Leprince de Beaumont, Madame. *Bella y la Bestia. (Beauty and the Beast)* Illus: Angela Barrett. Translated by Miguel Ángel Mendo. Madrid: Kókinos, 2006. 64p. ISBN: 84-96629-03-1. $21.95. Gr. 2–5.

Barrett's exquisitely refined, detailed illustrations sensitively convey the magic and drama of the ever popular tale about *Bella* (Beauty), the good daughter, who through her capacity to love releases a handsome prince from the spell that had made him an ugly beast. The sense of excitement is further enhanced by Mendo's powerful Spanish rendition that makes the characters entirely believable, Beaumont's moralistic voice praising *Bella's virtudes* (virtues) and condemning the sisters' *corazones y toda la malicia que encierran* (hearts and all the evilness they contain). Young Spanish speakers (and their parents) will make this their favorite version of the classic story.

Montejo, Víctor. *Blanca Flor: Una princesa maya. (White Flower: A Maya Princess)* Illus: Rafael Yockteng. Toronto: Tigrillo/Groundwood/ Distributed Publishers Group West, 2005. 36p. ISBN: 0-88899-600-4. $16.95. Gr. 2–5.

Set in the ancient Maya kingdom during the reign of the feared Witz Ak'al, this adaptation of the traditional Spanish folktale, *Blanca Flor,* features a strong female protagonist, a beautiful and resourceful Mayan princess who constantly outsmarts her demanding father and marries the young prince, Witol Balam. Yochteng's soft, pencil-and-watercolor illustrations provide an imaginative perspective of the Maya landscape and culture. A few Latin American colloquialisms (e.g., *ahorita*) add to the rhetorical effect, especially to Spanish speakers of the Americas.

Percy, Graham. *La liebre y la tortuga. (The Hare and the Tortoise)* Illus: the author. Translated by P. Rozarena. Madrid: Ediciones SM, 2002. 29p. ISBN: 84-348-8682-0. $14.95. Gr. Preschool–2.

Based on Percy's retelling, originally published by David Bennet, London, this bouncy Spanish rendition of Aesop's fable about perseverance is just right for one-on-one reading/viewing. Percy's close-up, black-line and color illustrations (albeit small) provide endearing views of the haughty hare and the deliberative tortoise, especially with the snappy conclusion: *Sin prisa, pero sin pausa, has ganado la carrera.* A delightful version of a popular fable.

Perrault, Charles. *Cuentos de Charles Perrault. (Stories by Charles Perrault)* Illus: Clara Calvo Salvador. Barcelona: Juventud, 2005. 94p. ISBN: 84-261-3494-7. $30.95. Gr. 3–7.

In an attractive, luxury edition, this volume includes eight of the best-known tales by Charles Perrault, including such longtime favorites as *La Bella Durmiente del Bosque* (Sleeping Beauty), *El gato con botas* (Puss in Boots) and *Cenicienta* (Cinderella). The relaxed Spanish rendition is complemented by Calvo's impressionable black-and-white and full-page color illustrations. Also included are the concluding *moralejas* (aphorisms), some offering an additional contrasting point of view. Not surprisingly, young Spanish speakers (and their parents) always delight in reading or listening to these classic tales.

Perrault, Charles. *Pulgarcito. (Tom Thumb)* Illus: Jean-Marc Rochette. Translated by Remedios Diéguez Diéguez. Barcelona: Blume, 2005. ISBN: 84-9801-035-7. $16.99. Gr. K–3.

This fluid Spanish rendition of the classic tale maintains the gore and meanness of the flesh-eating ogre and the cleverness and courage of *Pulgarcito* (Tom), the smallest of seven brothers, who repeatedly saves them and brings back riches to his poor family. Appropriately somber and dark full-page color as well as black-and-white line illustrations add interest to the original tale. Despite a few Peninsular Spanish pronouns and conjugations, Spanish speakers from the Americas will enjoy *Pulgarcito* and its concluding *Moraleja* (Moral).

Shua, Ana María. *Este pícaro mundo. (This Scheming World)* Illus: Noemí Villamuza. Madrid: Anaya, 2007. 108p. ISBN: 978-84-667-6267-0. pap. $11.95. Gr. 4–7.

Lighthearted and easy-to-read, this collection of sixteen brief tales highlights the everlasting appeal of tricksters around the world. In European tales the fox is considered both astute and crafty; the Sioux (United States) and Ashanti (Africa) regard the spider as the most intelligent animal; the Guaraní (South America) credit the turtle with great abilities; and in China, Russia and the Middle East clever humans trick the powerful to right injustices and punish the greedy. Regretfully, the lifeless, thick black-and-white line illustrations are unpleasant distractions. Nonetheless, readers will appreciate the intrinsic charm of tricksters who are always ready to lie, to plot and to jest.

Valeri, Maria Eulália. *The Hare and the Tortoise/La liebre y la tortuga.* Illus: Max. ISBN: 0-8118-5057-9.
Vallverdú, Josep. *Aladdin and the Magic Lamp/Aladino y la lámpara maravillosa.* Illus: Pep Montserrat. ISBN: 0-8118-5061-7.
Ea. vol.: 32p. Translated into English by Elizabeth Bell. San Francisco: Chronicle, 2006. $14.95. Gr. K–3.

Like the most recent titles in this bilingual series of retellings of popular tales, these include simple English texts, followed by clear and accessible Spanish renditions, with facing illustrations. Despite Max's insipid pastel watercolors, it is always a pleasure to follow the tortoise's small steps as she beats the boastful hare in *The Hare and the Tortoise/La liebre y la tortuga.* Fortunately, Montserrat's imaginative watercolors, executed in rich earth tones, depict the alluring middle Eastern flavor of the original *Aladdin and the Magic Lamp/Aladino y la lámpara maravillosa.*

Ward, Helen. *Las mejores fábulas de Esopo. (Unwitting Wisdom: An Anthology of Aesop's Fables)* Illus: the author. Translated by Marta Pagés. Barcelona: Parramón, 2004. 60p. ISBN: 84-342-2642-1. $21.95. Gr. 3–6.

Aesop's fables are always popular in the Spanish-speaking world, hence this stunningly illustrated, large-format publication of 12 fables is sure to be a winner with both children and adults. Originally published in the United Kingdom and now exquisitely rendered in Spanish, it combines the at times grandiose language with everyday expressions that all children understand: *Soy la más veloz de todas, solía decir de una forma muy irritante* ("I am the master of faster," was how he so irritatingly put it.") From *Las uvas verdes* (Sour Grapes) to *una tortuga que siempre tenía la cabeza en las nubes* (a tortoise that always had her head in the clouds), Spanish speakers will relish the beautiful pen and watercolor double-page spreads, well-told narrations and concluding moral statements.

Language

Palomar de Miguel, Juan. *Mis primeras letras de palabras mexicanas. (My First Words of Mexicanisms)* Illus: Cecilia Rébora. Mexico:

Destino/Planeta, 2004. 32p. ISBN: 970-37-0096-9. $13.95. Gr. Preschool–2.

The Spanish alphabet serves as a template to this ABC that introduces words characteristic of Mexican Spanish. Although most of the words are well-known by Mexican children (i.e., *comal, huarache, paleta*), some readers will need to refer to the glossary at the back of the book to find the meaning of such words as *alebrije, itacate,* and *xocoyote.* Despite the colorful yet pedestrian illustrations, this is a noteworthy, representative sample of Spanish words that originated in Mexico and continue to enrich the Spanish language.

Scarry, Richard. *Best Word Book Ever/El mejor libro de palabras.* Illus: the author. Translated by Alicia Fontán. New York: Northland, 2004. 64p. ISBN: 0-87358-873-8. $16.95. Gr. Preschool–3.

Young children are introduced to common objects and activities in both English and Spanish in this large-format pictorial vocabulary book with Scarry's characteristic tiny pen and watercolor illustrations. From familiar actions at home in the morning, to playing at the playground, to a visit to the doctor, to describing things people do, this well-conceived bilingual book provides English—and Spanish—language learners practice in naming basic words and concepts.

Science

Adamson, Thomas K. *Júpiter/Jupiter.* ISBN: 0-7368-5879-2.
———. *Marte/Mars.* ISBN: 0-7368-5880-6.
———. *Mercurio/Mercury.* ISBN: 0-7368-5881-4.
———. *Neptuno/Neptune.* ISBN: 0-7368-5882-4.
———. *Plutón/Pluto.* ISBN: 0-7368-5883-0.
———. *Saturno/Saturn.* ISBN: 0-7368-5884-9.
———. *La Tierra/Earth.* ISBN: 0-7368-5878-4.
———. *Urano/Uranus.* ISBN: 0-7368-5885-7.
———. *Venus/Venus.* ISBN: 0-7368-5886-5.

Ea. vol.: 24p. Translated by Martín Luis Guzmán Ferrer. (Exploremos la Galaxia/Exploring the Galaxy) Mankato, MN: Capstone, 2006. $15.93. Gr. K–1.

Eye-catching, full-page color photos and drawings and a most simple bilingual text (one or two sentences per page) introduce English and Spanish young learners to nine planets—Jupiter, Mars, Mercury,

Neptune, Pluto, Saturn, Earth, Uranus, Venus. The English text and the clear Spanish rendition, which follows in the bottom part of the page, describe basic facts about every planet. Each title includes a glossary, Internet sites and an index in both languages.

Albee, Sarah. *Trevor el ingenioso. (Clever Trevor)* Illus: Paige Billin-Frye. ISBN: 978-1-57565-263-4.

Herman, Gail. *Enterrado en el jardín. (Buried in the Back Yard)* Illus: Jerry Smath. ISBN: 978-1-57565-262-7.

Luke, Melinda. *El perro verde. (Green Dog)* Illus: Jane Manning. ISBN: 978-1-57565-264-1.

Penner, Lucille Recht. *Osos en la mente. (Bears on the Brain)* Illus: Lynn Adams. ISBN: 978-1-57565-261-0.

Ea. vol.: 32p. Translated by Alma B. Ramírez. (Science Solves It! en español). New York: Kane Press, 2008. pap. $5.95. Gr. 1–2.

Just as lively and appealing as the original English series, these engaging Spanish renditions feature a contemporary protagonist who *piensa como un científico* (thinks like a scientist) as he/she observes closely, asks questions, measures carefully and makes predictions. Almost cartoonish color illustrations, common situations and an easy-to-read text encourage young Spanish speakers to use simple scientific skills to solve real-life problems. The concept of levers is depicted in *Trevor el ingenioso* as Trevor figures out how to use an uneven seesaw to teach Buzz and his buddies a lesson and thus reclaim the playground. The importance of measurement is highlighted in *Enterrado en el jardín* as Ryan and Katie discover what they think is a dinosaur bone. While pet-sitting, Teddy uses science (deduction) to solve a mystery in *El perro verde*. By comparing tracks in Oscar's backyard to pictures in a library book, Oscar and his friends find out who has been eating his mother's red flowers in *Osos en la mente*. Each title includes a final page with simple suggestions for adults to talk about science with the young.

Aloian, Molly, and Bobbie Kalman. *Cadenas alimentarias del bosque tropical. (Rainforest Food Chains) ISBN: 978-0-7787-8533-0.*

Crossingham, John, and Bobbie Kalman. *Cadenas alimentarias de la costa marina. (Seashore Food Chains)* ISBN: 0-7787-8531-9.

Kalman, Bobbie. *Cadenas alimentarias del bosque. (Forest Food Chains)* ISBN: 0-7787-8529-7.

———. *Las cadenas alimentarias y tú. (Food Chains and You)* ISBN: 0-7787-8528-9.

————, and Kelley MacAulay. *Cadenas alimentarias del desierto. (Desert Food Chains)* ISBN: 0-7787-8530-0.

————, and Kylie Burns. *Cadenas alimentarias de los pantanos. (Wetland Food Chains)* ISBN: 978-0-7787-8532-3.

Ea. vol.: 32p. Illus: Barbara Bedell and others. Translated by translations.com. (Cadenas Alimentarias) New York: Crabtree, 2006–2008. $18.95. Gr. 2–4.

The importance and ubiquitousness of food chains in nature—a succession of organisms, each kind serving as a source of nourishment as it consumes a lower member and in turn is preyed upon by a higher member—are simply and clearly explained in these fluid Spanish renditions. Each title includes sharp color photos, easy-to-understand charts and a clean layout and design. The delicate balance of life maintained in lush Southeast Asian tropical rain forests is depicted in *Cadenas alimentarias del bosque tropical.* The unique environment where water meets land, the microscopic aquatic organisms that kick start food chains and the migratory animals that come in and out of seashore food chains as well as the dangers of pollution are described in *Cadenas alimentarias de la costa marina.* Temperate forest food chains including plants, herbivores, carnivores and omnivores of this habitat are explained in *Cadenas alimentarias del bosque.* How the transfer of energy takes place from the sun to various plants, animals and people is clarified in *Las cadenas alimentarias y tú.* The adaptation of plants and animals in the Sonoran Desert and the dangers to its food chains are depicted in *Cadenas alimentarias del desierto.* The interaction between plants and animals in a specific wetland—the marsh—is explained in *Cadenas alimentarias de los pantanos.*

Aloian, Molly, and Bobbie Kalman. *El ciclo de vida de la flor. (Life Cycle of a Flower)* ISBN: 978-0-7787-8671-9.

————. *El ciclo de vida del escarabajo. (Life Cycle of a Beetle)* ISBN: 978-0-7787-8669-6.

Crossingham, John, and Bobbie Kalman. *El ciclo de vida del tiburón. (Life Cycle of a Shark).* ISBN: 978-0-7787-8673-3.

Kalman, Bobbie. *El ciclo de vida de la abeja. (Life Cycle of a Honeybee)* Illus: Margaret Amy Reiach and Bonna Rouse. ISBN: 0-7787-8666-8.

————. *El ciclo de vida de la lombriz de tierra. (Life Cycle of an Earthworm)* ISBN: 978-0-7787-8670-2.

————. *El ciclo de vida de la mariposa. (Life Cycle of a Butterfly)* Illus: Margaret Amy Reiach. ISBN: 0-7787-8662-5.

——. *El ciclo de vida del mosquito. (Life Cycle of a Mosquito)* Illus: Barbara Bedell and Katherine Kantor. ISBN: 0-7787-8667-6.

——, and Amanda Bishop. *El ciclo de vida de un león. (Life Cycle of a Lion)* Illus: Bonna Rouse and others. ISBN: 0-7787-8664-1.

——, and Robbie Johnson. *El ciclo de vida del pingüino emperador. (Life Cycle of an Emperor Penguin).* ISBN: 978-07787-8672-6.

——, and Kathryn Smithyman. *El ciclo de vida de la araña. (Life Cycle of a Spider)* ISBN: 978-0-7787-8668-9.

——. *El ciclo de vida de la rana. (Life Cycle of a Frog)* Illus: Bonna Rouse. ISBN: 0-7787-8663-3.

——. *El ciclo de vida del árbol. (Life Cycle of a Tree)* Illus: Barbara Bedell. ISBN: 0-7787-8665-X.

Ea. vol.: 32p. Translated by translations.com. (Ciclos de Vida) New York: Crabtree, 2005–2007. $18.90. Gr. 2–4.

With excellent, clear, color photos and drawings and simple, easy-to-understand texts, these well-done Spanish renditions introduce children to nature's life cycles. *El ciclo de vida de la abeja* discusses such important aspects as how bees gather nectar and pollen from flowers, build strong beehives using beeswax in a specific design of hexagonal cells, and protect themselves from cold temperatures by utilizing resin from plants. Especially well-described are the members of a bee colony and the specific functions of the queen bee, the drones and the worker bees. It concludes with an explanation of how beekeepers maintain apiaries to raise honey, the problems of pesticide use, and how young people can help and learn more about bees. Each title includes a glossary, albeit, some without definite articles. How will Spanish learners know that it should be *el néctar* and many others? *El ciclo de vida de la flor* describes the growth of a flower from seed to the time it is a mature plant capable of producing new seeds. *El ciclo de vida del escarabajo* features the growth and development of beetles. The growth, development, feeding and mating habits of sharks are described in *El ciclo de vida del tiburón. El ciclo de vida de la lombriz de tierra* follows earthworms from birth to maturity. The life cycle of the monarch butterfly, the large orange and black butterflies that migrate long distances, is described in *El ciclo de vida de la mariposa.* The life cycle of a mosquito and how in these two-winged insects the females suck blood and sometimes transmit diseases are explained in *El ciclo de vida del mosquito.* The life cycle, hunting patterns, territorial boundaries, and male dominance of lions are characterized in *El ciclo de vida de un león. El ciclo de vida del pingüino emperador* explains the role of penguin fathers in caring for their newborns, their survival skills and the predators of emperor penguins. *El ciclo de vida de la araña* chronicles the growth and development of spiders. The life cycle of frogs, from egg to tadpole, froglet and adult, are explored in *El ciclo de vida de la rana*. The life cycle of trees, from the production of seeds, to the role of trees in a forest, to the importance of trees to avoid erosion are explained in *El ciclo de vida del árbol*.

Aloian, Molly, and Bobbie Kalman. *El ciclo de vida de los insectos. (Insect Life Cycles)* ISBN: 0-7787-8499-1.
——. *El cuerpo de los insectos. (Insect Bodies)* ISBN: 0-7787-8496-7.
——. *Insectos que trabajan en equipo. (Insects that Work Together)* ISBN: 0-7787-8498-3.
——. *Insectos útiles y dañinos. (Helpful and Harmful Insects)* ISBN: 0-7787-8497-5.
Ea. vol.: 32p. Translated by translations.com. (El Mundo de los Insectos) New York: Crabtree, 2006. $17.94. Gr. 2–4.
The world of insects is explained to young Spanish speakers through a simple text and spectacular color photos. Each title includes informative sidebars, a glossary and an index. The changes that different species of insects go through before they become fully grown are described in *El ciclo de vida de los insectos*. The physical features of insects and the importance of each body part are defined in *El cuerpo de los insectos*. How insect colonies work together to ensure the survival of their colonies is narrated in *Insectos que trabajan en equipo*. The importance and potential damage of insects to other living things on Earth are highlighted in *Insectos útiles y dañinos*.

Aloian, Molly, and Bobbie Kalman. *Muchos tipos de animales. (Many Kinds of Animals)* ISBN: 0-7787-8832-6.
Kalman, Bobbie. *Ranas y otros anfibios. (Frogs and Other Amphibians)* ISBN: 978-0-7787-8837-9.
——, and Kristina Lundblad. *Animales llamados mamíferos (Animals Called Mammals)* ISBN: 978-0-7787-8836-2.
Lundblad, Kristina, and Bobbie Kalman. *Animales llamados peces. (Animals Called Fish)* ISBN: 0-7787-8833-4.
MacAulay, Kelley, and Bobbie Kalman. *Reptiles de todo tipo. (Reptiles of all Kinds)* ISBN: 0-7787-8835-0.
Sjonger, Rebecca, and Bobbie Kalman. *Aves de todo tipo. (Birds of all Kinds)* ISBN: 0-7787-8834-2.

Ea. vol.: 32p. Translated by translations.com. (¿Qué Tipo de Animal Es Ese?) New York: Crabtree, 2006–2007. $17.94. Gr. 1–3.

Beginning Spanish-speaking readers are introduced to the world of animals through a simple, easy-to-understand text and clear color photos and drawings. Each title describes major characteristics and focuses on particular features. Various groups of animals, such as several types of mammals, fish, reptiles, birds and anthropods are introduced in *Muchos tipos de animales*. The bodies, senses, habitats and behavior of frogs, salamanders and caecilians are described in *Ranas y otros anfibios*. Primates, rodents, marsupials and other mammal groups are featured in *Animales llamados mamíferos*. How fish breathe underwater, how they use their fins and how they defend against predators are explained in *Animales llamados peces*. The bodies, feeding habits, and natural habitats of different reptiles such as snakes, lizards and turtles are described in *Reptiles de todo tipo*. Basic facts about the bodies and behavior of birds are discussed in *Aves de todo tipo*. The fluid Spanish renditions make this appealing series especially engaging to the young. The only caveat in this otherwise excellent Spanish series is that the labels accompanying the illustrations do not include the definite articles, which are absolutely necessary to beginning Spanish readers (and learners).

Aloian, Molly, and Bobbie Kalman. *Un hábitat del bosque tropical. (A Rainforest Habitat)* ISBN: 978-0-7787-8333-6.

——. *El hábitat de la Antártida. (The Antarctic Habitat)* ISBN: 978-0-7787-8332-9.

——. *Un hábitat de pantano. (A Wetland Habitat)* ISBN: 978-0-7787-8328-6.

——. *El hábitat del Ártico. (The Arctic Habitat)* ISBN: 978-0-7787-8330-5.

——. *Hábitats acuáticos. (Water habitats)* ISBN: 978-0-7787-8325-1.

——. *Hábitats subterráneos. (Underground Habitats)* ISBN: 978-0-7787-8331-2.

Kalman, Bobbie. *Un hábitat de bosque. (A Forest Habitat)* ISBN: 978-0-7787-8327-5.

——, and John Crossingham. *Hábitats terrestres. (Land Habitats)* ISBN: 978-0-7787-8324-4.

——, and Rebecca Sjonger. *Un hábitat de sabana. (A Savanna Habitat)* ISBN: 978-0-7787-8329-9.

MacAulay, Kelley, and Bobbie Kalman. *Un hábitat de desierto. (A Desert Habitat)* ISBN: 978-0-7787-8326-8.
——. *Un hábitat de pastizal. (A Grassland Habitat)* ISBN: 978-0-7787-8334-3.
——. *Hábitats de jardín. (Backyard Habitats)* ISBN: 978-0-7787-8335-0.
Ea. vol.: 32p. Translated by translations.com. (Introducción a los Hábitats) New York: Crabtree, 2007. $18.90. Gr. K–2.

With attractive, colorful illustrations and easy-to-read Spanish texts, this well-designed series introduces the very young to twelve different habitats. Each title includes *Palabras para saber* (Words to Know) and an index. The only caveat in this otherwise exquisitely rendered Spanish translation is that the labels do not include the definite articles. How will Spanish learners know if it is *el* or *la flor*, or *el* or *la ave*, and many others? The large trees, beautiful flowers, and animals of the South American tropical rain forests are described in *Un hábitat del bosque tropical*. The different species of birds, seals, and whales that live in the freezing Southern Ocean are shown in *El hábitat de la Antártida*. (An unfortunate typo on the cover and title page mar this book.) The plants and animals that live in wetlands are featured in *Un hábitat de pantano*. How plants and animals have adapted to the harsh environment in the Arctic is explained in *El hábitat del Ártico*. Different water habitats, such as oceans, lakes, rivers and swamps are portrayed in *Hábitats acuáticos*. The diverse plants and animals of the world's underground habitats are defined in *Hábitats subterráneos*. The plants and animals of temperate mixed forests arc described in *Un hábitat de bosque*. Land habitats, including mountains, deserts, grasslands, and forests are explained in *Hábitats terrestres*. The plants and animals of the grasslands of Africa are depicted in *Un hábitat de sabana*. The weather, plants and animals of the Sonoran Desert are portrayed in *Un hábitat de desierto*. The plants and animals that make their homes in prairies are featured in *Un hábitat de pastizal*. Plants and animals that survive in backyard habitats are shown in *Hábitats de jardín*.

Arnold, Nick. *Esa caótica química. (Chemical Chaos)* 158p. ISBN: 978-84-2722-052-2.
——. *Esos sufridos científicos. (Suffering Scientists)* 192p. ISBN: 978-84-272-2067-7.
Ea. vol.: Illus: Tony de Saulles. Translated by Josefina Caball. (Esa Horrible Ciencia) Barcelona: RBA Libros, 2008. pap. $10.95. Gr. 5–8.

Through cartoonish, black-and-white drawings, witty explanations, amusing sidebars and a lighthearted text, the *Esa Horrible Ciencia* series provides a most enjoyable and approachable introduction to science and noteworthy scientific achievements. From a family from the Stone Age where a normal mama discovered the well-known method of *ensayo y errores* (trial and error), to unknown Chinese scientists who discovered gunpowder in 250 A.D., to Archimedes's *bla, bla, bla* theories and Aristotles's accomplishments as well as *errores garrafales* (terrible errors), to Francis Bacon's *método científico* (scientific method), to intrepid astronomers, Galileo Galilei's and Johannes Kepler's ruthless persecution by the Church, to modern astronomers, chemists, biologists and physicists up to Albert Einstein's *teoría de la relatividad* (Theory of Relativity) and Niels Bohr's *mecánica cuántica* (quantum mechanics) as explained by Bohr: *a lo mejor significa que . . . no, esto no puede ser* (maybe it means . . . no, this can not be), *Esos sufridos científicos*, an attractively designed paperback, is science without pomposity or unnecessary obfuscation. The most chaotic aspects of chemistry, beginning with *espantosos alquemistas* (frightening alchemists) and unnecessarily troublesome words and with examples of *química culinaria* (culinary chemistry), useful discoveries such as nylon, the atom, chlorine and recycling plastics, *Esa caótica química* highlights the importance of chemists and chemistry in our lives.

Arnold, Nick. *Esa poderosa energía. (Killer Energy)* 144p. Translated by Josefina Cabal Guerrero. ISBN: 84-272-2093-6.
———. *Esos experimentos explosivos. (Explosive Experiments)* 192p. Translated by Conchita Peraire del Molino. ISBN: 84-272-2094-4.
Ea. vol.: Illus: Tony De Saulles. (Esa Horrible Ciencia) Barcelona: Molino/Planeta, 2003. pap. $9.95. Gr. 5–8.

Like the previous twenty-five titles of this delightful, easy-to-understand series, originally published by Scholastic, London, these unassuming paperback publications with numerous black-and-white cartoonish drawings, witty explanations, and amusing sidebars and a lighthearted text will certainly appeal to reluctant scientists-to-be. From *¿Qué es la energía?* (What is energy?) to energy as a source of usable power, to energy consumption and the big bang theory are discussed in *Esa poderosa energía*. Explosive experiments that have been done around the world from Galileo to William Harvey to amazing brain and unusual experiments in chemistry, light and electricity are explained in *Esos experimentos explosivos*.

Arnold, Nick. *Esos asquerosos bichos. (Ugly Bugs)* Illus: Tony de Saulles. Translated by Josefína Cabal Guerrero. (Esa Horrible Ciencia) Barcelona: RBA Libros, 2006. 127p. ISBN: 84-272-2059-6. pap. $9.95. Gr. 5–8.

In a lighthearted and easy-to-understand manner, Arnold explains numerous "repulsive" facts and habits about bugs. From flies' disgusting eating habits, to ants' horrible customs, to spiders' mortal poison, readers will learn both positive and negative characteristics of the world of insects. Originally published by Scholastic, London, this unassuming paperback with black-and-white cartoonish drawings will encourage all readers to learn more about insects.

Arnold, Nick. *Manual del cuerpo humano. (The Body Owner's Handbook)* Illus: Tony De Saulles. (Esa Horrible Ciencia) Barcelona: Molino, 2003. 160p. ISBN: 84-272-2095-2. pap. $9.95. Gr. 5–8.

Like the previous twenty-four titles of this most enticing series, originally published by Scholastic as *Horrible Science*, this includes amusing black-and-white cartoon illustrations and an entertaining text explaining basic characteristics of the human body. From such automatic functions as breathing and yawning, to essential care including *Desayuno del monstruo* (Monster Breakfast), to suggestions for dealing with annoying pimples, boils and blackheads, this is just the information that children need to care for their bodies.

Asimov, Isaac. *Asteroides. (Asteroids)* ISBN: 0-8368-3853-X.
———. *Júpiter. (Jupiter)* ISBN: 0-8368-3854-8.
———. *La Luna. (Moon)* ISBN: 0-8368-3855-6.
———. *Marte. (Mars)* ISBN: 0-8368-3856-4.
———. *Mercurio. (Mercury)* ISBN: 0-8368-3857-2.
———. *Neptuno. (Neptune)* ISBN: 0-8368-3858-0.
———. *Plutón y Caronte. (Pluto and Charon)* ISBN: 0-8368-3859-9.
———. *Saturno. (Saturn)* ISBN: 0-8368-3860-2.
———. *El Sol. (The Sun)* ISBN: 0-8368-3861-0.
———. *La Tierra. (Earth)* ISBN: 0-8368-3862-9.
———. *Urano. (Uranus)* ISBN: 0-8368-3863-7.
———. *Venus. (Venus)* ISBN: 0-8368-3864-5.

Ea. vol.: 32p. Revised by Richard Hantula. Translated by Carlos Porras and Patricia D'Andrea. (La Biblioteca del Universo del Siglo XXI) Milwaukee: Gareth Stevens, 2004. $23.93. Gr. 3–6.

Updated by Richard Hantula, this smooth Spanish rendition preserves Isaac Asimov's engaging overview about the universe. An easy-to-understand text, appealing design, and numerous color and black-and-white photos and drawings on every page explain the origins, physical makeup, and unique characteristics of our solar system. Each of the twelve titles in this series includes suggestions for further reading (in English only), English-language Web sites, places to visit, and a glossary.

Atlas visual Océano de botánica. (Océano's Visual Atlas: Botany) Barcelona: Editorial Océano, 2004. 84p. ISBN: 84-494-1279-X. pap. $10.95. Gr. 9–adult.

Like the other eleven titles in this series designed for high school students, this is not a simple overview to botany; rather it is a comprehensive survey of plant life, including the characteristic features and biology of plant habitats around the world. Numerous color maps, charts and diagrams on almost every page and a detailed text describe the plant world—from tropical rain forests to aquatic vegetation. Unfortunately, it does not include an index.

Baredes, Carla, and Ileana Lotersztain. *¿Por qué es tan guapo el pavo real? y otras estrategias de los animales para tener hijos. (Why Is the Peacock so Beautiful? And Other Strategies of Animals to Have Babies)* Illus: Esteban Tolj. ISBN: 987-20830-4-5.
———. *¿Por qué está trompudo el elefante? y otras curiosidades de los animales a la hora de comer. (Why Do Elephants Have a Long Trunk? And Other Curiosities of Animals at Eating Time)* Illus: Gonzalo García Rodríguez. ISBN: 987-98042-4-4.
———. *¿Por qué se rayó la cebra? y otras armas curiosas que tienen los animales para no ser devorados. (Why Does the Zebra Have Stripes? And Other Weapons that Animals Have to Defend Themselves)* Illus: Gonzalo García Rodríguez. ISBN: 987-98042-3-6.
Ea. vol.: 60p. (¡Qué Bestias!) Buenos Aires: Iamiqué, 2003–2004. pap. $10.95. Gr. 3–6.

With humorous, computer-generated color cartoon illustrations and a most amusing text, this lighthearted series explains why animals are the way they are. The strategies of such animals as elephants, fish and birds to seek a mate to preserve their species are explained in *¿Porqué es tan guapo el pavo real?* The strange habits of various animals—sharks, crocodiles, lions and others—to obtain food are described in *¿Porqué está trompudo el elefante?* The defensive mechanisms of animals such as porcupines' quills that stick into the attacking animal and lizards' abilities to grow a new tail are highlighted in *¿Porqué se rayó la cebra?* Published in Argentina and written in Argentinean Spanish, this series presents inherent animal characteristics in a most simple, unique and refreshing manner.

Bernhard, Emmanuel. *La meteorología. (Weather)* ISBN: 84-7864-922-0.
Nessmann, Philippe. *El color. (Color)* ISBN: 84-7864-921-2.
Zeitoun, Charline. *El cuerpo humano. (The Human Body)* ISBN: 84-7864-919-0.
    Ea. vol.: 24p. Illus: Peter Allen. Translated by Ana Gasol. (¿Qué Es?) Barcelona: Combel, 2005. $9.95. Gr. 3–5.
    Cartoonish illustrations, color photos and easy-to-follow, at-home experiments encourage children to discover and understand basic scientific phenomena. The combination of the sun, air and water and its effects on the weather are explained through simple experiments in *La meterología*. What is color and how to observe and separate colors are clarified in *El color*. Basic facts about the structure of the human body are described in *El cuerpo humano*. Originally published by Jeunesse, France, this series provides all measurements in the metric system, which is easier to understand by children from Hispanic America and Spain.

Bilgrami, Shaheen. *Animales increíbles: Libro de esqueletos mágicos. (Incredible Animal Discovery: A Magic Skeleton Book).* ISBN: 970-690-793-3.
    ———. *Dinosaurios increíbles. (Amazing Dinosaur Discovery).* ISBN: 970-690-794-7.
    Ea. vol.: 14p. Illus: Mike Phillips and others. México: Planeta, 2003/ Dist. by Planeta Publishing, 2003. $14.95. Gr. K–3.
    Sturdy, sliding pull-tabs, simple narratives, cartoon-style color drawings and amusing balloons with running comments of children and their parents while visiting two different museums add zest to these informative introductions to five large animals and to dinosaurs. *Papá* and *mamá* spend a day at the museum with Lucía, Juan and Miguel viewing, discussing and learning about whales, boa constrictors, bald eagles, crocodiles and elephants in *Animales increíbles*. Tomás, who loves dinosaurs, is delighted to spend Sunday with his father at the *museo de dinosaurios*. As they view the skeletons, Tomás consults his notebook and reviews basic facts and pictures of five different species: *Apatosaurio, Estegosaurio, Tiranosaurio Rex, Coritosaurio* and *Triceratops*

in *Dinosaurios increíbles.* Originally published by Sterling, London, these are indeed lively and playful guides.

Bourges R., Héctor. *Nutrición y vida. (Nutrition and Life)* ISBN: 970-35-0407-8.
Carrillo Trueba, César. *La diversidad biológica de México. (Biological Diversity of Mexico)* ISBN: 970-35-0406-X.
   Ea. vol.: 64p. (Tercer Milenio) Mexico: Conaculta, 2004. pap. $7.50. Gr. 9–adult.
   In a concise and not especially attractive format, this paperback series offers a panorama of specific issues related to Mexico. More informative of the two is *Nutrición y vida*, which explains basic aspects of the process by which the human body assimilates and uses food. Of special interest to people of Mexico are such factors as the importance of corn in the diet, traditional Mexican cuisine, undernourishment and the increase of obesity in Mexico. In contrast to *La diversidad biológica de México, Nutrición y vida* includes numerous two-tone photographs, drawings and charts that, albeit small, help clarify meaning along with informative captions and sidebars. *La diversidad biológica de México* provides an overview of the biological diversity of Mexico, including the processes that maintain it as well as those that destroy it. Unfortunately, the tiny and many unclear two-tone drawings, maps and photos and small font detract from its value. Serious students, however, will appreciate the easy-to-understand text, sidebars and recommended bibliography, which includes Mexican Web sites.

Bredeson, Carmen. *Astronautas. (Astronauts)* ISBN: 0-516-24441-8.
——. *Despegue. (Liftoff!)* ISBN: 0-516-25100-7.
——. *La Luna. (Moon)* ISBN: 0-516-24447-7.
——. *Nave espacial. (Living on a Space Shuttle)* ISBN: 0-516-25101-5.
——. *El sistema solar. (Solar System)* ISBN: 0516-24446-9.
   Ea. vol.: 32p. Translated by Eida Del Risco. (Rookie Español-Ciencias) New York: Children's Press, 2004. $17.00. Gr. K–2.
   Through clear color photos on almost every page and an easy-to-read Spanish text, young Spanish speakers are introduced to basic facts about space. *Astronautas* describes the work of astronauts, including special activities and simple experiments. *Despegue* provides an overview of some of the preparations leading up to the launch of a space shuttle. *La Luna* explores the physical characteristics and the ex-

ploration of the moon. *Nave especial* describes how astronauts aboard a space shuttle perform various activities. *El sistema solar* explains basic facts about our solar system and other features such as asteroids, comets and moons. Each title includes an index and a glossary, albeit without definite articles—a serious disadvantage for young Spanish speakers.

Candell, Arianna. *Los colores. (Colors)* ISBN: 0-7641-2994-5.
———. *Los contrarios. (Opposites)* ISBN: 0-7641-2993-7.
———. *Las formas. (Shapes)* ISBN: 0-7641-2995-3.
———. *Los números. (Numbers)* ISBN: 0-7641-2996-1.
Ea. vol.: 36p. Illus: Francesc Rovira. (El Osito Estudiante) New York: Barron's, 2004. pap. $6.95. Gr. Preschool–1.

Especially designed for the very young, this attractive paperback series features children and their teddy bears learning about colors, opposites, shapes and numbers through everyday activities at home and at play. The cheerful ink-and-watercolor illustrations and easy-to-understand texts are followed by suggested activities and a page for parents and teachers with further recommendations.

Claybourne, Anna, and others. *Enciclopedia del planeta Tierra. (The Usborne Encyclopedia of Planet Earth)* Illus: John Russell and Nicola Butler. Translated by Antonio Navarro Gosálvez. New York: Scholastic/Usborne, 2005. 160p. ISBN: 0-439-68127-8. pap. $5.99. Gr. 3–6.

Excellent color photos and digital illustrations, appealing layouts, and a brief, easy-to-understand text introduce Planet Earth's physical geography. Divided into seven chapters—*Planeta Tierra* (Planet Earth), *Terremotos y volcanes* (Earthquakes and Volcanoes), *El clima* (Climate), *El tiempo* (Weather), *La flora y la fauna* (Flora and Fauna), *El ciclo geológico* (Geological Cycles), *Los ríos y los mares* (Rivers and Oceans)—and followed by high-interest appendices, such as well-known scientists, world records and useful English and Spanish-language Web sites, this is indeed an informative overview to scientific concepts about the Earth.

Crossingham, John, and Bobbie Kalman. *¿Qué es la hibernación? (What Is Hibernation?)* ISBN: 0-7787-8758-3.
Kalman, Bobbie. *¿Qué son las plantas? (What Is a Plant?)* ISBN: 0-7787-8759-1.
———. *¿Qué son los reptiles? (What Is a Reptile?)* ISBN: 0-7787-8762-1.

———. *¿Qué son los seres vivos? (What Is a Living Thing?)* ISBN: 0-7787-8760-5.

———, and Heather Levigne. *¿Qué son los murciélagos? (What Is a Bat?)* ISBN: 0-7787-8763-X.

———, and Jacqueline Langille. *¿Qué son los anfibios? (What Is An Amphibian?)* ISBN: 0-7787-8761-3.

Ea. vol.: 32p. Translated by translations.com. (La Ciencia de los Seres Vivos). New York: Crabtree, 2005. $16.95. Gr. 3–5.

Like the previous six titles in this well-designed series, these are excellent introductions to living things. Originally published in English, these smooth Spanish renditions include clear, color photographs or drawings in every page, as well as boxed background pictorials, easy-to-understand labels and bold-faced typography. The techniques that various animals use to hibernate are described in *¿Qué es la hibernación?* The growth and importance of different plants are explained in *¿Qué son las plantas?* Survival mechanisms and appearance of reptiles are depicted in *¿Qué son los reptiles?* Basic facts about living things are introduced in *¿Qué son los seres vivos?* The lifestyle and survival of bats are presented in *¿Qué son los murciélagos?* The life cycle and survival mechanisms of various types of amphibians are related in *¿Qué son los anfibios?*

Crossingham, John and Bobbie Kalman. *¿Qué es la migración? (What Is Migration?)* ISBN: 978-0-7787-8769-3.

Kalman, Bobbie. *¿Cómo encuentran alimento los animales? (How Do Animals Find Food?)* ISBN: 978-0-7787-8768-6.

———, Kalman, Bobbie. *¿Cómo se adaptan los animales? (How Do Animals Adapt?)* ISBN: 978-0-7787-8767-9.

———, and Hannelore Sotzek. *¿Qué es un perro? (What Is a Dog?)* ISBN: 978-0-7787-8765-5.

———, and Heather Levigne. *¿Qué es un caballo? (What Is a Horse?)* ISBN: 978-0-7787-8766-2.

Walker, Niki, and Bobbie Kalman. *¿Qué es un dinosaurio? (What Is a Dinosaur?)* ISBN: 978-0-7787-8764-8.

Ea. vol.: 32p. Translated by translations.com. (La Ciencia de los Seres Vivos) New York: Crabtree, 2007. $18.90. Gr. 3–5.

More new titles in this attractively designed series with clear color photos and drawings that add interest to the text. The ever-changing world of animals and the need of animals to adapt to their habitats are explained in *¿Cómo se adaptan los animales?* How dogs use their senses and instincts in their daily lives and their efforts to help people are described in *¿Qué es un perro?* The special characteristics of horses, ponies, asses and zebras as well as their behavior and foraging habits are introduced in *¿Qué es un caballo?* From the study of fossils to the feeding and hunting habits of dinosaurs, including theories about their extinction, are discussed in *¿Qué es un dinosaurio?* It is unfortunate that despite the well-done Spanish renditions, the glossaries do not include definite articles. How will Spanish learners know that it should be *la especie* and *el fósil?*

Davis, Kenneth C. *Todo lo que hay que saber sobre el espacio. (Don't Know Much About Space)* Illus: Sergio Ruzzier. Translated by Joan Carles Guix. Barcelona: Oniro, 2004. 138p. ISBN: 84-9754-097-2. pap. $10.95. Gr. 3–5.

In a lively, question-and-answer format, Davis provides basic information about astronomy, the sun, stars, planets and space travel. With such questions as *¿Por qué fue encarcelado Galileo?* (Why was Galileo imprisoned?) and *¿Cómo se preparan los astronautas para la ingravidez?* (How do astronauts train for weightlessness?) as well as witty cartoons, charts, black-and-white photos, and informative sidebars and biographical boxes, this is a spirited introduction to space. Includes a timeline, glossary and bibliography (in English only).

DeRubertis, Barbara. *Una colección para Kate. (A Collection for Kate)* Illus: Gioia Fiammenghi. ISBN: 978-1-57565-240-5.
Dussling, Jennifer. *¡Lo justo es justo! (Fair Is Fair!)* Illus: Diane Palmisciano. ISBN: 978-1-57565-269-9.
Pollack, Pam, and Meg Belviso. *Gallinas de aquí para allá. (Chickens on the Move)* Illus: Lynn Adams. ISBN: 978-1-57565-268-9.
Ea. vol.: (Math Matters en Español) Translated by Alma B. Ramírez. New York: Kane, 2008. 32p. pap. $5.95. Gr. 1–3.

Unfortunately, the jaunty tone of the English originals is lacking in these at times awkward Spanish renditions with lively color cartoon illustrations that describe how young Spanish speakers can solve real-world problems by using simple mathematical skills. After Kate adds up the items in her classmate's collection, she comes up with her own collection and has enough items to share in *Una colección para Kate.* Although his father is not convinced, Marco uses bar graphs to persuade him that his allowance is not fair compared to what his friends are receiving in *¡Lo justo es justo!* Tom, Gordon and Anne are delighted with *abuelo's* surprise, but they have trouble finding the right place for the chicken coop. As they move the fence to accommodate the chickens, they try different shapes for their coop—rectangular, triangular, square—in *Gallinas de aquí para allá*. Each title concludes with simple questions about the concept discussed (bar graphs, perimeter) and suggested follow-up activities that require adult direction.

Durand, Jean-Benoît. *La vida a tu alcance. (Life Within Your Reach)* 76p. Illus: Robin Gindre. Translated by Núria Martí. ISBN: 84-9754-184-7.
——, and Georges Feterman. *El bosque a tu alcance. (Forests Within Your Reach)* 78p. Illus: Robin Gindre. Translated by Núria Martí. ISBN: 84-9754-185-5.
Girardet, Sylvie. *La prudencia a tu alcance. (Safety Within Your Reach)* 47p. Illus: Puig Rosado. Translated by Núria Martí. ISBN: 84-9754-212-6.
Le Duc, Michel, and Nathalie Tordjman. *La ciudad a tu alcance. (The City Within Your Reach)* 79p. Illus: Yves Calarnou. Translated by Núria Martí. ISBN: 84-9754-211-8.
——. *La geología a tu alcance. (Geology Within Your Reach)* 78p. Illus: Robin. Translated by Núria Martí. ISBN: 978-84-9754-251-7.
Michel, François. *La ecología a tu alcance. (Ecology Within Your Reach)* 79p. Illus: Marc Boutavant. Translated by Núria Martí. ISBN: 84-9754-187-1.
Mira Pons, Michéle. *El cielo a tu alcance. (The Sky Within Your Reach)* 64p. Illus: Robert Barborini. Translated by Núria Martí. ISBN: 84-9754-183-9.
Stern, Catherine. *El desarrollo sostenible a tu alcance. (Sustainable Development Within Your Reach)* 71p. Illus: Pénélope Paicheler. Translated by Gemma Gallart Alvarez. ISBN: 978-84-9754-293-7.
Ea. vol.: (Querido Mundo) Barcelona: Oniro, 2005-2007. pap. $11.95. Gr. 2–5.

In a spirited text with clear subheads, informative sidebars and most appealing pencil-and-watercolor cartoon illustrations, readers are introduced to our world. Each title in this snappy paperback series includes a *minidiccionario* (glossary) and a simple test followed by well-explained answers. From the Big Bang theory to the evolution of the species to puberty and the end of life, *La vida a tu alcance* is indeed a most enjoyable overview of living organisms. The wide diversity of trees, plants, underbrush and animals that coexist and interrelate in the forests of the world is explained in *El bosque a tu alcance*. Basic safety precautions—at home, outdoors and on the street—are explained in *La prudencia a tu alcance*. The history, development and uniqueness of cities around the world are described in *La ciudad a tu alcance*. The relationships between organisms and their environments, as well as the detrimental effects of human civilization on the environment, are discussed in *La ecología a tu alcance*. The origin, history and structure of the Earth are introduced in *La geología a tu alcance*. The upper atmosphere, the moon, the sun and galaxies are explored in *El cielo a tu alcance*. The benefits of sustainable development and the dangers to biodiversity of global warming are highlighted in *El desarrollo sostenible a tu alcance*.

Ehlert, Lois. *Cómo plantar un arco iris. (Planting a Rainbow)* Illus: the author. Translated by F. Isabel Campoy. Orlando, FL: Harcourt, 2006. 24p. ISBN: 0-15-205723-4. $6.95. Ages 2–4.

    With the same bold graphics and bright flat colors of its predecessor, *A sembrar sopa de verduras (Growing Vegetable Soup)*, this handsome board book exposes toddlers to the colors of the rainbow. After a mother and child plant flowers in the family garden, they see the bulbs sprout in spring, watch them grow and finally enjoy all the flowers in full bloom in six pages of varying size depicting each color of the rainbow. Despite the clear Spanish rendition, young Spanish speakers (and Spanish learners) will miss the definite articles in all of the labels. How will young readers/listeners know that it is *el clavel, los claveles, el áster* [sic] and *las violetas*?

Farmer, Jacqueline. *Calabazas. (Pumpkins)* Illus: Phyllis Limbacher Tildes. Translated by Eida del Risco. Watertown: Charlesbridge, 2006. 32p. ISBN: 1-57091-702-7. $16.95. Gr. 1–3.

    Spanish-speaking youngsters (and their parents) will certainly enjoy del Risco's almost conversational Spanish rendition that introduces the pumpkin plant as well as its history and its uses in the United States during Halloween. Although Halloween is not commonly known in many Spanish-speaking countries, many Latino children are eager to participate in the fun. This book, with attractive watercolor-and-pencil illustrations, provides simple instructions on pumpkin carving and other information to increase the enjoyment of this child-centered American holiday.

Farndon, John. *La enciclopedia de los hábitats*. *(Wildlife Atlas)* Translated by Fernando Bort Misol. Madrid: Ediciones SM, 2003. 128p. ISBN: 84-348-9093-3. $22.95. Gr. 6–10.

Divided into eight broad habitat types, this outstanding large-format book, originally published by Marshall Editions, London, describes each geographic location, its keystone animals, and its ecology. Sidebars on endangered species, emphasizing the relationship between climate, vegetation type, and the resident animals are included. Lavishly illustrated with clear photos, drawings, charts and maps on every page, this informative atlas concludes with a glossary and an index.

Firth, Rachel. *Astronomía*. *(Astronomy)* Illus: John Woodcock. Translated by Antonio Navarro Gonsálvez. (Descubre y Explora) Tulsa: EDC Publishing, 2004. 48p. ISBN: 0-7460-6389-X. pap. $8.95. Gr. 3–5.

Through clear, color photos, drawings and charts on every page, a simple text and informative sidebars, this attractive paperback introduces readers to the positions, motion and composition of celestial bodies. With numerous simple suggestions to observe the sky, it explains the explosions of the stars, the route of the comets and the evolution of the galaxies. Like the previous four titles in this series—*Aves* (Birds), *Dinosaurios* (Dinosaurs), *Serpientes* (Serpents), *Tiburones* (Sharks)—it encourages children to link to various Web sites. It also includes a glossary and an index.

Frost, Helen. *Alosaurio/Allosaurus*. ISBN: 978-0-7368-6683-5.

———. *Estegosaurio/Stegosaurus*. ISBN: 978-0-7368-6684-2.

———. *Mamut lanudo/Woolly Mammoth*. ISBN: 978-0-7368-6686-6.

———. *Tigre dientes de sable/Sabertooth Cat*. ISBN: 978-0-7368-6685-9.

———. *Tiranosaurio rex/Tyrannosaurus Rex*. ISBN: 978-0-7368-6688-0.

———. *Triceratops/Triceratops*. ISBN: 978-0-7368-6687-3.

Lindeen, Carol K. *Apatosaurio/Apatosaurus*. ISBN: 978-0-7368-7635-3.

———. *Braquiosaurio/Brachiosaurus*. ISBN: 978-0-7368-7636-0.

———. *Mastodonte americano/American Mastodon*. ISBN: 978-0-7368-7634-6.

———. *Velociraptor/Velociraptor*. ISBN: 978-0-7368-7641-4.

Riehecky, Janet. *Diplodocus/Diplodocus*. ISBN: 978-0-7368-7637-7.

———. *Iguanodonte/Iguanodon*. ISBN: 978-0-7368-7638-4.

———. *Megalodonte/Megalodon*. ISBN: 978-0-7368-7639-1.

———. *Pteranodonte/Pteranodon*. ISBN: 978-0-7368-7640-7.

Ea. vol.: 24p. Translated by Dr. Martín Luis Guzmán Ferrer. (Dinosaurios y Animales Prehistóricos/Dinosaurs and Prehistoric Animals) Mankato, MN: Capstone, 2007. $14.95. Gr. K–1.

In most simple and engaging bilingual texts and with eye-catching, full-page illustrations, this large-format series introduces the physical characteristics and unique behavior of fourteen dinosaurs and prehistoric animals—allosaurus, stegosaurus, woolly mammoth, sabertooth cat, tyrannosaurus Rex, triceratops, apatosaurus, brachiosaurus, American mastodon, velociraptor, diplodocus, iguanodon, megalodon, pteranodon. It includes such high-interest facts as: "Female diplodocuses laid their eggs while they walked. The eggs landed safely on the ground," followed by its equally well-stated Spanish rendition: *El diplodocus hembra ponía huevos mientras caminaba. Los huevos caían en el suelo sin lastimarse* (p. 16) with a corresponding illustration on a facing page. Glossaries in both languages are included. The only caveat in this otherwise outstanding series is that the Spanish rendition, which follows the English text, is in the exact color, size and style of font—which may confuse English and Spanish learners and beginning readers of both languages.

Fuller, Sue. *1001 datos sobre rocas y minerales. (1001 Facts about Rocks and Minerals)* 160p. Illus: Caroline Brooke. ISBN: 84-272-2374-9.
Stott, Carole, and Clint Twist. *1001 datos sobre el espacio. (1001 Facts about Space)* 192p. Illus: Fiona Watson. ISBN: 84-272-2372-2.
Ea. vol.: Translated by Alejandro Estallo and Josefina Caball. (Superenciclopedia de Bolsillo). Barcelona: Molino, 2002–2003. pap. $10.95. Gr. 4–7.

Numerous clear, color photos, drawings and diagrams on every page characterize this engaging, easy-to-understand, backpack-size (a bit larger than pocket-size), paperback series. Originally published by Dorling Kindersley, each title includes informative sidebars as well as a glossary, a reference section and an index. *1001 datos sobre rocas y minerales* provides a basic introduction to naturally formed minerals and a description of special minerals such as diamonds, silver, platinum, gold and others. *1001 datos sobre el espacio* describes the universe, galaxies, the solar system, planets and other aspects about space.

Gifford, Scott. *Piece=Part=Portion/Pedazo=parte=porción: Fractions =Decimals=Percents/Fracciones=decimales=porcentajes.* Photos by

Shmuel Thaler. Translated by Aurora Hernandez. Berkeley: Tricycle Press, 2007. 32p. ISBN: 978-1-58246-225-7. $14.95. Gr. 2–4.

With a minimum of text in both English and Spanish and through striking, easy-to-identify color photographs, this is a simple explanation of how, in the language of mathematics, fractions, decimals and percents describe the same parts of things. Because of the shortage of simple math books in Spanish, Spanish-speaking teachers and parents will find many uses for this basic introduction to important mathematical terms.

Gómez Roig, Edurne. *La clonación. (Cloning)* ISBN: 970-35-0733-6.
Miret, Maia F. *La evolución. (Evolution)* ISBN: 970-35-0732-8.
———. *El genoma. (Genome)* ISBN: 970-35-0734-4.
Ea. vol.: 24p. (Ciencias de la Vida) México: Conaculta, 2004. pap. $8.00 Gr. 4–7.

In a most accessible and easy-to-understand manner, this simple yet attractive paperback series introduces scientific concepts with up-to-date information. From photos of identical twins, to an explanation of DNA, to the process of making identical copies of a DNA sequence by dividing a cell, readers are exposed to cloning in *La clonación*. For example, it simply explains how Dolly, the sheep, was created from a clone cell, how cloning could be useful in medicine to create a new organ from a cell and important questions scientists must consider in this evolving field. Clear color drawings, diagrams and informative photos, and two or three paragraphs per page make this "sciences of life" (*Ciencias de la Vida*) series truly understandable. *La evolución* describes the changes in the genetic composition of living things as a result of natural selection. It also explains genetic variation, the development of new species, and the process of adaptation. *El genoma* expounds on the set of instructions in each cell that follows the genetic makeup of each organism and explains how chromosomes carry the genes that determine heredity as well as the importance of the Genome Project. Each title includes a simple-to-understand glossary. Spanish-speaking, middle-grade students will certainly welcome this comprehensible series on contemporary scientific topics.

Gomi, Taro. *Spring Is Here/Llegó la primavera.* Illus: the author. San Francisco: Chronicle, 2006. 36p. ISBN: 0-8118-4760-8. pap. $6.95. Gr. Preschool.

Winner of the Bologna Graphic Prize, Gomi's bold, simple watercolors and a minimal bilingual text engage English and Spanish learners as they follow the four seasons through an alluring calf. From a baby calf to *The calf has grown./El becerro ha crecido,* children experience melting snow, grass growing, a new harvest, snow falling and the arrival of spring. To reduce confusion to beginning readers, the English text is followed by the Spanish text in a different color font in facing pages.

Hall, Margaret. *Arañas/Spiders.* ISBN: 0-7368-6677-9.
——. *Grillos/Crickets.* ISBN: 0-7368-6678-7.
——. *Hormigas/Ants.* ISBN: 0-7368-6682-5.
——. *Mantis religiosas/Praying Mantises.* ISBN: 0-7368-6681-7.
——. *Mariquitas/Ladybugs.* ISBN: 0-7368-6680-9.
——. *Saltamontes/Grasshoppers.* ISBN: 0-7368-6679-5.
  Ea. vol.: 24p. Translated by Dr Martín Luis Guzmán Ferrer. (¡Criaturas Diminutas!/Bugs, Bugs, Bugs!) Mankato, MN: Capstone, 2007. $19.93. Gr. K–1.
  Exquisite, full-page, close-up color photos and one or two simple sentences per page in both English and Spanish describe the physical characteristics and habits of well-known insects—spiders, crickets, ants, praying mantis, ladybugs and grasshoppers. Young English and Spanish learners will appreciate the attractive, uncluttered design and well-done glossaries.

Heens, Caroline. *Mi gato Coque. (My Cat Coque)* ISBN: 84-263-4872-6.
——. *Mi perro Roque. (My Dog Roque)* ISBN: 84-263-4873-4.
  Ea. vol.: 28p. Illus: Clavis. Translated by P. Rozarena. Zaragoza: Luis Vives, 2002. $18.95. Gr. K–2.
  Originally published by Clavis, Belgium, these delightful books with witty black-ink and watercolor illustrations, simple texts, and well-constructed pop-ups and pull-the-tabs describe basic facts about cats and dogs. *Mi gato Coque* explains basic habits and special care of cats such as the meaning of various tail and hair positions and the importance of scratching columns. *Mi perro Roque* describes different types of dogs, their habits, body language and special commands for training.

Hipp, Andrew. *El árbol del olivo: Por dentro y por fuera. (Olive Trees, Inside and Out)* Illus: Fiammetta Dogi. Translated by Tomás González. ISBN: 1-4042-2865-9.
——. *El girasol: Por dentro y por fuera. (Sunflowers, Inside and Out)* Illus: Andrea Ricciardi di Gaudesi. Translated by María Cristina Brusca. ISBN: 1-4042-2868-3.

———. *El maíz: Por dentro y por fuera. (Corn, Inside and Out)* Illus: Andrea Ricciardi di Gaudesi. Translated by Tomás González. ISBN: 1-4042-2863-2.

———. *El roble: Por dentro y por fuera. (Oaks, Inside and Out)* Illus: Fiammetta Dogi. Translated by Tomás González. ISBN: 1-4042-2864-0.

Houghton, Gillian. *Abejas: Por dentro y por fuera. (Bees, Inside and Out)* Illus: Studio Stalio. Translated by Mauricio Velázquez de León. ISBN: 1-4042-2862-4.

———. *Arañas: Por dentro y por fuera. (Spiders, Inside and Out)* Illus: Studio Stalio. Translated by Tomás González. ISBN: 1-4042-2867-5.

———. *Búhos: Por dentro y por fuera. (Owls, Inside and Out).* Illus: Studio Stalio. Translated by Tomás González. ISBN: 1-4042-2866-7.

———. *Tortugas: Por dentro y por fuera. (Turtles, Inside and Out)* Illus: Studio Stalio. Translated by Tomás González. ISBN: 1-4042-2869-1. Ea. vol.: 28 p. (Explora la Naturaleza) New York: Buenas Letras/Rosen, 2004. $21.95. Gr. 2–5.

Through exquisite color photos, drawings, and straightforward Spanish text, this series encourages readers to explore nature. The first four titles—*El árbol del olivo: Por dentro y por fuera, El girasol: Por dentro y por fuera, El maíz: Por dentro y por fuera,* and *El roble: Por dentro y por fuera*—explain basic facts about the growth, reproduction, care, and special characteristics of olive trees, sunflowers, corn, and oak trees. The last four titles—*Abejas: Por dentro y por fuera, Arañas: Por dentro y por fuera, Búhos: Por dentro y por fuera* and *Tortugas: Por dentro y por fuera*—discuss the physical characteristics, behavior, reproduction, and life cycles of bees, spiders, owls, and turtles. Each title includes a well-done glossary and an index.

Jenkins, Steve, and Robin Page. *¿Qué harías con una cola como ésta? (What Would You Do with a Tail Like This?)* Translated by Laia Mercadé Roca. Barcelona: Juventud, 2004. 32p. ISBN: 84-261-3391-6. $15.95. Gr. K–3.

With the stunning cut-paper collage artwork of the original, this 2004 Caldecott Honor book is now available in this snappy Spanish rendition that is both intriguing and informative. Fascinating facts about the animal world follow a simple question: *¿Qué harías con una nariz/ unas orejas/unos ojos/una cola/una boca como ésta?* (What would you do with a nose/ears/eyes/tail/mouth like this?) illustrated with the body parts of several animals, followed by the animals and how each part functions. A picture glossary at the end of the book provides more information about each animal.

Kalman, Bobbie. *Ciclos de vida de los animales: Crecimiento y cambios. (Animal Life Cycles: Growing and Changing)* ISBN: 978-0-7787-8375-6.
———. *La fotosíntesis: De la luz del sol al alimento. (Photosynthesis)* ISBN: 978-0-7787-8372-5.
———. *La metamorfosis: Cuerpos que cambian. (Metamorphosis)* ISBN: 978-0-7787-8373-2.
———, and Rebecca Sjonger. *El ciclo del agua. (Water Cycle)* ISBN: 978-0-7787-8374-9.
———. *Las plantas de distintos hábitats. (Plants in Different Habitats)* ISBN: 978-0-7787-8377-0.
MacAulay, Kelley, and Bobbie Kalman. *Cambios del estado del tiempo: Las tormentas. (Changing Weather)* ISBN: 978-0-7787-8376-3.
Ea. vol.: 32p. Translated by translations.com. (Cambios Que Suceden en la Naturaleza) New York: Crabtree, 2007. $18.90. Gr. 2–4.

The ubiquitous changes in nature are simply explained through clear color photos, understandable charts, informative sidebars and a smooth Spanish rendition. Each title includes an index and a glossary, albeit without definite articles—a regrettable limitation. *Ciclos de vida de los animales: Crecimiento y cambios* describes the different ways animals grow and change—from embryos to adults. *La fotosíntesis: De la luz del sol al alimento* explains the process by which plants use light as an energy source to create food and oxygen. *La metamorfosis: Cuerpos que cambian* depicts how the bodies of different animals, including frogs, butterflies and beetles, change as they go through their life cycles. *El ciclo del agua* chronicles how different processes, such as evaporation, condensation, precipitation and run-off, work to move water from the ground to the air. *Las plantas de distintos hábitats* makes clear how, over time, plants have made remarkable adaptations to suit particular habitats. *Cambios del estado del tiempo: las tormentas* introduces the kinds of storms that take place each year, such as hurricanes, tornadoes, thunderstorms and blizzards.

Kalman, Bobbie. *¿Qué es el reino animal? (What Is the Animal Kingdom?)* ISBN: 0-7787-8757-5.
———. *¿Qué son los biomas? (What Is a Biome?)* ISBN: 0-7787-8755-9.

———, and Jacqueline Langille. *¿Qué es un ciclo de vida? (What Is a Life Cycle?)* ISBN: 0-7787-8754-0.

———. *¿Qué son las redes y cadenas alimentarias? (What Are Food Chains and Webs?)* ISBN: 0-7787-8756-7.

Ea. vol.: 32p. (La Ciencia de los Seres Vivos) New York: Crabtree, 2005. $16.95. Gr. 3–5.

With excellent color photographs, drawings, charts, and a most appealing design, these fluid Spanish renditions introduce students to basic aspects of animals, humans and plants. The classification of animals, from simple sponges to amphibians to reptiles to mammals, their special characteristics as well as threats to their habitats are explained in *¿Qué es el reino animal?* Life in major regional biotic areas—forests, deserts, grasslands, wetlands, oceans and arctic tundra—is described in *¿Qué son los biomas?* Numerous examples, beginning with plant life up to the human life cycle, that explain the basic concept of the life cycle are defined in *¿Qué es un ciclo de vida?* The connections between plants and animals and how they depend on each other to survive through food chains in various ecosystems are introduced in *¿Qué son las redes y cadenas alimentarias?*

Kalman, Bobbie and John Crossingham. *Los hogares de los insectos. (Insect Homes)* ISBN: 978-0-7787-8500-2.

———, and Rebecca Sjonger. *Insectos comunes. (Everyday Insects)* ISBN: 978-0-7787-8501-9.

Ea. vol.: 32p. Translated by translations.com. (El Mundo de los Insectos) New York: Crabtree, 2007. $18.90. Gr. 2–4.

Through exquisite close-up color photos, drawings, and a smooth Spanish text, children are introduced to the world of insects. *Los hogares de los insectos* describes the types of homes insects build, including the materials they use, and how social insects, such as ants and termites, work together to build homes. *Insectos comunes* highlights interesting facts about insects (beetles, ants, flies, grasshoppers and wasps) that children are likely to encounter in their everyday lives. Both titles include a glossary, albeit without definite articles.

Kalman, Bobbie, and Kelley MacAulay. *Los cobayos. (Guinea Pigs)* ISBN: 0-7787-8457-6.

MacAulay, Kelley, and Bobbie Kalman. *Los caniches o poodles. (Poodles)* ISBN: 978-0-7787-8461-6.

———. *Los cocker spaniel. (Cocker Spaniels)* ISBN: 978-0-7787-8458-6.

———. *Los dálmatas.* *(Dalmatians)* ISBN: 978-0-7787-8459-3.

———. *Los perros labradores.* *(Labrador Retrievers)* ISBN: 978-0-7787-8460-9.

Sjonger, Rebecca, and Bobbie Kalman. *Los cachorros.* *(Puppies)* ISBN: 0-7787-8455-X.

———. *Los hámsters.* *(Hamsters)* ISBN: 0-7787-8456-8.

Walker, Niki, and Bobbie Kalman. *Los gatitos.* *(Kittens)* ISBN: 0-7787-8454-1.

Ea. vol.: 32p. Photos by Marc Crabtree. Translated by translations.com. (El Cuidado de las Mascotas) New York: Crabtree, 2006–2007. $23.92. Gr. 2–3.

With exquisite color photographs and a most readable Spanish text, these well-done Spanish renditions introduce the young to the care, feeding, grooming and training of pets. The appeal of guinea pigs as friendly and affable and their special needs are explained in *Los cobayos.* The training and grooming requirements of poodles are described in *Los caniches o poodles.* *Los cocker spaniel* provides advice on caring for cocker spaniels. The history, training and grooming requirements of dalmatians are covered in *Los dálmatas.* The history, food and exercise needs of Labrador retrievers are explained in *Los perros labradores.* *Los cachorros* describes how to become successful dog owners, by caring and enjoying their puppies. Although hamsters sleep all day, children will learn what to expect from these nocturnal rodents in *Los hámsters.* The care of kittens and cats, including feeding, grooming and understanding kitten behavior, is explained in *Los gatitos.* Only caveat: The labels and glossaries do not indicate the definite articles. How are Spanish learners to know, *el* or *la nariz*?

Kalman, Bobbie, and Molly Aloian. *Tiburones espectaculares.* *(Spectacular Sharks)* ISBN: 978-0-7787-8401-2.

Smithyman, Kathryn, and Bobbie Kalman. *El bioma marino.* *(The Ocean Biome)* ISBN: 978-0-7787-8400-5.

Ea. vol.: 32p. Translated by translations.com. (La Vida en el Mar) New York: Crabtree, 2007. $18.90. Gr. 3–4.

These carefully edited Spanish-language titles, from the original The Living Ocean series, include the same clear charts, maps, illustrations and engaging color photos, and easy-to-understand texts. *Tiburones espectaculares* examines the habitats, behavior and bodies of sharks, dispelling shark myths and highlighting their importance in the food chain. *El bioma marino* describes why oceans and seas are the world's largest biome and their importance to the rest of the Earth.

Knox, Barbara. *Bajo las olas: vamos a contar la vida marina/Under the Sea: Counting Ocean Life.* ISBN: 978-1-4296-1199-2.
Marks, Jennifer L. *Vamos a ordenar por colores/Sorting by Colors.* ISBN: 978-1-4296-1196-1.
 Ea. vol.: 32p. Translated by Dr. Martín Luis Guzmán Ferrer (A+ Bilingüe/Bilingual) Mankato: Capstone, 2008. $22.60. Gr. Preschool–1.
 With striking color photos and a simple text in English and Spanish, these attractive large-format books encourage children to count from one to ten using a variety of creatures that live in the ocean (in *Bajo las olas: vamos a contar la vida marina/Under the Sea: Counting Ocean Life)* and to recognize various criteria by which sets are sorted (in *Vamos a ordenar por colores/Sorting by Colors).* Each title includes an interesting facts section, a glossary in both languages and an index.

Lessem, Don. *Dinosaurios con plumas. (Feathered Dinosaurs)* ISBN: 0-8225-6242-1.
——. *Los dinosaurios más inteligentes. (Smartest Dinosaurs)* ISBN: 0-8225-6245-6.
——. *Los dinosaurios más mortíferos. (Deadliest Dinosaurs)* ISBN: 0-8225-6240-5.
——. *Los dinosaurios más rápidos. (Fastest Dinosaurs)* ISBN: 0-8225-6241-3.
——. *Gigantes marinos de la época de los dinosaurios. (Sea Giants of Dinosaur Time)* ISBN: 0-8225-6244-8.
——. *Gigantes voladores de la época de los dinosaurios. (Flying Giants of Dinosaur Time)* ISBN: 0-8225-6243-X.
 Ea. vol.: 32p. Illus: John Bindon. Translated by translations.com. (Conoce a los Dinosaurios) Minneapolis: Lerner, 2007. $23.93. Gr. 2–4.
 Like the previous titles in this series, these highlight distinct characteristics of various extinct, often gigantic, carnivorous or herbivorous dinosaurs that existed millions of years ago. The dramatically detailed color illustrations, photographs, charts, maps and a most understandable Spanish rendition will capture the interest of young Spanish-speaking dino fans. Little-known or unusual aspects of feathered dinosaurs, including colorful feathers to attract a mate or large feathers to help them keep warm, are described in *Dinosaurios con plumas.* A range of dinosaurs, from smart Troodon dinosaurs that would dig small rodents out

of the ground to small but smarter microraptors, are discussed in *Los dinosaurios más inteligentes*. Deadly dinosaurs with pointy, destructive teeth and other rapacious dinosaurs are portrayed in *Los dinosaurios más mortíferos*. Fast dinosaurs that could outrun their raiders to Struthiomimus, the fastest, which could have run up to 60 miles per hour, are chronicled in *Los dinosaurios más rápidos*. Giant sea reptiles such as Archelon, an enormous turtle, and Mosasaurus, one of the deadliest, are depicted in *Gigantes marinos de la época de los dinosaurios*. Eight types of flying dinosaurs, known as *pterosaurios* (pterosaurs), winged creatures with hollow bones that allowed them to fly, are introduced in *Gigantes voladores de la época de los dinosaurios*. Each title includes a glossary, which unfortunately lacks definite articles. How will Spanish learners know if it is *la* or *el reptil*?

Lindeen, Carol K. *Caballitos de mar/Sea Horses*. ISBN: 978-0-7368-7647-6.
———. *Corales/Corals*. ISBN: 978-0-7368-7651-3.
———. *Focas/Seals*. ISBN: 978-0-7368-7649-0.
———. *Pez payaso/Clown Fish*. ISBN: 978-0-7368-7646-9.
———. *Pulpos/Octopuses*. ISBN: 978-0-7368-7648-3.
———. *Tiburones/Sharks*. ISBN: 978 0 7368-7650-6.
Ea. vol.: 24p. Translated by Dr. Martín Luis Guzmán Ferrer (Bajo las Olas/Under the Sea) Mankato, MN: Capstone, 2007. $14.95. Gr. K–2.

Simply and concisely, in easy-to-read bilingual texts, this series introduces the major physical characteristics and behavior patterns of six sea creatures—sea horses, corals, seals, clown fish, octopuses and sharks. Clear, excellent underwater photographs in full color on the right face one or two sentences of English text, followed by an equally well-written Spanish rendition. With easy-to-understand explanations, such as *Some sharks grow bigger than a car. Other sharks are the size of an adult's hand./Algunos tiburones son más grandes que un automóvil. Otros tiburones son del tamaño de la mano de un adulto* (p. 24), this series is sure to engage bilingual scientists-to-be. Straightforward bilingual glossaries are appended. The only caveat is that both the English and Spanish texts are in the exactly same font, which may confuse beginning readers of either language.

Llewellyn, Claire. *Así nace un árbol. (Starting Life Tree)* ISBN: 1-59437-449-X.
———. *Así nace un pato. (Starting Life Duck)* ISBN: 1-59437-448-1.

Ea. vol.: 25p. Illus: Simon Mendez. Translated by María Cristina Giraldo. Miami: Santillana USA, 2004. pap. $8.95. Gr. 2–4.

The life cycle is introduced to young readers through straightforward, easy-to-understand texts and full-page color illustrations. Like the original English editions, published by Andromeda, London, these feature pages on extra-heavy stock that gradually increase in size and allow children to flip each page. *Así nace un árbol* describes the growth of an apple tree from seed to sapling to a beautiful mature tree laden with fruit. *Así nace un pato* follows mallards from eggs to hatchlings to adults during a 12-month period. A glossary and a life cycle summary conclude these appealing paperbacks. The only caveat is that at times the captions appear on dark-colored backgrounds that make them difficult to see.

La mariposa. (Butterfly) ISBN: 84-236-6888-6.
El oso. (Bear) ISBN: 84-236-6887-8.
El pato. (Duckling) ISBN: 84-236-6886-X.
La rana. (Frog) ISBN: 84-236-6885-1.
Ea. vol.: 24p. Translated by Sara Sánchez. (Mira cómo crezco) Barcelona: Edebé, 2004. $10.95. Gr. 1–2.

With the exceptional color photographs of the originals, first published by Dorling Kindersley, this animal development series is an excellent introduction to the circle of life. Purists will certainly disapprove of the anthropomorphism in the simple first-person text in which *la mariposa* (butterfly), *el oso* (bear), *el pato* (duckling), *la rana* (frog) introduce themselves and describe their habitat, growth and functions of life. Nonetheless, the clear color photos and well-placed close-ups provide a most engaging view of the natural world for young Spanish speakers.

Markle, Sandra. *Los buitres. (Vultures)* ISBN: 978-0-8225-7731-7.
———. *Los demonios de Tasmania. (Tasmanian Devils)* ISBN: 978-0-8225-7733-1.
———. *Los glotones. (Wolverines)* ISBN: 978-0-8225-7732-4.
———. *Las hormigas legionarias. (Army Ants)* ISBN: 978-0-8225-7730-0.
Ea. vol.: 40p. Translated by translations.com. (Animales Carroñeros) Minneapolis: Lerner, 2008. $18.95. Gr. 3–5.

Maintaining the drama and tension of the original series, this eloquent Spanish rendition, translated with precision and pizzazz, discusses the lives of scavengers—nature's *la patrulla de la limpieza* (clean-up crew). Also engaging are the clear, close-up and telephoto action views of scavengers in their native habitats that support the text. The role of vultures in three different environments—the African savannah, the Gulf Coast of Florida and the Peruvian jungle—is described in *Los buitres*. It highlights the abilities of these magnificent fliers to cover great distances as they rely on their large wings and sharp eyesight to track carrion and care for their young. All titles in this series include a glossary (unfortunately, without definite articles), a bibliography (of English titles only), and a *Retrospectiva* (Look Again) section with suggestions for discussion. *Los demonios de Tasmania* provides a detailed depiction of Tasmanian devils, who with their superior sense of smell search their home range in search of carrion and protect themselves. The forests and open tundra of northern Europe, Siberia and North Africa are the home of wolverines, powerful creatures with sharp memories, strong jaw muscles, cone-shaped teeth and an exceptional sense of smell that allows them to track their prey (in *Los glotones*). The lifestyle of millions of army ants who as a colony devour dead or dying animals is discussed in *Las hormigas legionarias*.

Markle, Sandra. *Los cocodrilos. (Crocodiles)* ISBN: 0-8225-6492-0.
———. *Los leones. (Lions)* ISBN: 0-8225-6491-2.
———. *Los lobos. (Wolves)* ISBN: 0-8225-6489-0.
———. *Los tiburones blancos. (Great White Sharks)* ISBN: 0-8225-6490-4.
Ea. vol.: 40p. Translated by translations.com. (Animales Depredadores) Minneapolis: Lerner, 2007. $25.26. Gr. 2–5.

Excellent action color photos and an adept Spanish rendition describe the growth and maturation process of four skillful predators—crocodiles, lions, wolves, and great white sharks—and how they hunt for survival by stalking and attacking their prey. Each title describes their natural habitat and includes a glossary without definite articles, a review of special characteristics and recommended sources (in English only). This is indeed an eye-catching, appealing series for Spanish-speaking middle readers about the abilities and survival skills of four predators at the top of the food chain. Also, Spanish speakers will appreciate that all measurements are provided in U.S. customary units, followed by the metric system in parentheses.

Markle, Sandra. *Los perritos de las praderas. (Prairie Dogs)*. ISBN: 978-0-7613-3896-3.
———. *Los puercoespines. (Porcupines)* ISBN: 978-0-7613-3897-0.

———. *Los pulpos*. (*Octopuses*) ISBN: 978-0-7613-3898-7.

———. *Los zorrillos*. (*Skunks*) ISBN: 978-0-7613-3899-4.

Ea. vol.: 40p. Translated by translations.com. (Animales Presa) Minneapolis: Lerner, 2009. $25.26. Gr. 3–6.

Just as engrossing and revealing as the previous *Animales Carroñeros* (Animal Scavengers) and *Animales Depredadores* (Animal Predators) series, this noteworthy Spanish translation maintains the clarity and vigor of the original narrative as it details the defensive strategies used by prey animals and each animal species' place within the food chain of life. *Los perritos de las praderas* describes why prairie dogs find safety in large colonies and why hundreds of them live together in underground tunnels. Spectacular color close-up and telephoto action photos on the right capture the drama as the small animals come to the surface to nibble prairie grasses, always watching for eagles, coyotes or black-footed ferrets. But if one prairie dog is captured, the group will attack and drive the predator away. Follow-up questions, a complete glossary, an index and additional sources (in English only) complement this impressive series about predators and preys. *Los puercoespines* shows how porcupines can drive their long sharp quills into their enemies' skin to protect themselves from their predators. *Los pulpos* explains how octopuses use their eight arms to catch crabs and shellfish to eat and squirt ink into the water to escape from their enemies. *Los zorrillos* features the striped skunks that live in the North American forests and how they are equipped with a foul-smelling liquid that they can spray to keep their enemies away.

McGrath, Barbara Barbieri. *Cuenta con el béisbol. (Baseball Counting Book)* Illus: Brian Shaw. Translated by Yanitzia Canetti. Watertown, MA: Charlesbridge, 2005. 32p. ISBN: 1-57091-608-X. pap. $7.95. Gr. Preschool–2.

Baseball lovers will learn numbers from 1 to 20 as they review the rules and culture of the game in Canetti's spirited rhyming Spanish rendition. From an encouraging *Ven a jugar béisbol* (Come to play baseball) to 20 baseball cards that explain baseball terms, young Spanish-speaking fans will enjoy the enticing rhymes and acrylic illustrations as they play nine fun innings. Readers, however, will wonder why only English words are framed within the illustrations.

Mettler, René. *Álbum Visual de la Naturaleza y sus cambios mes a mes. (Nature: Month to Month)* Translated by Aquilino Álvarez. Madrid: Bruño, 2008. 33p. ISBN: 978-84-216-8031-5. $40. Gr. 2–4.

The change of seasons is described through the eyes of the author. Double-page spreads and foldouts with beautiful nature scenes complement this personal view of the seasons.

Muñoz Puelles, Vicente. *El viaje de la evolución: El joven Darwin. (The Journey of Evolution: Young Darwin)* Illus: Federico Delicado. Madrid: Anaya, 2007. 149p. ISBN: 978-84-667-6251-9. pap. $11.95. Gr. 5–8.
Written in the first-person point of view and based on the writings of Charles Darwin, this engrossing biography recounts Darwin's journey around the world in 1865 and explains how this trip changed his perceptions about nature. In a matter-of-fact and easy-to-understand narrative, Muñoz depicts through amusing anecdotes Darwin's observations about geology, flora and fauna that helped him understand how species of organisms arise and develop through natural selection. Not surprisingly, he concludes with the early conflicts between evolutionists and creationists. Despite the prosaic color illustrations, which sadly detract from the narrative, this is a captivating introduction to Darwin and his theories.

Nelson, Robin. *Cómo se mueven las cosas. (Ways Things Move)* ISBN: 978-0-8225-7811-6.
———. *Empujar y jalar. (Push and Pull)* ISBN: 978-0-225-7810-9.
———. *Flotar y hundirse. (Float and Sink)* ISBN: 978-0-8225-7808-6.
———. *La gravedad. (Gravity)* ISBN: 978-0-8225-7807-9.
———. *Los imanes. (Magnets)* ISBN: 978-0-8225-7809-3.
Ea. vol.: 24p. (Mi Primer Paso al Mundo Real. Fuerzas y Movimiento) Minneapolis: Lerner, 2008. $18.90. Gr. K–2.
With clear, candid, color photos and a brief, most accessible Spanish text—one sentence per page—this well-conceived series explains simple facts about force and motion in a manner that even young Spanish-speaking children can understand. Basic demonstrations about how things move by pushing or pulling are depicted in *Cómo se mueven las cosas. Empujar y jalar* describes a pulley and how a push or a pull is a force that makes something move, or stops it from moving. Why some things float and others sink are explained in *Flotar y hundirse. La gravedad* illustrates that gravity always pulls everything towards the center of the Earth. *Los imanes* makes clear that magnets have a north and south pole and attract metals. Each title includes a one-page summary with a facing diagram, an important facts section, an index and a glossary, albeit without definite articles. How will the young know that it is *el ancla* or *el metal*? This is truly a regrettable omission in an otherwise excellent series for the young.

Nelson, Robin. *El gusto. (Tasting)* ISBN: 0-8225-6224-3.
————. *El oído. (Hearing)* ISBN: 0-8225-6221-9.
————. *El olfato. (Smelling)* ISBN: 0-8225-6223-5.
————. *El tacto. (Touching)* ISBN: 0-8225-6225-1.
————. *La vista. (Seeing)* ISBN: 0-8225-6222-7.
Ea. vol.: 24p. Translated by translations.com. (Los Sentidos) Minneapolis: Lerner, 2007. $18.60. Gr. K–1.

Through candid color photos and one sentence per page, young children are introduced to their five senses. Each title highlights one sense and the different things that children can taste (*El gusto*), hear (*El oído*), smell (*El olfato*), touch (*El tacto*) and see (*La vista*). Glossaries (albeit without definite articles) complement each title. Despite the high quality of these Spanish renditions, the examples of what children like or do not like to eat (in *El gusto*) are most unfortunate. According to the text, children like pizza and hot dogs, but dislike fish and peas. This is, nutritionally speaking, a regrettable message to give to young Spanish speakers who, generally, like their vegetables.

O'Leary, John. *El profesor Topo y sus máquinas. (Professor Mole's Machines)* Illus: John O'Leary. Adapted by Emilia Hernández. Barcelona: Combel, 2004. 10p. ISBN: 84-7864-917-4. $17.29. Ages 3–6.

Simple text, pull-the-tabs, flaps and three-dimensional color images show the use and operation of Professor Topo's machines—elevator, washing machine, excavator, space rocket.

Poskitt, Kjartan. *Esas mortíferas mates. (Murderous Maths)* (Esa Horrible Ciencia) Illus: Trevor Dunton. Translated by Conchita Peraire del Molino. Barcelona: RBA Libros, 2006. 144p. ISBN: 84-272-2056-1. pap. $10.95. Gr. 5–8.

With the same tongue-in-cheek writing style, black-and-white cartoons, and whimsical sidebars of the previous titles in this series, this unpretentious paperback introduces reluctant students of mathematics to such concepts as Roman numerals, the decimal system, time measurement, prime and superior numbers as well as important mathematicians such as Archimedes and Euclid. Spanish speakers are sure to enjoy the lighthearted tone of this series, originally published by Scholastic, London.

Randolph, Joanne. *All about a Day/Los días*. ISBN: 978-1-4042-7627-7.
————. *All about a Month/Los meses*. ISBN: 978-1-4042-7628-4.

———. *All about a Season/Las estaciones.* ISBN: 978-0-4042-7629-1.

———. *All about an Hour/Las horas.* ISBN: 978-1-4042-7626-0.

Ea. vol.: 24p. Translated by María Cristina Brusca. (It's About Time!/Los Libros del Tiempo) New York: Editorial Buenas Letras/ Rosen, 2008. $21.25. Gr. K–1.

Just right for beginning English- and Spanish-speaking readers, this simply written series shows how days are part of passing time (in *All about a Day/Los días)*, the 12 months in a year (in *All about a Month/Los meses)*, the four seasons (in *All about a Season/Las estaciones)* and the 24 hours in a day (in *All about an Hour/Las horas)*. Especially noteworthy are Brusca's fluid Spanish rendition that never attempts a literal translation; rather, it is as playful as it is informative, as well as the easily identified English text in a boldface followed by the Spanish text in a lighter font. Each title includes *Words to Know/Palabras que debes saber* and an index.

Roca, Núria. *Los 5 sentidos. (The 5 Senses)* ISBN: 0-7641-3313-6.

———. *Los 4 elementos. (The 4 Elements)* ISBN: 0-7641-3315-2.

Ea. vol.: 35p. Illus: Rosa M. Curto. Barcelona: Gemser/Dist. by Barron's, 2005. pap. $6.99. Gr. 2–3.

Through perky, cartoon-type pastel illustrations and a lighthearted text, children discover their five senses—hearing, sight, smell, touch, and taste—(in *Los 5 sentidos)* and the four basic elements—air, water, earth, and fire—(in *Los 4 elementos)*. These are not detailed introductions to the senses or elements; rather, they are delightful overviews featuring children engaged in playful activities in which the senses and the elements take center stage. Each book includes an afterword with suggested activities for children and a two-page *guía para los padres* with thoughtful teaching suggestions for parents.

Roca, Núria, and Rosa M. Curto. *Cuidemos a nuestro gatito nuevo. (Let's Take Care of Our New Cat)* Barcelona: Gemser/Dist by Barron's, 2006. 35p. ISBN: 978-0-7641-3453-1. pap. $6.99. Gr. 2–5.

Pedro and Paula have a new kitten that they name Rufo. Soon they learn that caring for Rufo is a lot of work—they learn to keep the food bowl, water bowl, and sandbox clean. Also, they learn that cats need and want their independence and that they are a delight to play with. Guidelines with advice and basic instruction on cat and kitten care are appended. The cartoon-type ink-and-watercolor illustrations and the easy-to-understand text will appeal to Spanish-speaking cat lovers and their parents.

Simon, Seymour. *Tiburones. (Sharks)* Translated by Alberto Jiménez Rioja. New York: Rayo/HarperCollins, 2004. 32p. ISBN: 0-06-056496-2. pap. $6.99. Gr. 2–4.

An easy-to-understand Spanish rendition introduces the world of sharks through excellent, full-color photographs and an informative text on the opposite page. From general information about their variety, habits, life cycles, and physical characteristics to simple rules to avoid shark attacks, this is indeed an engrossing introduction to these fascinating fishes.

Smith, Alastair, and Judy Tatchell. *En el mar. (Under the Sea)* Illus: Peter Scott and Keith Furnival. Translated by Germa Alonso de la Serna. Tulsa: EDC Publishing, 2004. 16p. ISBN: 0-7460-6398-9. $11.95. Gr. Preschool–1.

Sea fauna are introduced to young children through full-page color illustrations and well-placed lift-the-flaps that show dolphins, sharks, sea horses, octopuses, and other fish as they play, feed, and interact with each other and protect themselves. Some adults will rightfully object to a certain degree of anthropomorphism; nonetheless, this is a thoughtful view of life under the sea.

Tang, Greg. *Come una y cuenta 20: Acertijos matemáticos para despertar la mente. (The Grapes of Math: Mind Stretching Math Riddles)* ISBN: 84-241-8075-5.

———. *Un, dos, tres el año se fue: Acertijos matemáticos para despertar la mente. (Math for All Seasons: Mind Stretching Math Riddles)* ISBN: 84-241-8074-7.

Ea. vol: Illus: Harry Briggs. (Colección Rascacielos) León: Everest, 2004. 44p. $12.95. Gr. 1–3.

Maintaining the playful tone of the original English versions, these lively Spanish rhymes encourage the young to look for set patterns, symmetries and visual groupings as they count, subtract and multiply. Briggs's crisp, clear computer-generated illustrations further assist young Spanish speakers to think creatively as they try to solve these enjoyable math riddles. From a complicated pattern of strawberry seeds (*La mejor de las sorpresas/es que en el bosque haya fresas*) to counting mushroom slices on pizza (*Un buen consejo mereces:/cuenta la mitad dos veces)* children will see patterns and combinations in *Come una y cuenta 20: Acertijos matemáticos para despertar la mente.* From counting tulips in springtime to multiple scoops of ice cream to counting Christmas gifts (*Suma incluyéndolos en vertical/y réstalos de la cuenta final)* readers will appreciate seasonal changes amid the math in *Un, dos, tres el año se fue: Acertijos matemáticos para despertar la mente.* Both titles include illustrated solutions and explanations at the back of each book.

Tielmann, Christian. *Conozcamos nuestro cuerpo. (Let's Find Out About Our Body)* Illus: Anne Möller. ISBN: 84-261-3507-2.
———. *¡Vamos a tener un bebé! (We Are Going to Have a Baby!)* Illus: Jan Lieffering. ISBN: 84-261-3509-9.
Ea. vol.: 29p. Translated by Christiane Reyes. (Mi Cuerpo) Barcelona: Juventud, 2006. $15.95. Gr. 2–4.

In a delightfully carefree, almost conversational style, this series, originally published by Verlag, Germany, explains basic facts about the human body. Appealing and at times witty, pencil and watercolor illustrations are complemented by engaging foldouts that further explain each topic. Beginning with simple questions that children can understand, such as *¿Por qué no oímos nada con la nariz, pero sí con las orejas?* (Why can't we hear with our nose, but we can with our ears?), *Conozcamos nuestro cuerpo* introduces the structure and functions of the skeleton, muscle, respiratory, circulatory and digestive systems as well as the brain and senses with clear examples that even the young can appreciate. At dinner, Father announces to young Eva and Martin, *Vamos a tener un bebé* (We are going to have a baby), which Mother proceeds to clarify in *¡Vamos a tener un bebé!* To answer the question how Papa and Mama made the baby, children are provided with straightforward descriptions about male and female reproductive organs, how the sperm enters the ovary, the development of the fetus and the process of birth. Prudish adults will certainly object to this explicit introduction with candid fully nude male and female drawings, but inquisitive Spanish-speaking children will appreciate the honest, no-nonsense explanations and drawings.

Tielmann, Christian. *María va a la pediatra. (María Goes to the Pediatrician)* ISBN: 978-84-261-3589-6.
———. *¿Por qué tenemos que comer? (Why Must We Eat?)* ISBN: 978-84-261-3587-2.

Ea. vol.: 26p. Illus: Jan Lieffering. Translated by Maria Antònia Torras. (Mi Cuerpo) Barcelona: Juventud, 2007. $20.95. Gr. 2–4.

Highlighting children's likes and dislikes about certain foods, *¿Por qué tenemos que comer?* explains, simply and matter-of-factly, the importance of good nutrition to be able to run, play or do somersaults. Lieffering's cartoonish black-ink and watercolor illustrations capture the world of children and their favorite and not-so-favorite foods with wit and pizzazz. Beginning with the book cover in which a girl and a boy are playing tug of war over a bowl of spaghetti to the title page where a boy is relishing his french fries and later is disgusted with his aunt's vegetable soup, to a girl and her father making a mango "tower" and children enjoying fresh fruit juices, this is not a dull repetition of proper eating habits. Rather, it describes how a well-balanced diet can be realistically integrated into a child's daily life. It concludes with two-page spreads: one describes organic farming, the other *Países distintos, comidas distintas* (Different countries, Different foods) contrasting eating styles in France, Ethiopia, Japan and China. María is not feeling well. So, *papá* has to take her to the pediatrician in *María va a la pediatra*. Through María, children are exposed to a visit at the doctor's office and to common diseases in children—*los resfriados* (colds), *la varicela* (chicken pox), *el sarampión* (measles) and *las alergias* (allergies). Well-placed flaps further explain such facts as the body's defenses against germs and inflammation of the tonsils.

Torok, Simon, and Paul Holper. *Ciencia extravagante. (Weird! Amazing Inventions and Wacky Science)* Illus: Stephen Axelsen. Barcelona: Oniro, 2005. 93p. ISBN: 84-9754-163-4. pap. $10.95. Gr. 4–6.

In a humorous, easygoing manner, this collection of scientific anecdotes briefly describes *descubrimientos fascinantes* (amazing discoveries), *experimentos estrambóticos* (odd experiments), *teorías extrañas* (strange theories) and other high-interest scientific/technical inventions and misstatements such as velcro, Frisbee, chewing gum and *La televisión no durará* (Television won't last). With witty, black-and-white cartoons and amusing subheads, this collection will appeal to determined and/or reluctant scientists-to-be.

Twina, Alice. *Bears/Osos.* ISBN: 978-1-4042-7634-5.
———. *Cats of the Wild/Gatos salvajes.* ISBN: 978-1-4042-7631-4.
———. *Ducks/Patos.* ISBN: 978-1-4042-7633-8.
———. *Horses/Caballos.* ISBN: 978-1-4042-7630-7.

——. *Monkeys/Monos.* ISBN: 978-1-4042-7635-2.

——. *Seals/Focas.* ISBN: 978-1-4042-7632-1.

Ea. vol.: 24p. Translated by José María Obregón. (Baby Animals/
Animales Bebé) New York: Editorial Buenas Letras/Rosen, 2008.
$21.25. Gr. K–2.

Concise, easy-to-read bilingual texts (English text in boldface
followed by the Spanish text in a lighter font) face sharp, candid color
photos of baby animals in their natural environments. Each title includes *Words to Know/Palabras que debes saber* and an index. This is
indeed an appealing series that introduces the special characteristics,
adaptations, lifestyles and growth patterns of baby bears, wild cats,
ducks, horses, monkeys and seals.

Vaisman, Sylvia. *Mi planeta y yo. (My Planet and Me)* Illus: Bruno Heitz.
Translated by Gabriela Peyrón. Mexico: Tecolote, 2004. 51p. ISBN:
968-7381-79-5. pap. $10.95. Gr. 2–5.

Through most amusing color cartoons and in an easy-to-understand graphic format, this lively introduction to the importance of con-
servation provides vivid examples of the misuse of natural resources—
air, water, the environment—and offers simple suggestions for their
protection. From common polluting activities, to waste disposal, to recycling, and genetically modified organisms (with specific facts about
pollution in Mexico), conservationists-to-be will be convinced. Although a glossary is included, it, unfortunately, lacks an index.

Walker, Sally M. *El calor. (Heat).* ISBN: 978-0-8225-7718-8.

——. *La electricidad. (Electricity)* ISBN: 978-0-8225—7717-1.

——. *La luz. (Light)* ISBN: 978-0-8225-7719-5.

——. *El magnetismo. (Magnetism)* ISBN: 978-0-8225-7720-1.

——. *La materia. (Matter)* ISBN: 978-0-8225-7721-8.

——. *El sonido. (Sound)* ISBN: 978-0-8225-7722-5.

Ea. vol.: 48p. Photos by Andy King. Translated by translations.com.
(Libros de Energía para Madrugadores) Minneapolis: Lerner, 2008.
$26.60. Gr. 3–5.

Through clear explanations, numerous examples and simple experiments children are introduced to basic concepts of energy and matter. Each title, in this well-done Spanish series, includes a *Mensaje para
los adultos* (Note to Adults) with suggested questions and ideas, a list
of recommended books and Web sites (in English only), an index and a
glossary, albeit without definite articles. How will Spanish learners

know if it is *el* or *la corriente?* The fundamentals of heat are explained in *El calor.* How electricity works including electrons, protons and neutrons is described in *La electricidad.* Photons, color, refraction, light rays, and waves are clarified in *La luz.* The central principles of magnetism including protons, neutrons and electrons are made clear in *El magnetismo.* Volume, mass, and how matter changes state are conveyed in *La materia.* The main concepts of sound such as vibration and how sound travels are imparted in *El sonido.*

Walker, Sally M., and Roseann Feldman. *Palancas. (Levers)* ISBN: 0-8225-2972-6.
———. *Planos inclinados. (Inclined Planes)* ISBN: 0-8225-2970-X.
———. *Poleas. (Pulleys)* ISBN: 0-8225-2980-7.
———. *Ruedas y ejes. (Wheels and Axles)* ISBN: 0-8225-2982-3.
———. *Tornillos. (Screws)* ISBN: 0-8225-2974-2.
———. *Trabajo. (Work)* ISBN: 0-8225-2984-X.
Ea. vol.: 48p. Photos by Andy King. Translated by translations.com. (Libros de Física para Madrugadores) Minneapolis: Lerner, 2006. $25.26. Gr. 2–4.

With clear, candid, color photos on every page and simple, easy-to-understand explanations and diagrams, this informative series introduces basic concepts of simple machines and how things work. Originally published in English as Early Bird Physics Series, the smooth Spanish renditions will assist young Spanish speakers to gradually understand each concept presented. Each title includes suggestions for further reading of English-language books, a glossary (without definite articles) and an index.

Wells, Robert E. *¿Hay algo más rápido que un guepardo? (What's Faster than a Speeding Cheetah?)* ISBN: 82-261-3501-3.
———. *¿Hay algo más viejo que una tortuga gigante? (What's Older than a Giant Tortoise?)* ISBN: 84-261-3436-X.
Ea. vol.: Illus: Robert E. Wells. Translated by Raquel Solá. Barcelona: Juventud, 2005. 32p. $15.95. Gr. 2–4.

As in his previous books—*¿Cómo se mide el tiempo? (How Do You Know What Time It Is?)*, *¿Sabes contar hasta un Googol? (Can You Count to a Googol?)*, *¿Hay algo más pequeño que una musaraña? (What's Smaller Than A Pygmy Shrew?)* and *¿Hay algo más grande que una ballena azul? (Is a Blue Whale the Biggest Thing There Is?)*—Wells introduces the meaning of "old" and "speed" through whimsical, colorful ink-and-acrylic cartoons and a simple text. Young Spanish speakers will appreciate Solás's smooth Spanish renditions while following a fast runner, who is outpaced by an ostrich, which in turn is left behind by a cheetah. Of course airplanes, meteorites and, subsequently, a beam of light proves to be the fastest, as depicted in *¿Hay algo más rápido que un guepardo?* Spanish speakers from the United States will be confused by the metric measurements (e.g., an ostrich runs at 70 kph, instead of 45 mph, cheetahs at 110 kph, not 70 mph). *¿Hay algo más viejo que una tortuga gigante?* shows a 150-year-old *tortuga gigante* on a magic carpet that encounters an even older giant sequoia, followed by even older Egyptian pyramids, Meteor Crater in Arizona, fossilized mammoths, Mount Everest, concluding with the universe. Illustrated charts and brief notes complete these amusing views of age and speed.

Wells, Robert E. *¿Sabes contar hasta un googol? (Can You Count to a Googol?)* Illus: the author. Translated by Lilian Weikert. Barcelona: Juventud, 2004. 32p. ISBN: 82-261-3361-4. $16.95. Gr. 2–4.

To introduce the concepts of large numbers up to a googol (number 1 followed by 100 zeroes) and multiples of ten, Wells uses humorous, colorful ink-and-acrylic cartoons and simple explanations. From a girl balancing one banana on her nose, to a monkey balancing 10, to 100 eagles pulling a basket of children, followed by 1000 scoops of ice cream up to *un googol*, children are reminded that numbers go on forever because *siempre puedes añadirle un cero* (You can always add a zero). Some mathematicians will question the simple notion of just adding zeros instead of multiplying by 10, but this understandable Spanish rendition is an enjoyable depiction of large numbers.

Wormell, Christopher. *Dientes, colas y tentáculos: Un libro de animales para contar. (Teeth, Tails and Tentacles: An Animal Counting Book)* Illus: the author. Translated by Elodie Bourgeois Bertín. Barcelona: Juventud, 2006. 60p. ISBN: 84-261-3555-2. $25.95. Gr. Preschool–3.

Just as dramatic as the highly acclaimed English original, Wormell's sparkling linoleum block prints introduce numbers 1–20 through the special physical characteristics and behavior of 20 animals followed by extensive notes that describe the habitat and intriguing information about each one. The very young will delight in counting *1 cuerno de rinoceronte* (1 rhinoceros horn), *2 jorobas de camello* (2 camel humps), up to *20 bálanos en* . . . (20 barnacle shells . . .). Older children will appreciate the appended notes with special facts, such as why chameleons are capable of changing color and why zebras have distinctive black-and-white markings.

Zumbusch, Amelie von. *Cheetahs/Guepardos.* ISBN: 978-1-4042-7604-8.
———. *Elephants/Elefantes.* ISBN: 978-1-4042-7605-5.
———. *Giraffes/Jirafas.* ISBN: 978-1-4042-7606-2.
———. *Hippos/Hipopótamos.* ISBN: 978-1-4042-7607-9.
———. *Lions/Leones.* ISBN: 978-1-4042-7608-6.
———. *Zebras/Cebras.* ISBN: 978-1-4042-7609-3.
Ea. vol.: 24p. Translated by Ma. Pilar Sanz. (Safari Animals/Animales de Safari) New York: Rosen/Buenas Letras, 2007. $21.25. Gr. K–1.

Simply written, brief bilingual texts—two sentences per page—face crisp, candid color photos of animals in their natural environments in this well-conceived *Safari Animals/Animales de Safari* series. Highlighting important aspects of their lives, *Cheetahs/Guepardos* describes their adaptation to the environment, how they get their food, their preference to live alone and how they play. Especially important to English and Spanish learners is the fact that the English text in bold font is followed by a dark black line that separates the Spanish text in a lighter font, thereby avoiding unnecessarily confusing English—or Spanish—beginning readers. A simple bilingual *Words to Know/Palabras que debes saber* and *Index/Índice* are also included. Other titles focus on the habitats, behaviors and adaptations to the environment of elephants, giraffes, hippos, lions, and zebras.

Technology

Ellis, Catherine. *Cars and Trucks/Autos y camiones.* ISBN: 978-1-4042-7624-6.
———. *Helicopters/Helicópteros.* ISBN: 978-1-4042-7621-5.
———. *Planes/Aviones.* ISBN: 978-1-4042-7622-2.
———. *Ships/Barcos.* ISBN: 978-1-4042-7623-9.
———. *Submarines/Submarinos.* ISBN: 978-1-4042-7620-8.
———. *Tanks/Tanques.* ISBN: 978-1-4042-7619-2.
Ea. vol.: 24p. Translated by María Cristina Brusca. (Mega Military Machines/Megamáquinas Militares) New York: Rosen/Buenas Letras, 2007. $21.25. Gr. K–1.

Simple bilingual texts (two sentences per page) and clear color photos introduce the very young to six military machines: cars and trucks, helicopters, planes, ships, submarines and tanks. Each title highlights the special capabilities of each in a manner that the young can understand, such as [military cars] "are bigger and stronger than everyday cars. . . . *son más grandes y fuertes que los autos comunes*" (p. 4). Beginning English and Spanish readers will appreciate the clearly distinguished fonts—the English text, which is darker, is separated by a dark line and followed by a fluid Spanish rendition in a lighter font. Simple bilingual glossaries are included.

Marshall, Pam. *De la idea al libro. (From Idea to Book)* (De Principio a Fin) Translated by translations.com. Minneapolis: Lerner, 2007. 24p. ISBN: 0-8225-6495-5. $18.60. Gr. K–2.

In a simple text with a color photograph on each facing page, this book describes how an author gets an idea for a book, proceeds to write it, sends it to a publisher, illustrates it, followed by the technical processes at the publishing house. Young Spanish speakers will appreciate the lucid explanations even though the photos show the production of an English-language book, *It's Not My Fault!* Unfortunately, the glossary lacks definite articles, a serious obstacle for young readers and Spanish-language learners.

Navarrete, Néstor. *Grandes inventos. (Great Inventions)* Illus: Marcel Socías. Barcelona: Parramón, 2004. 31p. ISBN: 84-342-2606-5. $16.95. Gr. 3–6.

The purpose of this well-designed publication is to interest young readers in the world of technology through some of the most interesting inventions. Beginning with the ax and the wheel, it also includes the compass, mechanical watches, telescope, printing press, camera, radio, helicopter, television, cellular telephone, and laser. Each invention is described in two-page, profusely illustrated spreads, easy-to-understand brief texts and clear labels. A chronology of inventions from stone tools to video/cellular phones is appended.

Health and Medicine

Canales, Claudia. *La comidilla: Un libro-revista de alimentación. (La Comidilla: A Book about Nutrition)* Illus: Heyliana Flores. Mexico: Serpentina, 2006. 79p. ISBN: 968-5950-11-3. pap. $12.95. Gr. 9–12.

This is indeed one of the best books about nutrition for Spanish-speaking adolescents I have ever seen. In a clear, easy-to-understand and at times chatty manner, it explains basic aspects about food, health and nutrition with many references to Mexican culture, good Mexican eating habits—*tacos de frijoles* (bean tacos)—and malnutrition and diabetes in Mexico. Although a few examples pertain to Mexico, all Spanish speakers will recognize such issues as constipation; soft drinks and sugar; the benefits of exercise—*sacudir el esqueleto* (shake the skeleton); dangerous substances; amphetamines and other stimulants; and anorexia and bulimia. This is not a preachy book about the benefits of healthful habits; rather, its lucid explanations and colorful, witty illustrations are sure to enlighten and convince adolescents because *Las proteínas son como el fútbol* (proteins are like soccer) and other verities. An informative glossary is included.

DeGezelle, Terri. *Cómo cuidar mi pelo/Taking Care of My Hair.* ISBN: 978-0-7368-7654-4.
———. *Cómo cuidar mi piel/Taking Care of My Skin.* ISBN: 978-0-7368-7656-8.
———. *Cómo cuidar mis dientes/Taking Care of My Teeth.* ISBN: 978-0-7368-7657-5.
———. *Cómo cuidar mis manos y pies/Taking Care of My Hands and Feet.* ISBN: 978-0-7368-7655-1.
———. *Cómo cuidar mis ojos/Taking Care of My Eyes.* ISBN: 978-0-7368-7653-7.
Schuette, Sarah L. *Cómo cuidar mis oídos/Taking Care of My Ears.* ISBN: 978-0-7368-7652-0.
Ea. vol.: 24p. Translated by Dr. Martín Luis Guzmán Ferrer. (Cuido Mi Salud/Keeping Healthy) Mankato, MN: Capstone, 2007. $19.93. Gr. Preschool–2.

In a most simple and accessible first-person bilingual text, and with large, attractive, color photographs of young multiethnic children, the *Cuido Mi Salud*/Keeping Healthy series introduces beginning Spanish and English readers to the benefits of good personal health and hygiene. Beginning with a short sentence ("Hair grows all over my body./*El pelo crece por todo mi cuerpo*"), *Cómo cuidar mi pelo/Taking Care of My Hair* explains that hair is made of keratin, that it can be different colors, and that it needs to be cut, washed, combed and checked. Easy-to-understand glossaries in both languages will assist English and Spanish learners to further comprehend the subjects discussed in each title. Other titles describe how children should care for their skin, teeth, hands and feet, eyes and ears.

Gaff, Jackie. *¿Por qué debo comer de forma saludable? (Why Must I Eat Healthy Food?)* ISBN: 978-84-241-7882-6.

———. *¿Por qué debo hacer ejercicio? (Why Must I Exercise?)* ISBN: 978-84-241-7883-3.

———. *¿Por qué debo lavarme las manos? (Why Must I Wash My Hands?)* ISBN: 978-84-241-7881-9.

———. *¿Por qué debo lavarme los dientes? (Why Must I Brush My Teeth?)* ISBN: 978-84-241-7880-2.
Ea. vol.: 34p. Photos by Chris Fairclough. Translated by María Nevares Domínguez. (*¿*Por Qué Debo . . . ?) León: Everest, 2007. pap. $8.95. Gr. 2–4.

With a simple, understandable text, colorful photos, clear charts and comprehensible sidebars, this well-done paperback series, originally published by Evans, London, encourages children to take care of their health. The relevance of healthful eating, a balanced diet and the reasons to avoid eating too much sugar and fat are described in *¿Por qué debo comer de forma saludable?* In addition it offers a simple description of the digestive system and provides numerous suggestions for good snacks and the reasons to avoid junk food. Young Spanish speakers will appreciate the appended Spanish Web sites about health and nutrition as well as the bibliography and index. *¿Por qué debo hacer ejercicio?* reminds children about the relationship between sports, exercise and health including suggestions for exercising alone or with friends. *¿Por qué debo lavarme las manos?* explains the importance of keeping the body clean, the function of soap and the harmful effect of germs. *¿Por qué debo lavarme los dientes?* illustrates how children should brush their teeth, why children lose their baby teeth and describes a visit to the dentist.

Kaufer Horwitz, Martha. *Asuntos de mucho peso: Un libro sobre aciertos y errores en la alimentación. (Serious Matters: A Book about Nutrition Successes and Mistakes)* Illus: Iris Alcázar and Rey David Rojas. México: Serpentina, 2007. 79p. ISBN: 978-968-595-029-9. pap. $12.95. Gr. 6–10.

With appealing, modernist, color illustrations and a straightforward, conversational text, the author explains the causes and effects of obesity and overweight conditions in young people, proper nutrition, exercise, and special diets. It is important to note that it describes fruits, vegetables and dishes well-known in Mexico such as *nopales, mamey,* and other Mexican delicacies such as *sopes* and *tostadas.* Adolescents in search of guidelines for healthful eating habits will appreciate the easy-to-understand recommendations for a balanced lifestyle. Although it includes a table of contents and a glossary, it lacks an index.

Ochoa, Anabel. *Los anticonceptivos explicados a los jóvenes. (Contraceptives Explained to Teens)* Mexico: Aguilar/Santillana, 2005. 269p. ISBN: 970-770-227-3. pap. $14.95. Gr. 9–12.

In a candid, almost colloquial style, Anabel Ochoa, a well-known sex educator and writer in Mexico, explains in a well-organized manual basic information about the advantages, disadvantages and common quandaries about more than fifteen contraceptive methods—from the pill to the patch, vaginal rings, injections, male and female condoms, to vasectomies and abstinence. Readers will note that she mentions the free availability of contraceptives for teens in Mexico's public health clinics as well as the *macho* attitudes of Mexican males regarding sex. She states: "*No es culpa de ellos pero sí del machismo en el que hemos crecido. Creen que la mujer nació para el sacrificio y ellos para el gozo.*" (It is not their fault; it is the fault of the *machismo* in which we grow up. They believe that women are born for sacrifice and they for enjoyment.) An unfortunate shortcoming is the lack of illustrations to explain how to use some of the devices. Yet, the overall message, especially to teen girls, " . . . *con derecho al placer, dueña de su sexualidad y de su cuerpo*" (with the right to pleasure, master of her own sexuality and her own body) is conveyed in a manner that teens can appreciate.

Schuh, Mari C. *El agua potable/Drinking Water*. ISBN: 0-7368-6670-1.
———. *El grupo de la leche/The Milk Group*. ISBN: 0-7368-6669-8.
———. *El grupo de las carnes y los frijoles/The Meat and Beans Group*. ISBN: 0-7368-6668-X.
———. *El grupo de las frutas/The Fruit Group*. ISBN: 0-7368-6666-3.
———. *El grupo de las verduras/The Vegetable Group*. ISBN: 0-7368-6672-8.
———. *El grupo de los cereales/The Grain Group*. ISBN: 0-7368-6667-1.
———. *Mantenerse activo/Being Active*. ISBN: 0-7368-6665-5.
———. *Meriendas saludables/Healthy Snacks*. ISBN: 0-7368-6671-X.
Ea. vol.: 24p. Translated by Dr. Martin Luis Guzmán Ferrer (Comida Sana con Mi Pirámide/Healthy Eating with My Pyramid) Mankato, MN: Capstone, 2007. $19.93. Gr. K–1.

With short, simple sentences in English followed by just as simple sentences in Spanish texts, this bilingual series encourages beginning readers of either language to learn the importance of healthful eating and physical activity. Each title includes candid color photos, bilingual glossaries and clear suggestions conducive to desirable nutrition and exercise. The importance of drinking water and having fun with water are described in *El agua potable/Drinking Water*; milk products in *El grupo de la leche/The Milk Group*; meat and beans in *El grupo de las carnes y los frijoles/The Meat and Beans Group*; different fruits in *El grupo de las frutas/The Fruit Group*; various vegetables in *El grupo de las verduras/The Vegetable Group*; whole grains in *El grupo de los cereales/The Grain Group*; the importance of being active and examples of how to stay active in *Mantenerse activo/Being Active*; examples of healthful snacks and ways to enjoy them in *Meriendas saludables/Healthy Snacks*.

Vargas de González Carbonell, Gabriela, and Yordi Rosado. *Quiúbole con . . . tu cuerpo, el ligue, tus cuates, el sexo, tu familia, las drogas y todo lo demás: Manual de supervivencia para hombres. (What's Up? With Your Body, Flirting, Buddies, Sex, Family, Drugs and Everything Else).* México, D.F.: Santillana Ediciones Generales, 2006. ISBN: 970-770-409-8. pap. Gr. 7–adult.

Written in an easy colloquial style with numerous subheads and illustrated with witty color cartoons, this engaging *Manual de supervivencia para hombres* (Survival Manual for Men) is just right for adolescents. Such chapters as your body, friends, sex, family, drugs and "everything else" include suggestions on how to say no, driving with friends, sexual orientation and other subjects of perennial interest to boys, youth and their parents.

Villegas, María, and Jennie Kent. *Púberman. (Puberman)* Illus: Ivan Chacón. Bogotá: Villegas Editores, 2006. 271p. ISBN: 958-8156-77-7. pap. $16.95. Gr. 7–12.

With striking full-color drawings and an eye-catching cover featuring *Púberman* (a clever combination of *pubertad* [puberty] and man), this paperback intermingles graphic vignettes, suggestive cartoons and modernistic collages with fonts of varying styles and sizes to discuss with candor and complete honesty more than 50 topics of interest to teen boys. From a sweet boy who faces *la inevitable transformación* (the inevitable transformation) to such questions as *fantasías sexuales* (sexual fantasies), pornography, homosexuality, high-risk Internet "chats," tattoos, *montadores* (bullies), and suggestions for kissing, this is not a sanitized discussion of adolescence that conventional adults would prefer; rather, it is a most realistic, at times humorous, review of important and not-so-important themes and issues confronting adolescents today.

Zepeda, Monique. *Ser chavo no es fácil: Trucos para sobrevivir. (Being a Teen Is Not Easy: Tricks for Survival)* Illus: Patricia Márquez and Arturo Ruelas. México: Pax México, 2005. 152p. ISBN: 968-860-755-X. pap. $11.95. Gr. 5–7.

    In a most accessible, conversational style, Zepeda guides teens through some of the changes and frustrations experienced during adolescence. With such colloquialisms as *Qué onda con los adolescentes* (What's up with teens) and *¿Qué hacer después de 'llegarle' a una chava?* (What to do after you've hit it off with a girl?), she provides simple suggestions about understanding adults, tolerating teachers, dealing with friends, recognizing love, and other aspects concerning life. The black-and-white cartoons and the relaxed layout and fonts add to its appeal. This is not an in-depth discussion for reflective adolescents (the subject of sex is barely mentioned); rather, it is a lighthearted, fun how-to guide.

The Arts

Abbado, Claudio. *Yo seré director de orquesta. (I Will Be an Orchestra Conductor)* Translated by Anna Coll-Vinent. Barcelona: Corimbo, 2007. 46p. ISBN: 978-84-8470-052-4. $19.95. Gr. 4–7.

    Claudio Abbado (1933), the much-celebrated Italian conductor, dedicated this book to young musicians with whom he has worked for many years. In this clear, straightforward Spanish rendition, he tells about his music-loving family, including his father's demanding style: *sus críticas eran despiadadas* (his faultfinding was cruel), and his early happy experiences as a performer and conductor. The second part is a description of different types of music such as chamber music and symphonies as well as a detailed introduction to the instruments of an orchestra. The thick black-line and watercolor illustrations in soft brown, yellow and grey tones add a lighthearted tone to Abbado's youth and a most engaging view to the world of music. Originally published by Babalibri, Milan, this book will especially appeal to young music fans and, perhaps, might awaken the interest of less-inspired music aficionados.

Aliki. *¡Oh, música! (Ah, Music!)* Illus: the author. Translated by Graziella
Bodmer. Barcelona: Editorial Juventud, 2004. 48p. ISBN: 84-261-3343-6
$18.95. Ages 2–4.

Aliki's always-expressive cartoonish illustrations, accompanied
by well-placed word balloons, sidebars, captions, and a simple Spanish
rendition, introduce readers/viewers to music—its origins, its history,
and its ubiquity in all aspects of life. With such chapters as *¿Qué es la
música?* (What is music?), *Instrumentos de la orquesta* (Instruments of
the Orchestra) and *música popular en un mundo pequeño* (Popular music in a Small World), this is indeed an enticing introduction to great
music and great composers, including pop, jazz and dance music.

Andrews-Goebel, Nancy. *La vasija que Juan fabricó. (The Pot that Juan
Built).* Illus: David Díaz. Translated by Eunice Cortés. New York: Lee
& Low, 2003. 30p. ISBN: 1-58430-229-1. $16.95 Gr. K–5.

Through this cheerful Spanish rendition, which combines the life
story of Juan Quezada, one of Mexico's most remarkable potters, with
a joyous cumulative refrain modeled after "The House that Jack Built,"
(here: *Ésta es la vasija que Juan fabricó.* [This is the pot that Juan
built.]), Spanish-speaking readers/listeners can celebrate this traditional
art form. Younger children will delight in the captivating rhymes about
the flames that fire Juan's beautiful pot: *Son éstas las llamas que nunca
están fijas/que crepitan, titilan y cuecen la vasija,/la hermosa vasija
que Juan fabricó*, and Diaz's original, stylized yellow, brown and blue
illustrations highlighting the landscape of Chihuahua, Mexico. On facing pages a simple narrative tells about this great artist and his re-
discovery of the pottery-making process of the Casas Grandes people.
An afterword, with color photographs, further explains Juan Quezada's
story.

Antoine-Andersen, Véronique. *El arte para comprender el mundo. (Understanding the World through Art)* Illus: Henri Fellner. Translated from
the French by Conrado Tostado. Mexico: Abrapalabra/Serres, 2005.
95p. ISBN: 970-9705-15-6. pap. $16.50. Gr. 5–9.

In a carefree, easy-to-understand manner, the author describes the
vitality of art through the centuries and its power to understand the
world. With excellent color reproductions and humorous black-and-
white cartoons, it explains that art has been used to conquer beauty, to
express emotions, to represent the world, to act and to reflect. From a
Paleolithic cave painting in France, to Egyptian art, religious icons, the

Renaissance and contemporary art, this is an inspiring overview that is never ponderous; rather, it is fun and enlightening.

Blake, Quentin. *Cuéntame un cuadro.* *(Tell Me a Picture)* Illus: the author. Translated by José Morán. Barcelona: Serres, 2005. 126p. ISBN: 84-8488-218-7. pap. $21.95. Gr. 2–6.

Based on an exhibit that Blake designed at the National Gallery in London, this well-illustrated book provides humorous guidance for studying and discussing 26 paintings and illustrations from European children's books. Arranged alphabetically by author, each reproduction is followed by Blake's two-tone, whimsical caricatures with children's candid reactions to each work: *Nadie compraría eso.* (Nobody would buy that.), *Parece una pesadilla.* (It looks like a nightmare.) Informative end notes with title, date, location, and brief descriptions and comments conclude this amusing invitation to art appreciation.

Browne, Anthony. *Las pinturas de Willy.* *(Willy's Pictures)* Illus: the author. Mexico: Fondo de Cultura Económica, 2000. 22p. ISBN: 968-16-5959-7. $16.95. Gr. 4–8.

Browne's well-known chimp, Willy, is happy to show his mischievous re-creations of art masterpieces and to offer humorous comments in the captions, which add insight and whimsy to each work. From *El Primer Traje*, a parody of Botticelli's "The Birth of Venus," with the comment, *¡Rápido, cúbrete!* (Quick, cover yourself!) to *Casi un Autorretrato* based on Frida Kahlo's self-portrait with monkeys in the background, with the comment, *Algunos de mis amigos querían ayudar.* (Some of my friends wished to help.), this is an ingenious introduction to famous paintings in which monkeys substitute for humans. A gatefold index with the original paintings and Browne's personal thoughts about each work conclude this inspiring large-format publication. Artists-to-be and Spanish learners will enjoy.

Giménez, Toni. *La vuelta al mundo en 25 canciones.* *(Around the World in 25 Songs)* Illus: Pep Brocal. Barcelona: La Galera, 2005. 40p. ISBN: 84-246-2059-3. pap. $18.00. Gr. K–5.

Divided into five chapters—*Africa, América, Asia, Europa* and *Oceanía*—this well-designed paperback publication includes 25 traditional children's songs from around the world. Brocal's witty, vividly colored cartoon illustrations are as joyful as Giménez's selections, which include such longtime favorites as *Juan Pestañas* (Mexico), *Dame un hogar* (Home on the Range) (United States), and *Hine Ma Tov* (Israel). Although most of the lyrics have been adapted into Spanish, some are offered only in the original languages. And despite the fact that it includes musical arrangements and a CD, accompanied by Giménez, a well-known Spanish singer, teachers and parents will note the absence of either a general introduction or a preface introducing each song. Nonetheless, all children will want to participate in the feelings of joy and camaraderie that embrace these selections.

Knight, Joan MacPhail. *Charlotte en París. (Charlotte in Paris)* Illus: Melissa Sweet. Translated by Miguel Ángel Mendo. Barcelona: Serres, 2005. 52p. ISBN: 84-8488-154-7. $12.50. Gr. 4–7.

Like its predecessor *Charlotte en Giverny (Charlotte in Giverny)*, this fictional journal of the young daughter of American artists living in Giverny, France, in 1893 recounts a pleasure-filled trip to Paris to attend an Impressionist art exhibition and other well-known Parisian sites. Mendo's fluid Spanish rendition peppered with numerous French words and expressions and Sweet's graceful watercolors and collages make this an enticing view of Impressionism and Paris. It also includes painting credits, biographical notes and an author's afterword.

Le Saux, Alain, and Grégoire Solotareff. *Pequeño museo/Little Museum.* Translated into Spanish by Margarida Trias, into English by Esther Sarfatti. Barcelona: Corimbo, 2004. 308p. ISBN: 84-8470-170-0. $30.95. Gr. 1–4.

Illustrated with details from 149 paintings by world-renowned painters, such as Bellini, Rubens and Picasso, this attractive 6½" × 6½", "little museum" introduces 149 words in Spanish in alphabetical order—from *águila*/eagle to *zapatos*/shoes—followed by the English translation. Each reproduction includes notes in both languages noting artist, title, date, and museum. Painter indexes are also included. Despite the caveat that definite articles are not provided (How will Spanish learners know that it is *el águila, el árbol*, and *la torre?),* young artists-to-be will be intrigued.

Mason, Antony. *El arte contemporáneo: en los tiempos de Warhol. (At the Time of Warhol: The Development of Contemporary Art)* Translated by Lourdes Hernández Fuentes. ISBN: 85-7416-241-8.

————. *El arte impresionista: en los tiempos de Renoir. (At the Time of Renoir: The Impressionist Era)* Translated by Martha Isabel Leñero Llaca. ISBN: 85-7416-229-9.

————. *El arte moderno: en los tiempos de Picasso. (At the Time of Picasso: The Foundations of Modern Art)* Translated by Lourdes Hernández Fuentes. ISBN: 85-7416-240-X.

————. *El arte renacentista: en los tiempos de Miguel Ángel. (At the Time of Michelangelo: The Renaissance Period)* Translated by Martha Isabel Leñero Llaca. ISBN: 85-7416-228-0.

Ea. vol.: 48p. (El Arte Alrededor del Mundo) São Paulo: Callis Editora, 2005. pap. $12.95. Gr. 3–6.

Highlighting important artists of each period, this well-designed paperback series features the major changes that influenced different artistic styles. Each title includes a straightforward text, informative sidebars, and numerous color reproductions and photographs on every page as well as a chronology, glossary and index. From expressionism to American realism to minimalism to multimedia installations are described in *El arte contemporáneo: en los tiempos de Warhol.* Landscapes, light and impressionism, Monet, Renoir, Degas, Cézanne and other artists of the era are featured in *El arte impresionista: en los tiempos de Renoir.* From the influence of fauvism, to the birth of cubism, to Klee, Miró, Chagall, Matisse and Picasso are presented in *El arte moderno: en los tiempos de Picasso.* Medieval manuscripts, religious art, and great Renaissance artists such as Leonardo da Vinci, Velázquez and Michelangelo are introduced in *El arte renacentista: en los tiempos de Miguel Ángel.* Simple and appealing introduction to art.

Merberg, Julie, and Suzanne Bober. *Un picnic con Monet. (A Picnic with Monet)* Translated by Raquel Mancera. Barcelona: Serres, 2005. 24p. ISBN: 84-8488-201-2. $11.95. Ages 3–5.

In a well-constructed board book, the very young are invited to a picnic with the French painter and founder of impressionism, Claude Monet. A simple rhyming text introduces each painting highlighting the artist's spontaneous reaction to landscapes and outdoor events. Originally published by Chronicle Books, parents and caregivers will enjoy sharing this Monet picnic with the little ones.

Roca, Núria. *Cine. (Movies)* ISBN: 0-7641-2707-1.

————. *Música. (Music)* ISBN: 0-7641-2706-3.

———. *Pintura y escultura. (Painting and Sculpture)* ISBN: 0-7641-2704-7.

———. *Teatro. (Theater).* ISBN: 0-7641-2705-5.

Ea. vol.: 36p. Illus: Rosa Maria Curto (¿Qué es el Arte?) Hauppauge, NY: Barron's, 2004. pap. $6.95. Gr. 2–4.

In a sprightly, easy-to-understand text and cheerful, full-page black-ink, mixed media and watercolor, almost cartoonish illustrations, this well-designed paperback series introduces five art forms to children. In addition, simple explanations and suggestions encourage children to participate in different art activities. In *Cine*, children visit a movie theater, discover how a movie projector works, and learn about sound stages, sets, and the illusion of motion. Singing, musical instruments, the difference between happy and sad music, and the fundamentals of music notation, including the names of the notes in Spanish- and English-speaking countries, e.g., "C (*do*), D (*re*), E (*mi*)" are described in *Música*. Colors, shapes, shadows, the graphic arts, crayons, paints and a visit to an art museum are explained in *Pintura y escultura*. In *Teatro*, Ana and her friends visit a theater, learn about the stage, lighting, props, puppets and acting. Each title includes simple activities to do at home or in the classroom. Kudos for the arts depicted in this series.

Vilchis, Alfredo. *La revolución imaginada. (The Imagined Revolution)* Illus: the author. Mexico: Serres, 2005. 140p. ISBN: 970-9705-08-3. $31.95. Gr. 9–adult.

As noted in the prologue, this book intermingles three histories— the history of the Mexican Revolution (1910–1920), the history of *exvoto* (a traditional votive offering, given or dedicated in fulfillment of a religious vow), and the history of Alfredo Vilchis, *pintor del barrio* (loosely translated as "painter of the slums"). It includes 54 excellent, full-page color reproductions of Vilchis's powerful *exvotos* depicting personal views of historical aspects of the Mexican Revolution. Like the traditional *exvotos*, the accompanying labels, also reprinted in facing pages, are written in the robust vernacular of Mexico's underprivileged, with extravagant forms and usages. As an example of a particularly provocative one: *Hago patente este retablo . . . una presiosa [sic] mujer que por mas [sic] puta que fue . . . los hombres son muy malos prometen muchos regalos y lo que dan son puros palos* (p. 52) (I clarify in this retable . . . a beautiful woman, although having been a whore . . . men are evil, they promise many gifts but what they give are only beatings). The reproduction depicts a dead, badly beaten nude woman. This is indeed a strikingly commanding "imagined" view of Mexico's Revolution for mature readers/viewers.

Recreation and Sports

Baptiste, Baron. *Mi papá es de plastilina. (My Daddy Is a Pretzel)* Illus: Sophie Fatus. Translated by Librada Piñero. Barcelona: Molino/Planeta, 2005. 48p. ISBN: 84-7871-415-4. $15.95. Gr. 2–5.

A yoga teacher teaches her students nine yoga postures, relating them to the jobs of each of the students' parents. Hence, Laura's mother is a gardener, so hers is the tree pose; Pablo's parents are veterinarians, his is the downward dog post; Juan's mother is an architect, his is the triangle post; and so on. Fatus's ink-and-watercolor illustrations, which humorously depict each parent's occupation, also provide detailed, step-by-step instructions to practice each posture. Baptiste provides both practical suggestions and insightful comments to assist children to attain spiritual and physical vitality. Originally published by Barefoot Books, London.

Bretón, Marcos. *Home is Everything: The Latino Baseball Story.* Photos by José Luis Villegas. Translated by Daniel Santacruz. El Paso, TX: Cinco Puntos Press, 2002. 143p. ISBN: 0-938317-70-9. pap. $25.95. Gr. 7–adult.

Highlighting the racism, struggles, disappointments and occasionally enormous success of some Latin American baseball players in the United States, this attractive bilingual publication with exquisite candid color photographs on almost every page is sure to appeal to baseball fans. In such chapters as "Home is Everything," "Forgotten Ones" and "The Immortals & Heroes," it tells about the loneliness, feelings of alienation, injuries and erratic performances that lead to the release of 90 to 95 percent of the "1000 or so Latino prospects brought to the U.S. every year" (p. 21) as well as the successes and achievements of such star performers as Chico Carrasquel and Miguel Tejada. The lack of an index is a serious detriment.

Crossingham, John. *Fútbol Americano en acción. (Football in Action)* ISBN: 0-7787-8573-4.
———. *Patinetas en acción. (Skateboarding in Action)* ISBN: 0-7787-8574-2.
———. *Porristas en acción. (Cheerleading in Action)* ISBN: 0-7787-8575-0.

——, and Sarah Dann. *Basquetbol en acción. (Basketball in Action)* ISBN: 0-7787-8572-6.

Dann, Sarah, and John Crossingham. *Béisbol en acción. (Baseball in Action)* ISBN: 0-7787-8571-8.

Walker, Niki, and Sarah Dann. *Fútbol en acción. (Soccer in Action)* ISBN: 0-7787-8570-X.
Ea. vol.: 32p. Illus: Donna Rouse and others. Translated by translations.com. (Deportes en Acción) New York: Crabtree, 2006. $23.92. Gr. 3–5.

With appealing, candid color photos, clear illustrations and diagrams, and easy-to-understand explanations, these well-done Spanish renditions introduce young Spanish speakers to the techniques, equipment, rules and safety requirements of football, skateboarding, cheerleading, basketball, baseball and soccer. These are not tedious rules; rather, they present essential information about each sport in a lively yet comprehensive manner.

Dayton, Connor. *Choppers/Choppers.* ISBN: 978-1-4042-7612-3.
——. *Cool Bikes/Motos cool.* ISBN: 978-1-4042-7613-0.
——. *Dirt Bikes/Dirt Bikes.* ISBN: 978-1-4042-7610-9.
——. *Street Bikes/Motos de calle.* ISBN: 978-1-4042-7614-7.
——. *Superbikes/Superbikes.* ISBN: 978-1-4042-7611-6.
——. *Tricks with Bikes/Trucos con la moto.* ISBN: 978-1-4042-7615-4.
Ea. vol.: 24p. Translated by Eduardo Alamán. (Motorcycles: Made for Speed!/Motocicletas a Toda Velocidad) New York: Rosen/Buenas Letras, 2007. $21.25. Gr. 1–2.

Young motorcycle enthusiasts will be delighted with this simple bilingual series about the design, history, and special likes and abilities of the riders of choppers, superbikes, cool dirt and street bikes as well as the excitement of bike tricks. Candid color photos face an easy-to-read English text, followed by a smooth, easy Spanish rendition in a lighter font. Simple bilingual glossaries with English pronunciation guides make this series even more appealing to English and Spanish beginning readers.

Gifford, Clive. *La enciclopedia del fútbol. (Soccer: The Ultimate Guide to the Beautiful Game)* Translated by Jimena Licitra. Madrid: Ediciones SM, 2003. 96p. ISBN: 84-348-9228-6. $18.95. Gr. 6–9.

From the history of soccer to the rules, skills, tactics and profiles of legendary players, this attractive book is sure to please soccer aficionados. A succinct text, informative sidebars and numerous computer-generated images and color photos on every page provide a wealth of information about the sport. The only disappointment to Spanish speakers from the Americas is that the appendixes highlight information about *Fútbol español* (Soccer in Spain) and Web sites from Spain. Despite this caveat, all Spanish speakers will appreciate the glossary, index, and practical information about this popular sport.

Hoffman, Mary Ann. *Alex Rodríguez: Baseball Star/Estrella del béisbol.* ISBN: 978-1-4042-7598-0.
———. *David Ortiz: Baseball Star/Estrella del béisbol.* ISBN: 978-1-4042-7599-7.
———. *Dwyane Wade: Basketball Star/Estrella del baloncesto.* ISBN: 978-1-4042-7602-4.
———. *LeBron James: Basketball Star/Estrella del baloncesto.* ISBN: 978-1-4042-7600-0.
———. *Peyton Manning: Football Star/Estrella del fútbol americano.* ISBN: 978-1-4042-7601-7.
———. *Shaun Alexander: Football Star/Estrella del fútbol americano.* ISBN: 978-1-4042-7603-1.
Ea. vol.: 24p. Translated by Eduardo Alamán. (Amazing Athletes/Atletas Increíbles) New York: Rosen, 2007. $21.25. Gr. 1–3.

Young sports fans, both English- and Spanish-speaking, will enjoy reading highlights in the lives of six well-known stars from three popular sports: baseball (Alex Rodríguez and David Ortiz), basketball (Dwyane Wade and LeBron James), football (Peyton Manning and Shaun Alexander). Especially important for beginning readers of either language, the well-done, simple Spanish text (two sentences per page) follows the English in a different color and style font. To avoid the resulting confusion of other bilingual books, both texts are also separated by a dark black line. Complete glossaries and suggestions for further reading in both languages are included. Candid color photos on all facing pages showing each athlete in action complement this appealing, high-interest/low-vocabulary series.

Mortimer, Gavin. *Locos por el fútbol. (Football Fanatic's File)* Illus: John Cooper. Translated by David Ponsà. Barcelona: La Galera, 2005. 32p. ISBN: 84-246-2055-0. $10.95. Gr. 3–6.

Soccer fans will find many practical suggestions and techniques to improve their playing abilities. In an easy-to-follow format, it describes training schedules, referee signals, special characteristics of good goalkeepers, defenders, midfielders, forwards, the ideal coach and other soccer tidbits. Unfortunately, it basically highlights European, especially Spanish, players and teams, which may disappoint soccer fans in the Americas.

Nik. *Gaturro 4.* (*Gaturro 4)* Illus: the author. Buenos Aires: Ediciones de la Flor, 2004. 96p. ISBN: 950-515-761-4. pap. $8.95. Gr. 7–12.

This collection of comic strips features the big-cheeked, big-eyed *Gaturro*, an inquisitive naïve cat that offers quick-witted observations to life's normal and not-so-normal situations. Two to six panels per page present self-contained scenes in which *Gaturro* comments on difficult-to-please *chicas*, presumptuous men, productive and unproductive work, misunderstood people and other lifelike predicaments. Written in the vernacular of Argentina with amusing wordplay and illustrated with witty, expressive cartoons in bright colors. *Gaturro* will charm fans of the genre.

Literature

Cárdenas, Teresa. *Cartas a mi mamá (Letters to My Mother)* Toronto: Groundwood, 2006. 104p. ISBN: 978-0-88899-723-4. pap. $6.95. Gr. 6–9.

Demoralized by the death of her mother and by the constant abuse she receives from her aunts and cousins, a ten-year-old African-Cuban girl composes loving letters to her *Querida mamá*. In brief, terse, moving letters, she describes the insults she endures because of her dark skin and thick lips; her grandmother's superstitions; her aunt's violent boyfriends, which include sexual abuse; a white friend who is ashamed of his prostitute mother; and, finally, her hopes of finding her unknown father. Cárdenas, who writes with a cadence and style that is firmly rooted in Cuban rhetorical tradition, will touch Spanish-speaking adolescents around the world who will appreciate her honesty and unrestrained candor.

Letria, José Jorge. *Animales fantásticos. (Fantastic Animals)* Illus: André Letria. Translated by Xosé Ballesteros. Sevilla: Kalandraka, 2007. 40p. ISBN: 978-84-96388-41-3. $20.95. Gr. 3–6.

Twenty mythological animals that in the worldview of people explain aspects of the natural world or delineate the psychology, customs or ideals of society are featured in this beautifully designed book. In striking colorful double-page spreads and an appropriately allegorical rhyming text, it tells about such well-known, supernatural beings as *El Ave Fénix* (Phoenix) the bird in Egyptian mythology that consumed itself by fire and rose renewed from its ashes; *El Centauro* (Centaur) in Greek mythology, a monster with the head, arms and trunk of a man and the body and legs of a horse; *El Cíclope* (Cyclops), Greek mythology, one-eyed giant reputedly descended from Titans; and *El Minotauro* (Minotaur) a half-man and half-bull monster from Greek mythology. Unfortunately, the lack of a table of contents, index or introduction limit its use; nonetheless, this is indeed a most intriguing introduction to mythological creatures.

Manguel, Alberto. *Diario de lecturas. (A Reading Diary)* Translated by José Luis López Muñoz. Madrid: Alianza, 2004. 233p. ISBN: 84-206-5667-4. pap. $10.95. Gr. 9–adult.

 Manguel's characteristic passion and gusto for books and reading are tastefully captured in López Muñoz's delightful Spanish rendition. From June 2002 to May 2003 Manguel set out to reread twelve of his favorite books as he traveled from his native Buenos Aires to London— *una de las ciudades más incómodas del mundo* (one of the most uncomfortable cities in the world)—to Paris and other cities. He intermingles his personal impressions of the places he visits, his beloved books—from Adolfo Bioy Casares's *La invención de Morel (The Invention of Morel)* to Joaquim M. Machado de Assis's *Memorias póstumas de Blas Cubas (Epitaph of a Small Winner)*—his reactions to the world after 9/11, and his disapproval of the war in Iraq and the policies of the Bush administration. Spanish-speaking book lovers, discriminating travelers and critical thinkers will appreciate Manguel's thoughtful and candid observations.

Osborne, Mary Pope. *La Tierra de los Muertos: Cuentos de la Odisea. (Tales from the Odyssey II: The Land of the Dead)* Illus: Julián De Narváez. Translated by Laura Quintana. Bogotá: Grupo Editorial Norma, 2006. 106p. ISBN: 958-04-9500-9. pap. $10.95. Gr. 4–8.

 Maintaining the swiftly paced episodes and the simple, engaging narrative with brief chapters and succinct sentences of the original, Quintana's lucid Spanish rendition relates the second volume in which *Odiseo* (Odysseus) and his fleet continue their difficult journey home. Before they can return to *Ítaca* (Ithaca), they must defeat giant cannibals, outwit Cerce, a beautiful witch and travel to the feared *Tierra de los Muertos* (Land of the Dead). An extensive afterword by Héctor Hoyos presents information about major Greek gods and goddesses, Greek beliefs, Homer and compares Greek and Latin American heroes. Spanish speakers, especially from the Americas, will appreciate this sleek introduction to Homer and Greek mythology.

Pablo, Eladio de. *El ingenioso hidalgo don Quijote de la Mancha. (The Ingenious Knight Don Quijote de la Mancha)* Illus: José Pérez Montero. León: Everest, 2005. 106p. ISBN: 84-241-1619-4. pap. $10.95. Gr. 5–8.

Based on Cervantes's masterpiece and maintaining the original humor and witty dialogue of the original, this play recounts, in the style of Cervantes, some well-known and amusing incidents of the legendary knight who roamed the world avenging wrongs and righting injuries. From the first scene where Don Quijote talks to courageous *Caballero de la Ardiente Espada* to the last scene where Don Quijote reads on his deathbed the most famous first line of the best loved and admired novel of the Spanish-speaking world: *En un lugar de la Mancha de cuyo nombre no quiero acordarme* . . . (In a village of La Mancha the name of which I have no desire to recall . . .), young readers/listeners will enjoy this truly accessible depiction of Don Quijote's idealistic dreams and poetic fantasies. Some readers from the Americas may be initially disturbed by the Peninsular Spanish pronouns and conjugations, but Don Quijote and Sancho Panza are hard to resist and Montero's lively, watercolor illustrations add to the fun.

Poniatowska, Elena. *Obras reunidas I: Narrativa breve. (Collected Works I: Short Stories)* Mexico: Fondo de Cultura Económica, 2005. 310p. ISBN: 968-16-7469-3. $19.95. Gr. 9–adult.

Four short stories by the acclaimed Mexican author and journalist Elena Poniatowska (1932) are included in this volume. It includes *Lilus Kikus*, her first book, in which the author relates her impressions of Eden Hall, a convent where she was educated. This is followed by *Querido Diego, te abraza Quiela* (known in English as *Dear Diego*), a re-creation of the letters that Angelina Beloff might have sent Diego Rivera; *De noche vienes*, which highlights feelings of love, solitude, children, patience and kindness; and *Tlapalería,* a collection of eight tales about her grandmother, her favorite canaries, her life as a reporter and her friends. Especially appealing to adolescents is the author's eleven-page prologue in which she tells about her childhood in Paris as well as her early years as a journalist and writer.

Torres, José Alejandro. *Refranero del Quijote. (Quijote's Book of Proverbs)* Mexico: Lectorum, 2005. 117p. ISBN: 970-732-091-5. pap. $10.45. Gr. 8–adult.

More than 300 proverbs, aphorisms, maxims and sayings from Miguel de Cervantes's classic work, *El ingenioso hidalgo don Quijote de la Mancha*, are included in this modest paperback publication. A brief explanation or summary follows each proverb. Spanish speakers will recognize such proverbs as *Pagan justos por pecadores* (When someone does not deserve to be punished), *Donde una puerta se cierra, otra se abre* (Good times follow bad times), *Cosa pasada es cosa juzgada* (When something is done, it's done), *Más vale buena queja que mala paga* (Hope is better than bad payment) and other short, pithy sayings that are in widespread use in the Spanish-speaking world. This is not a scholarly essay about *el Quijote*; rather, this collection highlights Cervantes's genius as a collector of the wisdom, ideas, basic truths and practical precepts of the common people of Spain. Even though it lacks an index and a table of contents, it is still a lighthearted introduction to Quijote's and Sancho Panza's adventures.

Woolf, Virginia. *Un cuarto propio. (A Room of One's Own)* Translated by Jorge Luis Borges. Madrid: Alianza, 2003. 125p. ISBN: 84-206-5526-0. pap. $9.95. Gr. 9–adult.

First published in 1929, Woolf's excellent essay describing the relationship between the feminine condition and literature is now available in this superior Spanish rendition. Borges's masterful talent as a translator convey to Spanish readers the author's sensitivity and powerful ideas about women, life and creativity.

Poetry

Alarcón, Francisco X. *Poems to Dream Together/Poemas para soñar juntos.* Illus: Paula Barragán. New York: Lee & Low, 2005. 32p. ISBN: 1-58430-233-X. $16.95. Gr. 3–5.

Alarcón celebrates families, communities and life in this bilingual collection of poems. Especially appealing are his short poems that tell about dreams, nightmares, real questions and happy feelings. Others, with a not-so-subtle didactic intent, (helping *Mamá* with household chores, working in the family garden) will remind readers of family sermons or preachy verses. Nonetheless, Barragán's pencil, cut paper and gouache digital renditions with a strong Latino flavor add a more joyful imaginative tone.

Ciria, Carmen, and José Antonio García. *Jrj.poemas (jrj.Poems).* León: Everest, 2006. 141p. ISBN: 84-241-1303-9. pap. $11.95. Gr. 8–12.

A well-written introduction to the life and work of Juan Ramón Jiménez (1881–1958), the 1956 Spanish Nobel laureate and poet who introduced modernism to Spanish verse and selections of some of his most accessible poems provide a thoughtful perspective to the significance of this much-acclaimed author of the popular *Platero y yo.* Of special interest to adolescents are Jiménez's unconventional spelling (e.g., *recojido, ánjeles),* which openly differed from the *Real Academia de la Lengua Española,* and his brief poems *Adolescencia* and *Abril.*

Del Paso, Fernando. *Encuentra en cada cara lo que tiene de rara. (Find What's Strange in Each Face)* Illus: the author. Mexico: Cidcli, 2002. 26p. ISBN: 968-494-125-0. $14.95. Gr. 2–4.

Sophisticated Spanish speakers will enjoy the wordplay, rhythm and nonsense of these brief rhymes that encourage children to find what's strange in each face. Perhaps the full-page, brightly colored collage illustrations are too bizarre for most children. Yet some will have fun as they note: *Mucho se adorna Teresa/con su boca de hamburguesa* with an eccentric cartoon illustration of a girl's face with a hamburger shaped as her mouth. And *Cejas de chile poblano/se mandó hacer Cayetano* with an outlandish full-page collage of a man's mustachioed face with *chile poblano* eyebrows.

The Golden Age: Poems of the Spanish Renaissance. Selected and translated by Edith Grossman. New York: W. W. Norton, 2006. 201p. ISBN: 0-393-06038-1. $26.95. Gr. 9–adult.

This is not a comprehensive nor scholarly anthology of poems by Spanish-speaking poets from the sixteenth and seventeenth centuries; rather, it is a tantalizing selection of the translator's favorite poems by some of her favorite authors—Jorge Manrique, Garcilaso de la Vega, Fray Luis de León, San Juan de la Cruz, Luis de Góngora, Lope de Vega, Francisco de Quevedo and Sor Juana Inés de la Cruz. Grossman explains that instead of separating rhyme from rhythm, which "might well be barbarous," she focused on re-creating meter. The results are eminently readable English translations that appear side by side of the original Spanish texts. Spanish-speaking adolescents will especially enjoy Manrique's deeply felt *Verses Written on the Death of His Father,* Lope de Vega's tongue-in-cheek *Instant Sonnet,* and Sor Juana Inés's quick-witted poems. In addition, poetry enthusiasts will appreciate Billy Collins's introduction, the brief notes on the poets and the black-and-white illustrations.

Red Hot Salsa: Bilingual Poems on Being Young and Latino in the United States. Edited by Lori M. Carlson. New York: Holt, 2005. 140p. ISBN: 0-8050-7616-6. $14.95. Gr. 8–12.

Through deeply felt bilingual poems, Latino authors portray their personal histories and special feelings about growing up Latino in the United States. From Gary Soto's amusing "Spanish is a matter/of rolling 'rrrrrs'" to Luis S. Rodríguez's adorable *Tia Chucha* to Martín Espada's powerfully symbolic *piñata* to lesser known poets, these are written in a lively mix of "streety English hip-hop," conventional Spanish and a composite of both that are a testimony to the wealth and diversity of the two languages. It is unfortunate that, although the English translations maintain the lyricism and beauty of the original Spanish poems, several of the Spanish translations are awkward and confusing, e.g., *Mi poema a la comida más corto* [sic] (p. 15) and *sin embargo anhelo vivir y quedarme vivo* (p. 115). What a disappointment!

Silverstein, Shel. *Batacazos: Poemas para reírse. (Falling Up)* Illus: the author. Translated by Daniel Aguirre Oteiza. Barcelona: Ediciones B, 2004. 176p. ISBN: 84-406-9295-1. $19.99. Gr. 3–7.

Just as clever, delightful and witty as its predecessors—*Donde el camino se corta (Where the Sidewalk Ends)* and *Hay luz en el desván (Light in the Attic)*—, Silverstein's slightly subversive and humorously naughty poems and facetious pen-and-ink cartoons are sure to appeal to Spanish speakers. From a *Papá con mando a distancia* (Remote-a-Dad) that can be easily controlled, to *un gnomo viejo y gordo/que intentaba pegar a un mosquito* ("I saw an ol' gnome/Take a gknock at a gnat"), to the stork that not only brings babies but also *actúa al revés/y recoge a la gente de más edad/cuando le llega la hora de marchar* ("comes and gets the older folks/When it's their time to go"), this charming Spanish rendition maintains the improbable characters, unconventional thoughts and offbeat humor that all children enjoy. In addition to the Peninsular

Spanish conjugations (*cosedme, podéis*), Spanish speakers from the Americas will note a few judicious adaptations, e.g., *gramos* and *kilos* for pounds and *pesetas* for dollars.

Geography

Aloian, Molly, and Bobbie Kalman. *Explora América del Norte. (Explore North America)* ISBN: 978-0-7787-8292-6.
———. *Explora América del Sur. (Explore South America)* ISBN: 978-0-7787-8293-3.
———. *Explora Europa. (Explore Europe)* ISBN: 978-0-7787-8291-9.
Kalman, Bobbie, and Rebecca Sjonger. *Explora Africa. (Explore Africa)* ISBN: 978-0-7787-8287-2.
———. *Explora la Antártida. (Explore Antarctica)* ISBN: 978-0-7787-8288-9.
———. *Explora Asia. (Explore Asia)* ISBN: 978-0-7787-8289-6.
———. *Explora Australia y Oceanía. (Explore Australia and Oceania)* ISBN: 978-0-7787-8290-2.
Ea. vol.: 32p. Translated by translations.com. (Explora los Continentes) New York: Crabtree, 2008. $18.95. Gr. 2–4.

Attractive and informative, the *Explora los Continentes* series introduces the world's seven continents to beginning Spanish readers. The easy-to-understand Spanish rendition is presented in a large, clear typeface and simple, captioned color maps, charts and photographs. Each title concludes with a useful glossary and index. *Explora América del Norte* describes the mountains, islands, lakes, plant and animal life in North America's forests, grasslands and desert biomes. From the unique fauna of the *islas Galápagos* (Galápagos Islands), to the beautiful blue butterflies of the tropical forests of the Amazonia, to life in the Atacama desert, where in some parts *no ha llovido en más de 400 años* (it hasn't rained in more than 400 years), to traditional dances in Bolivia, soccer in Argentina and carnival in Brazil are beautifully depicted in *Explora América del Sur. Explora Europa* features Europe's peninsulas, mountain systems, bodies of water and fauna. *Explora África* highlights Africa's mountains, valleys, waterways, culture and tourist attractions. *Explora la Antártida* describes Antarctica's chilly geography, mountains, seas, animals and mile-thick layer of ice. *Explora Asia* introduces the largest continent on Earth—Asia—including its major regions, bodies of water, landforms, forests and deserts. *Explora*

Oceanía presents the Great Barrier Reef in Australia, the fauna in Tasmania and geysers in New Zealand.

Becker, Michelle Aki. *Arizona. (Arizona)* ISBN: 0-516-25106-6.
Bredeson, Carmen. *Florida. (Florida)* ISBN: 0-516-25108-2.
———. *Texas. (Texas)* ISBN: 0-516-25110-4.
De Capua, Sarah. *California. (California)* ISBN: 0-516-25107-4.
———. *Nueva York. (New York)* ISBN: 0-516-25109-0.
   Ea. vol.: 32p. Translated by Eida Del Risco. (Rookie Español-Geografía)
   New York: Children's Press, 2004. $17.00. Gr. K–2.
   Clear color maps and photos on every page and easy-to-understand
Spanish texts introduce young readers to the people, landmarks, geography and animals of five states: Arizona, Florida, Texas, California and
New York. Each title includes an index and, unfortunately, an incomplete glossary. Although each glossary correctly states *Palabras que
sabes* (Words you know), none includes a definite article. How can
young Spanish learners know if it is *la* or *el fósil, bosque/puma* and
other new words?

Burgan, Michael. *Nuevo México: Tierra de encanto. (New Mexico: Land of
   Enchantment)* ISBN: 0-8368-5725-9.
———. *Puerto Rico y otras áreas periféricas. (Puerto Rico and Outlying
   Areas)* ISBN: 0-8368-5726-7.
   Ea. vol. 48p. (World Almanac Biblioteca de los Estados) Milwaukee:
   World Almanac Library, 2005. $22.50. Gr. 5–8.
   Highlighting the geographical contrasts and cultural traditions
that add to the beauty and uniqueness of New Mexico as a state where
old traditions intermingle with high-tech industries, *Nuevo México:
Tierra de encanto* provides a vivid overview that will encourage readers to learn more about the state. Especially interesting to Spanish
speakers is the role that Latinos and Hispanics have played in various
aspects of its history, politics, economy, and culture. *Puerto Rico y
otras áreas periféricas* describes the special relationship of the island as
a self-governing commonwealth in the Caribbean with the United
States. Like the other eight titles in this attractive and informative series, these are smooth Spanish renditions with clear, easy-to-understand
graphs, charts, sidebars, maps and timelines. Each title includes numerous sharp color photographs and a factual profile that present the state's
history, people, government, economy, culture, lifestyle and special attractions.

Elias, Megan. *Colorado: El estado del centenario. (Colorado: The Centennial State)* ISBN: 0-8368-5724-0.

Martin, Michael. *Arizona: El estado del Gran Cañon. (Arizona: The Grand Canyon State)* ISBN: 0-8368-5723-2.

    Ea. vol.: 48p. (World Almanac Biblioteca de los Estados) Milwaukee: World Almanac Library, 2005. $22.50. Gr. 5–8.

    Highlighting the natural beauty of the state as well as its distinctive history, *Colorado: El estado del centenario* provides an engrossing overview of its uniqueness and varied economy. With numerous color and period photographs, charts, maps and compelling sidebars such as *Tragedia nacional* (National Tragedy), which reports on the Columbine High School massacre in Littleton, Colorado in April 1999, this smooth Spanish rendition offers students basic facts and enlightening discussions. In addition to informative reviews, it provides lively descriptions on such topics as the beginning of the gold fever in 1858, the tragic lives of coal miners in the early 1900s, women's suffrage, and the natural amphitheater in Red Rocks where Stravinsky, the Beatles and U2 have performed. Like the eight other titles in this series, it includes a section on noteworthy *Coloradenses*, a timeline, calendar of events and an index. The history, people, geography, government, economy, culture and lifestyle of the Grand Canyon state are described in *Arizona: El estado del Gran Cañon*. From the Anasazi, to the Spanish explorers, to the Treaty of Guadalupe Hidalgo, to the Central Arizona Project that provides much-needed water to the state, to the beauty of Organ Pipe Cactus in the Sonora desert, Spanish-speaking readers will find useful facts and intriguing information.

History

Brill, Marlene Targ. *Allen Jay y el ferrocarril subterráneo. (Allen Jay and the Underground Railroad)* Illus: Janice Lee Porter. ISBN: 978-0-8225-77-84-3.

———. *Bronco Charlie y el Pony Express. (Bronco Charlie and the Pony Express)* Illus: Craig Orback. ISBN: 0-8225-2991-2.

Figley, Marty Rhodes. *Salvar a la Campana de la Libertad. (Saving the Liberty Bell)* Illus: Kevin Lepp. ISBN: 0-8225-3094-5.

Patrick, Jean L.S. *La niña que ponchó a Babe Ruth. (The Girl Who Struck Out Babe Ruth)* Illus: Jeni Reeves. ISBN: 978-0-8225-7785-0.

Roop, Peter, and Connie. *Botones para el general Washington. (Buttons for General Washington)* Illus: Peter E. Hanson. ISBN: 0-8225-6261-8.

———. *Mantén las luces encendidas, Abbie. (Keep the Lights Burning, Abbie)* Illus: Peter E. Hanson. ISBN: 0-8225-3098-8.

Ross, Alice, and Kent Ross. *La Dama de Cobre. (Copper Lady)* Illus: Leslie Bowman. ISBN: 0-8225-6262-6.

Schulz, Walter A. *Will y Orv. (Will and Orv)* Illus: Janet Schulz. ISBN: 0-8225-6263-4.

Welch, Catherine A. *La Bandera de Estrellas Centelleantes: El Himno Nacional. (The Star-Spangled Banner)* Illus: Carrie H. Warwick. ISBN: 0-8225-3114-3.

Wetterer, Margaret K. *Kate Shelley y el tren de medianoche. (Kate Shelley and the Midnight Express)* Illus: Karen Ritz. ISBN: 0-8225-3096-1.

———, and Charles M. Wetterer. *Caminando bajo la nieve. (Snow Walker)* Illus: Mary O'Keefe Young. ISBN: 978-0-8225-7786-7.

Ea. vol.: 48p. Translated by translations.com. (Yo Solo Historia) Minneapolis: Lerner, 2006-2008. $23.93. Gr. 2–4.

Young Julius Miller's greatest wish is to ride horses, especially after hearing stories about the Pony Express. Maintaining the easy-to-read and exciting text of the original, this zestful Spanish rendition tells the tale of the audacious rider, who despite rain, darkness and unknown forests, became Bronco Charlie, the youngest rider of the Pony Express, in *Bronco Charlie y el Pony Express*. Vivacious illustrations complement this fascinating depiction of a boy and the early mail service in the United States. Other titles in this lively historical fiction series recount how Allen Jay, a young Quaker boy, helped a passenger on the *Ferrocarril Subterráneo* (Underground Railroad) escape from slavery in 1842 in *Allen Jay y el ferrocarril subterráneo*; feature the efforts of eleven-year-old Johnny Mickley to keep *La Campana de la Independencia* safe from the British during the Revolutionary War in *Salvar a la Campana de la Libertad*; narrate the day in 1931 when in an exhibition game, seventeen-year-old Jackie Mitchell, a female professional baseball player, struck out Babe Ruth and Lou Gehrig in *La niña que ponchó a Babe Ruth;* re-create the dangerous missions of spies during the Revolutionary War through young John Darragh in *Botones para el general Washington*; highlight the bravery of Abbie Burgess and her struggles to keep the oil lamps of their lighthouse burning in the winter of 1856 in *Mantén las luces encendidas, Abbie*; reconstruct the history of the Statue of Liberty as a symbol of friendship between France and the United States in *La Dama de Cobre*; recount the first flight of

Wilbur and Orville Wright and their young helper, Johnny Moore, in *Willy y Orv*; portray the courageous actions of fifteen-year-old Kate to prevent a train disaster in *Kate Shelly y el tren de medianoche*; narrate how Frances Scott Key's poem became the Star-Spangled Banner, the National Anthem of the United States in *La Bandera de Estrellas Centelleantes*; tell how in 1888 in New York twelve-year-old Milton Daub ventures into a dangerous blizzard to bring food and medicine to his helpless neighbors in *Caminando bajo la nieve*. This is an excellent series to entice Spanish-speaking beginning readers (and Spanish learners) to appreciate well-known events in the history of the United States.

Cerdá, Marcelo, and others. *El cine no fue siempre así. (Movies Were Not Always Like This)* ISBN: 978-987-1217-10-6.
Glasman, Gabriel, and Ileana Lotersztain. *Los libros no fueron siempre así. (Books Were Not Always Like This)* ISBN: 978-987-1217-11-3.
Kukso, Federico, and Ileana Lotersztain. *El baño no fue siempre así. (Bathrooms Were Not Always Like This)* ISBN: 978-987-1217-09-0.
Ea. vol.: 36p. Illus: Javier Basile. (Las Cosas No Fueron Siempre Así) Buenos Aires: Iamiqué, 2006-2007. pap. $11.95. Gr. 3–7.

Humorous, computer-generated color cartoon illustrations and a most animated text are sure to entice young readers to learn about the history and development of the bathroom and its now ubiquitous devices such as toilets, soap, tooth brushes, toilet paper and showers. With well-designed *Sabías que . . .* (Did You Know . . .) sidebars and easy-to-follow timelines on every spread, as well as amusing, interesting-to-know historical facts and anecdotes (A *servidor de la silla* would wipe with his hand the behind of King Henry the VIII after every bowel movement), this is indeed a unique and refreshing presentation of unsanitary and now-discredited practices as well as the development and re-introduction of more hygienic customs and inventions. The development of books from tablets, papyrus and parchment to digital books and censorship is described in *Los libros no fueron siempre así. El cine no fue siempre así* introduces the pioneer work in cinematography of Auguste and Louis Lumière, up to Hollywood, television and animation. Each title includes a bibliography and Spanish-language Web sites.

Chrisp, Peter. *Al descubierto el Antiguo Egipto. (Ancient Egypt Revealed)* Translated by José Ochoa. Madrid: Pearson/Alhambra, 2003. 38p. ISBN: 84-205-4070-6. $14.95. Gr. 3–6.

Like other Dorling Kindersley titles, this attractive introduction to Ancient Egypt includes numerous crisp color photos and drawings on every page, brief texts and informative sidebars. In addition, clear acetate overlays depict inside/outside views of royal tombs, an Egyptian ship, and the temple at Abu Simbel. An index complements this excellent overview of the history and achievements of Ancient Egypt.

Clare, John D. *Los aztecas. (Aztec Life)* Translated by Elizabeth Hahn Villagrán. ISBN: 968-24-7061-7.

———. *Los indios del Norte de América. (North American Indian Life)* Translated by Javier Parra Chapa. ISBN: 968-24-7065-X.

Clements, Jonathan. *Los chinos. (Chinese Life)* Translated by Javier Parra Chapa. ISBN: 968-24-7063-3.

Drew, David. *Los incas. (Inca Life)* Translated by Javier Parra Chapa. ISBN: 968-24-7066-8.

Guy, John. *Los egipcios. (Egyptian Life)* Translated by Elizabeth Hahn Villagrán. ISBN: 968-24-7059-5.

———. *Los griegos. (Greek Life)* Translated by Elizabeth Hahn Villagrán. ISBN: 968-24-7062-5.

———. *Los romanos. (Roman Life)* Translated by Elizabeth Hahn Villagrán. ISBN: 968-24-7064-1.

———, and Richard Hall. *Los vikingos. (Viking Life)* Translated by Elizabeth Hahn Villagrán. ISBN: 968-24-7060-9.

Ea. vol.: 32p. (Grandes Civilizaciones) Mexico: Trillas, 2004. pap. $9.75. Gr. 4–7.

Highlighting the beauty and achievements as well as the ruthless and oppressive aspects of Aztec life, *Los aztecas* presents a most engaging and informative overview of this pre-Columbian civilization. In an easy-to-understand Spanish rendition, it describes such facts as the religious meaning of *el juego de pelota* (ball game), their high standards of personal hygiene in contrast to European people of the times, and their constant need for human blood to appease their gods. Like the other seven titles of this well-illustrated series on early civilizations, originally published by Ticktock Publishing, London, it includes numerous color drawings and photos on every page, brief texts, informative sidebars and an index. Readers will appreciate the two-page format discussing such topics as food, games, jewelry, art and architecture, health and medicine, war and religion.

Deary, Terry. *Caballeros. (Knights)* 94p. Translated by Raquel Mancera Francoso. ISBN: 978-84-7871-879-5.

———. *Esa bárbara edad media. (The Measly Middle Ages)* 128p. Translated by Rosa Roger. ISBN: 84-272-2033-2.

———. *Esos supergeniales griegos. (The Groovy Greeks)* 128p. Translated by Josefina Caball Guerrero. ISBN: 978-84-2722-031-7.

Ea. vol.: Illus: Martin Brown. (Esa Horrible Historia) Barcelona: RBA/Planeta, 2006-2007. pap. $10.95. Gr. 5–8.

Like the previous titles in this delightful, facetious series, these are written in Deary's irreverent style with witty cartoon illustrations that are sure to entice reluctant historians-to-be. *Caballeros* describes *detalles repugnantes* (repugnant details) about knights and knighthood during the Middle Ages in which *muchos eran estúpidos asesinos* (many were stupid murderers). In contrast to the other two, this volume includes color cartoons and an index. *Esa bárbara edad media* highlights important aspects of the Middle Ages from *Los antipáticos normandos* (The Disagreeable Normans) up to the murderous rampage of San Carlos de Blois from France. *Esos supergeniales griegos* begins with a *Cronología de esos supergeniales griegos* (A Groovy Greek Timeline) up to the Roman destruction of *el país más inteligente del mundo* (the most intelligent country in the world).

Deary, Terry. *La horrible historia del mundo. (The Wicked History of the World)* Illus: Martin Brown. Translated by Josefina Caball Guerrero. Barcelona: Molino, 2003. 93p. ISBN: 84-272-2050-2. $19.95. Gr. 5–8.

In contrast to Deary's previous paperback series *Esa Horrible Historia* (Horrible History) with Brown's characteristic black-and-white cartoon illustrations, this large-format edition is vividly illustrated with Brown's always-witty, now color cartoons. In Deary's inimitable style, he describes *los seres más abominables, perversos crueles y horribles* (the most detestable, perverse, cruel and horrible beings) in history. From "horrible" aspects of prehistoric men, to the "grim" laws of Mesopotamia, to "depravities" in ancient Rome up to the terrible wars of the 20th century, he concludes in the epilogue by quoting Hegel: *No aprendemos nada de la historia . . . pero aprendemos mucho de los horrores de la historia.* (We don't learn anything from history . . . but we learn a lot from history's horrors.) Purists may be offended, but reluctant history readers will welcome this candid and witty approach to history.

Dresser, Denise and Jorge Volpi. *México: Lo que todo ciudadano quisiera (no) saber de su patria. (Mexico: What Every Citizen Would Like to (Not) Know About His Country)* Mexico: Santillana, 2007. 335p. ISBN: 970-770-401-2. pap. $34.95. Gr. 9–adult.

More sarcasm, irony and humor than history, this extensively illustrated and well-designed "textbook" presents the history of Mexico as *un parque temático* (theme park) and disputes the official history of a country *donde los malos siempre son extranjeros (de preferencia gringos), y donde a pesar de que hemos peleado en desventaja, perdemos (siempre) con el honor intacto y el humor también* (p. 17) (Where the bad ones are always foreigners (preferably gringos [disparaging term for American people]), and although we have fought at a disadvantage, we (always) lose with complete honor and with humor too). It discusses the myths that enable Mexicans to sleep well at night, such as *El mito del país mestizo, incluyente, tolerante (mientras no seas indio, homosexual o mujer)* (p. 21) (The myth of a mestizo, inclusive, tolerant country [as long as you are not an Indian, homosexual or woman]); Mexican people's experiences with democracy; how to survive the Mexican Constitution; the disastrous 19th century in Mexico; the most hated Mexican personages; good things about Mexico *la comida más rica, el mejor clima, las playas más bonitas, las mujeres más hermosas, . . . la cultura más gloriosa* (p. 269) (the best food, the best climate, the nicest beaches, the prettiest women, . . . the most glorious culture); and concludes with a plea *Vota. Exige. Denuncia. Vigila. Edúcate* (p. 321) (Vote. Demand. Denounce. Watch out. Educate yourself). Numerous charts, cartoons, color photographs and maps add interest to this most amusing, exaggerated, farcical view of Mexico. Righteous historians will be offended but irreverent readers will smile and, perhaps, agree.

Green, Jen. *La tumba de Tutankamón. (Tutankhamen's Tomb)* Illus: Gary Slater. Translated by Begoña Oro. Madrid: Bruño, 2007. 28p. ISBN: 978-84-216-8009-4. $21.95. Gr. 3–6.

With exquisitely designed pop-ups, pull tabs, wheels and flaps, this book is an enticing depiction of archaeologist Howard Carter's journey to Egypt that culminated with his discovery in 1923 of Tutankhamen's tomb. It brings to life important highlights of the culture of the ancient Egyptians such as the great Pyramid of Khufu, the Great Sphinx of Giza, the Valley of the Kings, mummification techniques, and their belief in an afterlife. An easy-to-read text and informative sidebars add to this hard-to-resist exploration of the treasures and secrets of ancient Egypt.

Johansson, Patrick K. *Zazanilli, la palabra enigma: Acertijos y adivinanzas de los antiguos nahuas (Zazanilli, the Enigmatic Word: Puzzles and Riddles of the Ancient Nahuatl)* Mexico: McGraw-Hill, 2004. 90p. ISBN: 970-104478-9. pap. $10.95. Gr. 9–adult.

Serious students will appreciate this informative overview of the games, puzzles, and riddles of the ancient Nahuatl. This is not for the young; rather, it is a well-written description of the pastimes that occupied the spare time of the Aztecs from word games to double-entendres to metaphors to contemporary riddles. Lavishly illustrated with color photos and digital artwork, this attractive publication also includes numerous footnotes, sidebars, and a bibliography.

Labastida, Jaime. *La Semana Santa cora. (Cora Holy Week)* Illus: Felipe de la Torre. Mexico: Siglo XXI, 2004. 48p. ISBN: 968-23-2539-0. pap. $10.95. Gr. 6–9.

Written as a tribute to Konrad Theodor Preuss who, from 1905 to 1907, studied the Cora people of the mountains of Western Mexico, this large-format publication describes Cora ceremonies and myths. Despite the lavish watercolor spreads, a large type and ample space between lines, this is not a simple depiction of Cora people and beliefs; rather, it is a reverent treatise with thoughtful observations about their sacred rituals and celebrations that serious students will appreciate.

Labastida, Jaime. *Los cinco soles. (The Five Suns)* Illus: Felipe de la Torre. Mexico: Siglo XXI, 2003. 48p. ISBN: 968-23-2479-3. pap. $10.95. Gr. 6–9.

Based on codices from Mesoamerica and texts written by 16th-century Spanish monks, this imaginative rendition of the Nahuatl (Aztec) creation myth, *Cinco Soles* (Five Suns), tells about the birth of man, how the Earth came to be, the beginnings of the great city, Tenochtitlan, and why the Earth is surrounded by water. The powerful earth-tone watercolor spreads, full of magic and symbolism, add a sense of awe to this inspiring interpretation of the mythology of Mesoamerica. Although it lacks a glossary, younger readers will appreciate the large type and ample space between lines.

Libura, Krystyna M., and others. *Ecos de la guerra entre México y los Estados Unidos. (Echoes of the Mexican-American War)* Toronto: Groundwood/Distributed by Publishers West, 2004. 317p. pap. ISBN: 0-88899-604-7. $35.00. Gr. 9–adult.

Using contemporary letters from soldiers to their families, news reports, official documents and accounts from American and Mexican historians, this exquisitely illustrated book presents a vivid chronicle of the war between Mexico and the United States (1846–1848) from both the Mexican and American perspectives. Especially informative are the captions and sidebars alongside the narrative and striking color and black-and-white daguerreotypes, maps and period reproductions that make this a most accessible introduction to what Thoreau called *una contienda injusta* (an unjust war) and Lincoln denounced as *la ilegalidad de la guerra* (the illegality of war). Serious readers will appreciate the well-selected original documents with opposing views; budding historians will be engrossed by the illustrations and carefully selected cartoons depicting the passions and misunderstanding of a war in which there are and have been *una gran diversidad de opiniones* (a great diversity of opinions). Like its predecessor, *Ecos de la conquista*, this is indeed an insightful read, which, fortunately, is also available in an English rendition. An extensive bibliography is included, but in contrast to the English edition, this Spanish edition lacks an index. Bilingual readers will be glad to know that both editions have identical pagination. The editors have taken great care to keep most of the same text on the corresponding page of both editions.

Navarrete, Federico. *La invención de los caníbales (The Invention of the Cannibals)*. Illus.: Joel Rendón. México: Castillo, 2006. 52p. ISBN: 970-20-0774-7. pap. $12.95. Gr. 6–10.

In twenty-five brief, one-page chapters with facing powerful black-and-white woodcuts the author explains why Christopher Columbus and other Europeans of the 15th and 16th centuries, based on their own fears and prejudices, concluded that the indigenous people of the Americas were cannibals. Hence, the Spanish conquerors decided to make them their slaves and, according to the author, cannibalism justified the conquest of Mexico. He describes how cannibalism has been subjected to numerous misinterpretations and the reasons for cannibalism in pre-Columbian America. Not exactly sensationalistic, this paperback presents an intriguing and at times hair-raising discussion of cannibalism, slavery and war.

Obregón, José María. *California/California*. Translated by María Cristina Brusca. (The Bilingual Library of the United States of America) New York: Rosen/Buenas Letras, 2005. 32p. ISBN: 1-4042-3069-6. $22.50. Gr. 1–2.

Simply and succinctly, this bilingual (English-Spanish) volume in The Bilingual Library of the United States of America series introduces beginning readers (or learners of either language) to basic facts about California. Two or three sentences per page—the English in darker font, followed by a smooth Spanish rendition—highlight such aspects as California missions, the gold rush and the movie business in Hollywood. Candid color photos, a timeline, calendar of events, state facts and famous people are included in each of the 52 volumes of this series. Other titles are:

Alabama/Alabama. ISBN: 1-4042-3065-3.
Alaska/Alaska. ISBN: 1-4042-3066-1.
Arizona/Arizona. ISBN: 1-4042-3067-X.
Arkansas/Arkansas. ISBN: 1-4042-3068-8.
Colorado/Colorado. ISBN: 1-4042-3070-X.
Connecticut/Connecticut. ISBN: 1-4042-3071-8.
Delaware/Delaware. ISBN: 1-4042-3073 4.
District of Columbia/Distrito de Columbia. ISBN: 1-4042-3072-6.
Florida/Florida. ISBN: 1-4042-3074-2.
Georgia/Georgia. ISBN: 1-4042-3075-0.
Hawaii/Hawai. ISBN: 1-4042-3076-9.
Idaho/Idaho. ISBN: 1-4042-3077-7.
Illinois/Illinois. ISBN: 1-4042-3078-5.
Indiana/Indiana. ISBN: 1-4042-3079-3.
Iowa/Iowa. ISBN: 1-4042-3080-7.
Kansas/Kansas. ISBN: 1-4042-3081-5.
Kentucky/Kentucky. ISBN: 1-4042-3082-3.
Louisiana/Luisiana. ISBN: 1-4042-3083-1.
Maine/Maine. ISBN: 1-4042-3084-X.
Maryland/Maryland. ISBN: 1-4042-3085-8.
Massachusetts/Massachusetts. ISBN: 1-4042-3086-6.
Michigan/Michigan. ISBN: 1-4042-3087-4.
Minnesota/Minnesota. ISBN: 1-4042-3088-2.
Mississippi/Misisipi. ISBN: 1-4042-3089-0.
Missouri/Misuri. ISBN: 1-4042-3090-4.
Montana/Montana. ISBN: 1-4042-3091-2.
Nebraska/Nebraska. ISBN: 1-4042-3092-0.

Nevada/Nevada. ISBN: 1-4042-3093-9.
New Hampshire/Nuevo Hampshire. ISBN: 1-4042-3094-7.
New Jersey/Nueva Jersey. ISBN: 1-4042-3095-5.
New Mexico/Nuevo México. ISBN: 1-4042-3096-3.
New York/Nueva York. ISBN: 1-4042-3097-1.
North Carolina/Carolina del Norte. ISBN: 1-4042-3098-X.
North Dakota/Dakota del Norte. ISBN: 1-4042-3099-8.
Ohio/Ohio. 1-4042-3100-5.
Oklahoma/Oklahoma. ISBN: 1-4042-3101-3.
Oregon/Oregón. ISBN: 1-4042-3102-1.
Pennsylvania/Pensilvania. ISBN: 1-4042-3103-X.
Puerto Rico/Puerto Rico. ISBN: 1-4042-3104-8.
Rhode Island/Rhode Island. ISBN: 1-4042-3105-6.
South Carolina/Carolina del Sur. ISBN: 1-4042-3106-4.
South Dakota/Dakota del Sur. ISBN: 1-4042-3107-2.
Tennessee/Tennessee. ISBN: 1-4042-3108-0.
Texas/Texas. ISBN: 1-4042-3109-9.
Utah/Utah. ISBN: 1-4042-3110-2.
Vermont/Vermont. ISBN: 1-4042-3111-0.
Virginia/Virginia. ISBN: 1-4042-3112-9.
Washington/Washington. ISBN: 1-4042-3113-7.
West Virginia/Virginia Occidental. ISBN: 1-4042-3114-5.
Wisconsin/Wisconsin. ISBN: 1-4042-3115-3.
Wyoming/Wyoming. ISBN: 1-4042-3116-1.

Putnam, James. *Momias. (Mummy)* Photos by Peter Hayman. Translated by Alquimia ediciones. Madrid: Pearson Educación, 2005. 72p. ISBN: 84-205-4384-5. pap. $13.95. Gr. 4–8.

This engrossing introduction to mummies that begins with a brief chapter *¿Qué son las momias?* (What are mummies?), followed by a description on how bodies were embalmed after death by the ancient Egyptians, beautiful masks, coffins, sarcophagi and Tutankhamen's treasures. It also delineates ancient Greek and Roman mummies, animal mummies and mummies from the Andes region in South America. Like other titles originally published by Dorling Kindersley, London, it is profusely illustrated with excellent sharp color photographs on every page and concludes with *datos sorprendentes* (amazing facts), a chronology, Web sites, a glossary, and an index.

Vargas Llosa, Mario. *Israel/Palestina: Paz o Guerra Santa (Israel/Palestine: Peace or Holy War)* Photos by Morgana Vargas Llosa. Lima: Santillana, 2006. 187p. ISBN: 9972-848-13-2. pap. $14.95. Gr. 9–adult.

In the summer of 2005, Vargas Llosa, one of the most esteemed contemporary writers of the Spanish-speaking world and a long-time admirer of the state of Israel, traveled to the Gaza Strip and the West Bank to ascertain how Israelis and Palestinians reacted to Ariel Sharon's unilateral decision to evict the settlements in Gaza. With passion, energy and with his cogently distinctive voice, he chronicles the experiences and thoughts of the leaders, intellectuals and ordinary people on both sides of this tragic conflict. From the controversial wall and military checkpoints to life in Hebron and the appalling Palestinian refugee camps, he concludes *Parece mentira que la hermosa gesta de los sionistas . . . haya terminado en esta vergüenza* (p. 187). (It seems a lie that the beautiful Zionist achievements . . . ended in this ignominy.) Whether optimists or skeptics, serious readers of the Israel–Palestinian conflict will be moved by the artful writing and thoughtful narrative. Candid color photos by the author's daughter add insight and perspective to this human drama. First published in the Spanish newspaper *El País* and in numerous publications in Europe and Latin America, this book is dedicated to *the justos de Israel* (fair-minded people of Israel).

Williams, Brian. *4 de julio de 1776: La declaración de Independencia Americana. (4 July 1776: The Declaration of American Independence)* 31p. ISBN: 84-241-1601-1.
Malam, John. *12 de octubre de 1492: Colón llega a América. (12 October 1492: Columbus Reaches the Americas)* 47p. ISBN: 84-241-1600-3.
———. *11 de noviembre de 1918: Primera Guerra Mundial (11 November 1918: The World War I Armistice)* 47p. ISBN: 84-241-1602-X.
———. *1 de septiembre de 1939: Hitler invade Polonia. (1 September 1939: Hitler Invades Poland)* 31p. ISBN: 84-241-1603-8.
———. *6 de agosto de 1945: La bomba de Hiroshima. (6 August 1945: The Bombing of Hiroshima)* 31p. ISBN: 84-241-1604-6.
Williams, Brian. *22 de noviembre de 1963: Asesinato del Presidente Kennedy. (22 November 1963: The Assassination of President Kennedy)* 31p. ISBN: 84-241-1605-4.
Malam, John, and Hilary. *21 de julio de 1969: El hombre llega a la Luna. (21 July 1969: First man on the Moon)* 47p. ISBN: 84-241-1606-2.

Williams, Brian. *10 de noviembre de 1989: La caída del muro de Berlín.* *(10 November 1989: The Fall of the Berlin Wall)* 47p. ISBN: 84-241-1607-0.

Malam, John. *11 de febrero de 1990: La liberación de Nelson Mandela. (11 February 1990: The Release of Nelson Mandela)* 31p. ISBN: 84-241-1608-9.

Williams, Brian. *11 de septiembre de 2001: Ataque a las Torres Gemelas. (11 September 2001: Attack on America)* 47p. ISBN: 84-241-1609-7. Ea. vol.: Translated by Liwayway Alonso Mendoza. (Fechas para la Historia) León: Editorial Everest, 2004. pap. $10.95. Gr. 4–7.

In the crisp, engaging style of the original series, first published by Evans, London, these books explore key dates in history by describing the event and providing background and its consequences. Each title includes clear, color photos and maps on every page, a timeline and a glossary. Highlighting the importance of *La Declaración de Independencia* (Declaration of Independence) to the representatives of the 13 colonies and its adoption on the 4th of July 1776 and stressing the ideas that continue to influence democratic governments around the world, as well as the events that led to the American war for independence, the revolutionary struggle and the ratification of the Constitution in 1787, *4 de julio de 1776: La declaración de Independencia Americana* provides a vivid introduction to the importance of these events in the history of the United States. Columbus's four trips to the New World are explained in *12 de octubre de 1492: Colón llega a América.* World War I is described from the assassination of Archduke Francis Ferdinand in 1914 to the signing of the Armistice in 1918 in *11 de noviembre de 1918: Primera Guerra Mundial.* Adolf Hitler's role in launching World War II are depicted in *1 de septiembre de 1939: Hitler invade Polonia.* The destruction of Hiroshima by the atomic bomb is explained in *6 de agosto de 1945: La bomba de Hiroshima.* The controversies regarding the assassination of President Kennedy are related in *22 de noviembre de 1963: Asesinato del Presidente Kennedy.* Neil Armstrong's momentous landing on the moon and its effects on the space race are narrated in *21 de julio de 1969: El hombre llega a la Luna.* The divisions between East and West in Europe and the fall of the Berlin Wall are explored in *10 de noviembre de 1989: La caída del muro de Berlín.* The policy of apartheid in South Africa and the liberation of Nelson Mandela are discussed in *11 de febrero de 1990: La liberación de Nelson Mandela.* The tragedy of the attacks against the World Trade Center in New York, terrorism, and the war in Afghanistan are described in *11 de septiembre de 2001: Ataque a las Torres Gemelas.* These unassuming paperback publications are indeed well-written, simple introductions to dramatic events in the history of humankind that are just right for reluctant historians-to-be or as high-interest, low-vocabulary texts.

Biography

Adams, Simon. *Alejandro: El joven que conquistó el mundo. (Alexander: The Boy Soldier Who Conquered the World)* Translated by Patricia Helena Hernández. ISBN: 970-770-741-0.

Kramer, Ann. *Mandela: El rebelde que dirigió a su nación a la libertad. (Mandela: The Rebel Who Led His Nation to Freedom)* Translated by Patricia Helena Hernández. ISBN: 970-770-739-9.

Malam, John. *Leonardo Da Vinci: El genio que definió el Renacimiento. (Leonardo Da Vinci: The Genius that Defined the Renaissance)* Translated by Wendy P. López. ISBN: 970-770-765-8.

McCarty, Nick. *Marco Polo: El hombre que viajó por el mundo medieval. (Marco Polo: The Boy Who Traveled the Medieval World)* Translated by Wendy P. López. ISBN: 970-770-763-1.

Steele, Philip. *Galileo: El genio que se enfrentó a la Inquisición. (Galileo: The Genius Who Faced the Inquisition)* Translated by Patricia Helena Hernández. ISBN: 970-770-740-2.

———. *Marie Curie: La mujer que cambió el curso de la ciencia. (Marie Curie: The Woman Who Changed the Course of Science)* Translated by Wendy P. López. ISBN: 970-770-764-X.

Ea. vol.: 64p. (Biografías de Personajes Importantes en la Historia del Mundo) México: Santillana, 2006. $28.95. Gr. 4–7.

Originally published by Marshall Editions, London, these attractively designed biographies present the lives and accomplishments of outstanding people in the history of the world. With clear color photos, a brief text, numerous sidebars and simple timelines, these are indeed engaging, easy-to-understand introductions to the times and achievements of each personage. Each title includes a glossary, bibliography and an index. The most important successes in the life of Alexander the Great are described in *Alejandro: El joven que conquistó el mundo.* Mandela's political ventures and the turmoil that affected South Africa for over a century are included in *Mandela: El rebelde que dirigió a su nación a la libertad.* The genius of Leonardo Da Vinci as a scientist, painter, sculptor, architect, inventor and musician is highlighted in

Leonardo Da Vinci: El genio que definió el Renacimiento. Marco Polo's life as a ceaseless explorer is featured in *Marco Polo: El hombre que viajó por el mundo medieval.* Galileo's influence in the development of modern mathematical physics is explained in *Galileo: El genio que se enfrentó a la Inquisición.* Marie Curie's contributions to the discovery of radioactivity, radium and polonium are described in *Marie Curie: La mujer que cambió el curso de la ciencia.* These are indeed noteworthy biographies for young Spanish speakers.

Barber, Nicola. *Dickens: Su vida y su tiempo. (Dickens)* ISBN: 968-24-7098-6.

Middleton, Haydn. *Shakespeare: Su vida y su tiempo. (Shakespeare)* ISBN: 968-24-7099-4.

Ea. vol.: 32p. Translated by Elizabeth Hahn Villagrán. (Grandes Escritores) Mexico: Trillas, 2004. pap. $9.75. Gr. 4–7.

In a brief, well-written Spanish text and profusely illustrated with clear, color period photos and drawings on every page, readers are introduced to the major events in the life of the British author Charles Dickens (1812–1870) in *Dickens: Su vida y su tiempo.* Well-placed captions focus on important incidents that influenced his life and works such as the horrific poverty of his era, his father's imprisonment in a debtor's prison, his own work as a child laborer in a shoe factory as well as his later success and recognition as an international celebrity whose novels have been translated around the world. Just as appealing and informative is *Shakespeare: Su vida y su tiempo,* which provides an overview of the English Renaissance and how it influenced the life and work of one of the world's major playwrights and poets, William Shakespeare (1564–1616). Originally published by Ticktock, London, these engrossing Spanish renditions are indeed the best introductions to young Spanish speakers to the life and works of these great writers. Each title includes an index, chronology, revealing sidebars, and concludes with humorous ¿Sabías que . . . (Did you know?) episodes.

Barrera, Norma Anabel. *La niña de las nueve estrellas: La vida de la escritora Rosario Castellanos. (The Girl of the Nine Stars: The Life of the Writer Rosario Castellanos)* ISBN: 970-37-0101-9.

Suárez del Solar, Angeles. *Entre flores de cactos: La vida de la bióloga Helia Bravo Hollis. (Between Cactus Flowers: The Life of the Biologist Helia Bravo Hollis)* ISBN: 970-37-0104-3.

Ea vol.: 63p. (Vidas de Mexicanos Ilustres) México: Destino, 2004. $10.95. pap. Gr. 5–8.

The lives and times of Rosario Castellanos (1925–1974), one of Mexico's most important female writers and feminists, and Helia Bravo Hollis (1901–2001), Mexico's first biologist and pioneer ecologist, are related in these modest paperback publications. Despite almost didactic tones that at times verge on adulation, they provide an introduction to critical aspects of their lives: youth, travels, professional achievements, and death. Black-and-white photos, a bibliography, and suggestions for furthering reading complement each volume.

Bermejo, Victoria. *La más divertida historia de Mozart niño. (The Most Amusing Story about Mozart's Childhood)* Illus: Miguel Gallardo. Barcelona: Galera, 2006. 32p. ISBN: 84-246-2341-X. $16.95. Gr. 2–5.

In an amusingly conversational, almost irreverent style, Bermejo narrates the childhood of Wolfgang Amadeus Mozart by recounting significant aspects of his impressive musical talents as well as his human frailties, such as his big nose, which he compensated by changing his hairdo and wearing his father's shirts. The exuberant black-line and bright watercolor illustrations beautifully complement this enjoyable introduction to a child genius whose early successes as a composer and performer impressed all the kings, emperors, queens and noblemen of Europe. Although some adults may object to some of the vernacular expressions (*pinchazo en la barriga* (literally, a big pinch in the tummy) and (*el culo rojo* [red butt])), this is certainly the way to introduce young Spanish speakers to a master. A brief afterword provides biographical notes and a list of works.

Boothroyd, Jennifer. *Susan B. Anthony: Una vida de igualdad. (Susan B. Anthony: A Life of Fairness)* ISBN: 0-8225-6234-0.

Kishel, Ann-Marie. *Rosa Parks: Una vida de valentía. (Rosa Parks: A Life of Courage)* ISBN: 0-8225-6239-1.

———. *Thomas Jefferson: Una vida de patriotismo. (Thomas Jefferson: A Life of Patriotism)* ISBN: 0-8225-6238-3.

Nelson, Robin. *George Washington: Una vida de liderazgo. (George Washington: A Life of Leadership)* ISBN: 0-8225-6235-9.

Rivera, Sheila. *Abraham Lincoln: Una vida de respeto. (Abraham Lincoln: A Life of Respect)* ISBN: 0-8225-6236-7.

———. *Martin Luther King Jr.: Una vida de determinación. (Martin Luther King Jr.: A Life of Determination)* ISBN: 0-8225-6237-5.

Ea. vol.: 32p. Translated by translations.com. (Libros para Avanzar) Minneapolis: Lerner, 2007. $22.60. Gr. 1–2.

Simply and succinctly, beginning Spanish-speaking readers are introduced to the life and times of six protagonists in American history—Susan B. Anthony, Rosa Parks, Thomas Jefferson, George Washington, Abraham Lincoln, and Martin Luther King Jr. With two to three sentences per page facing black-and-white and a few color photos and understandable captions, these clear Spanish renditions highlight the most memorable achievements of each man and woman. Each title includes a brief chronology, important facts, a glossary (albeit without definite articles) and English-language Web sites.

Contró, Arturo. *Cristiano Ronaldo*. ISBN: 978-1-4042-7669-7.
———. *Gianluigi Buffon*. ISBN: 978-1-4042-7668-0.
———. *Landon Donovan*. ISBN: 978-1-4042-7666-6.
———. *Rafael Márquez*. ISBN: 978-1-4042-7667-3.
Obregón, José María. *David Beckham*. ISBN: 978-1-4042-7665-9.
———. *Ronaldinho*. ISBN: 978-1-4042-7664-2.
Ea. vol.: 24p. (World Soccer Stars/Estrellas del Fútbol Mundial). New York: Rosen/Editorial Buenas Letras, 2008. $21.25. Gr. 1–3.

Simple bilingual text and candid color photos describe the lives and achievements of six world soccer stars—Cristiano Ronaldo, Gianluigi Buffon, Landon Donovan, Rafael Márquez, David Beckham, and Ronaldinho.

Da Coll, Ivar. *¡Azúcar! (Sugar!)* Illus: the author. New York: Lectorum, 2005. 40p. ISBN: 1-930332-65-3. $14.99. Gr. 2–4.

Highlighting the optimism and playful personality of the Cuban-born singer of salsa, the popular form of Latin-American dance music, this affectionate biography describes the life of Celia Cruz and her fascination for Caribbean music—*guarachas, guaguancós, boleros, sones, guajiras*. It is unfortunate that the author stressed didactic messages that young readers should learn from the artist—*no discutas* (don't argue), *no te vayas a dormir enojado y con rencor* (don't go to bed angry and with bitterness)—rather than sticking to the facts surrounding this lively and much-loved singer. And although some readers will disagree with the political reference to Castro's regime, all will enjoy Celia's passion for shoes, dresses and wigs. Nonetheless, the easygoing text, full of colloquialisms and sprinkled with Cuban vernacular expressions, and the folkloric-type, color illustrations, brimming with Cuban sights and motifs, make this an appealing tribute to Celia.

Erdrich, Lise. *Sacagawea.* (*Sacagawea*) Illus: Julie Buffalohead. Translated by translations.com. Minneapolis: Lerner, 2005. 40p. ISBN: 0-8225-3191-7. $16.95. Gr. 3–6.

The life story of Sacagawea, the young Shoshone woman who assisted Lewis and Clark as an interpreter and guide, is now available in this polished Spanish rendition with the original, striking full-page oil paintings that poignantly convey a sense of time and place. Although the bibliography includes only English titles, Spanish speakers will appreciate this informative introduction to a brave young woman and her role in the discovery expedition to the West in the early 1800s. An afterword, timeline, and a map are appended.

Gisbert, Montse. *Salvador Dalí: Píntame un sueño. (Salvador Dalí: Paint Me a Dream)* Illus: the author. Barcelona: Serres, 2003. 42p. ISBN: 84-8488-127-X. $21.95. Gr. 3–5.

In a first-person point of view, Salvador Dalí, *el pintor de los sueños* (the painter of dreams), tells about *mi fascinante mundo de formas y colores* (my fascinating world of forms and colors). Exquisite collage illustrations, reminiscent of the art of the renowned Spanish surrealist artist (1904–1989), and a lively text provide highlights of his life and times. Miniature reproductions at the back of the book include title, date, medium and size. An author's afterword is also included.

Gómez, Juan, and Nando Caballero. *Introducción a Frank Zappa. (Introducing Frank Zappa)* Lleida: Milenio, 2004. 188p. ISBN: 84-9743-121-9. pap. $17.00. Gr. 10–adult.

Rock 'n' roll fans are sure to be delighted with this engaging introduction to the life and work of Frank Zappa. Written in two parts by two admirers of the prolific musician and composer who they describe as *provocador, obsceno, surrealista, genial, grandilocuente, prolífico, incisivo, excesivo, riguroso, loco* (provocative, obscene, surreal, genius-like, pretentious, sarcastic, excessive, rigorous, crazy) and provide numerous examples of these traits. In the first part, Gómez narrates personal incidents, concerts and Zappa's relationships with other musicians. In the second, Caballero discusses his music and achievements. Some adults may be offended by Zappa's rough humor and raw language, yet music lovers will be moved by the passion and energy depicted in this memorable biography. A discography and a list of videos and bootlegged discs are also included.

Mandela, Nelson. *Nelson Mandela. (Nelson Mandela)* Illus: William Wilson. Translated by Arturo Vázquez Barrón. Mexico: Tecolote, 2004. 46p. ISBN: 968-7381-82-5. pap. $13.95. Gr. 4–6.

In a striking, large-format presentation, Mandela's poignant voice describes the humiliations and indignities he suffered as a child and later as an adult under apartheid, the official policy of racial segregation practiced in the Republic of South Africa. Excellent candid photos are interspersed amid colorful, childlike collages and a boxed text highlighting Mandela's lifetime of sacrifice and his commitment to racial equality. A detailed biographical sketch is included as an afterword.

Muñoz Puelles, Vicente. *El pintor de las neuronas: Ramón y Cajal, científico. (The Painter of Neurons: Ramón y Cajal, Scientist)* Illus: Pablo Torrecilla. Madrid: Anaya, 2006. 158p. ISBN: 84-667-5196-3. pap. $11.95. Gr. 6–9.

The early life of Santiago Ramón y Cajal (1852-1934), one of Spain's foremost scientists, who shared a Nobel Prize for research on the structure of the nervous system, is related in a fast-paced narrative. Despite the at times dramatized aspects of his life—a most severe father, a horribly mean teacher—this biography will certainly awaken readers' interest and enthusiasm in Ramón y Cajal. It highlights his numerous childhood pranks and rowdy behavior as well as his love for painting. Although it lacks a chronology and the illustrations are neither exciting nor informative, it does provide thoughtful insights into Ramón y Cajal's critical thinking abilities and candidly depicts the dearth of interest in the sciences in Spain.

Muñoz Puelles, Vicente. *El viaje de la evolución: El joven Darwin. (The Journey of Evolution: Young Darwin)* Illus: Federico Delicado. Madrid: Anaya, 2007. 149p. ISBN: 978-84-667-6251-9. pap. $11.95. Gr. 5–8.

Written in the first-person point of view and based on the writings of Charles Darwin, this engrossing biography recounts Darwin's journey around the world in 1865 and explains how this trip changed his perceptions about nature. In a matter-of-fact and easy-to-understand narrative, Muñoz depicts through amusing anecdotes Darwin's observations about geology, flora and fauna that helped him understand how species of organisms arise and develop through natural selection. Not surprisingly, he concludes with the early conflicts between evolutionists and creationists. Despite the prosaic color illustrations, which sadly detract from the narrative, this is a captivating introduction to Darwin and his theories.

Poole, Josephine. *Ana Frank. (Anne Frank)* Illus: Angela Barrett. Translated by Ana Nuño. New York: Lectorum & Barcelona: Lumen, 2005. 32p. ISBN: 1-930332-87-4. $17.99. Gr. 4–7.

Nuño's affecting Spanish rendition of the exquisite picture-book biography of the incomparable Ana Frank maintains the refined, intense tone of the original. With Barrett's forcefully realistic double-page spreads, Spanish-speaking children are introduced to Ana's early years in Hitler-dominated Germany, the persecution of Jews, the family's strenuous confinement, her father's survival and the recovery of Ana's diary. A brief excerpt from the diary, an afterword and a chronology add to the educational and emotional value of this tribute to this world-recognized heroine.

Rodríguez, Alex. *¡Jonrón! (Out of the Ballpark).* Illus: Frank Morrison. New York: Harper Collins, 2007. 32p. ISBN: 978-0-06-115197-2. $16.99. Gr. 2–4.

Highlighting Alex Rodríguez's first time in a playoff game in which *mientras más se esforzaba, peor le salía todo* (the harder he tried, the worse he played), the well-known third baseman relates his efforts to learn from his mistakes, practice his skills, focus on his math class and, finally, hit a grand slam that won his team their first championship. The tone of the story and a final letter from the star to the reader almost verges on the didactic: *estudié mucho, me mantuve lejos de las drogas y siempre fui respetuoso con mis amigos y mis mayores* (I studied hard, stayed away from drugs, and showed respect for my friends and elders). Nonetheless, the simple Spanish rendition and Morrison's supple and engaging illustrations, full of energy and baseball lore, as well as a charming collection of family photos, will attract baseball fans. Interestingly, Rodríguez's family connection to their native Dominican Republic is never mentioned.

Uslar Pietri, Arturo. *Gandhi. (Gandhi)* Illus: Joanna Gutiérrez. Caracas: El Nacional, 2004. 40p. ISBN: 980-388-110-8. pap. $10.95. Gr. 4–7.

Based on a text written by one of Venezuela's foremost writers, this is not only the life history of Mohandas Gandhi (1869–1948), the

Indian nationalist and spiritual leader, but it also includes boxed biographical sketches on other civil rights leaders and authors such as Martin Luther King, Nelson Mandela, Octavio Paz, V. S. Naipaul and Rabindranath Tagore. Notwithstanding the at-times cluttered design, with numerous color and black-and-white photos and drawings on every page, a well-written text presents the life and achievements of an extraordinary man who, through his leadership, was able to *ponerle fin a lo que parecía muy difícil de erradicar: el dominio de un gran imperio colonial . . . simplemente por un movimiento de tipo espiritual* (p. 5) (bring to an end what seemed very difficult to eradicate: the domination of a great colonial empire . . . by a simple spiritual-type movement). It includes a timeline, but no index.

Walcker, Yann. *Ludwig van Beethoven. (Ludwig van Beethoven)* ISBN: 84-7864-959-X.
———. *Wolfgang Amadeus Mozart. (Wolfgang Amadeus Mozart)* ISBN: 84-7864-958-1.
Ea. vol.: 13p. CD. Illus: Charlotte Voake. Narrated by Manuel Veiga and Dolores Martínez. (Descubrimos a los Músicos) Barcelona: Combel, 2005. $15.95. Gr. K–2.

Numerous attractive period color photographs, amusing ink-and-watercolor pastel illustrations and brief simple texts introduce young children to the childhoods and work of two great musicians. Especially appealing to Spanish learners are the accompanying CDs that include narrated versions of the texts as well as fragments of some of each composer's best known works. Perhaps least appealing are the somewhat intrusive "activity" sidebars that include suggested musical games and experiments. *Ludwig van Beethoven* describes his birth, in December 1770 in Bonn, Germany, and his early successes including a brief introduction to his sonatas, symphonies and opera. From Wolfgang's birth in Salzburg, Austria in 1756, through his performances in the Austrian emperor's court and for the French king up to his visit to the Sistine Chapel in Rome, including brief descriptions of his chamber music, symphonies, opera and sacred music are presented in *Wolfgang Amadeus Mozart*.

Warhola, James. *Mi tío Andy. (Uncle Andy's)* Illus: the author. Translated by Marta Ansón Balmaseda. Barcelona: Serres, 2004. 32p. ISBN: 84-8488-131-8. $12.95. Gr. 1–4.

In the same carefree, relaxed tone of the original, the author introduces his famous uncle, the artist Andy Warhol. Through amusing watercolor spreads, full of family life and off-beat art, and a breezy Spanish rendition, he tells about his father's junk business and the family's visit to Warhol's art-filled house in New York City where Andy's twenty-five cats, soup cartoons, numerous wigs and exciting artwork were joyous sources of inspiration. An author's note presents the eccentric artist and the author's loving grandmother. Young Spanish-speaking artists-to-be will enjoy the mess amid the art.

Publishers' Series

Baquedano, Elizabeth. *Aztecas, incas y mayas. (Aztecs, Incas and Mayas)* Photos by Michel Zabé. ISBN: 0-7566-0410-9.

Clarke, Barry. *Anfibios. (Amphibian)* Photos by Geoff Brightling and Frank Greenaway. ISBN: 0-7566-0414-1.

McCarthy, Colin. *Reptiles. (Reptile)* ISBN: 0-7566-0412-5.

Parker, Steve. *Cuerpo humano. (Human Body)* ISBN: 0-7566-0420-6.

———. *Peces. (Fish)* ISBN: 0-7566-0418-4.

Van Rose, Susanna. *La Tierra. (Earth)* ISBN: 0-7566-0416-8.

Ea. vol.: 64p. (Guías Visuales) New York: DK Publishing, 2004. $15.99. Gr. 4–9.

Now available for sale in the United States, these exquisite, large-format DK guides in Spanish with magnificently detailed, color photographs and drawings, sidebars and brief, easy-to-understand texts introduce readers/browsers to three pre-Columbian cultures and several scientific topics. Details about Aztec, Inca and Maya history, lifestyle, agriculture and religion are depicted in *Aztecas, Incas y Mayas*. The habitat, life cycle and natural world of frogs, toads, newts and salamanders are described in *Anfibios*. The evolution, anatomy, and life cycle of various reptiles are explained in *Reptiles*. The major systems and organs of the human body are explored in *Cuerpo humano*. The evolution, life style and natural history of fish are depicted in *Peces*. From the composition and formation of the planet to oceanography, seismology up to paleontology are included in *La Tierra*.

Berendes, Mary. *Animals/Los Animales.* ISBN: 978-1-59296-7957.

———. *Body/El cuerpo.* ISBN: 978-1-59296-7964.

———. *Feelings/Las emociones.* ISBN: 978-1-59296-7971.

———. *Food/La comida.* ISBN: 978-1-59296-7988.

———. *Machines/Las máquinas.* ISBN: 978-1-59296-7995.

———. *People/Las personas.* ISBN: 978-1-59296-8008.

———. *Seasons and Weather/Las estaciones y el tiempo.* ISBN: 978-1-59296-8015.

———. *Sports and Games/Los deportes y los juegos.* ISBN: 978-1-59296-8022.

Ea. vol.: 24p. Illus: Kathleen Petelinsek. (Word Books/Libros de Palabras) Mankato: Child's World, 2007–2008. $19.93. Ages 3–6.

Spanish and English learners will appreciate these attractively designed bilingual wordbooks. Simple, colorful illustrations help learners identify common words in both languages about animals, the body, feelings, food, machines, people and seasons and weather. Each title includes approximately 100 words in each language and a word list.

Burnie, David. *Pájaro. (Bird)* ISBN: 0-7566-0634-9.

Macquitty, Miranda. *Tiburón. (Shark)* ISBN: 0-7566-0636-5.

Norman, David, and Angela Milner. *Dinosaurio. (Dinosaur)* ISBN: 0-7566-0632-2.

Stott, Carole. *El espacio. (Space Exploration)* ISBN: 0-7566-0635-7.

Ea. vol.: 72p. Translated by Alquimia Ediciones. (Guías Visuales) New York: DK Publishing, 2004. $15.99. Gr. 4–7.

Originally published by Dorling Kindersley, London, as part of the Eyewitness Books, these smooth Spanish renditions with DK's exquisite, double-spread clear color photos and charts provide readers/viewers with stunning, large-format guides to the natural world and ancient history. From dinosaurs to the natural history, behavior and life cycle of birds are presented in *Pájaro.* Ancient Egypt is introduced through its pharaohs, mummies, religion, pottery and other objects in *El mundo antiguo de Egipto.* The physical characteristics, behavior, and life cycle of various types of sharks are described in *Tiburón.* The world of dinosaurs, from their habitats to myths and legends, is explored in *Dinosaurio. Pirámide* highlights the pyramids, temples and sites of ancient Egypt, and concludes with Maya and Aztec pyramids. The rockets, exploratory vehicles, space stations and the life and work of astronauts are described in *El espacio.* Each title includes a glossary and an index.

Cortázar, Julio. *La autopista del sur. (The Southern Thruway)* 39p. Illus: César Cortés. ISBN: 970-09-0732-5.

Fuentes, Carlos. *El prisionero de Las Lomas (The Prisoner of Las Lomas)* 62p. Illus: Ricardo Peláez Goycochea. ISBN: 970-09-1004-0.

Neruda, Pablo. *Veinte poemas de amor y una canción desesperada. (Twenty Love Poems and a Song of Despair)* 47p. Illus: Margarita Sada. ISBN: 970-09-0733-3.

Rulfo, Juan. *¡Diles que no me maten! (Tell Them Not to Kill Me!)* 26p. Illus: Alfredo Aguirre. ISBN: 970-09-1003-2.

Ea. vol.: (Clásicos Latinoamericanos Ilustrados) Mexico: Grupo Editorial Norma, 2003–2006. $12.95. Gr. 9–adult.

This excellent selection of some of the best short stories and poems by Latin American authors is presented in a large format with full-page color illustrations. Set in an expressway near Paris where drivers and passengers must deal with hours/days of endless frustration, Julio Cortazár's (Argentina) *La autopista del sur* is as disconcerting as it is engrossing. Unfortunately some of the illustrations are mere decorations. The dark history of a luxurious and most admired mansion in Mexico City is narrated in Carlos Fuentes's (Mexico) compelling *El prisionero de Las Lomas*. Peláez Goycochea's appropriately rough and suggestive full-page color illustrations are realistic as Fuentes's depiction of the falsehoods and deceits common among the politicians and wealthy people of Mexico. Pablo Neruda (Chile), considered by many as America's Poet, is represented by his *Veinte poemas de amor y una canción desesperada,* a collection of his bittersweet, realistic love poems that highlight the pain, passion and sensuality of love. Sada's imaginative watercolors are just as evocative and sensuous. The chaos, cruelty and misery of life in rural Mexico is depicted in Juan Rulfo's (Mexico) *¡Diles que no me maten!* Aguirre's strikingly robust full-page illustrations underscore the protagonist's fear of being executed by an all-powerful colonel. Although written for adults, this is indeed an accessible, representative sample of some of the most esteemed Latin American writers.

Ganeri, Anita. *El cuerpo humano. (Get a Move On!)* 155p. Translated by Alberto Jiménez Rioja. ISBN: 84-241-1689-5.

Manning, Mick, and Brita Granström. *Ciencias. (Science School)* 48p. Translated by María Luisa Rodriguez Pérez and Alfredo Ramón Díez. ISBN: 84-241-1312-8.

———. *Teatro. (Drama School)* 48p. Translated by María Luisa Rodriguez Pérez. ISBN: 84-241-1311-X.

Ea. vol.: (Mi Primer Libro) León: Everest, 2005–2006. $19.95. Gr. 3–5.

With most inviting candid, color photographs and clear color charts, including some microscopic photographs, *El cuerpo humano* describes in a simple, easy-to-understand Spanish rendition and clear labels the function of muscles, bones, nerves and the brain. Also, it includes chapters on the respiratory and digestive systems, blood and the senses as well as a glossary and an index. Witty, colorful cartoon-type illustrations and easy-to-follow instructions encourage children to try simple science experiments about matter, heat, forces, sound, electricity and other areas of physics in *Ciencias* and to put on various types of stage shows—from discussing scripts, acting, working backstage and other aspects of preparing a show in *Teatro*.

Guibert, Francois de. *Caballos y ponis. (Horses and Ponies)* Illus: Béatrice Rodriguez. ISBN: 84-8332-614-0.
———. *Los piratas. (Pirates)* Illus: Marie Delafon. ISBN: 84-8332-612-4.
———. *El zoo. (The Zoo)* Illus: Isabelle Assímat. ISBN: 84-8332-611-6.
Vandewiele, Agnès. *Los bomberos. (Firemen)* Illus: Robert Barborini. ISBN: 84-8332-609-4.
———. *Sobre ruedas. (On Wheels)* Illus: Pronto. ISBN: 84-8332-613-2.
———. *El lobo. (Wolf)* Illus: Ronan Badel. ISBN: 84-8332-610-8.
Ea. vol.: 37p. (Tu Pequeña Enciclopedia Vox) Barcelona: SPES Editorial, 2005. $13.95. Gr. 1–3.

With most appealing, simple and witty color illustrations on every page and an easy-to-understand, easy-to-read text, this well-designed series, originally published by Larousse, Paris, introduces young readers to high-interest topics. Basic facts about horses and ponies, including such aspects as the birth of a colt, their training and care and how to mount and ride them are described in *Caballos y ponis*. *Los piratas* is a simple historical overview about piracy and pirates. From exotic birds such as pink flamingos to common zoo animals such as lions, tigers and elephants are discussed in *El zoo*. The training, equipment and work of firefighters are portrayed in *Los bomberos*. The development and progressive use of wheels in transportation—from a baby carriage, to tricycles, skates, cars and trucks—are defined in *Sobre ruedas*. The lifestyle and survival of foxes are explained in *El lobo*. Each title concludes with an *¡Es cierto!* (It Is True!) section that highlights notable details.

Hoena, B.A. *La biblioteca/The Library.* ISBN: 978-0-7368-7913-2.
———. *La estación de bomberos/The Fire Station.* ISBN: 978-0-7368-7912-5.

————. *La granja/The Farm.* ISBN: 978-1-4296-0082-8.
Murphy, Patricia J. *La huerta de manzanas/The Apple Orchard.* ISBN: 978-1-4296-0081-1.
 Ea. vol.: 24p. Translated by translations.com. (Una Visita a/A Visit to) Mankato, MN: Capstone, 2008. $14.95. Gr. K–1.
 Simple bilingual texts on the left face full color photos in this appealing large-format series about places in the community. Two easy-to-read sentences in English are followed by short sentences in Spanish in the same size and color. The things children can do in the library, such as using a computer and checking out books, are depicted in *La biblioteca/The Library.* A visit to the fire station including fire engines, ladders and firefighters are shown in *La estación de bomberos/The Fire Station.* Farm buildings and farm animals are introduced in *La granja/The Farm.* Picking, washing, sorting and enjoying apples are featured in *La huerta de manzanas/The Apple Orchard.* Each title includes a glossary and an index in both English and Spanish.

Moore-Mallinos, Jennifer. *Somos adoptados. (We Are Adopted)* ISBN: 978-0-7641-3788-4.
————. *Tengo asma. (I Have Asthma)* ISBN: 978-0-7641-3786-0.
Roca, Núria. *¿Cómo nos movemos? (How We Move Around)* ISBN: 978-0-7641-3654-2.
————. *¿De qué están hechas las cosas? (What Are Things Made Of?)* ISBN: 978-0-7641-3652-8.
————. *Las tres erres: reutilizar, reducir, reciclar. (The Three R's: Reuse, Reduce, Recycle)* ISBN: 978-0-7641-3582-8.
————. *Tu árbol genealógico. (Your Family Tree)* ISBN: 978-0-7641-3580-4.
 Ea. vol.: 36p. Illus: Rosa M. Curto. (¿Qué Sabes Acerca de?) Barcelona/New York: Barron's, 2007. pap. $6.99. Gr. 2–4.
 Written in a most engaging, almost conversational style, this easy-to-understand paperback series with amusing black-line and watercolor illustrations with up-close and exaggerated perspectives against a white background invites Spanish-speaking children (and their parents) to consider different topics. A little girl, who had been adopted in Russia, is now looking forward to a baby brother, also to be adopted in Russia in *Somos adoptados.* Despite having asthma, a respiratory disease marked by labored breathing, chest constriction and coughing, a young boy enjoys playing in the soccer team in *Tengo asma.* Different ways of movement—some babies crawl, some children need crutches, some animals walk on four legs, spiders on eight, frogs leap, butterflies glide—are

discussed in *¿Cómo nos movemos?* This is not a serious study on movement; rather, it provides enough information to make the act of moving interesting. One has to hope that the four pages of activities for children and a two-page *Guía para los padres* (Parents' Guide) that conclude each book will add to, not spoil, the reading. *¿De qué están hechas las cosas?* describes how familiar objects are either made from material directly from nature—cheese, wool—or from man-made products like plastic and glass. *Las tres erres: reutilizar, reducir, reciclar* encourages children to reduce pollution by reusing common objects, reducing throw aways and recycling products by placing them in special collection areas. Through young Martín's family tree, children are exposed to extended family members including *tatarabuelos* (great-great-grandparents) and other more remote ancestors in *Tu árbol genealógico*.

Fiction

Easy Books

Abadi, Ariel. *Un rey de quién sabe dónde. (A King from Who Knows Where)*
Illus: the author. Buenos Aires: Ediciones del Eclipse, 2003. 26p. ISBN:
987-9011-57-0. $9.95. Gr. 2–5.

    A king sitting on his throne is followed by another king from an-
other kingdom, who in turn is followed by another king, and then by a
would-be king, followed by an anything-but king, which culminates in
a big fight among kings. This results in a barely dressed, no-kingdom
king, a bruised king from another kingdom, which concludes in a se-
verely injured now-I-don't-care-to-be-king and finally by a happy,
playful, definitely-never-king. Whimsical black-ink and watercolor cartoon illustrations beautifully complement this one phrase per page facetious depiction of power. The only undesirable aspect of this picture
book is the small size: 3" × 6". What a shame!

Abeyà, Elisabet. *Hansel and Gretel/Hansel y Gretel.* Illus: Cristina Losan-
tos. ISBN: 0-8118-4793-4.
Ros, Roser. *The Musicians of Bremen/Los músicos de Bremen.* Illus: Pep
Montserrat. ISBN: 0-8118-4795-0.
Ea. vol.: 24p. Translated into English by Elizabeth Bell. San Francisco:
Chronicle, 2005. $14.95. Gr. 1–3.

    Maintaining the rhythm and cadence of the original Spanish-
language adaptations, these bilingual editions with modernist watercolor-
and-ink illustrations present an updated look of these classic tales.
Whether enjoyed as read alouds or independent reading, English and

Spanish speakers will celebrate as Gretel and Hansel delight in the mean witch's treasures in *Hansel and Gretel/Hansel y Gretel*, and as four aging animals find a new home after outwitting a gang of robbers in *The Musicians of Bremen/Los músicos de Bremen.*

Abril, Paco. *Colores que se aman. (Colors That Love Each Other)* Illus: Anne Decis. León: Everest, 2005. 32p. ISBN: 84-241-7989-7. $16.95. Gr. K–2.

Dedicated to Lucrecia Pérez from the Dominican Republic who was murdered in Spain and to others who have suffered the hatred of racists, this simply written story depicts fear and love as experienced by Luca, a five-year-old black boy. Narrated in the first-person, Luca tells about hearing unhappy words outside, a shot, and screams in the street. Then he hears his grandmother's voice reassuring him. When screams continue, Luca is ready to cry. But Luca's grandmother, who is white, knows exactly how to make him laugh. Despite the strong didactic message, the easy-to-read text and eye-catching double-page spreads, this story could be used as a discussion starter about ethnic differences with young children.

Allison, Catherine. *El oso del abuelo (Brown Paper Bear)* Illus: Neil Reed. Translated by Josefina Caball i Guerrero. Barcelona: Juventud, 2005. 30p. ISBN: 84-261-3438-6. $19.95. Ages 3–6.

When Ruth awakens in the night, she finds an abandoned, lively teddy bear who eagerly takes her to an old-fashioned land. She delights in playing with his somewhat antique friends, including a train ride and dancing a waltz with a *bella muñeca de porcelana* (beautiful porcelain doll). In the morning, a loving grandpa hugs her and says: ¡*Vaya, Ruth, has encontrado mi oso!* (I see you found my teddy bear.) Like the original English edition, first published by Fernleigh, London, 2004, this fluid Spanish rendition is printed on sturdy, brown butcher paper in a square, oversize format with Reed's detailed watercolors in up-close and unusual perspectives that certainly will command the attention of young Spanish-speaking readers or listeners.

Amado, Elisa. *Primas. (Cousins)* Illus: Luis Garay. Translated by Elena and Leopoldo Iribarren. Toronto: Groundwood Books/Douglas & McIntyre/ Distributed by Publishers Group West, 2004. 32p. ISBN: 0-88899-548-2. $16.95. Gr. 2–4.

Maintaining the tender tone of the original, this gentle Spanish rendition with Garay's rich, earth-tone illustrations warmly depicts a young Latina's feelings about the Catholic religion amid the contrasting worlds of her two grandmothers. Narrated in the voice of the child, the protagonist, who tells about Mimi's beautiful things and *abuela* Adela's Catholic lifestyle, the girl still has the strength to go to the priest and later confront her family about her three sins. Fortunately, everyone understands and forgives her.

Andersen, Hans Christian. *El árbol de Navidad. (The Christmas Tree)* 24p. ISBN: 84-241-1628-3.
———. *La cerillera. (The Little Match Girl)* 24p. ISBN: 84-241-1632-1.
———. *El porquerizo. (The Swineherd)* 24p. ISBN: 84-241-1627-5.
———. *La Reina de las Nieves. (The Snow Queen)* 32p. ISBN: 84-241-1629-1.
———. *La sirenita. (The Little Mermaid)* 47p. ISBN: 84-241-1633-X.
———. *El soldadito de plomo. (The Steadfast Tin Soldier)* 24p. ISBN: 84-241-1630-5.
———. *El traje nuevo del emperador. (The Emperor's New Clothes)* 24p. ISBN: 84-241-1631-3.
Ea. vol.: Adapted by Arnica Esterl. Illus: Anastassija Archipowa. Translated by María Victoria Martínez Vega. León: Everest, 2005. $18.95. Gr. 2–4.

As in the originals, most of these stories—*La cerillera* (The Little Match Girl); *El porquerizo* (The Swineherd); *La Reina de las Nieves* (The Snow Queen); *La sirenita* (The Little Mermaid); *El soldadito de plomo* (The Steadfast Tin Soldier)—depict the heavenly rewards as well as the loneliness and suffering that are necessary for happiness and growth. The snappy, fluid Spanish texts, which are just right for individual reading or reading aloud, are accompanied by detailed, full-page, pastel illustrations that complement the tone and message of each story. Although these fresh Spanish renditions based on Esterl's adaptations omit some details, they nevertheless follow Andersen's stories fairly closely. My favorites are: *El porquerizo,* a lively and accessible retelling of the familiar story about the rejected prince who disguises himself as a swineherd and ultimately rejects the arrogant princess, and *El traje nuevo del emperador*, an equally spirited rendition of one of Andersen's most popular stories in which everyone, except a child, is afraid to tell the ostentatious emperor the truth about his clothes. Despite a few Peninsular Spanish pronouns and conjugations (e.g., *dejadlo, tendríais, vosotras*), Spanish speakers from the Americas will enjoy.

Andersen, Hans Christian. *La pequeña cerillera.* *(Little Match Girl)* Illus: Judit Morales and Adrià Gòdia. ISBN: 84-667-3674-3.
———. *El valiente soldadito de plomo.* *(The Steadfast Tin Soldier)* Illus: Javier Sáez Castán. ISBN: 84-667-3673-5.
Comotto, Agustín. *Nuevos vecinos.* *(New Neighbors)* ISBN: 84-667-3675-1.
Villamuza, Noemí. *Mirando fotografías.* *(Looking at Photographs)* ISBN: 84-667-3676-X.
Ea. vol.: 24p. (Sopa de Cuentos) Madrid: Grupo Anaya, 2004. $10.95. Gr. 2–4.

Distilling the essential narratives of Andersen's classic stories, these smooth retellings include a full-page illustration on the right page facing a simple text on the left page. Soft watercolor illustrations accompany *La pequeña cerillera,* a cold and hungry young girl who, after trying to sell matches, attempts to warm herself as she imagines a happy holiday with her grandmother. Full-page dramatic illustrations with varied perspectives add interest to *El valiente soldadito de plomo,* the one-legged tin soldier's perilous adventures that culminate in the flames with his beloved ballerina. Beginning readers will appreciate the simple texts—one or two sentences per page—and modernist almost cartoon illustrations of the two stories. In *Nuevos vecinos,* Fabián is surprised by his new neighbors, until he finds out they work at a circus. In *Mirando fotografías,* Darío learns about his family and himself when he finds a family photograph album. A few Peninsular Spanish pronouns and conjugations will not confuse Spanish speakers from the Americas.

Andersen, Hans Christian. *La tetera.* *(The Teapot)* Illus: Elia Manero. Translated by Enrique Bernárdez. ISBN: 84-667-4733-8.
Grimm, Jacob, and Wilhelm Grimm. *El Enano Saltarín.* *(Rumpelstiltskin)* Illus: Marina Seoane. Translated by María Antonia Seijo Castroviejo. ISBN: 84-667-4732-X.
Ea. vol.: 24p. (Sopa de Cuentos) Madrid: Anaya, 2006. $8.95. Gr. 1–3.

Like the previous titles in this joyful series, these are indeed compelling Spanish renditions that resonate with the beauty and rhythm of the Spanish language. The vivid narratives on the left side of page, which face full-page, imaginative color illustrations, are certain to appeal to beginning readers or young listeners. Although not as well-known as other

Andersen tales, *La tetera* tells about the misfortunes of a proud teapot who declines in status, from serving tea, to serving as a pot, to becoming trash in the street with only her cherished memories. The always-popular *El Enano Saltarin* (Rumpelstiltskin in the English-language world) is eager to help the beautiful miller's daughter spin gold, yet ultimately loses out.

Argueta, Jorge. *Moony Luna/Luna, lunita lunera.* Illus: Elizabeth Gómez. San Francisco: Children's Book Press, 2005. 32p. ISBN: 0-89239-205-3. $16.95. Gr. K–2.

Although *mami* and *papi* reassure five-year-old Marisol that school is a fun place, she worries about ugly monsters with scary voices that live there. Even if she is now "*soy grande como la luna llena/*as big as the full moon," she still worries and hides under a table as soon as she arrives. But, after spending a happy day with her kind teacher and friendly classmates, she knows that "*En esta escuelita no viven monstruos feos/*no monsters live at my school." It is regrettable that Argueta's simple bilingual text—the Spanish text is followed by the English in the same font and size—may confuse beginning readers of either language. Despite this caveat, Gómez's whimsical, bright illustrations, brimming with a loving Latino family and a childlike monster that is seen disappearing as Marisol is convinced that "*En esta escuelita no viven monstruos feos/*no monsters live at my school," will gently remind readers/listeners of other personal fears/monsters that also seem to disappear.

Arispe, Nicolás, *Té de palacio. (Palace Tea)* Illus: the author. Buenos Aires: Ediciones del Eclipse, 2007. 24p. ISBN: 978-987-9011-86-7. $15.95. Gr. 2–4.

When an important king in a faraway kingdom notices an unexpected guest—a cat—at his table, he is definitely upset. His assistants provide most ingenious explanations: a bear would be too hungry, a hedgehog would have flashing spines, a giraffe would be too tall, a seal would have been a risk for the fine china. Finally convinced, the majestic, but *timorato* (chicken-hearted) king orders a large cup of chocolate for the cat. Arispe's colored pencil illustrations complement the facing jocose, rhyming text. Despite the small size—4½" × 9½"—this is an unconventional tongue-in-cheek depiction of royalty.

Ashbé, Jeanne. ¡*Es hora de recoger! (Pick Up Time!)* ISBN: 84-8470-163-8.
——. *La hora del baño. (Bath Time)* ISBN: 84-8470-165-4.

———. *¡Mira cómo te has puesto! (What a Mess!)* ISBN: 84-8470-162-X.

———. *¡Oh!, está oscuro! (Oh! It's Dark)* ISBN: 84-8470-164-6.
  Ea. vol.: 16p. Illus: the author. Translated by Anna Coll-Vinent. (Edi y
  Tedy) Barcelona: Corimbo, 2004. $8.95. Ages 1–3.

  Thick black lines against flat colors used on the background are
just what is needed to portray Edi, a charming toddler, and his toy bear,
Tedy, as they enjoy their daily activities with gusto and a bit of mischief. Well-constructed flaps and fold outs encourage toddlers to pick
up Edi's toys in *¡Es hora de recoger!;* participate during bath time in *La
hora del baño*; prepare for and clean up after dinner in *¡Mira cómo te
has puesto!*; get ready for bedtime in *¡Oh!, está oscuro!* This delightful
series was originally published by L'ecole des loisirs, Paris.

Banks, Kate. *La gran casa azul. (The Great Blue House)* Illus: Georg Hallensleben. Translated by Christiane Reyes. Barcelona: Juventud, 2005.
  34p. ISBN: 84-261-3484-X. $19.95. Gr. Preschool–2.

  As summer ends, a family packs their suitcases and the children
cry out, *¡Adiós, casa!* (Goodbye house!) Although the vacation house is
locked, the house celebrates the passing of the seasons from a quiet fall
when *una araña teje su red* (a spider weaves her web) to winter when
las cañerías se hielan (the pipes freeze) to spring when rain *viene a despertar el jardín* (comes to awaken the garden), to a joyous summer
when the family returns and *un nuevo bebé llora* (a new baby cries).
Reyes's spare, evocative Spanish rendition and Hallensleben's spectacular, thickly brushed, impressionistic illustrations provide a sense of
wonder to the rhythm and cycle of life and nature.

Banks, Kate. *Si la luna pudiera hablar. (And If the Moon Could Talk)* Illus:
  Georg Hallensleben. Translated by Mireia Porta i Arnau. Barcelona: Juventud, 2003. 34p. ISBN: 84-261-3131-X. $18.95. Ages 2–5.

  In a simple, almost poetic Spanish rendition, an unseen narrator
describes what the moon would tell if it could talk: a child gets ready
for bed, papa reads a story, a lion cares for her cubs, a toy rabbit listens
to the radio, and mama comes in to say *Buenas noches* (Good night).
Hallensleben's bold, double-page spreads add a dreamy quality to this
quiet bedtime story.

Baumbach, Martina. *Los fines de semana veo a papá. (Weekends I See Father)* Illus: Jan Lieffering. Translated by Christiane Reyes. Barcelona:
  Juventud, 2006. 26p. ISBN: 84-261-3552-8. $18.95. Gr. K–3.

Leo, who is about eight, is especially close to Rita, the family's dog. At home he notices that papa and mama's arguments continue to escalate. After a particularly tense day, he hears, *Nos separamos* (We'll separate), which means that papa is leaving home. Leo's feelings about his parent's separation, eventual divorce, and life at home with his mother and weekends with his father and his father's girlfriend are described in a poignant, yet reassuring manner. Particularly when Leo is allowed to keep Rita and his mother convinces him that despite the divorce papa and mama will never separate from him because that promise *¡No se puede romper jamás de los jamases!* (Can never ever be broken!) Lieffering's realistic, pencil-and-watercolor illustrations are as down-to-earth as Leo's story. In contrast to many children's books in Spanish about divorce, this matter-of-fact Spanish rendition, originally published by Verlag, Germany, depicts, honestly and candidly, this difficult subject from the child's point of view.

Bebés dinámicos. (Dynamic Babies) ISBN: 84-7864-689-2.
Bebés juguetones. (Playful Babies) ISBN: 84-7864-690-6.
　　Ea. vol.: 10p. Illus: Thierry Courtin. Barcelona: Combel Editorial, 2003. $10.95. Ages 1–3.
　　Thick black lines and bright colors against flat colorful backgrounds, simple rhyming texts, and well-constructed lift-the-flaps characterize these sturdy board books, originally published by Pinwheel Limited, London. Through well-placed lift-the-flaps, energetic babies/toddlers demonstrate how they can bend down and touch their feet, turn around, play hide-and-seek and other activities in *Bebés dinámicos*. *Bebés juguetones* features playful toddlers behind lift-the-flaps as they play ball, ride a hobby horse, slide down a slide and other fun games.

Berner, Rotraut Susanne. *¡Ay, no! (Oh, No!)* Illus: the author. Translated by Moka Seco Reeg. ISBN: 978-84-667-6234-2.
Gutiérrez Serna, Mónica. *Si fuera . . . (If I Were . . .)* Illus: the author. ISBN: 978-84-667-6437-7.
　　Ea. vol.: 24p. (Sopa de Cuentos) Madrid: Anaya, 2007. $12.95. Gr. K–2.
　　With simple texts, these recent titles from the Sopa de Cuentos series are just right for beginning readers. *¡Ay, no!* features *gallina blanca* (White Hen) who complains about everything and *gallina negra* (Black Hen) who always finds a solution. But when they go on a picnic they discover that things are not always black and white. The lively, colorful

illustrations against a flat background add a touch of humor to the hens' contrasting views. With more sophisticated collage illustrations, *Si fuera* . . . is a cheerful, lyrical play on words in which an unseen child asks, *Si fuera una zanahoria . . . /sería una nariz.* (If I were a carrot . . . /I would be a nose.), followed by *Si fuera una nariz . . . /sería una montaña.* (If I were a nose . . . /I would be a mountain.). And so on, until Mama reassures the child that, if she were a star, she would watch over her every night.

Berner, Rotraut Susanne. *El libro de la primavera. (The Book of Spring)* ISBN: 84-667-4526-2.
———. *El libro del invierno. (The Book of Winter)* ISBN: 84-667-4013-9.
———. *El libro del otoño. (The Book of Fall)* ISBN: 978-84-667-6496-4.
———. *El libro del verano. (The Book of Summer)* ISBN: 84-667-5212-9.
Ea. vol.: 16p. Illus: the author. Madrid: Anaya, 2004–2005. $19.95. Gr. Preschool–2.

In delightful large-format board books, these wordless picture books with lively, detailed pen-and-watercolor illustrations, originally published by Verlag, Germany, depict busy scenes of families, friends and their animals getting ready to enjoy spring, summer, fall and winter activities. In *El libro de la primavera* people and animals are eager to enjoy the good weather. They go to a farm, take a train, visit a museum and a library, shop in a plaza and a large department store and have fun at the park. In *El libro del invierno* snow arrives, Christmas decorations are everywhere and the park is stirring with winter sports. Typical fall activities such as a pumpkin growing contest are highlighted in *El libro del otoño*. The bustle of a fun-filled summer, which includes *¡Recolecta tus propias fresas!* (picking your own strawberries), selecting *Las ofertas del verano* (Summer Sales), shopping at a *Librería* (Bookstore) and, finally, *Vuelta al Cole* (Back to School) is depicted in *El libro del verano*. The appropriately placed labels, framed within the illustrations, will assist beginning Spanish readers to identify a *Gasolinera* (gas station), *Salidas* (Departures), *Frutas y Verduras* (Fruits and Vegetables) and other pertinent areas. Amid the whimsy, lovers of detail will enjoy the bustle of the seasons.

Berner, Rotraut Susanne. *Miguel juega al fútbol. (Miguel Plays Soccer)* Translated by Moka Seco Reeg. Madrid: Anaya, 2006. 40p. ISBN: 84-667-5223-4. $18.95. Gr. 2–4.

Miguel, a child rabbit, loves to play soccer on Sundays with his rabbit family. *Mamá* rabbit is the referee and even *abuela* (grandma) and other uncles and cousins join the game. With delightful ink-and-watercolor cartoonish illustrations and through an easy-to-follow dialogue among the players, readers are exposed to basic soccer rules such as unintentional headers and the difference between yellow and red cards. Although the game ends in a tie, *abuela* proclaims that both teams won and offers cake and hot chocolate to all the players. A glossary with basic soccer terms concludes this enjoyable romp, originally published by Verlag, Germany. Soccer fans should not miss the fun.

Besora, Ramón. *¿Quién lo adivinará? (Who Can Guess?)* Illus: Judit Morales and Adrià Gòdia. Barcelona: Edebé, 2004. 50p. ISBN: 84-236-6016-8. $16.95. Gr. 1–4.

This collection of 171 brief riddles about the weather, animals, food and other items well-known to children captures the elements of rhythm and sound intrinsic to the Spanish language. From simple riddles such as *Por el mismo camino andamos/y ni nos vemos ni nos encontramos* (Answer: shoes), to a more abstract *Qué es/que pasa por tus ojos/y no lo ves?* (Answer: air), these can be used for vocabulary building, phonemic awareness, or just plain fun. Unfortunately, the bland color illustrations are mere decorations. Also, it is regrettable that the riddles are not organized in some manner, e.g., riddles about food are interspersed with animals, kitchen items, clothing, and nature.

Bloom, Becky. *La liebre y la tortuga. (The Hare and the Tortoise)* Illus: Pawel Pawlak. Translated by Cristina Puerta. Bogotá: Norma, 2004. 34p. ISBN: 958-04-8042-7. pap. $7.40. Gr. 2–4.

Using the well-known tale about a persevering tortoise and a boastful hare as a takeoff, this contemporary version depicts athletic forest animals in constant disagreements with each other. To try to improve life in the forest, *señora búho* (Mrs. Owl) organizes a race. Although *señor liebre* (Mr. Hare) wins the race, he graciously offers the medal to *señorita tortuga* (Ms. Tortoise), because she deserves credit for bringing peace to the forest. Pawlak's amusing whimsical illustrations of animals engaged in serious athletic preparations are set against a modernist design that intermingles graphic art techniques with fonts of different styles and sizes. Young Spanish speakers will enjoy this easygoing Spanish rendition.

Bloom, Suzanne. *Un amigo de veras maravilloso. (A Splendid Friend, In-deed)* Illus: the author. Translated by Aída E. Marcuse. Honesdale, Pennsylvania: Boyds Mills, 2007. 32p. ISBN: 978-1-59078-489-1 $15.95. Gr. Preschool–2.

When a friendly, loquacious goose approaches a serious, pensive polar bear and constantly interrupts him by questioning every activity—*¿Estás leyendo?* (Are you reading?), *¿Estás escribiendo?* (Are you writing?), *¿Estás pensando?* (Are you thinking?)—and imitating him, the polar bear stoically looks at him. But when goose writes a note stating *Tú eres mi amigo maravilloso.* (You are my splendid friend.), polar bear excitedly agrees that he is also *mi amigo maravilloso.* The striking, double-page spreads in bright shades of blue and white, and Marcuse's animated Spanish rendition, which maintains the energy and brevity of the original English dialogue, make a perfect combination for reading aloud as well as cordial discussions about friendship and "irritating" friends.

Boada, Francesc. *The Princess and The Pea/La princesa y el guisante.* Illus: Pau Estrada. ISBN: 0-8118-4451-X.; pap. ISBN: 0-8118-4452-8.
———. *Puss in Boots/El gato con botas.* Illus: José Luis Merino. ISBN: 0-8118-3923-0. pap. ISBN: 0-8118-3924-9.
Escardó i Bas, Mercè. *The Ugly Duckling/El patito feo.* Illus: Max. ISBN: 0-8118-4454-4.; pap. ISBN: 0-8118-4455-2.
Valriu, Caterina. *Thumbelina/Pulgarcita.* Illus: Max. ISBN: 0-8118-3927-3; pap. ISBN: 0-8118-3928-1.
Ea. vol.: 24p. San Francisco: Chronicle Books, 2004. HC. $13.95; pap. $6.95. Gr. K–3.

As opposed to the first three pedestrian bilingual titles in this series—*Jack and the Beanstalk/Juan y los frijoles mágicos, Little Red Riding Hood/Caperucita Roja,* and *Goldilocks and the Three Bears/Ricitos de Oro y los tres osos*—these bilingual editions will appeal to both English and Spanish young readers/listeners. Simple English texts followed by clear and easy Spanish renditions on the left side of the page face modernist, full-page watercolor illustrations. Simply and succinctly, in both languages, a girl proves she is a true princess by feeling a pea through twenty mattresses and twenty featherbeds in *The Princess and The Pea/La princesa y el guisante.* Especially appealing is the rhythmic Spanish text that depicts a resourceful *gato con botas (Con las botas puestas y el saco a cuestas . . .)* who outwits the evil ogre to gain a fortune for his master in *Puss in Boots/El gato con botas.* An ugly duckling's sad experiences with several animals and his joyous welcome as a beautiful swan are presented in matter-of-fact bilingual renditions in *The Ugly Duckling/El patito feo*. Straightforward Spanish and English adaptations of Andersen's always-popular tale about the tiny, courageous heroine who is stolen by a big, ugly toad and later is rescued by a swallow are presented in *Thumbelina/Pulgarcita*.

Bolliger, Max. *Matías y la estrella. (Matías and the Star)* Illus: Gianni de Conno. Translated by Christiane Reyes. Barcelona: Juventud, 2003. 26p. ISBN: 84-261-3341-X. $16.95. Gr. K–3.

Two thousand years ago in the Middle East, Matías, a young jester, is eager to become a wise man. As he follows a star to meet the newborn child and offer him his most precious belongings, Matías encounters three children in need. He doesn't hesitate to give them his gifts, but arrives empty-handed. Nonetheless, he knows he found the king and the wisdom he aspired. Originally published by Bohem, Zurich, under the title *Der Weihnachtsnarr* (The Christmas Buffoon), this gentle Spanish rendition with imaginative, richly colored double-page spreads depicting dreamy, starlit landscapes touchingly portrays the spirit of Christmas.

Bravi, Soledad. *El libro de los ruidos. (The Book of Sounds)* Translated by Rafael Ros. Barcelona: Corimbo, 2006. 104p. ISBN: 84-8470-232-4. $15.95. Ages 1–3.

More than fifty sounds are identified for the very young through uncluttered illustrations featuring well-known items and simple sentences. Beginning with *El asno hace hi ha hi ha* (The donkey goes hi ha hi ha), and *El tambor hace ram-pa-ta-plan* (The drum goes ram-pa-ta-plan), to a silent snail, and a kiss that goes *muak,* this well-constructed board book, originally published by L'école des loisirs, Paris, introduces Spanish learners to familiar concepts. The bold black lines and bright colors against flat backgrounds will appeal to Spanish speakers (or learners).

Bridges, Shirin Yim. *El deseo de Ruby. (Ruby's Wish)* Illus: Sophie Blackall. Translated by Marta Ansón. Barcelona: Serres, 2005. 28p. ISBN: 84-8488-206-3. $16.95. Gr. 2–4.

Ruby, who loves to wear red, her favorite color and the color of celebration, is especially interested in getting a good education. Fortunately, her wealthy, Chinese grandfather supports her wishes to go to the university. Blackall's gouache illustrations with joyous touches of red perfectly convey life amid a large Chinese family. Despite a few Peninsular Spanish conjugations, young Spanish speakers from the Americas will get a glimpse of traditional Chinese customs where girls receive fewer gifts than boys and are only expected to get married, cook and embroider.

Browne, Anthony. *En el bosque. (Into the Forest)* Illus: the author. Translated by Juana Inés Dehesa. Mexico: Fondo de Cultura Económica, 2004. 26p. ISBN: 968-16-7218-6. $17.95. Gr. 2–5.

After a particularly blustery night, a boy wakes up to find a sad *mamá* and his *papá* gone. Obviously dejected and eager to see his *papá*, his *mamá* sends him to take a cake to grandma. As he walks through the forest, he encounters unfriendly fairy-tale characters. Feeling cold, he grabs a bright red jacket and remembers the story of the bad wolf. Though scared, he knocks at grandma's house, runs in to embrace a happy smiling *abuela* and sees his cheerful delighted *papá*. Browne's characteristic pencil-and-watercolor illustrations, depicting the fantastic imagery of a forlorn boy, realistically capture the boy's initial consternation, which ends with a loving delighted *mamá*. Dehesa's spare Spanish rendition is as powerful and ultimately as reassuring as the original.

Browne, Anthony. *El juego de las formas. (The Shape Game)* Illus: the author. Translated by Ernestina Loyo. Mexico: Fondo de Cultura Económica, 2004. 26p. ISBN: 968-16-7184-8. $24.95. Gr. K–3.

Browne describes in this autobiographical story *un día que cambió mi vida para siempre* (a day that changed my life forever). Although *papá* and his brother Jorge are bored, his *mamá* makes this childhood trip to an art museum an interesting and participatory experience. Browne's engaging illustrations full of fantasy and mirth, and the straightforward Spanish rendition including *papá's* ridiculous jokes, might encourage young Spanish speakers to perhaps look forward to a trip to an art museum. If not, *mamá's juego de las formas* (shape game) is just as much fun.

Browne, Anthony. *Mi mamá. (My Mom).* Illus: the author. Translated by Andrea Fuentes. Mexico: Fondo de Cultura Económica, 2005. 24p. ISBN: 968-16-7375-1. $15.95. Gr. Preschool–2.

Maintaining the carefree tone of its predecessor, *Mi papá (My Dad)*, a child narrator now provides an exalted portrait of his/her mother. Introducing an average flowered-robe-clad mother as *Es linda mi mamá* (She's nice, my mom), she is also a *fantástica cocinera* (great cook), juggler, painter, gardener, fairy godmother, singer, who at times roars like a lion and is as forceful as a rhinoceros, yet *¡Sí que es Linda, LINDA, MUY LINDA, mi mama!* (She is really, really nice!) Browne's always-engaging, chalk-and-gouache, full-page illustrations with humorous allusions to Marilyn Monroe, Superwoman and other farfetched characters conclude with a loving mother fondly embracing the child narrator. Spanish-speaking parents and the little ones will appreciate the fancy amid the candor.

Brun-Cosme, Nadine. *¡Hoy lo hace papá! (Papa Will Do It!)* Illus: Michel Backès. Translated by Rafael Ros. Barcelona: Corimbo, 2004. 24p. ISBN: 84-8470-116-6. $15.95. Ages 3–6.

After school, Ana, a child fox, is delighted to come home and invite Julio, her best friend. But mama fox is in a bad mood and says no to all of Ana's suggestions. So when papa comes home, Ana only wants papa to help her, including putting her to bed and tells mama: *¡No, tú no! ¡Esta noche, lo hace papá!* (No, not you! Tonight, papa will do it!) Mama is hurt and explains to Ana that tonight she is very tired. Ana smiles and is now happy with mama's big hug. The bold colorful illustrations of a fox family at home add a tender touch to this realistic story about family feelings and misunderstandings.

¡Buenas noches, bebé!/Good Night, Baby! ISBN: 0-7566-0438-9.
¡Buenos días, bebé!/Good Morning, Baby! ISBN: 0-7566-0437-0.
Todo sobre bebé/All About Baby. ISBN: 0-7566-0436-2.

Ea. vol.: 20p. Photos by Jo Foord and others. (Bilingual Soft to Touch Books) New York: DK Publishing, 2004. $4.99. Ages 1–3.

With a delightful multiethnic cast, these well-constructed bilingual board books show babies getting ready for bedtime *(¡Buenas noches, bebé!)*, starting their day *(¡Buenos días, bebé!)*, and learning to crawl, to sit up straight, to clap and to play with friends *(Todo sobre bebé)*. The easy-to-understand Spanish rendition in bold is followed by the English text in a lighter, smaller font.

Burningham, John. *Eduardo: El niño más terrible del mundo (Eduardo, The Horriblest Boy in the Whole World)* Illus: the author. Translated by Ma. Fe González Fernández. Vigo: Faktoria K, 2006. 32p. ISBN: 978-84-934713-9-2. $19.95. Gr. Preschool–1.

Although Eduardo is just like any boy, demanding adults consider him *bruto, ruidoso, abusón, cruel, desordenado y sucio* (nasty, noisy, rude, cruel, unruly, and untidy). As adults overreact, he becomes even worse. But, gradually, people start admiring how he cares for plants, pets, children and escaped lions. They now hail him as *EL NIÑO MÁS BUENO DEL MUNDO* (The Best Boy in the World). The carefree Spanish rendition and Burningham's original humorous, almost cartoonish, black-ink with splashes of color illustrations will appeal to young Spanish speakers and their parents who will enjoy Eduardo's not-so-terrible behavior.

Canetti, Yanitzia. *Un poquito más. (A Little Bit More)* Illus: Ángeles Peinador. León: Everest, 2005. 32p. ISBN: 84-241-8760-1. $16.95. Gr. K–2.

Using a popular nursery rhyme as a takeoff (*Si un elefante se balanceaba sobre la tela de una araña*), an enthusiastic elephant is happily bouncing on a tree limb. When the limb breaks and he falls, all the animals come to his rescue. First comes a zebra, followed by a monkey, a camel, a hippo, and a penguin, but even altogether, they can't help the elephant stand up. When a small ant offers to help, the animals ridicule her, but the elephant accepts her kindly, and, finally, *¡lo lograron!* (They were successful!) Now the animals know *hasta un POQUITO puede ¡hacer la GRAN diferencia!* (Even a LITTLE BIT can make a BIG difference!) Despite the obvious message, children will enjoy the rhyming repetitive text and Peinador's expressive animal illustrations.

Cano Guijarro, Isabel. *Los alimentos. (Food)* ISBN: 84-667-4000-7.
———. *El colegio. (School)* ISBN: 84-667-3998-X.
———. *La naturaleza. (Nature)* ISBN: 84-667-4001-5.
———. *Las profesiones. (Careers)* ISBN: 84-667-3999-8.
Ea. vol.: 24p. Illus: Tae Mori. (Adivina y Pegatina) Madrid: Grupo Anaya, 2004. $11.95. Gr. K–2.

Like the previous four titles in this series—*Los animales* (Animals), *La ciudad* (The City), *En casa* (At Home), *Los juegos* (Games)—these encourage children to solve the riddle in each two-page spread, which include bold black fluid lines, bright watercolors and charming rhyming texts. Whether used for simple reading, vocabulary building, or child participation, all readers/listeners will enjoy such puzzles as *Cuanto más caliente, más fresco y crujiente*, with an appropriate outline of a *pan* (bread) and *Soy redondo y blando,/con leche me hacen/de vacas y cabras/que en el campo pacen* as a couple enjoys a picnic with *queso* (cheese) followed by nine other common foods, as featured in *Los alimentos*. (This title was awarded Spain's prestigious 2003 Premio Lazarillo for illustrations.) School activities can be interesting and fun, especially if you can paint, read, play, eat and discuss as portrayed in *El colegio*. From trees to stars to the sun and other aspects of nature are depicted in *La naturaleza*. Various careers such as mail carrier, carpenter and doctor are shown in *Las profesiones*. Some adults may object to the stickers of missing items included at the end of each book that children are supposed to attach to the correct outline. Despite this caveat, these are fun riddles.

Carle, Eric. *Don Caballito de Mar. (Mister Seahorse)* Illus: the author. Translated by Miguel Angel Mendo. Madrid: Kókinos, 2005. 34p. ISBN: 84-88342-79-9. $19.95. Gr. K–3.

Just as dazzling as the original English edition and with Mendo's always-endearing Spanish rendition, Carle's luminous tissue-paper collages, intermingled with acetate overlays, present a tender view of life undersea and the benefits of camouflage in nature. While *don Caballito de Mar* (Mister Seahorse) carries mother's eggs in his pouch before they hatch, he meets other fish fathers—*don Pez Espinoso* (Mr. Stickleback), *pez-león* (lionfish), *señor Tilapia* (Mr. Tilapia), *don Pez-Flauta* (Mr. Stonefish), *don Tiburón-Toro* (Mr. Bullhead Catfish)—who also are busy caring for the eggs. After little seahorses leave papa's pouch, a freshly hatched seahorse wants to go back in, but papa is serious *Sabes que te quiero mucho, pero ahora tienes ya que valerte por tí mismo.* (I do love you, but you are ready to be on your own.) This is an engaging story about fathers' roles in fish life with Carle's never-to-be-missed illustrations.

Carle, Eric. *10 patitos de goma. (10 Little Rubber Ducks)* Illus: the author. Translated by Miguel Ángel Mendo. New York: Rayo/HarperCollins, 2006. 32p. ISBN: 978-0-06-112623-9. $19.99. Gr. Preschool–1.

Based on a newspaper story about little rubber ducks falling off a cargo ship, Carle creates his distinctively colorful cut-paper collages featuring ten rubber ducks as they are swept away in various directions. From the first that drifts west, to the tenth that is adopted by a mother duck and her ducklings, Mendo's endearingly simple Spanish rendition with easily understood, appropriately repeated phrases throughout the story *el cielo y el mar, el cielo y el mar* (the sky and the sea, the sky and the sea) can be used as an enjoyable, large-format read-aloud or as a supplement to ordinal numbers, directional words and animals in their own habitat.

Carlson, Nancy. *Look Out, Kindergarten, Here I Come/¡Prepárate, Kindergarten! ¡Allá voy!* Illus: the author. Translated by Teresa Mlawer. New York: Viking, 2004. 32p. ISBN: 0-670-03673-0. $15.99. Gr. Preschool–2.

Although Henry, a mouse, is ready for his first day of kindergarten, his mother has to remind him to get dressed, brush his teeth, and eat breakfast. On the way, he eagerly questions his mother about school. Upon arrival, however, he hesitates, runs to his mother, and says: *¡Quiero irme a casa!* (I want to go home!) Kindly, his teacher invites him in. Soon he concludes: *¡El kindergarten va a ser muy divertido!* (Kindergarten is going to be fun!) In the lively and reassuring tone of the original, this bilingual edition with English text above and Spanish below Carlson's animated colored cartoons is sure to encourage reluctant preschoolers and their parents.

Chapra, Mimi. *Amelia's Show-and-Tell Fiesta/Amelia y la fiesta de 'muestra y cuenta.'* Illus: Martha Avilés. Translated by Cristián Pietrapiana. New York: HarperCollins, 2004. 30p. ISBN: 0-06-050255-X. $14.99. Gr. K–2.

Amelia is excited about her first show-and-tell in her new school in the United States. She joyfully decides to wear her special fiesta dress from Cuba only to find out that she may have made a mistake *muy grande*. An understanding teacher and classmates help her overcome her embarrassment as she shows her talking skirt and sings *La Bamba*. Despite the predictable ending, young children, especially from other countries who may not be familiar with "show-and-tell," will empathize with Amelia's confusion. Unfortunately, the fluid Spanish rendition, which follows the English text and appears in the same page in identical color font, size and face, may confuse beginning readers of either language. Avilés's lively, colorful illustrations perfectly portray the fun of a Cuban fiesta in an American school.

Chapra, Mimi. *Sparky's Bark/El ladrido de Sparky*. Illus: Viví Escrivá. Translated by Cristián Pietrapiana. New York: HarperCollins, 2006. 32p. ISBN: 0-06-053172-X. $16.99. Gr. K–2.

When young Lucy travels with her mother from an unnamed Latin American country (where there are banana groves, flamingos and lagoons) to visit Papi's family in Ohio, she is not only homesick, she also is upset because she can't communicate with Sparky, her cousin's playful dog. Fortunately, her cousin Robby agrees to teach her to speak English and thus she is able to play with him. The only caveat in this well-done bilingual (English-Spanish) rendition is that beginning Spanish and English readers are sure to be confused—the Spanish text follows the English in the same font, size and color. All readers/listeners, however, will delight in Escriva's tender watercolors featuring pink-cheecked characters and cozy Midwestern farm scenes.

Chen, Chi-Yuan. *Guji Guji. (Guji Guji)* Illus: the author. Translated by María Fernanda Pulido Duarte. La Jolla, CA: Kane/Miller, 2007. 32p. ISBN: 978-1-933605-34-0. pap. $7.95. Gr. Preschool–3.

    Raised from an egg by *Mamá pata* (Mother Duck), Guji Guji is delighted with his life as a duckling even though he doesn't look like one—he looks more like a crocodile. One day he meets three mean crocodiles who make fun of him and insist that he deliver his duck family for their dinner. But Guji Guji finds a way to outsmart the crocodiles and enjoy his life as a *cocopato* (crocoduck). Chen's engaging double-page illustrations, with warm blue and earth tones, are as satisfying as Pulido Duarte's fluid Spanish rendition. Young Spanish speakers will appreciate this loving family that ignores their differences and celebrates their uniqueness, originally published in Taiwan.

Chen, Chi-Yuan. *La mejor Navidad (The Best Christmas Ever)* Illus: the author. Translated by Aloe Azid. Barcelona: Thule, 2006. 40p. ISBN: 84-96473-50-3. $18.95. Gr. Preschool–2.

    Although things are difficult in *Osito's* house, *Osito* reassures his father, *Papá Oso*, that *Papá Noel* will not forget them. So on Christmas morning when *Osito* wakes up the family, under the small tree there is one gift for each family member. *Hermano Oso* finds his damaged kite, now mended. *Hermana Osa* recovers her lost umbrella. *Mamá Osa* is delighted with her newly found button, *Papá Oso* gets back his hat, and *Osito's* baseball glove is clean and polished like new. When *Mamá Osa* notices tiny footsteps around the tree, young readers/listeners will realize that *Osito* is responsible for the gifts. The bare, unadorned illustrations against flat backgrounds and Azid's cogent Spanish rendition make this particularly affecting holiday story as exceptional as the original, first published by Heryin Books, California.

Child, Lauren. *Humberto Horacio Herminio Bobton-Trent. (Hubert Horatio Bartle Bobton-Trent)* Illus: the author. Translated by Miguel Ángel Mendo. Barcelona: Serres, 2005. 46p. ISBN: 84-8488-225-X. $18.99. Gr. 1–3.

Child's exquisite satire about the *escandalosamente, pero lo que se dice escandalosamente ricos* (frightfully, frightfully rich) is now available in Mendo's jocular Spanish rendition. Humberto, a child genius, has to figure out a way to save his fun-loving, monopoly playing, lavish-spending parents from ruin. To his surprise, his parents not only love the modest apartment building Humberto selects but they are happier with their new neighbors and the whole family even enjoys a nightly hot *taza de cacao* (cup of chocolate) together. The ludicrous life of the very rich, with all its absurdity and silliness, is keenly depicted in Child's whimsical, collage-enhanced illustrations and playful fonts.

Child, Lauren. *La princesa y el guisante (The Princess and the Pea).* Photos by Polly Borland. Translated by Esther Rubio. Barcelona: Serres, 2005. 42p. ISBN: 84-8488-221-7. $19.95. Gr. 1–3.

Based on Hans Christian Andersen's *The Princess and the Pea* and with Rubio's playful Spanish rendition that maintains the contemporary and irreverent tone of the original, first published by Penguin, London, this updated classic has the irresistible charm of a long lost friend. Borland's photos of Lauren's enticing mixed-media collages and the signature fonts of varied shapes and sizes engagingly present a bedraggled young lady who claims to be a princess. Despite her impeccable manners, irresistible charm and stunning good looks, it is up to a tiny green pea hidden under *doce colchones de plumas* (twelve down mattresses) that proves that she is *una princesa de verdad* (a true princess).

Child, Lauren. *Soy demasiado pequeña para ir al colegio. (I'm Too Absolutely Small for School)* Illus: the author. Translated by Esther Rubio. Barcelona: Ediciones Serres, 2003. 32p. ISBN: 84-8488-111-3. $13.95. Gr. Preschool–1.

Although Totola's parents think she is ready for school, she is not so sure. She insists she is extremely busy doing important things at home. But her older brother, Juan, knows exactly how to convince her.

Upon her return from the first day of school, she proclaims: *Yo no estaba preocupada . . . yo estaba estupendamente* (I wasn't worried . . . I was delighted). Rubio's lighthearted Spanish rendition joyfully depicts young children's normal fears and apprehensions, which are further enhanced by the author's always-appealing collage illustrations and signature fonts in varied shapes and sizes.

Christelow, Eileen. *Cinco monitos brincando en la cama/Five Little Monkeys Jumping on the Bed.* Illus: the author. Translated by Victoria Ortiz. New York: Clarion, 2005. 30p. ISBN: 0-618-56442-X. $5.95. Ages 3–6.

As five little monkeys get ready for bed, mama expects a quiet good night. But they are ready for fun and bed-jumping. So, one by one, the little monkeys jump on the bed only to fall off and bump their heads. Christelow's soft, pastel illustrations add a humorous tone to this well-constructed bilingual counting book that, despite the doctor's repeated admonition: *¡Qué ya no brinquen en la cama los monitos!*/No more monkeys jumping on the bed, readers/listeners are sure to enjoy. The simple Spanish text in blue is followed by the English in black color font.

Christelow, Eileen. *En un árbol están los cinco monitos/Five Little Monkeys Sitting in a Tree.* Illus: the author. Translated by Victoria Ortiz. New York: Clarion, 2006. 30p. ISBN: 978-0-618-75248-5. $5.95. Gr. Preschool–2.

When mama takes a nap, five mischievous little monkeys climb a tree and discover, one by one, that teasing a crocodile *Es desagradable—¡y muy peligroso!/It's not nice—and it's dangerous.* The bright and cheery ink-and-watercolor illustrations are as lighthearted as the bilingual text. Notably, the simple Spanish rendition in a purple font is followed by the English text in a black font. The fact that English and Spanish learners can clearly distinguish between the two languages adds to the appeal of this well-constructed board book.

Cohn, Diana. *El tallador de sueños. (Dream Carver)* Illus: Amy Córdova. Translated by Rayo Ramírez. México: Destino/Planeta, 2003. 34p. ISBN: 970-690-854-4. $15.95. Gr. 1–3.

Young Mateo, who lives with his family in a small village in Oaxaca, Mexico, dreams of carving the dazzling, large, colorful animals he sees in his imagination, rather than the little *juguetes (toys)* that the family sells at village *fiestas*. Despite his father's disapproval, Mateo secretly carves his animals and displays them with great success at the *Día de Muertos fiesta*. This simple Spanish rendition and Córdova's brilliant double-spreads, rendered in acrylic on a gessoed ground and color pencils, are a beautiful testament to this much-admired folk-art tradition. A brief afterword tells about Manuel Jiménez, the modern creator of Oaxacan wood carving who inspired the story.

Cole, Babette. *Mamá no me contó . . . (Mummy Never Told Me)* Illus: the author. Translated by Marta Ansón Balmaseda. Barcelona: Ediciones Serres, 2004. 32p. ISBN: 84-8488-117-2. $13.00. Gr. Preschool–3.

With Cole's characteristic directness, humor and richly irreverent comical watercolors, she now approaches many grown-up secrets. From what are belly buttons for, to *Mamá no me había dicho que los niños y las niñas son distintos* (Mummy never told that boys and girls are different), to *¿Por qué mamá y papá se encierran con llave en su dormitorio?* (Why do Mummy and Daddy lock you out of their bedroom?), to a reassuring conclusion: *Mamá me lo explicará todo cuando llegue el momento* (Mummy will explain everything at the right time). This is not for prudish adults; rather it is a delightful invitation for young Spanish speakers (and their parents) to openly talk about life's important yet often unspoken mysteries.

Los colores/Colors. ISBN: 0-7566-0440-0.
Las formas/Shapes. ISBN: 0-7566-0441-9.
Los números/Numbers. ISBN: 0-7566-0439-7.
Ea. vol.: 26p. (First Concepts) New York: DK Publishing, 2004. $3.99. Ages 1–3.

Just right for the toddler set, these well-conceived, baby-sized ($3\frac{1}{4}$" χ $\frac{1}{4}$"), bilingual board books introduce colors, shapes and numbers through clear color photos and simple bilingual labels (Spanish in bold, followed by English in a smaller and lighter font).

Corentin, Philippe. *El ogro, el lobo, la niña y el pastel. (The Ogre, the Wolf, the Girl and the Cake)* Illus: the author. Translated by Anna Coll-Vinent. Barcelona: Corimbo, 2004. 24p. ISBN: 84-8470-157-3. $16.95. Gr. Preschool–1.

A big fat ogre is delighted with his catch—a wolf, a girl and a cake. The problem is, how can he keep all three for himself without the wolf eating the girl, or the girl eating the cake? Corentin's amusing black-ink and watercolor double spreads and the jaunty Spanish rendition are a perfect complement to this bad-ogre story with a most surprising double ending. Originally published by L'ecole de loisirs, Paris, this story is sure to please the young and engage their parents.

Cousins, Lucy. *¡Crick-ras-flash! Cuenta con Maisy. (Maisy's Twinkly Crinkly Counting Book)* Illus: the author. Barcelona: Serres, 2004. 12p. ISBN: 84-8488-121-0. $12.95. Ages 1–3.

Maisy's toddler fans will enjoy touching and feeling the cute mouse as they count to five amid bright, bold watercolors and alluring textures in this sturdy board book that invites lots of touching.

Cousins, Lucy. *Maisy va a la biblioteca. (Maisy Goes to the Library)* Illus: the author. Translated by Marta Ansón. Barcelona: Serres, 2005. 26p. ISBN: 84-8488-213-6. $12.95. Ages 2–5.

When Maisy, the cute mouse, goes to the library to find a quiet place to read, she discovers that she can also search the Web, listen to music, photocopy her favorite drawing, enjoy storytelling time, and check out her book. She then finds a quiet place to read under a tree. Young Spanish speakers will delight in the bold watercolor illustrations and the simple straightforward text.

Cousins, Lucy. *Los mejores amigos de Maisy. (Maisy's Best Friends)* Illus: the author. Translated by Paula F. Bobadilla. Barcelona: Serres, 2004. 12p. ISBN: 84-8488-123-7. $10.95. Gr. Preschool.

Maisy, the cute mouse, has many friends. She enjoys shopping with Rodrigo, playing tennis with Tula, gardening with Pepo, and going to the library with Flor, so she considers them her best friends. Like other Maisy titles, this well-constructed board book has bold watercolor illustrations in primary colors and a brief simple text.

Cousins, Lucy. *Sueños de colores, sueña con Maisy. (Maisy's Rainbow Dream)* Translated by Paula F. Bobadilla. Barcelona: Ediciones Serres, 2003. 26p. ISBN: 84-8488-108-3. $14.95. Gr. Preschool.

Fans of Maisy, the cute mouse, now have an oversize picture book that takes them on a fantastic nighttime journey. From a *mariquita roja* (red ladybug) to a *pez naranja* (orange fish) to other brightly colored animals, Maisy dreams about Rainbowland and wakes up to *un día precioso*. The cheerful, hand-lettered Spanish text beautifully matches this large format book that is just right for groups of young Spanish speakers.

Cowan, Catherine, adapter. *Mi vida con la ola. (My Life with the Wave)* Based on the story by Octavio Paz. Illus: Mark Buehner. Translated by Esther Rubio. Madrid: Kókinos, 2003. 30p. ISBN: 84-88342-45-4. $16.95.

First adapted into English, Octavio Paz's short story by the same title is now available in this flowing Spanish rendition that young Spanish speakers can understand. Buehner's original powerful humorous acrylic and oil paintings beautifully capture a young boy's special friendship with the wave as it progresses from a friendly, loving wave to a moody, monstrous wave that has to be carried back to the sea. To be sure, this is a delightful introduction for the young to the work of Mexico's only Nobel Prize laureate, Octavio Paz.

Cronin, Doreen. *Clic, clac, plif, pluf: una aventura de contar. (Click, Clack, Splish, Splash: A Counting Adventure)* Illus: Betsy Lewin. Translated by Alberto Jiménez Rioja. New York: Lectorum, 2006. 24p. ISBN: 1-933032-11-1. $10.40. Gr. Preschool–K.

Like the previous cheerful farmyard farces—*Clic, clac, muu: Vacas escritoras* and *Jajá, jijí, cuac*—Cronin and Lewin now introduce the very young to numbers 1 to 10 through Jiménez Rioja's joyful Spanish rendition. From *1 granjero está dormido* (1 sleeping farmer) to *10 peces que ansiosos esperan* (10 fish ready to go), this comical counting book with witty line-and-watercolor cartoons of *Pato* (Duck) eager to liberate the ten fish from the farmer's fish tank is playful and inviting.

Cronin, Doreen. *Dubi Dubi Muu. (Dooby Dooby Moo)* Illus: Betsy Lewin. Translated by Alberto Jiménez Rioja. New York: Lectorum, 2007. 38p. ISBN: 978-1-933032-33-7. $15.95. Gr. K–3.

Jiménez Rioja maintains the ingenious, deadpan fun of the original and adds a decidedly Spanish-sounding twist—*Guaca, guaca, cuac*—to this latest title of the amusing series about barnyard animals in search of mischief. Although *Granjero* Brown watches carefully over his animals, they still sneak off to a *Concurso de Talentos* (talent show) with jubilant results. Lewin's whimsical black lines with watercolors complement the romp.

Cronin, Doreen. *Pato para presidente. (Duck for President)* Illus: Betsy
Lewin. Translated by Alberto Jiménez Rioja. New York: Lectorum,
2004. 40p. ISBN: 1-930332-73-4. $15.99; ISBN: 1-930332-74-2. pap.
$5.99. Gr. K–2.

When *Pato* tires of doing his chores at the farm, he holds an elec-
tion to replace *Granjero* Brown. After he wins, *Pato* decides it's too
much work to run a farm, so he runs for governor, and subsequently for
president. Soon, however, he returns to the farm to write his *memorias*.
Like the original English edition, Jiménez Rioja's matter-of-fact Spanish rendition and Lewin's boisterous line-and-watercolor cartoons provide a humorous view of the U.S. electoral process.

Cronin, Doreen. *¡A tu ritmo! (Wiggle)* Illus: Scott Menchin. Translated by
Yanitzia Canetti. New York: Lectorum, 2007. 34p. ISBN: 978-1-933-
03205-4. $13.99. Gr. Preschool–K.

Translating Cronin's playful English text is certainly not an easy
task, yet Canetti's lively Spanish rendition will encourage young Spanish
speakers to be just as fun-loving and mirthful as the endearing dog who
shakes, jumps, dances, climbs, and swims *con alegría* (with joy). Of
course, Menchin's original ink-and-watercolor, cartoon-style illustrations
with appropriately placed collages depicting the high-spirited dog with
up-close and exaggerated perspectives add to the buoyant invitation,
¿Quieres divertirte más? (Do you want to enjoy yourself more?)

Crowther, Kitty. *¡Scric scrac bibib blub! (Scritch Scratch Bib Blub!)* Illus:
the author. Translated by Anna Coll-Vinent. Barcelona: Corimbo, 2005.
34p. ISBN: 84-8470-197-2. $17.95. Gr. K–2.

Jerónimo, a child frog, is afraid of darkness. Every night, *mamá*
and *papá* frog try to reassure him, but a constant noise *scric, scrac,
bibib, blub* won't let him sleep. Scared, Jerónimo goes to sleep in his
parents' bed and frustrated sleepy *papá* goes to sleep in Jerónimo's bed.
Suddenly, the same noise wakens *papá*, who now is eager to investigate. Together *papá* and Jerónimo find the culprit. Finally, they are
lulled to sleep by the *scric, scrac, bibib, blub* of a busy mole. The small
pencil and crayon illustrations of a close frog family and the simple text
make this a reassuring bedtime story. Originally published by L'ecole
des loisirs, Paris.

Cruz-Contarini, Rafael. *De la A a la Z con Cristóbal Colón. (From A to Z
with Christopher Columbus)* ISBN: 84-241-1818-9.

———. *De la A a la Z con Don Quijote.* *(From A to Z with Don Quijote)* ISBN: 84-241-1625-9.

———. *De la A a la Z con Mozart y la música.* *(From A to Z with Mozart and Music)* ISBN: 84-241-1697-6.

Ea. vol.: 32p. Illus: Rafael Salmerón. (Montaña Encantada) León: Everest, 2005–2006. pap. $9.95. Gr. 2–5.

Using the alphabet as a template, Cruz-Contarini's ingenious rhyming text and Salmerón's colorful computer-generated artwork introduce Columbus, Don Quijote and Mozart. From _A_merica to _I_ndias (*Las Indias por occidente,/eso creyó que encontró.*) to _S_anta María to _Z_arpar celebrate Christopher Columbus's explorations in *De la A a la Z con Cristóbal Colón.* From _A_venturas (Adventures) to _M_olinos (Windmills) to _Z_oraida introduce some of the best known characters, incidents, themes and places of Cervantes's classic novel in *De la A a la Z con Don Quijote.* From _A_madeus to _G_iovanni to _V_iolín and _Z_umbido highlight music and Mozart's life in *De la A a la Z con Mozart y la música.* These are not serious expositions; rather, they are lighthearted charming overviews that joyfully complement each topic.

Cucú—¡Te veo! (Peek-A-Boo). ISBN: 978-0-7641-6039-4.

Cucú—¡Te veo! En la selva (Peek-A-Boo-Jungle). ISBN: 978-0-7641-6040-0.

Ea. vol.: 10p. Illus: Francesca Ferri. New York: Barron's, 2007. $7.99. Ages 2–4.

Spanish-speaking toddlers will delight in playing peek-a-boo as they lift the well-constructed flaps while guessing which animal says *¡Miau, miau!,* or *¡Guau, guau!* or *¡Muu, muu!* up to a well-placed flap covering a mirror, surprising the young viewer (in *Cucú—¡Te veo!*). An elephant, a zebra, a giraffe, a hippo, a bear, a crocodile, and a lion can be discovered by lifting full-page flaps in *Cucú—¡Te veo! En la selva.* Especially appealing are the black-line and bright watercolors depicting cheery animals introducing themselves to the viewers.

Cumpiano, Ina. *Quinito's Neighborhood/El vecindario de Quinito.* Illus: José Ramírez. San Francisco: Children's Book Press, 2005. 24p. ISBN: 0-89239-209-6. $16.95. Gr. K–2.

In a simple, bilingual text, Quinito tells that his *mami* is a carpenter, his *papi,* a nurse, his *abuela* drives a big truck, and goes on to describe other people in his neighborhood: a dentist, a baker, a mailman, and a seamstress. Especially appealing are Ramirez's vivid illustrations

in bold primary colors depicting joyous scenes that resonate with the
tempo and tone of a busy Latino neighborhood.

Curtis, Jamie Lee. *Me gusto: Nunca viene mal un poquito de autoestima.*
(I'm Gonna Like Me: Letting Off a Little Self-Esteem) Illus: Laura Cor-
nell. Translated by Paula F. Bobadilla. Barcelona: Serres, 2005. 32p.
ISBN: 84-8488-149-0. $17.95. Gr.1–3.

In a cheerful lively mood, a boy and a girl encourage the young
to like themselves every single day and do all kinds of good deeds. Although the unrelenting, heavy-handed messages don't foster candid responses, these are provided in a most entertaining rhyming Spanish rendition that are made even more palatable by Cornell's always-ludicrous
ink-and-watercolor illustrations. Self-esteem with rhyme and humor.

Da Coll, Ivar. *El señor José Tomillo y María Juana. (Mr. José Tomillo and*
María Juana) Illus: the author. Bogotá: Grupo Editorial Norma, 2004.
48p. ISBN: 958-04-7662-4. pap. $11.95. Gr. K–2.

Two stories in rhyme are included in this unassuming paperback
publication. My favorite is *El señor José Tomillo*, which features the
protagonist *muy flaco y amarillo* (very thin and yellow) whose leisurely
walk is temporarily interrupted by a red louse. *María Juana* is a sweet
lady who enjoys taking care of her animals, who in turn watch over her.
The humorous, almost cartoonish illustrations and easy-to-read rhyming
text will appeal to beginning readers.

Danziger, Paula. *Es día de feria, Ámbar Dorado. (It's a Fair Day, Amber*
Brown) ISBN: 978-1-59820-596-1.
———. *Justo a tiempo, Ámbar Dorado. (It's Justin Time, Amber Brown)*
ISBN: 978-1-59820-595-4.
———. *Lista para segundo grado, Ámbar Dorado. (Get Ready for Second*
Grade, Amber Brown) ISBN: 978-1-59820-593-0.
———. *¡Qué viaje, Ámbar Dorado! (What a Trip, Amber Brown)* ISBN:
978-1-59820-592-3.
———. *Segundo grado es increíble, Ámbar Dorado. (Second Grade Rules,*
Amber Brown) ISBN: 978-1-59820-594-7.
Ea. vol.: 48p. Illus: Tony Ross. Translated by Enrique Mercado (A de
Ámbar) Miami: Alfaguara/Santillana USA, 2007. pap. $7.95. Gr. 1–3.

In the simple prose style of the original Amber Brown stories,
Mercado's clear Spanish renditions are just right for beginning Spanish
readers (and Spanish learners). Danziger's characteristic humor com-

bined with Ross's witty black-line and colorful spot artwork make
Ámbar Dorado's problems endearing, universal and ubiquitous. *Es día
de feria, Ámbar Dorado* shows Ámbar Dorado upset with her parents
for arguing on what she assumed would be a perfect day; instead, she
gets lost at a country fair. Unlike her best friend Justo, *Ámbar Dorado*
loves to measure time and hopes to receive a watch on her seventh
birthday in *Justo a tiempo, Ámbar Dorado.* Ámbar Dorado is nervous
about *Srta. Luz,* her new second grade teacher, but despite being in the
same class as mean Ana Burton, things turn out just fine in *Lista para
segundo grado, Ámbar Dorado.* Ámbar Dorado and her parents go to
the Poconos for two weeks with Ámbar's best friend Justo and his family, including his pesky younger brother, Dani, in *¡Qué viaje, Ámbar
Dorado!* Ámbar Dorado loves second grade, but she dislikes the rules,
especially when she needs to keep her desk clean in *Segundo grado es
increíble, Ámbar Dorado.*

Dautremer, Rébecca. *Enamorados. (In Love)* Illus: the author. Translated
by Esther Rubio and Chusa Hernández. Madrid: Kókinos, 2003. 34p.
ISBN: 84-88342-47-0. $17.95. Gr. 2–4.

   When Ernesto persists in annoying Salomé (by pulling her hair,
taking her hat, snatching her eyeglasses), her mother concludes that he
is in love with her but doesn't know how to tell her. Salomé, who
doesn't know what being in love means, is confused. Her friends, however, are eager to explain: Guillermo says that it's like a fall, Mateo says
that it's a fairy tale, Nicolás that it's being sad, Lucas that it's being hyp-
notized, Serena giggles and explains that lovers kiss, hold hands and
make babies and so forth. So, when Ernesto returns to pester Salomé,
she wishes that her friends would urgently explain to him what it means
to be in love. The dreamlike, cartoonish illustrations in bright reds and
pinks add a fantastic tone to this amusing definition of the always mys-
tifying condition. Some parents might object to Serena's views on love,
but children will appreciate the honesty and rejoice on the contradictions. Originally published by Hachette Livre, Paris.

Davis, Katie. *¿Quién salta? (Who Hops?)* Illus: the author. Translated by
F. Isabel Campoy. New York: Harcourt, 2005. 36p. ISBN: 0-15-205602-5.
Ages 2–4.

   Now available in board book format with the same stylized illustrations in flashy colors, thick outlines and bold black simple texts, this
is a lively review of animals that hop—frogs, rabbits and kangaroos—

in contrast to an animal that doesn't hop—a cow—with the explanation: *Las vacas mugen y dan leche; pero no saltan!* (Cows moo and give milk, but they don't hop!) Other animals swim, or crawl, or fly and are followed by an animal that obviously doesn't. This simple guessing game will appeal to the very young and their parents.

Delval, Marie-Hélène. *A Tigretón le gusta moverse. (Tigretón Likes to Move)* ISBN: 84-7864-709-0.
——. *Burrito escucha los ruidos. (Burrito Hears Noises)* ISBN: 84-7864-710-4.
——. *¿Cómo estás, Pequeño Panda? (How are You Little Panda?)* ISBN: 84-7864-707-4.
——. *Lolo y Lorito son muy educados. (Lolo and Lorito Are Very Well Educated)* ISBN: 84-7864-708-2.
Ea. vol.: 16p. Illus: Thierry Courtin. Translated by Emilia Hernández. (Palabras Menudas) Barcelona: Combel, 2004. $10.95. Ages 2–4.

Like the previous four titles in this delightful, well-constructed board book series, originally published by Bayard Jeunesse, Paris, these encourage the very young to take note and participate. Tigretón, a lively young tiger, enjoys a day in the park as he splashes in the water, slides, climbs, runs and swings in *A Tigretón le gusta moverse.* As Burrito, a busy donkey, cleans the house, he hears the vacuum cleaner, washing machine, hot water boiling and even the door bell in *Burrito escucha los ruidos.* Little Panda tells when he is feeling happy, surprised, upset, sad, fearful and proud in *¿Cómo estás, Pequeño Panda?* Lolo and Lorito, two friendly parrots, demonstrate their good manners in *Lolo y Lorito son muy educados.* Parents looking for attractive board books with colorful illustrations for their toddlers should certainly consider this series.

Denou, Violeta. *Teo en la nieve (Teo in the Snow)* Illus: the author. (Teo Descubre el Mundo) Barcelona: Planeta, 2005. 48p. ISBN: 84-7176-343-5. $17.95. Ages 4–7.

Like the previous 38 titles in this series with Denou's wonderfully detailed and amusing double-page spreads, this one features Teo and his friends on an overnight winter excursion in the mountains. A group of rambunctious boys and girls enjoy making a snow man, skating on a pond, going on a sleigh ride and, finally, skiing down the mountain. Although Teo falls and has to have his leg in a cast, he will soon be ready to run and play again. Two Peninsular Spanish conjugations (*soltádme* and *alborotéis*) will not bother young Spanish speakers from the Americas. But children will surely want to skip the dull, didactic guide at the end that will spoil all the fun winter activities.

Dodd, Emma. *Grande o pequeña es mi pelota: El libro de los contrarios. (Big, Small, Little Red Ball: A Changing Book of Opposites)* Illus: the author. Translated by Luz Orihuela. Barcelona: Combel, 2004. 18p. ISBN: 84-7864-816-X. $15.95. Ages 2–4.

The very young are introduced to opposites in this well-constructed board book where appropriately placed pull-the-tabs change the display featured in the acetate pictures. From *dormido* (asleep) to *despierto* (awake) to *arriba* (up) to *abajo* (down) preschoolers can participate in identifying opposites as they enjoy the colorful illustrations against a flat background.

Donaldson, Julia. *Un osito se cae de la cama. (One Ted Falls Out of Bed)* Illus: Anna Currey. Translated by Josefina Cabal i Guerrero. Barcelona: Juventud, 2006. 26p. ISBN: 84-261-3514-5. $15.95. Ages 2–4.

When teddy bear falls out of a boy's bed, he tries and tries to get back in. Because the boy is sound asleep, teddy bear reluctantly agrees to play with three mice, drink tea with six dolls, listen to nine frogs play music and other engaging activities. As a result of the commotion, the boy wakes up and, lovingly, reaches out for teddy bear. Now both are restfully back in bed. Currey's ink-and-watercolor illustrations provide the right tone to this warm large-format bedtime story, originally published by MacMillan, London.

Dunbar, Polly. *Azul. (Dog Blue)* Illus: the author. Translated by Raquel Mancera. Barcelona: Serres, 2004. 34p. ISBN: 84-8488-194-6. $15.95. Gr. Preschool–K.

Young Mario, who loves the color blue, is eager to have a blue dog. As he pretends he has a blue dog, a lonely spotted dog is looking for an owner. Although disappointed, Mario names his dog *Azul* (Blue) and they become the perfect couple. The endearing pencil-and-watercolor illustrations against soft pastel backgrounds and the easy-to-understand Spanish text will make dog lovers out of most young listeners/ viewers.

Dunbar, Polly. *Lola con alas. (Flyaway Katie)* Illus: the author. Translated by Raquel Mancera. Barcelona: Serres, 2004. 34p. ISBN: 84-8488-152-0. $12.95. Gr. Preschool–2.

Young Lola is feeling sad and everything looks gray to her. But when she gazes at a colorful painting in her bedroom, she decides that *Ese sí que sería un buen sitio para vivir.* (That would be a much better place to be.) Hence, she adds color to *un sombrero verde* (a green hat), *leotardos amarillos* (yellow tights), *zapatos azules* (blue shoes) until she has so much color that she begins to dance, smile and play with her imaginary friends. Finally, it's time to take a bath. The whimsical framed illustrations that build up to a multicolored splash of colorful birds and bright feathers and the simple Spanish text will encourage Spanish learners to join Lola's colorful reverie.

Duquennoy, Jacques. *Las cataratas del Niágara. (Niagara Falls)* ISBN: 84-263-5228-6.
—— . *Los fantasmillas. (The Little Ghosts)* ISBN: 84-263-5225-1.
—— . *Una sorpresa para Kiki. (A Surprise for Kiki)* ISBN: 84-263-5227-8.
—— . *Las travesuras de Nessie. (Nessie's Pranks)* ISBN: 84-263-5224-3.
—— . *¡Vivan los novios! (Long Live the Bride and Groom!)* ISBN: 84-263-5226-X.
Ea. vol.: 28p. Translated by Violante Krahe. (La Pandilla Fantasma) Zaragoza: Edelvives, 2004–2005. $11.95 Gr. 2–4.

With a minimum of text and attention-grabbing visuals, these graphic stories, full of humor and whimsy, are sure to entertain. Reluctant readers will be intrigued by the black background contrasted by the whimsically expressive lines of the white ghosts as they are involved in not-so-judicious endeavors. Four young ghosts survive a perilous canoe trip over the Niagara Falls in *Las cataratas del Niágara.* As the adult ghosts prepare dinner, the little ones find ways to be disruptive in *Los fantasmillas.* Kiki, a bored fish in a fish bowl, is happily surprised by the ghost-provoked flood in *Una sorpresa para Kiki.* Nessie, a green dinosaur, makes life difficult for the ghosts in *Las travesuras de Nessie.* Although the ghosts and *tatarabuela* (great-grandmother) Mimí are invited to a wedding, the bride and groom are definitely a surprise in *¡Vivan los novios!*

Duran, Teresa. *Mamás a porrillo. (Mothers Galore)* Illus: Quelot. Barcelona: La Galera, 2006. 24p. ISBN: 84-246-2339-8. $14.95. Gr. Preschool–2.
When little Juan complains about his mother to his big strong father, his father is eager to help him find another mother. He wants a mother that tickles him, and hugs him and lets him sleep in her bed.

Papa knows exactly where to find one. But Juan won't settle for *Mamá Clueca* (Mother Hen), nor for *Mamá Vaca* (Mother Cow), nor for *Mamá Raposa* (Mother Fox). He states: *¡Quiero a mi mamá!* (I want my mother!) And Papa agrees. He too prefers Juan's mother. Quelot's exaggerated, simply drawn watercolor illustrations with no details to break up the flat bright colors used on the background provide a humorous tone to the unconstrained childlike text and expressions. Spanish-speaking youngsters will empathize with Juan's feelings.

Eastman, P. D. *El mejor nido. (The Best Nest)* Illus: the author. Translated by Teresa Mlawer. New York: Lectorum, 2005. 64p. ISBN: 1-930332-84-X. $7.20. Gr. K–2.

    Sra. Pájaro (Mrs. Bird) is eager for a new place to build a nest, so *Sr. Pájaro* (Mr. Bird) reluctantly complies. After a discouraging search, they happily discover that *no hay mejor nido,/que un viejo nido* (the best nest is an old nest). Eastman's pencil-and-watercolor cartoons maintain the jocose tone in this playful rhyming Spanish rendition, just right for beginning readers.

Echevarría, Pablo. *Una amistad peligrosa. (A Dangerous Friendship)* Illus: the author. Madrid: SM, 2004. 30p. ISBN: 84-675-0284-3. $19.95. Gr. 1–3.

    Dorabella, a beautiful carrier pigeon, is eager to start her new job carrying messages. Her jealous colleagues make sure she is assigned to deliver the mail to *conde de Almaviva*, the much-feared fox of the forest. Confidently and with great pride, she finds his home, and, surprisingly, is received with kindness and exquisite gifts. When she shares her gifts with her mean colleagues they, in turn, feel remorseful. Dorabella now knows it is time to go. Fortunately, Echevarría's sensitive water color and meticulous silhouette illustrations, which received the 2004 award for illustrations by the Fundación Santa María, lighten the author's moralistic intent.

Eck, Kristin. *Colores en mi casa. (Colors In My House)* ISBN: 1-4042-7588-6.
———. *Opuestos. (Opposites)* ISBN: 1-4042-7586-X.
Harte, May. *1 2 3 en mi casa. (1 2 3 at Home)* ISBN: 1-4042-7585-1.
Zuravicky, Orli. *Caritas de bebé. (Babies Everywhere)* ISBN: 1-4042-7590-8.
    Ea. vol.: 16p. New York: Rosen, 2006. $10.75. Ages 1–3.

These attractive, well-constructed board books are the right size (5½" × 5½") and shape for the baby and toddler sets. White backgrounds, simple texts and clear color photographs encourage the young to find specific colors found in different rooms of a house (*Colores en mi casa*), identify opposites (*Opuestos*), count common objects (*1 2 3 en mi casa*) and identify babies' emotions (*Caritas de bebé*). As opposed to other titles in this series, these titles include the definite articles in the labels, which are certainly needed for all Spanish learners.

Eduar, Gilles. *El planeta de la A a la Z.* (*The Planet from A to Z*) Illus: the author. Translated by Elodie Bourgeois. Barcelona: Juventud, 2004. 50p. ISBN: 84-261-3384-3. $16.95. Gr. K–2.

With Adela, a giraffe, and Zobra, a zebra, readers are encouraged to travel the world to discover new landscapes, animals, pastimes, and customs while identifying 500 new words and images. From a farewell party in Africa to a carnival in Brazil, to a sleigh race in Alaska, this joyous introduction to the five continents, originally published by Jeunesse, Paris, has amusing watercolor illustrations in a large-format publication.

Eduar, Gilles. *¡Todos al tren!* (*Tralala Train Train*) Illus: the author. Translated by Elodie Bourgeois. Barcelona: Juventud, 2007. 14p. ISBN: 978-84-261-3562-9. $16.95. Ages 2–5.

This most appealing counting book with thick black lines and bright watercolor illustrations not only encourages toddlers to count to ten but it also follows the wedding of two hippos. After the wedding, they get on a train conducted by *1 tapir, 2 hipopótamos se quieren* (2 hippos in love), 3 crocodiles watch over the rings, up to *¡10 pasajeros están invitados a la boda más bonita del año!* (10 passengers are invited to the most beautiful wedding of the year!) Designed in a foldout format that can be easily opened to show happy animals on a fully loaded train in motion. Originally published by Jeunesse, Paris.

Ellery, Tom, and Amanda Ellery. *If I Had a Dragon/Si yo tuviera un dragón.* Illus: the authors. Translated by Teresa Mlawer. New York: Lectorum, 2006. 40p. ISBN: 1-933032-16-2. $12.99. Gr. Preschool–2.

Upset because his mother sends him to play with his toddler brother, a boy wishes that his brother could turn into a truly fun companion—like a huge, green dragon. But he really can't play basketball with the dragon, or swim in the pool, or play hide-and-seek, or go to a movie. So he concludes: *I guess a dragon doesn't make a very good playmate after all/Al fin y al cabo, quizás un dragón no sea el mejor compañero de juegos.* And he rushes home to play with his brother. The full-page, amusing cartoon illustrations with splashes of bright colors are as expressive as the originals in the English-only edition. The well-done Spanish rendition, which follows the English in the same color, size and font, will delight bilingual book devotees. However, newly independent readers as well as English and Spanish learners will be confused by the identical texts.

Ely, Lesley. *Cuidando a Louis. (Looking After Louis)* Illus: Polly Dunbar. Translated by Paula F. Bobadilla. Barcelona: Ediciones Serres, 2004. 26p. ISBN: 84-8488-115-6. $14.95. Gr. 1–3.

In the first-person point of view of a little girl who tells about Louis, an autistic boy in her class, young Spanish speakers are exposed to the detachment, constant repetition, isolation and other behavior of children afflicted with autism. Dunbar's almost cartoonish ink and watercolor illustrations realistically depict children in the classroom and in the playground encouraging Louis to get involved. And the unaffected Spanish rendition, with its kind and sensitive message: *Creo que podemos saltarnos las normas por la gente especial* (It's OK to break rules for special people), will be understood by the young. An afterword directed to adults explains the special needs of autistic children.

Emberley, Rebecca. *My City/Mi Ciudad.* ISBN: 0-316-00051-5.
———. *My Room/Mi Cuarto.* ISBN: 0-316-00052-3.
———. *My School/Mi Escuela.* ISBN: 0-316-00050-7.
Ea. vol.: 20p. Illus: the author. Boston: Little, Brown and Company, 2005. $6.95. Ages 2–4.

Like the previous titles in this series, these include colorful sculpted images through which the very young are introduced to the city, a bedrooom, and a school in these eye-catching bilingual (English-Spanish) board books. The simplicity and allure of the illustrations are just right for the little ones.

Escudié, René. *Paco y Álvaro. (Paco and Álvaro)* Illus: Alises Wensell. Translated by P. Rozarena. Zaragoza: Edelvives, 2004. 35p. ISBN: 84-263-5208-1. pap. $10.95. Gr. 2–4.

Paco, who lives in a trailer house with blue curtains, and his neighbor Alvaro, who lives in an apartment with green curtains, go to the same school. But their mothers don't allow them to play together because they insist that the boys are very different. After the boys get lost on a school field trip, they enjoy each other's company and even their mothers finally realize how similar their sons are. The playful, saccharin-free, full-page illustrations provide an honest tone to this story about friendship and intolerance.

Falconer, Ian. *Olivia Counts/Cuenta.* ISBN: 1-930332-89-0.
———. *Olivia's Opposites/Olivia y los opuestos.* ISBN: 1-930332-90-4.
Ea. vol.: 14p. Illus: the author. Translated by Sabrina Abreu. New York: Lectorum, 2005. $6.99. Ages 1–3.

Olivia, an enchanting little pig, will delight English and Spanish learners as they learn to count to ten (*Olivia Counts/Cuenta*) and discover the concept of opposites (*Olivia's Opposites/Olivia y los opuestos*). Especially appropriate for second-language-learners are the clear bilingual captions in different fonts—English text followed by the Spanish. Yet, it is Falconer's whimsical black-and-white illustrations with splashes of bright red that make these sturdy board books truly special.

Falwell, Cathryn. *Los dibujos de David. (David's Drawings)* Illus: the author. Translated by Eida de la Vega. New York: Lee & Low, 2005. 30p. ISBN: 1-58430-258-5. pap. $7.95. Gr. Preschool–2.

On his way to school, David, a shy boy, sees a beautiful tree, which he is eager to draw. When he does, his classmates contribute their own suggestions: more color, *hierba verde* (green grass), *una niña* (a girl), clouds and birds. At the end of the day, he has a beautiful *Dibujo de la clase* (Our Class Picture) and many delighted new friends. The happy multiethnic children are joyously depicted in Falwell's cut-paper-and-fabric collages. De la Vega's lucid Spanish rendition maintains the affable tone of the original.

Fleming, Candance. *¡Ñam!¡Ñam!¡Ñam! (Muncha! Muncha! Muncha!)* Illus: G. Brian Karas. Translated by Alejandra Schmidt. New York: Lectorum, 2007. 32p. ISBN: 978-1-933032-35-1. $15.95. Gr. K–2.

With the humor and irresistible perkiness of the original, Schmidt's Spanish rendition adds a decidedly playful Spanish onomatopoeia to *el señor McGreely's* dreams of soon enjoying his fresh vegetables: *¡Mmmmm, qué rico!* . . . *¡Muy pronto me llenaré la barriga con verduras frescas y crujientes! (Yum! Yum! Yummy!* . . . *I'll soon fill* *my tummy with crisp, fresh veggies!* Although *¡Tipi, tipi, tipi, tun!,* the three naughty rabbits insist on nibbling his crop, *el señor McGreely* is determined to protect his garden, but *¡Ñam! ¡Ñam! ¡Ñam!* the rabbits seem to always find a way to enjoy the delicious carrots. Karas's child-like pencil, gouache and acrylic illustrations amusingly convey the plucky determination of both gardener and rabbits. Young Spanish speakers will be as surprised with the rabbits' tenacity as the astonished farmer.

Gauch, Patricia Lee. *Tanya y las zapatillas rojas. (Tanya and the Red Shoes)* Illus: Satomi Ichikawa. Translated by Miguel Ángel Mendo. Barcelona: Serres, 2005. 32p. ISBN: 84-8488-197-0. $16.95. Gr K–3.

From the first *Baila, Tanya* (2002) *(Dance, Tanya)* to the subsequent titles in which young Tanya is eager to dance, she now dreams of discarding her old soft ballet slippers and flying on toe shoes. When the ballet teacher finally asks the students to dance with elegant, new point shoes, she finds out about blisters and pain and awkward movements. With the encouragement of her older sister, and with lots of practice and time, she becomes an accomplished *sur pointes* dancer. The world of determined ballet students is realistically depicted through Ichikawa's fluid, line-and-watercolor illustrations and Mendo's upbeat Spanish rendition, with a few Peninsular Spanish conjugations—*vais, tenéis.*

Gay, Marie-Louise. *Estela, princesa de la noche. (Stella, Princess of the Sky)* Illus: the author. Translated by Verónica Uribe. Caracas: Ekaré, 2004. 32p. ISBN: 980-257-304-3. pap $8.95. Gr. Preschool–1.

As in the previous Estela titles, the older sister now explains to her always-questioning younger brother, Samuel, why the sun is red at sundown, why raccoons wear masks, and other aspects about the natural world. In the same gentle reassuring tone of the original, first published by Groundwood, Uribe's simple Spanish rendition conveys comforting information about the sky, the sun, the stars, fireflies, and other night animals that the patient sister is keen to provide to her younger brother. Gay's whimsical watercolor illustrations add to this playful introduction to nighttime.

Gebhard, Wilfried. *Lo que Eduardo sabe hacer (What Eddie Can Do)* Illus: the author. Translated by Maria Fernanda Pulido Duarte. La Jolla, CA: Kane/Miller, 2007. 26p. ISBN: 978-1-933605-40-1. pap. $7.95. Gr. Preschool–1.

Although Eduardo is too busy to learn how to tie his shoelaces, he is eager to go deep-sea diving, to explore a cave and to travel through space. But when he attempts to save his neighbor from a frightening, two-tailed monster, he runs to mother for a quick lesson in shoelace tying. The humorous cartoonlike, ink-and-watercolor illustrations and Pulido Duarte's brief, straightforward Spanish rendition are sure to appeal to reluctant young Spanish speakers who have yet to master tying knots. Originally published in Germany.

Genechten, Guido van. *La pequeña canguro. (Little Kangaroo)* Illus: the author. Translated by Alberto Jiménez Rioja. New York: Lectorum, 2006. 26p. ISBN: 1-933032-00-6. $12.80. Gr. Preschool–K.

Despite Mama Kangaroo's encouragement, Little Kangaroo doesn't want out of her pouch. She prefers its comfort, warmth and peacefulness as opposed to the busy world around her. Yet, she quickly changes her mind when she sees a young kangaroo happily hopping nearby and doesn't hesitate to discover the world with him. The pleasing full-page illustrations, of a devoted Mama Kangaroo patiently reassuring her cautious little one, are as comforting as Jiménez Rioja's tender Spanish rendition. Some adults, however, may object to the anthropomorphism and the undisguised didactic intent.

Gisbert, Montse. *El abecedario fantástico de Patam, el elefante. (The Fantastic ABC of Patam, the Elephant)* Valencia: Tàndem, 2006. 48p. ISBN: 84-8131-524-9. $16.95. Gr. K–2.

In this fanciful ABC, Patam, a charming, five-legged elephant, highlights each letter of the Spanish alphabet. Appealing double-page watercolor illustrations, in soft pastel shades with splashes of bright colors, and a simple sentence focus on a specific letter (*Llena la BAÑERA de BOTONES; Da PERAS a los PECES*). Young Spanish learners will enjoy practicing their ABCs with a whimsical elephant.

Gotlibowski, Leicia, adapter. *La Caperucita Roja. (Little Red Riding Hood)* Illus: the adapter. Buenos Aires: Del Eclipse, 2006. 30p. ISBN: 987-9011-76-7. pap. $11.95. Gr. Preschool–2.

Gotlibowski's version of "Little Red Riding Hood" combines elements and illustrations of Queen Marie Antoinette of France (1774–1793) with modern appliances and a few Argentine Spanish terms (here *Caperucita Roja* takes a *tortilla* (Argentine cake) and *mantequilla* (butter) to her grandmother). As in the traditional version, she stops to chat with a sly wolf, who then hurries ahead of her, gobbles up *Abuelita,* and does the same thing to *Caperucita* when she arrives. And of course the *moraleja* warns young girls about dangerous wolves, especially the *Lobos empalagosos* (fawning wolves). This is indeed an interesting and most unique version of the popular tale with little-known historical references and observations.

Gray, Kes. *Mi hermanita es súper. (Ever So, Ever So)* Illus: Sarah Nayler. Translated by Marta Ansón Balmaseda. Barcelona: Serres, 2004. 26p. ISBN: 84-8488-125-3. $12.95. Gr. Preschool–2.

In an excited first-person voice, a young girl relates everyone's enthusiasm when *mamá* and *papá* bring home new-born Susana, who she describes as *súper-pequeña* (ever so small) and *súper-guapa* (ever so pretty). Although she dirties eight diapers, papá says she is *súper-inteligente* (ever so intelligent), *Tía* Debbie says she is *súper-fuerte* (ever so strong) and so forth. Only when the protagonist learns to care for baby Susana is she described as *súper-buena* (ever so good) and *súper-mayor* (ever so big sister). The bold humorous cartoon illustrations with bright colors and the simple repetitive text make this a fantastic depiction of children's feelings regarding a new sibling. Originally published by Hodder Children's Books, London.

Guilloppé, Antoine. *¿Cuál es mi color? (What Color Am I?)* Illus: Géraldine Alibeu. Translated by Ana Rey Kochinke. Madrid: Anaya, 2006. 32p. ISBN: 84-667-5194-7. $13.95. Gr. K–2.

In a first-person point of view, a black Muslim boy born in Spain describes his conflicting thoughts regarding his identity. The simple childlike black-line and watercolor illustrations, although a bit stark, poignantly complement the direct most accessible text. The boy's paradoxical speculations (*Para los árabes, soy español.* (For the Arabs, I am a Spaniard.) *Pero los españoles me dicen que soy un extranjero.* (But the Spaniards tell me I'm a foreigner.)) highlight the rejection and contradictions experienced by immigrant children. Fortunately, his beloved dog understands: *¡Él es de muchos colores!* (He is multi-colored!)

Gusti. *La mosca. (The Fly)* Illus: the author. Mexico: Serres, 2005. 34p. ISBN: 970-9705-03-2. $16.99. Gr. K–2.

When a jubilant fly wakes up, she tells herself, *Hoy me toca 'bañarme.'* (Today is my day to take a bath). After careful preparations, she takes a big dive and delights as she sings and dances in the water.

Suddenly, however, everything goes dark, a loud noise ensues and a strange, brown object drops down. When the water begins to swirl, the fly makes a quick escape and hears a voice *¡Mamá, mamá! He terminado* (Mama! Mama! I'm done). The annoyed fly promises herself never to take a bath again. The stylized watercolor and mixed-media illustrations, which combine paper sculptures, toys and fabrics, in exaggerated perspectives add a sense of mirth and mischief to this story that some purist adults will object to. Although a fly bathing in a toilet bowl and a young child relieving himself are certainly incongruous events, young Spanish speakers will find the story most amusing and the whimsical clear, easy-to-read text makes it even more fun.

Guy, Ginger Foglesong. *¡Perros! ¡Perros! Dogs! Dogs!* Illus: Sharon Glick. New York: Greenwillow, 2006. 32p. ISBN: 978-0-06-083574-3. $15.99. Gr. Preschool–2.

With mirth and pizzazz, young bilingual readers are introduced to a wide selection of dogs, who in turn demonstrate the concept of opposites. Glick's especially engaging and humorous illustrations, with bold black lines and bright watercolors, add a sense of energy to these fun-loving, yet diverse dogs. In simple bilingual phrases (*¡Muchos perros! Lots of dogs*) young readers follow *Perro grande. Perro chico. Big dog. Little dog* and many others, to find out *¿Adónde van? Where are they going?* with a concluding joyful *¡Splash!* into a pond. It is unfortunate, however, that the Spanish and English texts are presented in the same color, size and style of font, thereby certainly confusing both English and Spanish beginning readers.

Haan, Linda de. *Rey y rey (King and King)* Illus: Stern Nijland. Barcelona: Serres, 2004. 30p. ISBN: 84-8488-147-4. $12.95. Gr. K–3.

There is nothing traditional about this tale about an old queen who insists that the prince get married and take over as king. Although he asserts that *no conozco a ninguna princesa que me guste* (I don't know any princess that I like), the queen proceeds with a search for a suitable mate. He doesn't care for fat *princesa Aria* from Austria, or juggler *princesa* Dolly from Texas, or an ugly *princesa* from Greenland, or any other. But, as soon as he sees *príncipe Azul* (Blue Prince), he knows he is the right one. They fall in love, get married and live happily together. The avant-garde, colorful collages, with exaggerated comic and grotesque princesses and royalty, set the stage for this whimsical boy-meets-boy story that is sure to please cutting-edge readers/viewers and displease those with a more conventional bent. Originally published in Holland and later in an English translation.

Harper, Piers. *Osito blanco. (Snow Bear)* Illus: Piers Harper. Translated by Christianne Reyes. Barcelona: Juventud, 2003. 22p. ISBN: 84-261-3319-3 $16.95. Gr. Preschool–2.

   A young polar bear is eager to see the world. *Mamá* Bear encourages him to go, but warns him to stay close so she can watch him. *Osito* is marveled at the beautiful surroundings, plays with a young seal and a kind reindeer and, later, when he is hungry and tired, decides to find his mother. A friendly Eskimo girl knows exactly where to take him. A happy *Osito* cuddles in his mother's arms as he concludes, *pero estar en casa contigo es lo mejor* (but to be home with you is the best thing in the world). The eye-catching double-page spreads depicting gorgeous North Pole landscapes are further enhanced by a velvety-like material on soft-to-touch furry animals. Despite the bland story, young children will be attracted to the appealing oversized spreads with softly textured animal characters.

Hausfater-Douïeb, Rachel. *El niño estrella. (The Child Star)* Illus: Oliver Latyk. Zaragoza: Edelvives, 2003. 26p. ISBN: 84-263-5007-0. $16.95. Gr. 1–3.

   Using a six-pointed star as a metaphor, a young boy, who does not know its meaning, experiences the shame and rejection of having to wear one on his clothing. In a very simple direct text (*Hace años en un rico país,/un loco obligó/a los que consideraba distintos . . .* (Many years ago in a rich country/a crazy man commanded/those he considered different . . .)), this story narrates the horrors of the Nazi regime in Europe in a manner that even the young can understand. Without stressing the specific terrors committed against individual groups, it mentions the trains that took people away, the need for the boy to remain in hiding, and, finally, the kindness of some people who showed the boy how to enjoy sunlight again. Appropriately stark full-page watercolors against a deep blue or red sky convey strength and immediacy to the illustrations, which include a lonely innocent boy with a big yellow star on his shirt and the silhouettes of Nazi soldiers wearing a big bright swastika. Originally published by Casterman, Brussels, this is a poingnant portrayal of a sad period in Europe's history.

Heide, Florence Parry. *¡Qué horror! (Some Things Are Scary)* Illus: Jules Feiffer. Translated by Marta Ansón. Barcelona: Serres, 2004. 32p. ISBN: 84-8488-157-1. $12.95. Gr. Preschool–2.

This joyous Spanish rendition, which perfectly captures a small child's anxieties and fears, is made even more real with Feiffer's exaggerated felt-tip marker and watercolor cartoons. From *Un abrazo de alquien que no te gusta . . .* (Getting hugged by someone you don't like) to *Cuesta abajo, con patines y sin frenos* (Skating downhill when you haven't learned how to stop) and other stressful and comical situations, these unpleasant scenarios are as disagreeable as they are heartfelt and *¡Qué horror!* (scary). Young Spanish speakers will certainly identify with this honest depiction, from a child's viewpoint, of life's scary things.

Henkes, Kevin. *Owen. (Owen)* Illus: the author. Translated by Ma. Luz Castela Gil-Toresano. León: Everest, 2006. 24p. ISBN: 84-241-1519-8. pap. $10.95. Gr. Preschool–2.

Henkes's 1994 Caldecott Honor book about Owen, a resourceful mouse, who outmaneuvers his parents when they try to take away *Pelusilla*, his security blanket, is now available in paperback with Castela's joyous Spanish rendition. Spanish-speaking children will delight in Henkes's endearing watercolors and will rejoice with the satisfying ending, especially when *mamá* mouse cuts the blanket into handkerchiefs so that Owen can take his security with him wherever he goes. Despite the fact that security "blankets" are not as common in Spanish-speaking countries, young Spanish speakers and their parents will empathize with Owen's sad predicament.

Henkes, Kevin. *La primera luna llena de Gatita. (Kitten's First Full Moon)* Illus: the author. Translated by Osvaldo Blanco. New York: HarperCollins/Greenwillow, 2006. 30p. ISBN: 0-06-087223-3. $16.99. Gr. Preschool–K.

When *Gatita* (Kitten) mistakes the full moon for a bowl of milk, she is determined to reach it. Her efforts end up with *un insecto en la lengua* (A bug on her tongue), a hard tumble down the stairs and other frustrations. Finally, *mojada y triste y cansada y con hambre* (wet and sad and tired and hungry), she returns home to find a bowl of milk on the porch waiting for her. Henkes's expressive, 2005 Caldecott-award-winning black-and-white bold illustrations with soft shades of gray and cream are as outstanding as Blanco's always distinguished Spanish rendition that resonates with the simple rhythmic refrain of the original text. This is one of the best U.S. offerings for young Spanish speakers and Spanish learners published in 2006.

Hicks, Barbara Jean. *¡Ñec-Ñec, ris-ras! (Jitterbug Jam)* Illus: Alexis Deacon. Translated by Raquel Solà. Barcelona: Juventud, 2004. 32p. ISBN: 84-261-3382-7. $15.95. Gr. K–3.

Bubú, a young monster who is afraid to sleep in his own bed, is sure that a boy is hiding beneath it. Although Bubú's older brother thinks he is a *miedica* (fraidy-cat), *abuelo Bu* (grandpa Bu) knows exactly how to scare monsters away. Printed on elegant, buff-colored paper and with Deacon's original, ink-and-watercolor artwork that combines traditional florid illustrations with contemporary graphic novel design features, this fluid Spanish rendition will reassure young Spanish-speaking nighttime worriers as they confront their own *monstruos* (monsters). A few Spanish speakers from the Americas will note some Peninsular Spanish pronouns and conjugations, e.g., *os podéis, venid, sabéis.*

Hobbie, Holly. *Choni y Chano: En la cima del mundo. (Toot and Puddle: Top of the World)* Illus: the author. Translated by Teresa Blanch. Barcelona: Edebé, 2004. 32p. ISBN: 84-236-7027-9. $16.95. Gr. Preschool–2.

When Choni, a pig who loves to travel, takes a walk and doesn't return home, Chano worries and sets out to find him. Chano correctly guesses that Choni might have gone to Provenza, in France. Together they tour France and Nepal; finally they decide to return home. Originally published by Little Brown, this new title of the winsome pig adventures includes the same sweet endearing watercolors that always appeal to young Spanish-speaking travelers-to-be.

Hoff, Syd. *Danielito y el dinosaurio. (Danny and the Dinosaur)* Illus: the author. Revised translation by Teresa Mlawer. New York: Lectorum Publications, 2008. 64p. ISBN: 978-1-933032-38-2. pap. $7.20. Gr. 1–3.

Danny's adventures with the friendly dinosaur are now available in this revised Spanish translation for all Spanish-speaking readers to enjoy. The whimsical line illustrations and the fast-paced Spanish translation are as diverting as the original version.

Hong, Chen Yiang. *Pequeño Águila. (Little Eagle)* Illus: the author. Translated by Julia Vinent. Barcelona: Corimbo, 2004. 32p. ISBN: 84-8470-142-5. $19.95. Gr. K–3.

Set in 15th-century China, this gentle Spanish rendition tells about Master Yang and his longtime student, *Pequeño Águila*, who, through perseverance and hard work, learns the Chinese martial art, kung fu. Exquisite black-ink and watercolor illustrations depicting traditional Chinese scenes are interspersed with flexible fluid lines that portray the sharp blows and kicks characteristic of this sport. A brief historical introduction and an afterword explaining this martial art complements this well-told story, originally published by L'ecole des loisirs, Paris.

Horáček, Petr. *Mariposa, Mariposa. (Butterfly Butterfly)* Illus: the author. Translated by Esther Rubio. Madrid: Kókinos, 2007. 28p. ISBN: 978-84-96629-24-0. $15.95. Gr. Preschool–K.

Lucía is delighted to play with a beautiful butterfly, but the following day she can't see her anywhere. She finds *un gusano rosa* (a pink worm), *una araña marrón* (a brown spider), *un escarabajo verde* (a green beetle) and other colorful creatures. Tired, she lies down in the grass and, unexpectedly, the butterfly reappears (as it pops up from the double-page spread). Horáček striking acrylic illustrations, well-placed die holes and gorgeous pop-up butterfly are sure to intrigue nature lovers and color enthusiasts.

Isaías, Isabel. *¿Qué te picó la hormiga de los pies a la barriga? (What Did the Ant Bite You from Your Feet to Your Stomach?)* 16p. Illus: Pablo Prestifilippo. ISBN: 968-494-140-4.

Núñez, Alonso. *Dime Traviesa, ¿qué fruta es ésa? (Tell Me Traviesa, What Fruit Is That?)* 18p. Illus: Irina Botcharova. ISBN: 968-494-160-9.

——. *¿Dónde está Juan Perol, el caracol? (Where Is Juan Perol, the Snail?)* 18p. Illus: Claudia Legnazzi. ISBN: 968-494-139-0.

Serrano, Pablo. *Juego de dedos. (Finger Games)* 14p. Illus: Rogelio Rangel. ISBN: 968-494-161-7.

Solinis, Tessie. *Inés tres pies. (Three-feet Inés)* 22p. Illus: Alejandra Barba. ISBN: 968-494-162-5.

Ea. vol.: Mexico: Cidcli, 2003–2004. Gr. Preschool.

With a joyous, rhyming text and eye-catching color photos and illustrations, these charming well-constructed board books are sure to appeal to inquisitive toddlers. A pesky ant insists on annoying and biting a toddler in several parts of his/her body in *¿Qué te picó la hormiga de los pies a la barriga?* A little girl tells about how several fruits such as papayas, pineapples, avocados, and bananas grow in *Dime Traviesa,*

¿qué fruta es ésa? A friendly snail, Juan Perol, delights in visiting his surroundings in *¿Dónde está Juan Perol, el caracol?* Imaginative color photos and designs introduce the names of the fingers and the hands in *Juego de dedos.* Inés describes the advantages of having three feet in *Inés tres pies.*

Jadoul, Émile. *¡Todo el mundo va! (The Whole World Goes!)* Illus: the author. Translated by Violante Krahe. (Colección Luciérnaga) Zaragoza: Edelvives, 2004. 24p. ISBN: 84-263-5242-1. $10.95. Ages 1–4.

When Raúl's parents explain to his son that *el vaquero* (the cowboy), *la princesa* (the princess), *el papá* (father), and the entire world go to the toilet, he then decides he will go too. This well-designed board book with thick black lines and brightly colored illustrations of whimsical people running to the toilet is sure to resonate with toddlers who may or may not yet be convinced to go. Originally published by Casterman, Brussels, this is toilet training with humor and verve.

James, Simon. *León y Beto. (Leon and Bob)* Illus: the author. Translated by Ernestina Loyo. México: Castillo, 2006. 28p. pap. ISBN: 970-20-0844-1. $10.95. Gr. K–2.

Loyo's spare Spanish rendition and James's original charming watercolor-and-ink illustrations maintain the feelings of loneliness and friendship evident in the first English edition. León, whose father is away in the army, has an imaginary friend Beto, who accompanies him everywhere. When a new family moves in and León meets his new neighbor, Beto, León is delighted to play soccer with a "real" Beto.

James, Simon. *Pasito. (Little One Step)* Illus: the author. Translated by Chema Heras and Pilar Martínez. Vigo: Faktoría K, 2006. 26p. ISBN: 84-9346-410-4. $18.95. Gr. Preschool–2.

When three duckling brothers find they are lost and alone in the forest, the youngest one is too tired to proceed and asks for *mamá.* This tender Spanish rendition uses the rhythm of the Spanish language with even greater effect than the original English. Especially when the older ducklings encourage the youngest to keep walking by teaching him a game *paso a paso* (One step) and naming him *Pasito* (Little One Step). As he complains, his brothers remind him to continue: *Un paso, un paso, un paso* (One step—one step—one step), until they finally find their delighted *mamá.* James's ink-and-wash illustrations in warm tan and ocher tones provide the perfect background to this endearing do-not-give-up story.

Janisch, Heinz. *En casa. (At Home)* Illus: Helga Bansch. Translated by Cristina Rodríguez Aguilar. Madrid: Edelvives, 2004. 26p. ISBN: 84-263-5266-9. $15.95. Gr. K–3.

In a first-person point of view, a big, red hen asks herself if she would be as happy living elsewhere as she is at home. If she lived in a library, she would enjoy reading; if she lived in a clock tower, she could watch the storms much better; if she lived on a boat . . . no, she could get seasick; in a nest, she would sleep like a bird; in a tree, could you find her? and so on. But at home, with you, *¡me sentiría feliz a todas horas!* (I would be happy all the time!) Colorful double-page spreads depicting large stylized animals from unusual and exaggerated perspectives add a humorous tone to this delightful fantasy, originally published by Jungbrunnen, Vienna. The brief matter-of-fact Spanish rendition makes it even more fun.

Jäntti, Mariana. *¡Cuánta gente! ¿quiénes son? (How Many People! Who Are They?)* Illus: Mariana Jäntti and others. Montevideo: Hardenville, 2006. 22p. ISBN: 9974-7799-2-8. $15.95. Ages 3–5.

Three-year-old Francisco tells about his baby sister, his mother's delicious cooking, his father's busy day at the office, his kind *abuela* Lola and his many other uncles, aunts and cousins, who he can barely identify. His father gently reassures him, *sin apuro* (not to worry), you know the names of those close to you. The striking, full-page, childlike illustrations, with thick lines and bold colors, definitely convey the world from a child's viewpoint. Spanish-speaking youngsters will readily identify with the joy and confusion amid an extended family.

Jiménez Soria, Ángeles. *Arriba y abajo/Up and Down.* Illus: Pablo Prestifilippo. Translated by Esther Sarfatti. León: Everest, 2005. 38p. ISBN: 84-241-8750-4. pap. $9.95. Gr. K–3.

In an imaginative, bilingual text, two boys describe what they see both "*Aquí arriba/*Up here" and "*Aquí abajo/*Down here." From "*veo un cielo azul invadido por nubes de mil colores/*I see a blue sky filled with clouds of a thousand colors," to "*toco la tierra, el agua y el barro/*I touch earth, water and mud" this is a fanciful view of nature as experienced by a very tall and a very short boy. Prestifilippo's striking full-page spreads with exaggerated perspectives are further accentuated with bright colors and up-close views that compel attention. As opposed to bilingual texts that distort the syntax of one or both languages, these are carefree Spanish and English renditions.

Joosse, Barbara M. *¿Me quieres, mamá? (Mama, Do You Love Me?)* Illus: Barbara Lavallee. Translated by Diego Lasconi. San Francisco: Chronicle, 2004. 26p. ISBN: 0-8118-4341-6. $6.95. Ages 2–5.

Joosse's popular story about an Inuit mother's unconditional love for her young daughter is as reassuring in this tender Spanish rendition. Set in Alaska and enhanced by Lavallee's rich expressive illustrations of Inuit culture and traditions, this well-designed board book with its comforting *Pero aún así te querría* refrain can be used as a universal story of mother's love as well as a simple depiction of Inuit traditions.

Jungman, Ann. *La mezquita maravillosa. (The Most Magnificent Mosque)* Illus: Shelley Fowlcs. Translated by Miguel Ángel Mendo. Barcelona: Serres, 2004. 28p. ISBN: 84-8488-159-8. $13.95. Gr. 1–4.

Set in Spain at Córdoba's Great Mosque, this story tells about the beauty and significance of what once was the second largest mosque in the Islamic world. When three mischievous boys—Rashid, who is a Muslim, Samuel, who is Jewish and Miguel, a Christian—are punished for dropping oranges on people's heads in the gardens of the mosque they experience the freshness and elegance of its interiors. Years later, they convince the Christian king not to destroy the structure. Despite a few Peninsular Spanish pronouns and conjugations, Fowle's exquisitely detailed, colorful paintings and Mendo's brisk Spanish rendition provide a joyous testament to the tolerance among the three religions that prevailed in Islamic Spain. A brief author's note highlights the symmetry and historical meaning of the mosque.

Ketteman, Helen. *Armadillo el chismoso (Armadillo Tattletale)* Illus: Keith Graves. Translated by Miriam Fabiancic. New York: Scholastic, 2003, 32p. ISBN: 0-439-55119-6. pap $3.99. Gr. K–3.

With the cadence of a pourquoi cautionary tale, this whimsical Spanish rendition tells why *Armadillo* lost his orejas fenomenales (huge ears) and his bad habit of eavesdropping and misreporting what he hears. After *Armadillo* irritated several of his animal "friends" with his constant *chismes* (gossip), *don Cocodrilo* teaches him a lesson. Graves's spirited double-page spreads, rendered in acrylic, ink and colored pencil, make this tale even more appealing.

Kimiko. *El avión. (Airplane)* ISBN: 84-95150-54-9.
――. *El elefante. (Elephant)* ISBN: 84-95150-55-7.
――. *El gato. (Cat)* ISBN: 84-95150-52-2.
――. *El lobo. (Wolf)* ISBN: 84-95150-53-0.
Ea. vol.: 12p. Translated by Anna Coll-Vinent and Rafael Ros. Barcelona: Corimbo, 2004. $9.95. Ages 1–3.

Spanish speaking toddlers will have a great time with the pop-ups, pull-the-tabs, lift-the-flaps, bold black lines with bright illustrations and simple texts of these delightful board books, originally published by L'ecole des loisirs, Paris. A little red airplane plays in the sky, flies over mountains and visits his friends in *El avión.* Juan, a little pig, introduces himself and his favorite activities, including an audible oink as his mother holds him in *El cerdito.* A clownish elephant plays with his friends in *El elefante.* A vivacious, white kitten deserves a much-needed rest in *El gato.* A proud wolf enjoys scaring others, except at night in *El lobo.*

Kimiko. *El camaleón. (Chameleon)* ISBN: 84-8470-229-4.
――. *El cerdito. (Little Pig)* ISBN: 84-8470-140-9.
――. *El conejo. (Rabbit)* ISBN: 84-8470-203-0.
――. *El dinosaurio. (Dinosaur)* ISBN: 84-8470-171-9.
――. *El koala. (Koala)* ISBN: 84-8470-227-8.
――. *La ratita. (The Little Rat)* ISBN: 84-8470-205-7.
Ea. vol.: 10p. Translated by Rafael Ros. Barcelona: Corimbo, 2004–2006. $11.95. Ages 2–5.

Like the previous four titles—*El avión (Airplane), El lobo (Wolf), El elefante (Elephant), El gato (Cat)*—originally published by L'ecole des loisirs, Paris, these are delightful board books for the very young. With colorful illustrations against flat backgrounds and well-constructed pull-the-tabs, pop-ups, cutouts and an easy-to-understand, simple text, they encourage joyful interaction. Combining fantasy with well-known facts, they tell about chameleons, pigs, rabbits, dinosaurs, koalas and rats and can be used as vocabulary builders or just plain fun.

Kimmel, Elizabeth Cody. *Mi pingüino Oliver. (My Penguin Osbert)* Illus: H.B. Lewis. Translated by Esther Rubio. Madrid: Kókinos, 2004. 34p. ISBN: 84-88342-68-3. $19.95. Gr. Preschool–2.

Although each year at Christmas Juan writes a letter to *Papá Noel* specifying what he wants, there have been misunderstandings. Hence, this year Juan describes exactly what he wants. And Oliver is what he gets—a living, breathing, black-and-white penguin who wants to do all the things penguins do. Oliver wants to take cold baths, eat creamed herring for breakfast and play with ice cream. Despite his best efforts, Juan soon asks for a replacement. Lewis's tender watercolor and pastel illustrations and Rubio's playful Spanish rendition maintain the tongue-in-cheek, be-careful-what-you-wish-for tone of the original edition, first published by Walker, London.

Kimmel, Eric A. *Sopa de cactus. (Cactus Soup)* Illus: Phil Huling. New York: Marshall Cavendish, 2007. 34p. ISBN: 978-0-7614-5344-4. $16.99. Gr. 1–4.

Set during the Mexican Revolution (1910–1922) when different troops of soldiers roamed into defenseless towns, this straightforward Spanish rendition is a whimsical variant of the traditional *Stone Soup*. When a resourceful *Señor Capitán* manages to charm the reluctant *Señor Alcalde* (Mayor), the scared townspeople agree to help him make a delicious soup. Despite a few awkward expressions (*¿Pueden darnos algunos frijoles y tortillas?*), young Spanish speakers will delight with this happy *fiesta*, and enjoy the delicious *sopa de cactus* as well as the *tortillas, tamales, chorizos, camotes y varios cerdos gordos para asar.*

Especially appealing are Huling's slightly facetious watercolor and ink illustrations, in deep yellow and orange tones, which provide a nostalgic view of the Mexican countryside. Appropriately, an author's historical note concludes with portraits of Pancho Villa and Emiliano Zapata.

Knutson, Bárbara. *Amor y pollo asado: Un cuento andino de enredos y engaños. (Love and Roast Chicken: A Trickster Tale from the Andes Mountains)* Illus: the author. Translated by Judy Goldman and Wendy A. Luft. Minneapolis: Lerner, 2005. 40p. ISBN: 0-8225-3190-9. $16.95. Gr. K–3.

Although Cuy, a clever guinea pig, constantly escapes from *Tío Antonio*, a hungry fox, he is finally caught by a strong farmer. But again, the fast-talking guinea pig manages to outsmart the fox who vows he will never be tricked again. With the lively eye-catching woodcut-and-water illustrations of the English original, which vividly depict the fauna and flora of the Andes Mountains, this smooth Spanish rendition will delight young Spanish speakers (and learners) as they celebrate the antics of clever Cuy outsmarting powerful *Tío Antonio*.

Krahn, Fernando. *¿Quién ha visto las tijeras? (Who Has Seen the Scissors?)* Illus: the author. Pontevedra: Kalandraka, 2006. 50p. ISBN: 978-84-8464-602-0. $20.95. Gr. 1–3.

   Don Hipólito, a busy tailor, is surprised when his much-needed scissors suddenly take off. As they snip their way around town, they cause serious mischief: They cut a newspaper while a man is reading it, a girl's braid, the stems of a bouquet of flowers, an elderly lady's blanket, the string of a boy's kite and, after other *travesuras* (antics), they cut off Don Hipólito's mustache. Despite the obviously nonsensical and incongruous "mischief," the humorous ink-and-watercolor illustrations add a whimsical fantastic tone. Lovers of the absurd also will enjoy the simple text.

Krebs, Laurie. *Nos fuimos todos de safari. (We all Went on Safari)* Illus: Julia Cairns. Translated by Yanitzia Canetti. Cambridge: Barefoot, 2005. 30p. ISBN: 1-905236-08-5. pap. $6.99. Gr. Preschool–2.

   As Arusha, Mosi, Tumpe and their Maasai friends set out on a safari through the grasslands of Tanzania, they encounter various animals. In a lively engaging text, they count the animals from one to ten in both Spanish and Swahili. Young Spanish speakers will enjoy the counting as they learn basic facts about Tanzania and its people. The colorful watercolor illustrations, map and informative notes about the animals, people and country make this a unique counting book.

Kulot, Daniela. *Leopoldo y Casilda. (Leopoldo and Casilda)* Illus: the author. Translated by Fe González. Vigo: Faktoria K, 2007. 26p. ISBN: 978-84-935122-1-7. $19.95. Ages 3–6.

   Leopoldo, a young frog, has a loving and understanding *mamá* who tells him stories at bedtime, lets him select the clothes he wants to wear, never washes his *patito de peluche* (stuffed animal) even though it's dirty and helps him write a note to his friend. Casilda, his frog friend, also has a loving *papá* who ties bows on her hair, never gets angry despite her mischief and is eager to take her on his motor scooter to play with Leopoldo. Not surprisingly, Casilda's *papá* frog and Leopoldo's *mamá* frog enjoy each other's company as much as the young ones. Kulot's black line and bright color illustrations add an even more endearing tone to this warm story about parent-and-child relationships and the joys of friendship.

Lach, William. *Con amor de bebé. (Baby Loves)* Paintings by Mary Cassatt. Barcelona: Serres, 2004. 38p. ISBN: 84-8488-172-5. $14.95. Ages 3–5.

Sixteen full-page paintings, pastels and prints by the American Impressionist Mary Cassatt illustrating baby's activities on one side of the page face simple rhymes, such as *bebé se sienta* (baby sits), *bebé aplaude* (baby claps), *bebé bebe* (baby drinks) in this tender view of motherly love. The easy-to-understand text makes this book especially appealing to young language learners and their caregivers. Artists-to-be will appreciate the miniature reproductions with notes indicating title, date, medium and size.

Lasky, Kathryn. *El pirata Bob. (Pirate Bob)* Illus: David Clark. Translated by María Lucchetti. Barcelona: Editorial Juventud, 2006. 32p. ISBN: 978-84-261-3568-1. $17.99. Gr. K–3.

El pirata Bob (Pirate Bob), like all other pirates, is mean, greedy and heartless, but what he really fears is losing his pirate friend, *Jack el Amarillo*. After burying his treasure, he looks for true friends and, as opposed to other bandit-pirates, *el pirata Bob* wonders: *seré feliz . . . creo* (I will be happy . . . maybe). Clark's exaggerated ink-and-watercolor illustrations are as enjoyable as Lucchetti's lively Spanish rendition. Originally published by Charlesbridge Publishing, London, this pirate story will appeal to young Spanish speakers in search of buccaneer action and close friends.

Lionni, Leo. *Tili y el muro. (Tillie and the Wall)* Illus: the author. Translated by Teresa Mlawer. New York: Lectorum, 2005. 30 p. ISBN: 1-930332-82-3. $6.99. Gr. K–2.

In contrast to the other mice, Tili, an inquisitive, determined mouse, is eager to discover what lies on the other side of the wall. In the same simple, fable-like style of the original, Mlawer's clear Spanish rendition celebrates Tili's perseverance that results in happy mice joyously passing freely back and forth from one side to the other. Lionni's colorful collages add to the jubilant mood as mice explore the unknown.

Lobel, Arnold. *El mago de los colores. (The Great Blueness and Other Predicaments)* Illus: the author. Translated by Margarida Trias.

Barcelona: Corimbo, 2004. 30p. ISBN: 84-8470-178-6. $24.95. Gr. K–3.

A great wizard, who lives in a gray world, decides to bring color to his surroundings. So he invents the color blue and paints everything blue. But when blue isn't the perfect color, he invents yellow, which also has problems. This is followed by red, and, finally, a wonderful intermingling of colors that results in a perfect multicolored world. Lobel's detailed witty illustrations add a buoyant tone to a fantastically colored world.

Losantos, Cristina. *Los campamentos.* *(Campgrounds)* ISBN: 84-246-3835-2.
——. *El circo.* *(The Circus)* ISBN: 84-246-3834-4.
——. *La nieve.* *(Snow)* ISBN: 84-246-3831-X.
——. *El parque de atracciones.* *(An Amusement Park)* ISBN: 84-246-3832-8.
——. *La playa.* *(The Beach)* ISBN: 84-246-3836-0.
——. *El zoológico.* *(The Zoo)* ISBN: 84-246-3833-6.
Ea. vol.: 10p. (Espacios) Barcelona: La Galera, 2003–2005. $10.95. Ages 1–4.

In a most appealing manner, these well-constructed, wordless, board books depict humorous scenes of families and groups of children going to a campground, a circus, an amusement park, a beach, a ski resort and a zoo. The tiny witty illustrations in full color will encourage lots of sharing and laughs. In addition, toddlers and caregivers will appreciate the foldout format, depicting scenes from a campground, a circus, an amusement park, a beach, a ski resort and a zoo and, on the other side, the clear, simple glossaries with drawings and definite articles. These are indeed amusing introductions to fun places for young Spanish speakers and, most definitely, Spanish learners.

Madonna. *Las manzanas del Sr. Peabody.* *(Mr. Peabody's Apples)* Illus: Loren Long. Translated by Daniel Cortés. New York: Scholastic, 2003. 30p. ISBN: 0-439-62279-4. $19.95. Gr. K–3.

Inspired on a tale by Baal Shem Tov, this Spanish rendition maintains Madonna's overbearing, didactic tone with its strong message about the dangers of gossip. When Tommy Tittlebottom falsely accuses *Señor* Peabody of stealing an apple after every Little League game, the whole town turns against the kind-hearted teacher. After realizing his mistake, little Tommy apologizes but learns that it is impossible to undo the damage done by rumor. Long's playful, sensitive full-page illustration depicting scenes of a small American town are the most appealing part of this story.

Máquinas de rescate/Rescue Machines. ISBN: 0-7566-0445-1.
Máquinas duras/Tough Machines. ISBN: 0-7566-0447-8.
Máquinas rápidas/Speedy Machines. ISBN: 0-7566-0446-X.
Máquinas trabajadoras/Busy Machines. ISBN: 0-7566-0444-3.
    Ea. vol.: 22p. (Machines) New York: DK Publishing, 2004. $3.99. Ages 1–3.

    These attractive small bilingual board books (3¼" x 3¼") include clear color photographs and simple concise Spanish labels in bold (with definite articles) on top of each page, followed by English labels in a lighter smaller font. From bulldozers, to diggers, to freight trucks are depicted in *Máquinas duras/Tough Machines*; from an ambulance, to a police motorcycle, to a fire rescue truck in *Máquinas de rescate/Rescue Machines*; from a sports car, to fighter planes, to a race car in *Máquinas rápidas/Speedy Machines;* from a car, to bicycles, to a pickup truck in *Máquinas trabajadoras/Busy Machines.*

Mari, Iela. *Las estaciones. (The Seasons)* Illus: the author. Sevilla: Kalandraka, 2007. 34p. ISBN: 978-84-96388-57-4. $19.95. Gr. Preschool–2.

    Clean, simple illustrations featuring a beautiful large tree in the middle of a field depict the change of seasons in this charming wordless book, originally published by Emme Edizioni, Italy. Alongside the black or white silhouette of the tree, a wide-eyed squirrel hibernates in the winter, followed by spring's rebirth as the squirrel emerges from the ground, the tree sprouts new leaves, birds return to their nest and grass covers the ground. Joyfully and serenely through elegant color strokes, dabs and fine lines, this book celebrates nature's seasonal grandeur.

Martínez, Rocío. *Matías pierde su lápiz. (Matías Lost His Pencil)* Illus: the author. Caracas: Ekaré, 2004. 22p. ISBN: 980-257-299-3. $15.95. Gr. Preschool–1.

    Matías, an otter-like child, is sad because he can't find his favorite pencil. As each of his friends come to visit, they remember the wonderful things they did together with the lost pencil and help him search for it. Despite the bland story, children will empathize with Matías's feelings, which are made even more real by the gentle illustrations of concerned animal friends looking for Matías's prized pencil.

Marzollo, Jean. *Descubro la Navidad: Un libro de adivinanzas visuales. (I Spy Christmas: A Book of Picture Riddles)* Photos by Walter Wick. Translated by P. Rozarena. Madrid: Altea/Santillana, 2003. 37p. ISBN: 84-372-2346-6. $15.95. Gr: Preschool–3.

Thirteen exquisite Christmas scenes with joyous rhyming riddles that challenge kids to find a variety of small objects in the purposefully crowded oversize pictures are just right for lovers of detail. As in the original English version and the 1995 Spanish edition published by Scholastic under the title *Veo Navidad: Un libro de advinanzas ilustradas*, Wick's crisp and clear, full-color, double-page spreads of seasonal scenes add glee to the holiday celebrations.

Max. *¡Cuánto ruido! (Too Much Noise!)* ISBN: 84-667-4431-2.
———. *De excursión (Hiking)* ISBN: 84-667-4429-0.
———. *Papá, ¿qué es . . . ? (Dad, What Is . . . ?)* ISBN: 84-667-4432-0.
———. *¡Vaya susto! (What a Scare!)* ISBN: 84-667-4430-4.
Ea. vol.: 20p. (Mi Primera Sopa de Libros) Madrid: Grupo Anaya, 2004. $8.95. Gr. Preschool.

Like the previous four titles of this sturdy board books series, with bold cartoon-like illustrations, these feature Dani, a child penguin, and Renata, his loyal frog friend. Dani complains of the noises around him that won't let him sleep in *¡Cuánto ruido!* Despite the fog, Dani enjoys going on a long hike with his parents in *De excursión.* Dani questions his father about different shapes in *Papá, ¿qué es . . . ?* Mama reassures Dani about fears, dreams and fantasies in *¡Vaya susto!* This series is just right for the very young to share with a parent or caregiver.

Mayhew, James. *Carlota y los bañistas. (Katie and the Bathers)* Illus: the author. Translated by Miguel Ángel Mendo. Barcelona: Serres, 2004. 32p. ISBN: 84-8488-193-8 $16.95. Gr. 2–4.

Like previous titles in this series in which Carlota, accompanied by her grandma, introduces young readers/viewers to the work of great artists. On a warm summer day, Carlota jumps into the water in Georges Seurat's *Bañistas en Asnières* and other paintings by the water. Later, she helps a woman hang up clothes in Camille Pissarro's *Mujer tendiendo y lavando.* Just before closing time at the museum, she asks the magician in Paul Signac's *Retrato de Félix Fénéon* for assistance in helping her clean up her mess. Mayhew's bright double-page spreads and the informative afterword provide just the right introduction to pointillism for the young. Originally published by Orchard Books, London.

McKee, David. *Negros y blancos. (Tusk, Tusk)* Illus: the author. Translated
by Juan Ramón Azaola. Madrid: Anaya, 2008. 27p. ISBN: 978-84-667-
7646-2. $7.95. Gr. K–2.

   White elephants hate black elephants and black elephants hate
white elephants, which result in a most unfortunate war. Fortunately,
new grey elephants now live in peace. Simple black line and bright watercolors complement this tale of war and peace.

Milbourne, Anna. *Viaje a la luna. (On the Moon)* Illus: Benji Davies.
Translated by Gemma Alonso de la Sierra. Tulsa, OK: Usborne/EDC,
2005. 24p. ISBN: 0-7460-6632-5. $9.95. Gr. Preschool–1.

   A young girl imagines a space flight to the moon including liftoff,
moon landing, wearing a space suit, the moon's surface and positioning
an American flag. The simple text and computer-generated illustrations
make this an accessible introduction to astronauts and space flights for
the very young.

Monreal, Violeta. *La araña violeta. (The Violet Spider).* ISBN: 84-667-
2683-7.
———. *El cuervo negro. (The Black Raven).* ISBN: 84-667-2677-2.
———. *El fantasma blanco. (The White Ghost).* ISBN: 84-667-2676-4.
———. *El gusano naranja. (The Orange Worm).* ISBN: 84-667-2679-9.
———. *El marciano azul. (The Blue Martian).* ISBN: 84-667-2682-9.
———. *El monstruo amarillo. (The Yellow Monster).* ISBN: 84-667-2680-2.
———. *La piraña roja. (The Red Piranha).* ISBN: 84-667-2678-0.
———. *El sapo verde. (The Green Toad).* ISBN: 84-667-2681-0.
Ea. vol.: 20p. (Papeles Rotos) Madrid: Grupo Anaya, 2003. $10.95. Gr.
Preschool–1.

   These appealing board books with enticing covers and modernist
design are not for the very young. Older children, however, will enjoy
these imaginative stories based on different colors. In *La araña violeta*, a
friendly violet-colored spider saves a butterfly from insect-eating plants. A
black raven and a wise witch build just the right black castle in *El cuervo
negro*. A white ghost becomes famous as a result of his magic apples in *El
fantasma blanco*. An orange worm evolves into a pink dinosaur in *El gusano naranja*. In search of powerful sun, a blue Martian designs a beautiful sunflower in *El marciano azul*. A yellow monster who doesn't like
frightening people finds his perfect home in *El monstruo amarillo*. A red,
sharp-toothed fish saves a red-haired mermaid in *La piraña roja*. A green
toad is changed into a handsome prince in *El sapo verde*.

Mora, Pat. *Doña Flor: Un cuento de una mujer gigante con un gran corazón. (Doña Flor: A Tall Tale about a Giant Woman with a Great Big Heart)* Illus: Raul Colón. Translated by Teresa Mlawer. New York: Knopf, 2005. 32p. ISBN: 0-679-98002-4. $17.99. Gr. K–3.

Set in a Latin American village where *las plantas de maíz . . . crecían tan altas como los árboles* (corn plants grew as tall as trees), this magical tall tale features Doña Flor, a giant lady with a big heart. Always ready to help her neighbors, she even makes delicious *tortillas*, which the families can also use for rafts. When a dangerous animal terrorizes the villagers, she is determined to find the culprit and to return peace to her village. Mlawer's straightforward Spanish rendition and Colón's whimsical scratchboard art maintain the uplifting tone of this satisfying tale.

Morales, Yuyi. *Nochecita (Little Night).* Illus: the author. New Milford, CT: Roaring Book/Neal Porter, 2007. 32p. ISBN: 978-1-59643-232-1. $16.95. Gr. Preschool–2.

With a distinctive Mexican quality, this fanciful tale contrasts the playful routine of *Nochecita* (Little Night) with the serious efforts of a loving and determined *Madre Cielo* (Mother Sky) to get her daughter ready for bed. *Madre Cielo* fills a tub with falling stars, unfolds a dress crocheted from clouds, serves her daughter stars dripping from the *Vía Láctea* (Milky Way) and finally both play moon ball in the sky. The gentle engaging Spanish rendition, including a few Mexicanisms (e.g., *ahorita*), is complemented by Morales's imaginative, fluid art, in rich Mexican colors with varying and exaggerated perspectives, graciously depicting whimsical views of Mexican traditional dress, hairstyles, furniture and other scenes reminiscent of old Mexico. Young Spanish speakers and their parents will delight with this *mamá . . . magna como el cielo* to whom this book is dedicated. Also available in an English edition.

Munson, Derek. *Pastel para enemigos. (Enemy Pie)* Illus: Tara Calahan King. Translated by Christiane Reyes. Barcelona: Juventud, 2004. 34p. ISBN: 84-261-3372-X. $18.95. Gr. K–3.

In a first-person voice, a young narrator tells about his perfect summer until Claudio García moves to his neighborhood and becomes enemy number one. When his father proposes to make a pie to get rid of his enemy, the narrator has to promise to spend a day with Claudio and *tienes que ser simpático con él* (be nice to him). After spending a fun day with Claudio and enjoying his father's delicious pie, the boy concludes that he just lost *mi mejor enemigo* (my best enemy). King's large, stylized illustrations, full of humor and color, perfectly depict children's feelings about friends and "enemies." One Peninsular Spanish conjugation will not bewilder Spanish speakers from the Americas.

Muth, Jon J. *Las tres preguntas.* *(The Three Questions)* Illus: the author. Translated by Susana Pasternak. New York: Scholastic, 2003. ISBN: 0-439-54564-1. pap. $5.99. Gr. 1–3.

Based on Tolstoy's story, Muth's simple version is now available in a gentle Spanish rendition in which young Nikolai seeks answers to three questions to become a good person. Because his animal friends can't give him the answers, he consults Live, *una tortuga vieja*, an old turtle who observes his actions and helps him discover the answers himself. The soft double-spread watercolors depicting beautiful landscapes while a young boy searches for important answers add a fable-like quality that many adults may want to discuss with the young: Hence, *sólo hay un momento importante y ese momento es ahora* (there is only one important time, and that time is now); *El ser más importante es siempre el que está a tu lado* (The most important one is always the one with you); *Y lo más importante es hacer el bien* (And the most important thing is to do good). A brief author's afterword explains the source of the story and the characters' names.

Naumann-Villemin, Christine. *El chupete de Gina.* *(Gina's Pacifier)* Illus: Marianne Barcilon. Translated by Rafael Ros. Barcelona: Corimbo, 2004. 26p. ISBN: 84-8470-184-0. $15.95. Gr. Preschool–K.

Despite mama's concern, Gina absolutely refuses to give up her pacifier—not even when she goes on a picnic, or swimming, or in the future when she gets married. But one day, an angry, horrible, hungry wolf threatens her, and, to calm him, she gives him her pacifier. Of course, he becomes a sweet, pleasant wolf. When mama questions her about it, she responds: *Se lo he dado a alguien que lo necesitaba mucho más que yo.* (I've given it to someone who needed it more than I.) Barcilon's pencil and watercolor illustrations add a tone of whimsy that devoted pacifier lovers will completely understand.

Nava, Emanuela, and Giulia Re. *Arrullos y caricias.* *(Kisses and Hugs)* ISBN: 84-667-5199-8.
———. *Una comida sorpresa.* *(A Surprise Meal)* ISBN: 84-667-5200-5.

———. *Gotas y goterones. (Raindrops and Showers)* ISBN: 84-667-5198-X.
———. *Una merienda de hielo. (Snack on Ice)* ISBN: 84-667-5197-1.
Ea. vol.: 24p. Translated by Mario Merlino (Mi Primera Sopa) Madrid: Anaya, 2006. $10.95. Ages 2–4.

These latest entries in this sturdy board book series will delight toddlers as they accompany *Pedro Conejo* in search of new friends around the world. Originally published by Carthusia, Milano, Italy, each title has a most appealing combination of bold black lines, colorful spreads and a simple one- or two-sentence text that young Spanish speakers (or learners) can understand. After a day of play in the forest, (in *Arrullos y caricias*) *Pedro Conejo* hands out pajamas to all his friends. When they moan and groan, he wonders *¿Por qué no duermen?* (Why aren't they sleeping?) He soon realizes that each needs a kiss, a hug or other endearments. For his friends in the jungle, *Pedro Conejo* delivers a sack full of carrots in *Una comida sorpresa.* Although *Pedro Conejo* is prepared to wash his friends in the prairie, rain drops and showers disturb the fun in *Gotas y goterones.* When *Pedro Conejo* arrives in the South Pole with his friend, *Pingüino*, they delight in offering ice drinks to their new friends in *Una merienda de hielo.*

Nesquens, Daniel. *¿Dónde está Gus?* (*Where Is Gus?*) Illus: Elisa Arguilé. ISBN: 84-667-4572-6.
———. *Una nube. (One Cloud)* Illus: Elisa Arguilé. ISBN: 84-667-4573-4.
Rodenas, Antonia. *Duerme. (Sleep)* Illus: Rafael Vivas. ISBN: 84-667-4570-X.
———. *Risa de cocodrilos. (Crocodile's Laughter)* Illus: Rafael Vivas. ISBN: 84-667-4571-8.
Ea. vol.: 16p. (Mi Primera Sopa) Madrid: Anaya, 2005. $9.95. Ages 2–4.

These are certainly not the typical board books for the very young. Rather, they are sophisticated depictions of common situations that some adults will enjoy discussing with the little ones. With avantgarde, dark red and black illustrations, toddler Gus tells about his early-morning fears when he can't find his favorite blanket in *¿Dónde está Gus?* The effects of a drop of water that falls from a cloud on a dog, a cat and a mouse are depicted in *Una nube.* Mama wolf, concerned mouse, mama kangaroo, tender bird and other animals put different young animals to sleep in *Duerme.* Although crocodile swallows *Pato Faustino* (Duck Faustino), Faustino knows exactly how to escape in *Risa de cocodrilos.*

Norac, Carl. *¿Me quieres o no me quieres? (Do You or Don't You Love Me?)*
Illus: Claude K. Dubois. Translated by Anna Coll-Vinent. Barcelona:
Corimbo, 2004. 26p. ISBN: 84-8470-155-7. $11.95. Gr. Preschool–1.

Lola, a child hamster, has a new baby brother. Impatiently, she
tries to hold him, to play with him and even to share her favorite toy.
But the baby only cries and Lola interprets his cry to mean *¡No hay
duda que no me quiere!* (There is no doubt he doesn't love me!) Finally,
one night Lola approaches him quietly and baby smiles at her. Lola is
now happy: *Creo que mi hermanito ya me quiere.* (I think my little
brother loves me now.) The tender pencil and watercolor illustrations in
soft natural colors will reassure children who are experiencing the joys
and tribulations of a new sibling. Originally published by L'ecole des
loisirs, Paris, this simple Spanish rendition is just right for the very
young.

Numeroff, Laura. *Si le haces una fiesta a una cerdita. (If You Give a
Pig a Party)* Illus: Felicia Bond. Translated by Teresa Mlawer. New
York: HarperCollins, 2006. 30p. ISBN: 0-06-081532-9. $15.99. Gr.
Preschool–2.

Like its predecessor *Si le das un panqueque a una cerdita (If You
Give a Pig a Pancake)*, this constantly demanding *cerdita* is not satisfied with a *fiesta*, she also wants balloons, her favorite dress, her special friends, which lead to entertaining distractions, pillow fights and
more. Mlawer's playful Spanish rendition is as crisp as Bond's humorous, ink-and-watercolor illustrations featuring an enthusiastic *cerdita*
and an expressionless, overly obliging girl caretaker.

O'Callaghan, Elena. *¿Se habrán vuelto locos? (Have They Gone Crazy?)*
Illus: Àfrica Fanlo. Barcelona: La Galera, 2006. 34p. ISBN: 84-246-
2337-1. $15.95. Ages 3–6.

In a charming first-person voice, a young boy describes the
strange things that have been happening at home for the last three
months. Witty colorful sculpted images depict contrasting home collage
scenes in facing pages: a calm mother sitting in an orderly living room
reading a newspaper faces a harried mother carrying a load of dirty
clothes, with the appropriate text: *Esa era mi mamá antes.* (This was
mother before.) and *Esta es mi mamá ahora.* (This is mother now.); a
calm papa gardening contrasted with a rushed papa engaged in seven
activities at the same time; and so on, until he explains that he doesn't
understand what has happened for the past three months, because

Suerte que yo me distraigo un montón con mi nueva hermanita . . . que cumplió tres meses. (Luckily, I amuse myself a lot with my new, three-month-old sister.) This is indeed an ingenuous depiction, from a child's viewpoint, regarding the commotion that results after the arrival of a new sibling.

O'Callaghan i Duch, Elena. *El color de la arena. (The Color of Sand)* Illus: María Jesús Santos Heredero. Zaragoza: Edelvives, 2005. 40p. ISBN: 84-263-5921-3. $18.95. Gr. 2–4.

Set somewhere in the Middle East in an Arab refugee camp, Abdulá, a barefooted boy, poignantly tells about his love of painting, which, unfortunately, he can now only do in the sand. As he paints Nadjma, the goat, his grandfather describes life before the war and the beauty of the ocean, which Abdulá will be able to see whenever they are set free. Meanwhile, he is delighted when a stranger arrives with color pencils and paper that allow him to paint and to dream. Santos Heredero's compelling double-page spreads with up-close and exaggerated perspectives powerfully depict Arab people and life in a barren desert. This book is dedicated to all who suffer in refugee camps.

Olten, Manuela. *Niños valientes. (Brave Boys)* Illus: the author. Translated by Juan Villoro. Mexico: Serres, 2005. 26p. ISBN: 970-9705-10-5. $15.95. Gr. Preschool–1.

Just before bedtime, two young boys are chatting in bed about girls. They conclude that girls are boring because they play with dolls, take their teddy bears to bed, wet their nightgowns and are afraid of *fantasmas* (ghosts). Upon reconsidering *¿Fa-fa-fantasmas?* they try to reassure each other . . . and run to grab their own teddy bears. Some adults may object to Olten's expressive cartoon-like watercolors featuring two boys trying to appear "brave," especially when they pull down their pajamas and show half their buttocks. Originally published by Verlag, Zurich, this is not a delicate depiction of "brave" boys, yet it is an open, comforting view of children's bedtime fears.

O'Neill, Alexis. *Estela en el mercado de pulgas. (Estela's Swap)* Illus: Enrique O. Sánchez. Translated by Eida de la Vega. New York: Lee & Low, 2005. 32p. ISBN: 1-58430-246-1. pap. $7.95. Gr. 2–4.

De la Vega's zesty Spanish rendition effectively depicts the liveliness of *el mercado de pulgas* (flea market) in Santa Ana, California.

When Estela, a young Mexican–American girl, accompanies her father to the *mercado,* she has high hopes to sell her music box for folk-dancing lessons at the *Ballet Folklórico.* But as a strong wind creates havoc and ruins the flowers an older woman was selling, Estela graciously assists her and gives her her music box. Kind Estela gets a beautiful skirt as a swap and pictures herself dancing with it. As in the original, Sánchez's luscious, acrylic illustrations joyously recreate the bustle of *mercados* while highlighting the young heroine's generosity and compassion. Although young Spanish speakers will wonder why only the English words "Swap Meet" are framed within the first illustration, *mercado de pulgas* is certainly an appropriate term.

Orihuela, Luz. *La Bella Durmiente/Sleeping Beauty.* Illus: Jordi Vila Delclòs. ISBN: 0-439-87199-9.
———. *Caperucita Roja/Little Red Riding Hood.* Illus: Francesc Rovira. ISBN: 0-439-77375-X.
———. *Cenicienta/Cinderella.* Illus: Maria Espluga. ISBN: 0-439-87195-6.
———. *La lechera/The Milkmaid.* Illus: Mabel Piérola. ISBN: 0-439-77377-6.
———. *El patito feo/The Ugly Duckling.* Illus: Irene Bordoy. ISBN: 0-439-77376-8.
———. *La princesa y el guisante/The Princess and the Pea.* Illus: Petra Steinmeyer. ISBN: 0-439-87197-2.
———. *La ratita presumida/The Conceited Little Rat.* Illus: Rosa M. Curto. ISBN: 0-439-77379-2.
———. *Los tres cerditos/The Three Little Pigs.* Illus: María Rius. ISBN: 0-439-77382-2.
Ea. vol.: 24p. Translated by Esther Sarfatti. New York: Scholastic, 2005–2006. pap. $3.50. Ages 3–6.

Originally published in Spanish by Combel (Spain), these simple bilingual (Spanish-English) renditions of the well-known tales will appeal to very young readers/listeners of either language. As opposed to numerous bilingual books, these are not literal translations; rather, each story has maintained the syntax and rhythm of the original Spanish adaptation, followed by a straightforward English text in a different font. Despite the reduced text—one or two sentences per page in each language—the lighthearted color illustrations and the everlasting allure of these popular tales make these unassuming paperbacks a good choice for those adults who insist on bilingual editions.

Orihuela, Luz. *La cigarra y la hormiga. (The Locust and the Ant)* Illus:
Bassa. ISBN: 84-7864-869-0.
——. *Las fresas. (Strawberries)* Illus: Irene Bordoy. ISBN: 84-7864-870-4.
——. *Pulgarcita. (Thumbelina)* Illus: Javier Andrada. ISBN: 84-9825-
028-5.
——. *El ruiseñor. (The Nightingale)* Illus: Max. ISBN: 84-9825-027-7.
Ea. vol.: 24p. (Caballo Alado Clásico) Barcelona: Combel, 2004–2005.
$7.95. Gr. K–2.

Adapted for beginning readers with simple texts and colorful full-
page illustrations, these well-known tales have maintained their long-
standing appeal. A carefree singing locust can't understand why the
busy ants insist on working all summer until winter arrives in *La cigarra y la hormiga*. A mean woman finally realizes that her stepdaughter
is as worthy as her own daughter in *Las fresas*. A kind swallow helps a
female Tom Thumb find a handsome young man her size in *Pulgarcita*.
A Chinese emperor regrets banishing a live nightingale from his forest
in *El ruiseñor*. Despite a few Peninsular Spanish pronouns and conjugations (e.g., *mirad, vosotras teméis*) in *La cigarra y la hormiga* and *El
ruiseñor,* young Spanish speakers from the Americas will enjoy reading
or listening to these stories.

Orlev, Uri. *El león de regalo. (A Lion as a Gift)* Illus: Jacky Gleich. Translated by Olga Martín. Bogotá: Grupo Editorial Norma, 2004. 30p.
ISBN: 958-04-7665-9. pap. $10.95. Gr. 1–3.

When Daniela gave a T-shirt with a picture of a gentle lion to her
younger brother for his birthday, she never expected Miguelito's reaction. He is so delighted that he wants to wear his new T-shirt to bed at
night, but the lion dislikes being called "gentle." As the lion demon-
strates his ferocious side, Miguelito becomes anxious and scared. Soon,
however, Miguelito and the lion resolve their misunderstanding and
Miguelito can go happily to sleep. Gleich's exuberant double-page
spreads, in rich natural tones, are as fantastic as Miguelito's gentle lion.
Originally published by Beltz, Berlin.

Ormerod, Jan. *Buenas noches. (Moonlight)* ISBN: 84-8488-170-9.
——. *Buenos días. (Sunshine)* ISBN: 84-8488-169-5.
Ea. vol.: 26p. Illus: the author. Barcelona: Serres, 2005. $13.95. Ages
2–4.

Ormerod's tender, yet action-filled, ink-and-watercolor illustrations make these wordless picture books ideal for joyful viewing, oral

discussions, creative dramatics or imaginative writing. In soothing shades of blue, a child is involved in routine bedtime activities with papa and mama appearing in different scenes in *Buenas Noches*. Especially engaging are their attempts to help the child fall asleep as they themselves become sleepier and sleepier. As the first rays of bright yellow and orange sunlight shine into a child's bedroom, she wakes up her parents and helps them prepare for their busy day in *Buenos días*. Like the originals, first published in 1981 with great success in English-speaking countries, these are sure to resonate with young Spanish speakers and their caregivers.

Pawagi, Manjusha. *La niña que odiaba los libros. (The Girl Who Hated Books)* Illus: Leanne Franson. Translated by Christiane Reyes. Barcelona: Juventud, 2006. 26p. ISBN: 84-261-3407-6. $25.95. Gr. 1–3.

Meena, who absolutely hates books and hates to read, lives in a home where books clutter everything; and, incredibly, her avid-reading parents keep buying more books. When Max, the family cat who shares her book phobia needs to be rescued from a tower of books, the books, pages and characters come tumbling down. As Meena attempts to get them back to their proper home, she reads the books aloud, which she joyfully enjoys. Although Franson's crammed watercolor illustrations are a bit repetitious, Reyes's Spanish rendition cleverly maintains the author's message. Despite a few Peninsular Spanish conjugations (e.g., *buscárais*), young Spanish speakers from the Americas will empathize with Meena's open defiance.

Pennart, Geoffroy de. *El lobo sentimental. (The Softhearted Wolf)* Illus: the author. Translated by Paula Vicens. Barcelona: Corimbo, 2004. 34p. ISBN: 84-8470-120-4. $14.95. Gr. Preschool–2.

When Lucas, a teen wolf, decides it is time for him to leave home and fend for himself, his father wolf gives him a list of what he should eat. Along the way he meets mama goat and her seven kids, Red Riding Hood, three little pigs, and Pedro, from Peter and the Wolf. Although he is hungry, he is too softhearted to eat them. But, when he meets a mean, rude ogre, the hungry Lucas devours him and frees Tom Thumb and his brothers. So he adds *OGRO* (ogre) to his father's list. Despite a few Peninsular Spanish pronouns and conjugations (e.g., *sois, os comeré, marchaos*) Spanish speakers from the Americas will enjoy this refreshing wolf and the charming black-ink and watercolor illustrations depicting well-known characters. Originally published by Kaléidoscope, Paris.

Pérez Escrivá, Victoria. *¡Ay!* *(Ouch!)* Illus: Claudia Ranucci. Madrid: Anaya, 2004. 26p. ISBN: 84-667-4472-X. $19.95. Gr. K–3.

When a mean magician turns María into a tea strainer, a frightened cook notices that every time he strains tea, the strainer sighs and says, *¡Ay!* (Ouch!) Hence, he treats the strainer with utmost care. To avoid the magician's wrath, he escapes with the strainer, and, suddenly, the enchantment breaks and María appears sitting on a tea cup. She never again has to say *¡Ay!* Against a white background, the avant-garde, stylistic watercolors, full of humor and whimsy, add a surrealistic tone to this incongruous story that will appeal to lovers of the fantastic. The brief text, which includes two English expressions "¡Horribol!" [sic] and "¡Wonderful!," and an exquisite, large-format design make this an out of the ordinary selection for story hour.

Perrault, Charles. *El gato con botas.* *(Puss in Boots)* Illus: Jean-Marc Rochette. Translated by Remedios Diéguez Diéguez. Barcelona: Blume, 2005. 27p. ISBN: 84-9801-031-4. $15.95. Gr. K–3.

Based on Perrault's original tale, this is a graceful Spanish rendition slightly pared down for young Spanish-speaking listeners, who are sure to rejoice as the clever cat wins a fortune for his master, along with the hand of a princess. The black-and-white line illustrations, which are intermingled with full-page, saccharin-free watercolors, the two concluding lighthearted *moralejas* (aphorisms) and a brief afterword about the author and the tale make this an appealing new interpretation of the classic story.

Perrault, Charles and others. *El gran libro feroz del lobo.* *(The Big Book of the Bad Wolf)* Illus: Ulises Wensell and others. Translated by Raquel Solà García. Barcelona: Juventud, 2005. 120p. ISBN: 84-261-3487-4. pap. $23.95. Gr. 2–5.

Featuring a big, bad wolf as the protagonist, this collection includes fifteen stories and songs, both classic and contemporary. From the conventional *Caperucita Roja* (Red Riding Hood) to an unusual *El lobo está cansado* (The Wolf Is Tired) these stories combine enough action and excitement to appeal to young readers/listeners. Some readers/viewers may object to a ferocious wolf pouncing on a scared *abuelita* and a trusting Red Riding Hood as well as several unnecessary admonitions to readers to behave. Nonetheless, the everlasting appeal of the bad wolf and the additional games that follow some of the stories make this collection a welcome addition to most libraries.

Pfister, Marcus. *El pez arco iris: colores/Rainbow Fish: Colors*. ISBN: 0-7358-1978-5.

——. *El pez arco iris: números/Rainbow Fish: Counting*. ISBN: 0-7358-1979-3.

Ea. vol.: 24p. Illus: the author. New York: North-South Books, 2005. $4.99. Ages 1–3.

The always-popular *pez arco iris*/Rainbow Fish, now in a simple bilingual board book edition, introduces toddlers to nine colors and ten numbers in two languages. Colorful images face bold labels in English and, in a lighter typeface, in Spanish. Pfister's uses his seductive iridescent fish scales only on the cover and last page of each title, announcing that there is "only one glittering Rainbow Fish/*Pero sólo un pez arco iris brillante*." Just right for parents looking for enticing, bilingual board books for their young.

Piquemal, Michel. *Mi miel, mi dulzura. (My Honey, My Sweetheart)* Illus: Elodie Nouhen. Zaragoza: Edelvives, 2005. 24p. ISBN: 84-263-5637-0. $18.95. Gr. 1–3.

Jadiya and her parents, who now live in Spain, are eager to visit *abuela* Zhora in Chott el-Yerid, a town in North Africa. With her loving *abuela,* she enjoys delicious figs, dates and sweet pastries, and especially the *Sherezad* tales and other traditional games that her affectionate grandma delights in recounting. When grandma dies, Jadiya and her mother are filled with pain. They console each other with *abuela's* hand-embroidered caftan and memories of her tales and nursery rhymes. Arabic words and expressions are intermingled in the tender Spanish text, which is further enhanced by the imaginative dream-like illustrations in exquisite shades of blue, silver and gold depicting Muslim motifs.

Pomés Leiz, Juliet. *Cumpleaños feliz. (Happy Birthday)* (Simón en) Illus: the author. Barcelona: Tusquets, 2005. 32p. ISBN: 84-8310-413-X. $15.95. Gr. Preschool–2.

As soon as Simón wakes up, he is eager to awaken his father to remind him that today is his birthday. Papa, of course, is ready with a special gift. While he is having breakfast, he gets calls from uncles, grandparents and from his mother who is away on a trip, but promises she will be home when he blows out his birthday candles. Simón's birthday is celebrated at school and has a wonderful party at home, meticulously planned and prepared by his father. Unfortunately, his mama's plane is late and she misses his party. But happily, she and *abuela* are there when he blows his candles. Mama and papa's role reversal and the lighthearted ink-and-watercolor illustrations, full of realistic details, and energetic children, add a contemporary tone to Simón's birthday.

Poole, Josephine. *Blancanieves. (Snow White)* Illus: Angela Barrett. Translated by Miguel Ángel Mendo. Madrid: Kókinos, 2007. 32p. ISBN: 978-84-96629-17-2. $21.95. Gr. 2–4.

Spanish-speaking children (and their parents) are devoted fans of the traditional Grimm fairy tales, yet Poole's version of the always-loved *Blancanieves* is certain to be an unforgettable experience—to listen to, to read, or to view. Barrett's exquisitely elegant double-page spreads, filled with the romance and tone of 18th-century Europe, and Mendo's graceful Spanish rendition, translated with charm and finesse, result in a spectacular and sophisticated, somewhat longer version of the traditional tale about the beautiful princess who takes refuge from her wicked stepmother in the cottage of seven dwarfs.

Portell, Raimon. *¡Quiero una corona! (I Want a Crown!)* Illus: Ignasi Blanch. Barcelona: La Galera, 2005. 36p. ISBN: 84-246-3924-3. $16.95. Gr. K–2.

Ever since Julia was three years old, she's always wanted a crown. Finally, her parents give her one, and off she goes to the palace. Although the guards are reluctant to let her in, she points to her crown and announces, *¡Soy la reina Julia!* (I am Queen Julia!) Thus begins Julia's encounter with the young king, where she learns what kings do—give orders—and he learns what girls do—all kinds of fun activities. A bit incongruous, perhaps, (such as the "king" and "queen" wiping chocolate off their hands on the palace's velvet curtains), yet Blanch's slapstick pencil and watercolor illustrations add a fantasy tone to this story with strong European themes and motifs.

Ramírez, Antonio. *Napí. (Napí)* Illus: Domi. Toronto: Groundwood, 2004. 40p. ISBN: 0-88899-611-X. $15.95. Gr. K–3.

In an informal, almost colloquial style, Napí, a Mazateca girl who lives in a village in the state of Oaxaca, Mexico, describes her feelings about her family and surroundings. Despite the slight story and at times befuddling text *(con un verde que se va oscureciendo poco a poco hasta verse como las partes más profundas del río)*, some children might appreciate the cultural references specific to the Mozatecas—*pachota, huipiles*. As in the English edition, the most appealing aspect of this book are Domi's vibrant double-page spreads, full of imagery and magical whimsy, depicting the different colors of nature on the bank of the river.

Ramos, Mario. *¡Mamá! (Mother!)* Illus: the author. Translated by Julia Vinent. Barcelona: Corimbo, 2004. 26p. ISBN: 84-8470-145-X. $17.95. Gr. Preschool.

Full of humor and whimsy, this ingenious counting book exposes children to numbers 1–10 through a startled boy in search of his *¡Mamá!* As he opens the door to his bedroom, he finds one big hippopotamus (and a tiny spider) and calls *¡Mamá!*; in the bathroom he finds a mama lion with her cub sitting on the toilet and calls *¡Mamá!*; in another bedroom he finds three giraffes and calls *¡Mamá!* This goes on until the last spread amid ten mice, he shouts *¡Mamá! Hay una araña en mi habitación.* (Mother! There is a spider in my bedroom.) Thick black lines and bright colors depict endearing animals in the most incongruous situations, in which the appropriate number (1–10) is embedded somewhere in the illustration. Originally published by L'ecole des loisirs, Paris, this imaginative counting book cannot be beat.

Rapaport, Gilles. *10 soldados. (10 Soldiers)* Translated by P. Rozarena. Zaragoza: Edelvives, 2003. 32p. ISBN: 84-263-4168-3. $16.95. Gr. 2–4.

In this satire, ten soldiers march to war with a flower in their rifles and a smile on their lips. They go to defend something but nobody knows what. Yet the queen urges them to fight until death. Along the way, the first soldier sprains an ankle, now there are nine. Another is allergic to flowers, hence: *Ya no quedan más que 8* (Now there are 8). Another is distracted, a different soldier is too tired, and so forth until a lonely soldier remains. He now gets rid of his red uniform, black hat and rifle—and walks away. Stark, compelling cartoon-style, black double-spread illustrations broken by splashes of bright watercolors against a white background add strength and immediacy to this intriguing view of ten soldiers and their reactions to war. Originally published by Circonflexe, Paris, this anti-war picture book with minimal art is not for the very young. Older children, however, will certainly react and discuss.

Rathmann, Peggy. *10 minutos y a la cama.* *(10 Minutes till Bedtime)* Illus: the author. New York: Putnam/Penguin, 2005. 44p. ISBN: 0-399-24359-3. $8.99. Ages 2–4.

As a father immersed in his newspaper announces *10 minutos y a la cama* (10 minutes till bedtime), his son sees a hamster family arriving for a visit. Although papa's countdown urges the boy to proceed with his bedtime routine—brushing his teeth, reading a story—numerous hamsters continue to arrive, which results in many bustling, even chaotic scenes. But a loving papa leaning over for a goodnight kiss adds the right tone to a soon-to-be-asleep boy. Rathman's ink-and-watercolor cartoons, full of busy details and lots of action, may confuse some youngsters, but the excitement of bedtime amid the bedlam will delight most little ones and their parents.

Recorvits, Helen. *Me llamo Yoon.* *(My Name Is Yoon)* Illus: Gabi Swiatkowska. Translated by Christiane Reyes. Barcelona: Juventud, 2003. 32p. ISBN: 84-261-3335-5. $16.95. Gr. K–2.

In contrast to the original edition, where learning the English language is the problem, here Yoon, a Korean-born girl, narrates in a graceful, first-person point of view her struggles to adjust and to learn to write in Spanish. Because she dislikes her name as written in Spanish, Yoon, which means *Sabiduría Resplandeciente,* refers to herself as *gato, pájaro,* and *Magdalena* as a way to feel accepted in her new school and new country. Swiatkowska's fanciful illustrations perfectly depict Yoon's initial sadness and feelings of alienation to an ultimately smiling and proud girl.

Reiser, Lynn. *My Way: A Margaret and Margarita Story/A mi manera: Un cuento de Margarita y Margaret.* Illus: the author. New York: Greenwillow, 2007. 32p. ISBN: 978-0-06-084101-0. $15.99. Gr. Preschool–1.

In most delightful parallel English and Spanish texts, Margaret and Margarita, two little girls, mirror their activities in their own special way. Although both fix their hair, greet their friends and make art, each girl has her special likes: Margaret eats a sandwich for lunch and Margarita enjoys a *quesadilla.* But both conclude: "*SIEMPRE me gusta hacer las cosas contigo*/I ALWAYS like to do them with you." The simple black pen and watercolor illustrations of the two girls engaged in their favorite activities are as charming as the bilingual text that sounds equally engaging in both languages. One caveat: Whereas the English text is always followed by the Spanish, both are presented in the same color, size and font—which will certainly confuse English and Spanish learners and, especially, beginning readers in both languages.

Repún, Graciela. *¿Quién está detrás de esa casa? (Who is Behind that House?)* Illus: Mónica Weiss. Buenos Aires: Ediciones del Eclipse, 2003. 30p. ISBN: 987-9011-59-7. pap. $8.95. Gr. 1–3.

In the energetic voice of a young smiling boy who asks, *¿Quién estará detrás de esa casa tan importante?* (Who might be behind that important house?) and his always-present dog, whose constant refrain, *Y yo* (And me), is as witty as it is intriguing. As the boy asserts that many people are behind this house such as painters; carpenters; electricians; plumbers; up to an architect (who happens to be his mother); and Father, who serves a cup of tea to his mother. But who is really always behind mother? *Yo* an estatic boy and a playful dog, who conclude: *¿No es cierto que soy importante?* (Truthfully, am I not important?) Weiss's flexible fluid illustrations with exaggerated perspectives and bold colors add a whimsical tone to this tongue-in-cheek story about homebuilding and family life.

Rius, María. *¡No quiero comer! (I Don't Want to Eat!)* Illus: Roser Rius. ISBN: 84-7864-839-9.
———. *¡No quiero hacer pipí en el orinal! (I Don't Want to Pee in the Potty)* Illus: the author. ISBN: 84-7864-840-2.
Ea. vol.: 18p. (Colección Cucú) Barcelona: Combel, 2004. $9.95. Ages 1–3.

Just right for the very, very young, these well-constructed board books with bold lines and watercolor illustrations against flat backgrounds will entice the little ones and their parents. In *¡No quiero comer!*, Blanca, who is about one and just learning to feed herself, tells her mother she is not hungry. Mama proceeds to play a game: If Blanca were a rabbit, she would eat a carrot; a duck, lettuce; a kitten, drink milk; a monkey, a banana; and, finally, empties her bowl. Interestingly, an informative afterword for parents encourages them to avoid overfeeding their children. In *¡No quiero hacer pipí en el orinal!* papa encourages toddler Raul to pee in the potty, which he angrily refuses. Papa then jokes and asks him if he wants to pee like a dog, or a cat, or a hen, or a donkey, or a baby. No, Raul is ready to pee in the toilet like his papa. Some adults may be put off by two illustrations: Father discreetly using the toilet and Raul openly urinating in the toilet. Most adults, however, will appreciate the tasteful candid illustrations as well as the straightforward afterword with suggestions for toilet training. Also in this series *¡No quiero bañarme! (I Don't Want to Bathe!)* and *¡No quiero dormir! (I Don't Want to Sleep!)*.

Robberecht, Thierry. *Perdí mi sonrisa. (I Lost My Smile)* Illus: Philippe Goossens. Mexico: Altea/Santillana, 2002. 26p. ISBN: 970-29-0667-9. $16.95. Gr. K–2.

In a first-person point of view a young girl relates how she lost her smile at school. Even Justine, her best friend, asks her if she is upset. At home, she tries to hide her mouth from her mother; and, although her father always makes her laugh, she now prefers to sit on his lap. As she worries about finding her missing smile, she confronts some bullies at school who just laugh at her. Even her *tia Gruñilda* "blames" her for smiling at everyone. Yet *mamá* reassures her that there are always enough smiles. Unexpectedly, when the boy who had her smile trips and falls, she happily regains her big smile. Some readers will question the puzzling, cruel tone of the story—mean bullies, an unpleasant aunt, a selfish friend—yet the eye-catching double-page spreads with exaggerated close-up perspectives amplify the emotional impact as a happy girl regains her smile.

Robleda, Margarita. *Números tragaldabas. (Glutton Numbers)* Illus: Natalia Gurovich. Mexico: Planeta/Destino, 2003. 24p. ISBN: 970-690-807-2. $13.95. Gr. Preschool.

Numbers 1 through 20 are introduced through amusing rhyming texts and whimsical illustrations. From *a la una cucharadas de luna.* (At one . . . spoonfuls of moon), to *a las dos . . . les encanta el arroz.* (At two . . . they love rice), to *a las veinte . . . muy feliz se siente* (at 20 . . . he feels very happy), these *números tragaldabas* will appeal to beginning readers and/or playful listeners/viewers.

Robleda, Margarita. *Ramón y su ratón. (Ramón and His Mouse)* ISBN: 1-59437-818-5.
——. *Rebeca. (Rebeca)* ISBN: 1-59437-819-3.
——. *Sana ranita, sana. (Get Well, Little One)* ISBN: 1-59437-820-7.
——. *Sueños. (Dreams)* ISBN: 1-59437-821-5.
Ea. vol.: 10p. Illus: Maribel Suárez. (Rana, Rema, Rimas) Miami: Santillana, 2004. $7.95. Gr. Preschool–K.

Despite the slight stories and at times flat illustrations, this easy-to-read series may appeal to beginning readers as they peruse one simple phrase or sentence per page. The best one of the series, *Ramón y su ratón,* is a creative rhyming story about an elderly Ramón, who hides a *jamón* (ham) inside a *jarrón* (vase) only to be outsmarted by a *ratón* (mouse). *Rebeca* is a dull recounting of a young girl's daily activities. Based on a traditional rhyme, *Sana ranita, sana* depicts a sick girl who gets well after a dose of cuddling, tickles, hugs, stories and an apple. Despite playing with his wooden horse, a boat and a mermaid, a little boy prefers to be embraced by his mother in *Sueños.*

Rohmann, Eric. *Clara y Asha. (Clara and Asha)* Illus: the author. Translated by Élodie Bourgeois Bertín. Barcelona: Juventud, 2006. 34p. ISBN: 84-261-3547-1. $18.95. Gr. Preschool–2.

With Rohmann's characteristic imaginative double-page spreads, full of fantasy and reverie, this spare Spanish rendition is as convincing as the original. When an unseen mama announces *¡Clara! Es hora de ir a la cama* (Clara! Time for bed.) Clara embarks on an imaginary escapade with her friend, Asha, an enormous, affable blue fish. Together they enjoy various adventures in the park, during bath time, in the snow and soaring in the sky. Finally, mama suggests *A dormir* (Go to sleep). Like Clara, Spanish-speaking youngsters will prefer to play with their magical friends.

Root, Phyllis. *La casa de Tomasa. (The House that Jill Built)* Illus: Delphine Durand. Zaragoza: Edelvives, 2005. 20p. ISBN: 84-263-5937-X. $17.95. Ages 3–5.

Using the nursery rhyme, "The House that Jack Built" as a take-off, Tomasa's simple house grows and grows to accommodate all her friends who knock on her door. With a delightful sense of Spanish rhyme, well-known characters take on a distinctly Hispanic flavor; hence, *Juanito Glotón* (Little Jack Horner), *la abuela Rosario* (Old Mother Hubbard), *la pastora Aleja* (Bo Peep), and *los tres osos* (the three bears) happily enjoy their new house. Durand's humorous ink-and-watercolor illustrations are further enhanced by the whimsical lift-the-flaps and well-constructed foldout and final pop-up.

Ross, Tony. *Figuras. (Shapes)* ISBN: 968-19-1486-4.
———. *Hora de dormir. (Bedtime)* ISBN: 968-19-1488-0.
———. *Mascotas. (Pets)* ISBN: 968-19-1485-6.
———. *El tiempo (Weather)* ISBN: 968-19-1487-2.

Ea. vol.: 16p. (La Pequeña Princesa) Miami: Santillana USA, 2004. $7.95. Ages 1–3.

Although *La Pequeña Princesa* (Little Princess) has been playing in the mud and obviously needs a bath before bedtime, mama and papa can't convince her. She washes her hands and her face, brushes her teeth, combs her hair and insists: *¡Uuuy! No quiero bañarme.* (Yuck! I don't want to take a bath.) Mama finally understands: *Porque hay una araña en la bañera.* (Because there is a spider in the bathtub.) and, besides, teddy bear is already in bed. Ross's witty, almost cartoonish, pencil and watercolor illustrations depicting an energetic toddler standing her ground in *Hora de dormir* will certainly resonate with Spanish-speaking toddlers. In other titles in this well-constructed board book series, *La Pequeña Princesa* has fun with shapes in *Figuras;* learns about taking care and feeding her pets in *Mascotas;* enjoys different activities according to the weather in *El tiempo.*

Rueda, Claudia. *Mientras se enfría el pastel. (While the Cake Cools Down)* Illus: the author. Mexico: Serres/Abrapalabra, 2005. 34p. ISBN: 970-9705-05-9. $13.95. Ages 3–5.

Mother hen bakes a cake to celebrate her five chicks' birthdays. While the cake cools, preparations begin for the party: *a la 1, llamar a las amigos* (at 1, call friends) *a las 2, limpiar la casa* (at 2, clean house) and so forth, until 12 when they are ready to celebrate. But when the cake is missing, *Cuatro pollitos dijeron no fui yo/Y Pilu, de tan malito,/ ni pío murmuró* (Four chicks denied they did it/Pilu, however was so sick,/he couldn't even say peep), Nonetheless, the guests have cookies to celebrate, although *alguien . . . en la cama se habrá de quedar* (someone will have to stay in bed). The simple easy-to-read text and the exuberant colored-pencil illustrations, with up-close and sensational perspectives, add a whimsical tone to this naughty-chick story who misses a wonderful party.

Ruillier, Jérôme. *¡Hombre de color! (Man of Color!)* Illus: the author. Translated by Christiane Reyes. Barcelona: Juventud, 2003. 28p. ISBN: 84-261-3357-6. $13.95. Gr. K–3.

Inspired by an African tale and narrated in a simple, rhyming text in the first-person voice of a black man, *Yo, hombre negro,* who compares himself to a white man *(Tú, hombre blanco).* The white man constantly changes his color—pink at birth, red when sunburnt, blue when cold, green when fearful, gray at death. Yet the black man never changes his own color. He concludes: *¡Y tú me llamas hombre de color!* (And you call me a man of color!) The bold child-like flat illustrations in primary colors of a consistently black man contrasted with an ever-changing colored white man add a humorous tone to this not-so-simple story about racial differences.

Rylant, Cynthia. *El caso del zorro nervioso. (The Case of the Fidgety Fox)* Illus: G. Brian Karas. Translated by Nicolás Posada. Bogotá: Grupo Editorial Norma, 2004. 56p. ISBN: 958-04-7749-3. pap. $9.95. Gr. 1–3.

When Melvin, *un zorrillo malgeniado* (an ill-tempered skunk), refuses to drive a bus because *¡Se me perdieron mis dados de la suerte!* (I lost my lucky fluffy dice!), Jack and Bony, two private detectives, come to the rescue of the frustrated passengers by successfully solving the mystery. Beginning Spanish readers will appreciate the simple sentences, humorous illustrations and comical situations.

Santiago, Esmeralda. *Una muñeca para el Día de Reyes. (A Doll for Navidades)* Illus: Enrique O. Sánchez. Translated by Nina Torres-Vidal. New York: Scholastic, 2005. 30p. ISBN: 0-439-75510-7. pap. $5.99. Gr. K–3.

Amid the smells of Christmas from Mami's kitchen and the neighbor's music, seven-year-old Esmeralda asks the *Reyes Magos* (Three Magi) for a baby doll like her cousin's. But, disappointingly, it's her younger sister Delsa who gets the baby doll. Incredibly, Esmeralda is satisfied to be the doll's *madrina* (godmother). Sánchez's sumptuous acrylic-on-canvas illustrations depicting a joyous Puerto Rican setting with all the Christmas trimmings and celebrations add a cheerful tone to this almost too-good-to-be-true memoir.

Schreiber-Wicke, Edith, and Carola Holland. *¡Cuidado! ¡Palabra terrible! (Careful! Terrible Word!)* Illus: the authors. Translated by Natalia García. Bogotá: Norma, 2005. 28p. ISBN: 958-04-8314-0. pap. $9.95. Gr. K–3.

Laura and Leo are best friends, but after a particularly bad day, Laura calls Leo: *¡Eres un . . . !"* (You are an . . . !") Although he doesn't know what . . . means, he knows it is not something nice. His feelings are definitely hurt and the ever-increasing . . . seems to follow him everywhere. Fortunately, both decide to talk to each other and the terrible . . . disappears. The pencil-and-watercolor cartoonish illustrations whimsically depict the children's fears and misunderstandings.

Originally published by Verlag, Germany, this fluid rendition will ring true to young Spanish speakers who occasionally use "bad" words.

Schwartz, David M. *Superabuelo. (Super Grandpa)* Illus: Bert Dodson. Translated by Martín Luis Guzmán. Santa Rosa, CA: Tortuga, 2005. 32p. ISBN: 1-889910-37-6. $18.95. Gr. K–3.

Just as uplifting as the English edition, this delightful Spanish rendition is sure to captivate bicycle enthusiasts and their grandparents. In a zippy lively text, it tells the story of a 66-year-old cyclist who competed in the Tour of Sweden and, to the surprise of the judges, finished first. The soft watercolors of the Scandinavian countryside amid an eager and determined cyclist add a tender touch to this persistent *superabuelo* whose dreams we all share. A CD is included.

Scieszka, Jon. *Pamplinas (Henry P.) (Baloney (Henry P.))* Illus: Lane Smith. Translated by Maria Villa. Bogotá: Grupo Editorial Norma, 2006. 32p. ISBN: 958-04-8753-7. $17.85. Gr. 1–4.

Unless Henry P. Pamplinas comes up with a good excuse for being late to school again, he faces permanent detention, which in Villas's admirably interpreted Spanish rendition results in *Quedas castigado de por vida.* To appease *señorita Callanecios* (an imaginative play on words on the original Miss Bugscuffle), Henry lets loose his fantastic imagination and proceeds to explain about his lost "zimulis," his trip to "skola" and his fall like a "uyarak." Smith's appropriately extravagant depictions of outer space are as amusing as Henry's conveniently borrowed foreign locutions, defined in a concluding *Decodificador.*

Scott, Ann Herbert. *En las piernas de mamá/On Mother's Lap.* Illus: Glo Coalson. Translated by Victoria Ortiz. New York: Clarion, 2006. 28p. ISBN: 978-0-618-75247-8. $5.95. Gr. Preschool–2.

In this well-constructed bilingual board book, Miguel (Michael in the English text), a small Eskimo boy, discovers that "*siempre hay lugar en las piernas de Mamá/*there is always room on mother's lap." Coalson's warm illustrations tenderly depict Miguel gathering his favorite toys, and his beloved Puppy. Although he initially objects to including his crying baby sister, he finally agrees: "*Así me gusta/*It feels good." To avoid confusion and to assist English and Spanish learners, the Spanish font in brown is followed by the English in black.

Segal, John. *Sopa de zanahoria (Carrot Soup)* Illus: the author. Translated by Teresa Mlawer. New York: Lectorum, 2006. 30p. ISBN: 1-933032-13-8. $12.99. Gr. Preschool–2.

Conejo (Rabbit) is delighted that spring has arrived. Patiently, he prepares for his favorite meal, *sopa de zanahoria* (carrot soup). After plowing, planting, watering and waiting for his carrots to grow, he is ready to harvest, but all his carrots are gone. Dejectedly, he questions each one of his friends, who express only sympathy. But *¡Sorpresa!* (Surprise!) when he arrives home he finds all his friends, a party and a delicious carrot soup. Young Spanish speakers (or listeners) will be charmed by the simple Spanish rendition and the black-line and soft watercolor illustrations, which ingeniously hide the party preparations in the background. It is important to note that in an introductory page the labels indicating the types of carrots are provided only in the original English.

Seuss, Dr. *El Gato Garabato. (The Cat in the Hat)* Illus: the author. Translated by P. Rozarena. Madrid: Altea/Santillana Ediciones, 2003. 64p. ISBN: 84-372-2394-6. $13.95. Gr. 1–3.

In contrast to the 1967 inferior Spanish bilingual (Spanish-English) edition available to children in the United States, this humorous Spanish rendition resonates with the joyful exuberance of *El Gato Garabato (The Cat in the Hat)*. Young Spanish speakers will delight when *Gato Garabato* comes to play one rainy nothing-to-do afternoon and proceeds to create a far-fetched mess. The only caveat for Spanish speakers from the Americas are the Peninsular Spanish pronouns and conjugations (e.g., *hacéis, echadlo, vuestra, miradme)*. Nonetheless, Dr. Seuss's original cartoon art is as enticing as the gross exaggerations and amusing word play that have appealed to generations of English speakers.

Seuss, Dr. *¡Hay un molillo en mi bolsillo! (There's a Wocket in my Pocket!)*. Illus: the author. Translated by Yanitzia Canetti. New York: Lectorum, 2007. 28p. ISBN: 978-1-933032-25-2. $8.99. Gr. K–2.

As an enjoyable vocabulary builder of common household words, Canetti's pleasing Spanish rendition makes language learning a fun experience. Assisted by Dr. Seuss's humorous cartoons and nonsense situations, beginning readers (and Spanish learners) will delight in finding *una CHARURA metida en la BASURA* (a *CHARURA* stuck in the waste basket), *¿O un GAVETORIO en tu ESCRITORIO?* (Or a *GAVETORIO* in your desk?), *¿O un ANTARIO en tu ARMARIO?* (Or an *ANTARIO* in your closet?). This is an undisguised Spanish lesson with entertaining wordplay and Seuss's always hilarious and unusual characters.

Seuss, Dr. *Un pez, dos peces, pez rojo, pez azul. (One Fish, Two Fish, Red Fish, Blue Fish)* Illus: the author. Translated by P. Rozarena. Madrid: Santillana, 2003. 64p. ISBN: 84-372-2305-9. $15.95. Gr. 1–3.

Rozarena's jocose Spanish rendition of Dr. Seuss's popular title from the Beginner Book series, first published in 1960, now includes the misadventures and unusual activities of *Zans Cabra, Yundo, Zalama,* and *Zato* who conclude, *Ha sido un día estupendo.* (It's been a wonderful day.) Despite a few Peninsular Spanish pronouns and conjugations *(os, veis, pensáis),* Spanish-speaking beginning readers will be amused by the ludicrous rhymes, lively cartoon art and inviting rhythm.

Seuss, Dr. *Un pez, dos peces, pez rojo, pez azul. (One Fish, Two Fish, Red Fish, Blue Fish)* Illus: the author. Translated by Yanitzia Canetti. New York: Lectorum, 2006. 67p. ISBN: 1-930332-83-1. $7.20. Gr. 1–2.

Dr. Seuss's easy-to-read rhymes about unusual animals with remarkable characteristics—*un camellón que tiene un solo chichón* (a one-humped Wump), or *las mascotas amarillas/todas se llaman Zedillas* (yellow pets called the Zeds)—are now available in the United States in Canetti's lilting Spanish rendition. Although some beginning readers may be confused by the lack of connection from one rhyme to the next, all will enjoy Dr. Seuss's always recognizable and vivacious cartoon art.

Seuss, Dr. *Y pensar que lo vi por la calle Porvenir. (And to Think that I Saw It on Mulberry Street)* Illus: the author. Translated by Yanitzia Canetti. New York: Lectorum, 2006. 32p. ISBN: 1-933032-07-3. $14.99. Gr. K–2.

With the freshness and whimsy of the original, Canetti's lively Spanish rendition retains Seuss's depiction of a boy's imaginative sights on his way home from school. *Un caballo y su carreta* (a horse and wagon) become a zebra pulling *un carro azul y dorado* (a blue and gold chariot), a reindeer pulling *un trineo lujoso* (a luxury sled) and even an elephant pulling *un Rajá, con rubíes, sentado en un trono* (a ruby-bedecked rajah enthroned on top). Despite the exuberance, Spanish-speaking youngsters will identify with the boy when he ultimately reports to his father that he only saw *un caballo y una carreta por la calle Porvenir* (a horse and a wagon on Mulberry Street).

Shannon, David. *Alicia el hada. (Alice the Fairy)* Illus: the author. New York: Scholastic, 2004. 32p. ISBN: 0-439-66203-6. $15.95. Gr. Preschool–1.

Alicia, a precocious energetic girl, is only *un hada Temporal* (temporary fairy). If she were *un hada Permanente* (permanent fairy), she could avoid eating broccoli, taking baths, and other things she hates. Just as convincing as Shannon's David books, Alicia captures the likes and dislikes of little girls through vivacious artwork and ingenious undertakings.

Shannon, David. *¡David huele! (David Smells!)* Illus: the author. (David en Pañales) New York: Scholastic, 2005. 14p. ISBN: 0-439-75511-5. $6.99. Ages 1–3.

David, the effusive, mischief-maker toddler, discovers his five senses by doing things not encouraged by an unseen caregiver. From petting a dog, to banging on a drum, to finally playing a joyful peek-a-boo, this board book with delightful illustrations of a snaggle-toothed, roundheaded toddler is pure fun and perhaps educational too.

Shannon, David. *¡Muy bien, Fergus! (Good Boy, Fergus!)* Illus: the author. New York: Scholastic, 2006. 32p. ISBN: 0-439-80294-6. pap. $3.99. Gr. K–2.

Fergus, the playful white terrier who goes wild when he sees a cat, won't come when he's called, eats the flowers, puddles in the mud, and dislikes bath time will now delight dog lovers in this simple Spanish rendition. Shannon's stunning, double-page spreads, full of canine action and expressions, are just what Spanish-speaking dog owners can identify with.

Shulman, Mark. *El gato grande. (The Big Cat)* Illus: Sally Chambers. Translated by Emilia Hernández. Barcelona: Combel, 2004. 10p. ISBN: 84-7864-822-4. $15.95. Ages 3–5.

Various animals introduce the concepts of big and little through common objects that the very young can readily understand. Especially engaging are the well-constructed pull-the-tabs that transform such items as a *camión grande* (big truck) into a *camión pequeño* (little truck). Charming watercolor illustrations and a joyous rhyming text make this full-sized board book, originally published by Pinsheel, London, even more fun.

Sierra, Judy. *¡Qué locura por la lectura! (Wild about Books)* Illus: Marc Brown. Translated by Yanitzia Canetti. New York: Lectorum, 2006. 34p. ISBN: 1-930332-85-8. $16.95. Gr. Preschool–2.

Sierra's sprightly story about librarian Moly who accidentally ended up in a zoo with her bookmobile retains its boisterous charm in Canetti's bouncy rhythmical Spanish rendition. When the animals run *para saber qué era aquello que se llamaba leer* (to learn all about this new something called reading) the birds and beasts find just the right book for each one. From *Libros escritos en chino* (Chinese books) for the pandas, to funny books for the hyenas, to *Crictor* for the boa constrictor, all the delighted animals *les ha dado, ¡locura por la lectura!* (are wild, simply wild about wonderful books). Brown's fanciful double-page spreads are as enticing as the originals.

Soto, Gary. *Chato y los amigos pachangueros. (Chato and the Party Animals)* Illus: Susana Guevara. Translated by Teresa Mlawer. New York: Puffin/Penguin, 2004. 32p. ISBN: 0-14-240033-5. pap. $7.99. Gr. K–3.

Chato, the coolest cat of the *barrio* first applauded in *Chato y su cena* (1997), is now engaged in celebrating his best friend, Novio Boy, who was raised in a pound and has never had a party. Although Chato forgot to invite the birthday boy, he appears just in time to enjoy this truly special *pachanga*. Spanish speakers will enjoy this smooth rendition of salsa and friendship with Guevara's original festive acrylic-on-scratchboard illustrations imbued with Latino folklore and traditions.

Stehr, Fréderic. *Las tres cerditas. (The Three Little Pigs)* Translated by Anna Coll-Vinent. Barcelona: Corimbo, 2006. 28p. ISBN: 978-84-8470-005-0. $ 24.50. Gr. Preschool–2.

This delightful version of the three little female pigs is a joyous tale of gender reversed. The first female pig, *cerdita,* is eaten by an elegantly clad wolf, *lobo*, disguised as a pig. The second female *cerdita* is also deceived by the disguised *lobo*. But the third *cerdita*, who manages to outwit the ferocious *lobo*, thrives in the admiration of all the male pigs. The appropriately witty line-and-watercolor full-page spreads will charm all boys and girls. Originally published by L'ecole des loisirs, Paris, in 1997.

Stewart, Amber. *No sin mi Mantita. (I Love My Cloth)* Illus: Layn Marlow. Translated by Teresa Mlawer. New York: Lectorum, 2007. 26p. ISBN: 978-1-933032-28-3. $12.00. Gr. Preschool–2.

Benita, a little bunny, who knows she is big enough to do many things, still insists that she won't go anywhere without her *Mantita* (blanket). Just in case her family takes it away, she hides it in a hollow log. But when she can't find it at bedtime, all her family tries to comfort her. Gradually, she forgets her beloved *Mantita* and the following spring she knows she has outgrown it. Mlawer's smooth Spanish rendition and the soft pastel watercolors will reassure young Spanish-speaking listeners as they confront their own losses and growing independence.

Stewart, Sarah. *La jardinera. (The Gardener)* Illus: David Small. Translated by Isabel Tenhamm. Caracas: Ekaré, 2005. 38p. ISBN: 980-257-308-6. pap. $10.95. Gr. K–3.

Set in the 1930s amid the economic difficulties of the Great Depression, this tender story, related through letters written by a little girl, is both touching and inspiring. Tenhamm's Spanish rendition, which maintains the simplicity of the original letters, and Small's eloquent ink-and-pastel illustrations movingly depict Lydia Gracia's efforts to gradually transform dour *tío* Jim and his drab shop and apartment through her love of and dedication to gardening. An editor's note briefly explains the effects of the Great Depression to many children and families in the United States.

Tan, Shaun. *El árbol rojo. (The Red Tree)* Illus: the author. Translated by Carlos Andreu and Albert Vitó. Cádiz: Barbara Fiore, 2005. 32p. ISBN: 84-933980-4-7. pap. $11.95. Gr. 2–5.

When a cheerless girl wakes up, a simple, omniscient voice explains: *A veces el día empieza vacío de esperanzas* (Sometimes a day begins without hope) *y las cosas van de mal en peor* (and things go from bad to worse). You have no idea what you must do . . . Suddenly, before you, just as you imagined . . . Soft-edged, realistic images of a sad distraught girl in a perplexing and at times fantastic environment evocatively depict the girl's sense of loneliness and confusion, which is contrasted with a bright red tree symbolizing the optimism the girl imagines. Originally published by Lothian, Australia, this large format publication with eye-catching, double-page spreads and collages and a few lines of text per page is not for the very young; rather, it is a personal and thoughtful depiction of bewildering thoughts and emotions that older children can understand.

Taylor, Sean. *Cuando nace un monstruo. (When a Monster is Born).* Illus: Nick Sharratt. Translated by María Lucchetti. Barcelona: Juventud, 2006. 32p. ISBN: 978-84-261-3564-3. $20.99. Gr. Preschool–1.

    Things happen when monsters live in *los bosques lejanos* (Far-away-in-the Forests Monsters) or *debajo de tu cama* (Under-Your-Bed Monsters). They either sit down quietly and play basketball or they eat the principal. The either/or scenarios will entrance young Spanish speakers as they wonder what monsters do when they dance, sleep, fall in love and have a baby monster. Sharratt's bright illustrations featuring lime-green and violet monsters are as engaging as Lucchetti's circular Spanish rendition.

Teague, Mark. *Detective LaRue: Cartas de la investigación. (Detective LaRue: Letters from the Investigation)* Illus: the author. Translated by Juan Pablo Lombana. New York: Scholastic, 2005. 32p. ISBN: 0-439-76070-4. pap. $6.99. Gr K–3.

    As in its predecessor *Querida Sra. LaRue (Dear Mrs. LaRue)*, Ike, the misunderstood dog, faces an unfair accusation. Although *señora Ondino's* cats mysteriously disappeared and he is captured with the *golosinas sorprendentemente deliciosas* (deliciously surprising treats), he manages to prove his innocence and become a hero. Lombana's tongue-in-cheek Spanish rendition is as amusing as Teague's oversize, acrylic illustrations of a self-assured dog who takes matters in his own *pezuñas* (paws).

Teague, Mark. *Querida Sra. LaRue: Cartas desde la Academia Canina. (Dear Mrs. LaRue: Letters from Obedience School)* Illus: the author. Translated by Miriam Fabiancic. New York: Scholastic, 2004. 32p. ISBN: 0-439-66128-5. pap. $4.99. Gr. K–3.

    With the jocose tone of the original, this Spanish rendition of the popular and misunderstood dog, Ike LaRue, who is sent to obedience school yet succeeds in convincing his owner that he must come home at once, will especially delight young Spanish-speaking dog lovers. Teague's always-pleasing, oversize acrylic illustrations of a resourceful dog and his clever letter-writing campaign where he insists *¡Esto es una CÁRCEL, no una escuela!* (This is a PRISON, not a school!) make this a wonderful selection for story time or individual reading/viewing.

Torres, Daniel. *Tom tu gran amigo: Juega al fútbol. (Your Friend Tom Plays Soccer)* Illus: Carlos Arroyo. Barcelona: Norma Editorial/Dist. by Public Square Books, 2004. 32p. ISBN: 159497-120-X. $17.95. Gr. 1–3.

Tom, a friendly dinosaur, is eager to join a group of boys playing soccer. Although he is too big to play goalkeeper, too strong to kick the ball, too loud to be a cheerleader, he becomes the perfect coach. Computer-generated cartoons and a lively easy-to-read text will please young soccer fans.

Tullet, Hervé. *Juego de azar. (Game of Chance)* ISBN: 978-84-96629-63-9.
——. *Juego de colores. (Color Game)* ISBN: 978-84-96629-12-7.
——. *Juego de construcción. (Construction Game)* ISBN: 978-84-96629-64-6.
——. *Juego de dedos. (Finger Game)* ISBN: 978-84-96629-10-3.
——. *Juego de formas. (Shapes Game)* ISBN: 978-84-96629-65-3.
——. *Juego de ojos. (Eye Game)* ISBN: 978-84-96629-11-0.
——. *Juego de sombras. (Shadow Game)* ISBN: 978-84-96629-09-7.
——. *Juego del circo. (Circus Game)* ISBN: 978-84-96629-62-2.
Ea. vol.: 16p. Madrid: Kókinos, 2007. $14.95. Gr. Preschool.

These sophisticated board books with appropriately placed cutouts and bright watercolors against flat backgrounds will encourage the very young to play with abstract figures (in *Juego de azar),* to play with colors (in *Juego de colores*), to play constructing various objects (in *Juego de construcción),* to play hide-and-seek with their fingers (in *Juego de dedos*), to play with forms as they touch and feel a circle, a square, a triangle and other interesting shapes and silhouettes (in *Juego de formas),* to view different eyes from various perspectives (in *Juego de ojos*), to play magical shadow games in a dark room (in *Juego de sombras*), to play with circus acrobats, clowns and animals (in *Juego del circo).* Originally published by Éditions du Panana, Paris, these are not conventional-type board books; rather, adults looking for different board books, with more participation from the young, will find them creatively engaging.

Ungerer, Tomi. *Los tres bandidos. (Three Robbers)* Illus: the author. Translated by Mark Taeger. Sevilla: Kalandraka, 2007. 38p. ISBN: 978-84-96388-56-7. $21.95. Gr. 1–3.

Although three ferocious robbers continue to terrify even the bravest townspeople, they are no match to the resourceful orphan,

Ursula, who questions their use of the stolen gold. Ungerer's bold, imaginative artwork, with black backgrounds contrasted by colorful silhouettes, adds a lighthearted tone to this cautionary tale of robbers-turned-orphan-saviors. Beginning Spanish readers will enjoy Taeger's fluid Spanish rendition.

Valverde, Mikel. *Paula en Nueva York.* *(Paula in New York)* Illus: the author. Madrid: SM/Dist. by Lectorum, 2005. 31p. ISBN: 1-933032-15-4. $12.00. Gr. 1–3.

While on a field trip with her teacher and friends in a small city in Spain, Paula asks a passing cloud if she would take her on a ride. Surprisingly, she wakes up in a big city full of tall buildings with a poster *Bienvenidos a Nueva York* (Welcome to New York). After a walk and eager to return home, she asks numerous kind and unique city dwellers—a giant whose tallness prevented him from playing basketball, a smiling policewoman, an opera singer—for directions. Finally, at Central Park a flock of geese agree to fly her back on their way home. Valverde's beautifully detailed ink-and-watercolor illustrations provide a most appealing view of New York City and its sundry inhabitants. This attractive, large-format publication was awarded the 2005 Fundación Santa María (Spain) award for its illustrations.

Van Allsburg, Chris. *El naufragio del Zéfiro.* *(The Wreck of the Zephyr)* Illus: the author. Translated by Teresa Farran i Vert. Barcelona: Juventud, 2006, 32p. ISBN: 84-261-3559-5. Gr. 2–4.

With Van Allsburg's original, dazzling artwork, with a subtle mix of reality and make-believe, and a most accessible Spanish rendition, young Spanish speakers will empathize when a boy tries to become the greatest sailor in the world. Despite a calm sea that sparkles with light and a star-filled night perturbed only by a magical ship flying through the sky, the boy misuses his new ability to sail his boat in the air.

Voutch. *Por quéééé.* *(Whyyyy)* Illus: the author. Translated by Marta Grech. (Los Chorlitos) Madrid: Dandelion, Ediciones, 2006. 24p. ISBN: 84-96568-08-3. Ages 2–5.

As soon as mama frog announces bedtime, little frog immediately questions, *¿Por quéééé?* (Whyyyy?), which results in endless witty and ironic responses and an increasingly frustrated mama. Voutch's carefree ink-and-watercolor cartoonish illustrations, full of humor and child sensitivity, add a realistic tone to this universally repeated bedtime routine that Spanish-speaking parents and their little ones will immediately recognize. Originally published by Editions Thierry Magnier, Paris, this well-constructed board book series—4½" × 4½"—also includes *Mi cerdito (My Little Pig), Papá en la oficina (Father at the Office), Mi almohada (My Pillow)*.

Waddell, Martin. *Duerme bien, Osito. (Sleep Tight, Little Bear!)* Illus: Barbara Firth. Translated by Esther Rubio. Madrid: Kókinos, 2005. 32p. ISBN: 84-88342-76-4. $19.95. Gr. Preschool–K.

When *Oso Pequeño* (Little Bear) finds a small cave that is just right for him, *Oso Grande* (Big Bear) encourages him to use it as a playhouse. After playing all day in *mi propia cueva* (his own cave), he now is ready for bedtime. But, feeling lonely, he goes back to *Oso Grande* and asks *Oso Grande* to read him a book. Soon *Oso Pequeño* falls asleep on his guardian's lap. Firth's tender artwork in gentle tones of grey and gold and Rubio's warm Spanish rendition beautifully depict *Oso Grande*'s mixed emotions and *Oso Pequeño*'s need for independence while yearning for protection.

Waring, Richard. *La gallina hambrienta. (Hungry Hen)* Illus: Carolina Jayne Church. Translated by Christiane Reyes. Barcelona: Juventud, 2003. 26p. ISBN: 84-261-3339-8. $16.95. Gr. Preschool–2.

With the simple, repetitive text and bright big appealing pen-and-ink and watercolor artwork of the original, Reyes's Spanish rendition will entrance the young as a very hungry red hen gobbles up a sneaky fox. The joyous depiction of the red hen that *comía y comía y crecía y crecía, y cuanto más comía, más crecía* (ate and ate, and grew and grew, and the more she ate, the more she grew) is contrasted with an increasingly emaciated fox who, in a surprising climax, results in a big happy, satisfied hen.

Weeks, Sarah. *Counting Ovejas. (Counting Sheep)* Illus: David Diaz. New York: Atheneum, 2006. 32p. ISBN: 0-689-86750-6. $17.99. Gr. K–2.

When a young boy can't fall asleep, he resorts to counting sheep in both Spanish and English. As *Una oveja Blanca/One white sheep* appears, he now has to find a way to remove it and declares: *Adios, oveja Blanca!/good-bye, white sheep!* This sheep is followed by two brown, three black and so on until he thanks them and wishes them *Buenas noches /Good Night*. Each simple bilingual refrain with a Spanish pronunciation guide is accompanied by Diaz's imaginative,

acrylic-and-pencil double-page spreads. Just right for Spanish learners and their parents or caregivers to learn to count or enjoy at bedtime.

Wells, Rosemary. *Only You/Sólo tú.* Translated by Teresa Mlawer. New York:
Viking, 2004. 18p. ISBN: 0-670-03692-7. $14.00. Gr. Preschool–1.
   In a gentle bilingual text, a little bear describes how much his
mother means to him. As opposed to literal translations, which are always dense and confusing, Mlawer's Spanish rendition aptly maintains
the meaning and loving intent of each thought—*I'm the apple of your
eye./Only you. De tus ojos soy la luz.* Preschoolers will enjoy Wells's
signature pencil-and-watercolor illustrations, which tenderly depict the
bear's loving relationship with his understanding mother, and their parents will appreciate the preface and afterword with excellent reminders
in both languages about life with their little ones.

Wild, Margaret. *¡Beso, beso! (Kiss, Kiss!)* Illus: Bridget Strevens-Marzo.
Translated by Verónica Uribe. Caracas: Ekaré, 2004. 24p. ISBN: 980-
257-310-8. pap. $8.95. Gr. Preschool–2.
   Bebé, Baby Hippo, is in such a hurry to go to play that he forgets
to give his mama a kiss. Wandering through the jungle, he repeatedly
hears *beso, beso* (kiss, kiss) as he sees a mama elephant kissing her
baby, then a papa lion kissing his cub, followed by a zebra and a chimp
kissing their babies. Suddenly, he remembers and rushes home to find
his mama and delightedly asks *¿Beso, beso?* The simple, repetitive text
and the lush detailed illustrations, full of action and affection, make this
an endearing reading/listening experience for the very young Spanish-
speaking crowd.

Willems, Mo. *El conejito Knuffle: Un cuento aleccionador. (Knuffle Bunny:
A Cautionary Tale)* Illus: the author. Translated by F. Isabel Campoy.
New York: Hyperion, 2007. 32p. ISBN: 978-1-4231-0566-4. $15.99.
Ages 2–6.
   When Trixie, *Papá* and *el conejito Knuffle* take a trip to the neighborhood *lavandería* (Laundromat), something jocularly wrong happens. Although toddler Trixie tries to communicate her distress to *papá*
in Spanish baby talk *¡Agugu yacaya magu!*, he is completely unaware
and even pleads, *por favor, no te pongas quisquillosa* (please don't get
fussy). *Mamá* realizes the problem and together they rush back; happily,
papá retrieves the missing toy and Trixie shrieks her first words: *¡Mi*

conejito! ¡Mi Knuffle! (Knuffle Bunny!). Young Spanish speakers and their parents won't resist Willems's vivacious cartoons superimposed over sepia-tone photographs depicting common parent-child scenes and Campoy's felicitous Spanish rendition.

Wilson, Henrike. *"Ya sé hacerlo todo solo", dice Lukas León. ("I Can Do Everything by Myself," says Lukas Lion)* Illus: the author. Barcelona: Edebé, 2003. 18p. ISBN: 84-236-6828-2. $11.95. Ages 1–3.

An audacious child lion, Lukas León, won't let any of his friends outdo him. Hence when Oscar Oso brags about dressing himself, Lukas León responds, *Yo también* (Me too). The same for going fast on a scooter, or properly eating spaghetti, or taking a nap, or building tall block towers, or cleaning up, or brushing his teeth. So when he brags to his parents, *Yo sé hacerlo todo solo* (I can do everything by myself), he is surprised by their answer: *¡Qué bien! Pues ahora, vete a la cama!* (That's great! Now, go to bed!) Originally published by Verlag, Munich, this charming board book with endearing watercolor illustrations of an enterprising child lion is certain to reassure intrepid toddlers.

Witte, Anna. *El loro Tico Tango. (Parrot Tico Tango)* Illus: the author. Cambridge, MA: Barefoot, 2004. 24p. ISBN: 1-84148-971-9. pap. $6.99. Gr. K–2.

Set in a lush rainforest reminiscent of Costa Rica, where the author states she first saw Tico Tango, this vividly illustrated cumulative rhyme is a pleasure to listen to and to behold. In a lively repetitive, rhyming Spanish narrative, it tells how a greedy *loro* (parrot) insists on taking fruit from the other animals of the rainforest until his beak can hold no more. Thus, the hungry repentant *loro* is forced to dance *un tango* to get *algo del mango* (a piece of the mango). Whether used with young Spanish listeners (or learners) as they hear about *el limón amarillo* (yellow lemon), *un higo morado* (a purple fig), *una cereza roja* (a red cherry) and other enticing fruits and colors, or as an amusing read-aloud, or as a playful introduction to the Costa Rican rainforest, this large-format book should not be missed, especially because of Witte's striking double-page spreads executed from paper, fabrics, acrylics, pastels and ink.

Wolfe, Frances. *Un deseo. (One Wish)* Illus: the author. Translated by Arturo Castán and Teresa Farrán. Barcelona: Juventud, 2004. 32p. ISBN: 84-261-3380-0. $15.95. Gr. K–3.

As a young girl narrates her greatest wish, she describes *una casa a la orilla del mar* (a cottage by the sea) where she could sit and sunbathe, take a toy boat to the water, walk along a sandy beach to feed hungry gulls, look for shells and other simple seaside pleasures. Originally published in Canada, this polished Spanish rendition maintains the lyrical style and evocative feelings of the English original. Although most youngsters won't be as enthusiastic as the elderly woman who realized her dream, the exquisite double-spread oil paintings, with an almost photographic quality, present a most inviting view of life by the sea that all children relish.

Wormell, Chris. *Dos ranas. (Two Frogs)* Translated by Élodie Bourgeois. Barcelona: Juventud, 2004. 32p. ISBN: 84-261-3354-1. $25.95. Gr. K–3.
Exquisite double-page spreads of two frogs debating the value of a stick, and other consequential dilemmas, are the perfect counterpart to this humorous cautionary tale. Maintaining the facetious tone of the original, first published by Jonathan Cape, London, this easy-to-read Spanish rendition will delight groups of young Spanish-speaking listeners/ viewers who will empathize with this surprised pair and their quick escapes.

Wright, Cliff. *Oso y barca. (Bear and Boat)* ISBN: 978-84-261-3610-7.
———. *Oso y caja.(Bear and Box)* ISBN: 978-84-261-3608-4.
———. *Oso y cometa. (Bear and Kite)* ISBN: 978-84-261-3604-6.
———. *Oso y pelota. (Bear and Ball)* ISBN: 978-84-261-3606-0.
Ea. vol.: 18p. Illus: the author. Translated by Élodie Bourgeois Bartín. Barcelona: Juventud, 2007. $9.95. Ages 3–5.
Delightfully simple and charmingly designed, the *Álbumes ilustrados* board book series introduces numbers, colors and opposites in an easy-to-understand straightforward manner. Exquisite black-ink and watercolor illustrations with a touch of nostalgia and classic conception depict *Oso Negro* (Black Bear) as he sails in his boat and counts *una barca* (one boat), *dos mariposas* (two butterflies) up to *¡diez amigos!* (ten friends). Babies, toddlers and caregivers will find lots to share in this beautiful counting book (*Oso y barca*), originally published by Templar Publishing, London. A final double-page spread in each book recounts the storyboard with illustrations and text. Oso Marrón and Oso Blanco introduce colors in *Oso y caja*. Oso Blanco (in *Oso y pelota*) and Oso Negro and his friends (in *Oso y cometa*) introduce the concept of opposites.

Yolen, Jane. *¿Cómo aprenden los colores los dinosaurios? (How Do Dinosaurs Learn Their Colors?)* ISBN: 0-439-87192-1.

———. *¿Cómo juegan los dinosaurios con sus amigos? (How Do Dinosaurs Play with Their Friends?)* ISBN: 0-439-87193-X.

Ea. vol.: 14p. Illus: Mark Teague. Translated by Pepe Alvarez-Salas. New York: Scholastic, 2006. $6.99. Ages 1–3.

Like the previous four titles in this charming well-constructed board book series with Teague's snappy dinosaurs, these dinosaurs encourage the very young to share their toys and play kindly with their friends (in *¿Cómo juegan los dinosaurios con sus amigos?*) and to learn their colors (in *¿Cómo aprenden los colores los dinosaurios?*). Alvarez-Salas's rhyming Spanish renditions are as enticing as thc original English versions.

Yolen, Jane. *¿Cómo cuentan hasta diez los dinosaurios? (How Do the Dinosaurs Count to Ten?)* ISBN: 0-439-66201-X.

———. *¿Cómo ordenan sus habitaciones los dinosaurios? (How Do Dinosaurs Clean Their Rooms?)* ISBN: 0-439-66202-8.

Ea. vol.: Illus: Mark Teague. Translated by Pepe Alvarez-Salas. New York: Scholastic, 2004. 14p. $6.99. Ages 1–3.

These amusing well-constructed board books will certainly encourage the very young to count to ten *(¿Cómo cuentan hasta diez los dinosaurios?)* and to pick up their rooms and put away their toys *(¿Cómo ordenan sus habitaciones los dinosaurios?)* as they delight in Teague's always spirited dinosaurs. Alvarez-Salas's rhyming Spanish renditions will especially captivate young Spanish-speaking listeners.

Yolen, Jane. *¿Cómo comen los dinosaurios? (How Do Dinosaurs Eat Their Food?)* ISBN: 0-439-76404-1.

———. *¿Cómo se curan los dinosaurios? (How Do Dinosaurs Get Well?)* ISBN: 0-439-54563-3.

Ea. vol.: 32p. Illus: Marc Teague. Translated by Pepe Alvarez-Salas. New York: Scholastic, 2003–2005. pap. $4.99. Gr. Preschool–1.

Just as sprightly as the originals, Alvarez-Salas's frolicsome Spanish renditions will resonate with young Spanish speakers who, in contrast to dinosaurs with terrible table manners, thcy always say *gracias* (thank you) and *por favor* (please) like the well-behaved dinosaurs (in *¿Cómo comen los dinosaurios?*) and despite feeling *de muy mala gana* (in a bad mood), these dinosaurs really drink lots of juice, rest, use a hankie and take their medicine (in *¿Cómo se curan los dinosaurios?*).

Teague's vividly colored, highly dramatic oversized dinosaurs even include the name of each species tucked somewhere in each double-
spread illustration.

Zullo, Germano. *Marta y la bicicleta.* *(Marta and the Bicycle)* Illus: Albertine. La Jolla, CA: Kane Miller, 2007. 28p. ISBN: 978-1-933605-38-8.
pap. $7.95. Gr. K–2.
    Marta, an orange-colored, bicycle-loving cow, is not like the other
cows. She is especially eager to win a bicycle race. To do so, she must
first build her own bike from old parts from the town junkyard. Then,
she had to teach herself to ride, which *no fue nada divertido* (was not
fun). *Se cayó. Mucho.* (She fell down a lot.) Albertine's preposterous
ink-and-watercolor illustrations are as engaging as the farcical Spanish
rendition that concludes with a victorious cow ruminating, *Si todos van
a montar en bicicleta, tendré que encontrar otra cosa que hacer* (If
everyone is going to ride bicycles, I'll have to find something else to
do.) Originally published by La Joie de Lire, Genève, this edition maintains the French signage within the illustrations.

General Fiction

Alcántara, Ricardo. *El aguijón del Diablo.* *(The Devil's Sting)* Zaragoza:
Edelvives, 2003. 139p. ISBN: 84-263-4849-1. pap. $10.95. Gr 9–12.
    Although Gustavo's hostility and bad habits are obvious, his
mother insists on pretending that if she gives him more money, which
she can't afford, he will become the son she cherishes. Soon Gustavo's
drug addiction affects the whole family: The father wants a divorce; his
sixteen-year-old brother Fernando has to work and forgo his soccer
practice to help pay for Gustavo's treatments; and his mother endures.
Despite the fact that this novel is not written from the viewpoint of the
young people and the mother's almost pathological denial of reality seems
extreme, this novel has been a great success with Spanish-speaking adolescents in Spain. Perhaps the theme of drug abuse and its negative consequences is the allure of this fast-paced, easy read.

Allende, Isabel. *Zorro: Una novela.* *(Zorro: A Novel)* New York: Harper-
Collins, 2005. 382p. ISBN: 0-06-077901-2. $24.95. Gr. 9–adult.
    With the tone and tempo of a flamboyant adventure story, Allende's
spirited retelling of the Zorro legend discloses the early life, during

undertakings, and gentlemanly deeds of Diego de la Vega, the handsome aristocrat who became the masked man to help the powerless and poverty-stricken. Set in Southern California and Barcelona in the 1800s, Allende's entertaining narrative includes such open-minded characters as *padre Mendoza* (Father Mendoza) who *confiaba en la ciencia casi tanto como confiaba en Dios* (p. 17) (trusted science almost as much as he trusted God), and Toypurnia and her mother, Lechuza Blanca, two assertive intelligent Native American women who became revered leaders of their people. Some adolescents may object to the 382 pages of small print, yet historical fiction fans will be thrilled by the duels, secret societies and romantic intrigues of this charming, fresh version of the famous Zorro legend.

Alonso, Manuel L. *Corriendo tras el viento. (Running After the Wind)* Madrid: Alianza, 2005. 150p. ISBN: 84-206-5901-0. pap. $10.95. Gr. 8–12.

Set in 1971 in Spain during the waning years of the Franco dictatorship, 17-year-old Inma and 23-year-old Luis are persuaded to leave their dull, difficult lives in Barcelona to go to an obscure forest in Portugal where, supposedly, they'll find a buried treasure. Despite too many coincidences that allow the two protagonists to evade a violent malefactor, this survival, fast-paced novel with likable characters will appeal to teens interested in a fast read. Especially engaging is the well-described setting that portrays, with great sensitivity and brio, life in Barcelona and other cities in Spain in the 1970s.

Alonso, Manuel L. *Rumbo sur. (Heading South)* Illus: Elena Odriozola. Zaragoza: Edelvives, 2005. 116p. ISBN: 84-263-5948-5. pap. $8.95. Gr. 4–7.

After a long separation, ten-year-old Clara, who lives in foster homes, and her father, who has been incarcerated for four years, are allowed to spend 15 days together. Without money, they decide to travel south towards Spain's beautiful beaches. Although Clara and her father survive (much too coincidentally) thanks to many generous strangers, and Clara's resentment and hostility seem to disappear (much too quickly), young Spanish speakers will enjoy the unconventional, trumpet-playing father who is ready to steal and to dedicate his life to his daughter's happiness. Odriozola's black-and-grey ink line illustrations add a realistic tone to Clara's trip.

Álvarez, Blanca. *El puente de los cerezos. (The Bridge of the Cherry Trees)* Illus: Federico Delicado. Madrid: Grupo Anaya, 2003. 159p. ISBN: 84-667-2719-1. $12.95. Gr. 8–12.

Seventeen-year-old Bei-Fang is sent against her will to live with her grandmother in a faraway village. Through her grandmother, she learns the secret language used by several generations of women who endured the power and absolute control of men—their husbands and lords. Set in China, this heartbreaking tale, based on traditional beliefs, highlights the tragic lives of women who were treated as useful objects—never allowed to complain or disagree with their masters. At times the spontaneity of the narrator's voice is lost amid adult voice-overs about the relationship between parents and adolescents and the meaning of life. Yet, the gripping setting, intriguing survival story and tenacious characters have the power to engage adolescents. The sensitive Chinese-style illustrations definitely reinforce the ambiance.

Andersen, Hans Christian. *La pequeña cerillera. (Little Match Girl)* Illus: Judit Morales and Adriá Gódia. ISBN: 84-667-4434-7.
———. *La princesa y el guisante. (The Princess and the Pea)* Illus: Elena Odriozola. ISBN: 84-667-4435-5.
———. *El valiente soldadito de plomo. (The Steadfast Tin Soldier)* Illus: Javier Sáez Castán. ISBN: 84-667-4433-9.
Ea. vol.: 24p. Translated by Enrique Bernárdez (Sopa de Cuentos) Madrid: Grupo Anaya, 2004. $10.95. Gr. 3–5.

In an appealing, small-size format (5" × 6"), these smooth renditions with numerous full-page illustrations of three of Andersen's most popular stories will entice independent readers. From the always-sad *La pequeña cerillera* to the surprising *La princesa y el guisante* to the dangerous adventures of *El valiente soldadito de plomo,* these titles are just right for Andersen's numerous fans.

Andersen, H. C. *El ruiseñor y otros cuentos. (The Nightingale and Other Stories)* Illus: Christian Birmingham. Translated by Francisco Antón. Barcelona: Vicens Vives, 2005. 143p. ISBN: 84-316-7165-3. pap. $12.95. Gr. 3–6.

Birmingham's stunningly delicate pastel and black-and-white illustrations add a touch of distinction to this luxury paperback collection of eight of Andersen's most beloved stories: *El traje nuevo del emperador (The Emperor's New Clothes), El firme soldado de plomo* (*The Steadfast Tin Soldier*), *La princesa y el guisante* (*The Princess and the Pea*), *El ruiseñor* (*The Nightingale*), *El patito feo* (*The Ugly Duckling*), *La pequeña cerillera* (*The Little Matchgirl*), *La sirenita* (*The Little Mermaid*), and *Pulgarcita* (*Thumbelina*). Some readers will appreciate the vocabulary footnotes, but children will gladly skip the tedious and unnecessary appended *Actividades* (Activities).

Andersen, Hans Christian. *La cerillera. (The Little Match Girl)* 27p. Illus: Toril Marö Henrichsen. ISBN: 84-241-1682-8.

———. *El compañero de viaje. (The Traveling Companion)* 31p. Illus: Elfriede and Eberhard Binder. ISBN: 84-241-1680-1.

———. *Los cisnes salvajes. (The Wild Swans)* 45p. Illus: Juan Ramón Alonso. ISBN: 84-241-1685-2.

———. *La hija del Rey de los Pantanos. (The Swamp King's Daughter)* 32p. Illus: Tiziana Gironi. ISBN: 84-241-1681-X.

———. *El patito feo. (The Ugly Duckling)* 47p. Illus: Tiziana Gironi. ISBN: 84-241-1686-0.

———. *Pulgarcita. (Thumbelina)* 28p. Illus: Toril Marö Henrichsen. ISBN: 84-241-1683-6.

———. *La Reina de las Nieves. (The Snow Queen)* 45p. Illus: Uwe Häntsch. ISBN: 84-241-1687-9.

———. *El ruiseñor. (The Nightingale)* 45p. Illus: François Crozat. ISBN: 84-241-1688-7.

———. *La sirenita. (The Little Mermaid)* 32p. Illus: Hubert Sergeant. ISBN: 84-241-1679-8.

———. *¡Totalmente cierto! (It's Absolutely True!)* 28p. Illus: François Crozat. ISBN: 84-241-1684-4.

Ea. vol.: Translated by María Victoria Martínez Vega. León: Everest, 2005. $17.95. Gr. 3–6.

Andersen's classic tales are always popular in the Spanish-speaking world. Especially so in 2005, which celebrated the 200th anniversary of his birth. Like other Spanish renditions, most of these are oversentimental renderings with a strong dose of religious overtones. Nonetheless, the full-page color illustrations will entice loyal Andersen fans. Spanish speakers from the Americas will note the Peninsular Spanish pronouns and conjugations used throughout, e.g., *comprendéis, matadme, os apartéis, vosotros, seguidme*. My favorites in this series are *El patito feo*, the beloved story of an unhappy ugly duckling who is ostracized by the other animals until he grows into a beautiful swan and

Totalmente cierto, one of Andersen's less-known works, which highlights the effects of gossip, particularly when an insignificant feather can result in five dead hens.

Andersen, Hans Christian. *Peiter, Peter y Peer y otros cuentos. (Peiter, Peter and Peer and Other Stories)* Translated by Enrique Bernárdez. Illus: Pablo Auladell. Madrid: Anaya, 2004. 286p. ISBN: 84-667-4012-0. $22.95. Gr. 4–7.

This smooth Spanish rendition of Samlede Eventyr of Historier, first published in 1874, includes 39 stories written by Andersen between 1865 and 1872 when he was over 60. Although none is as well known as his popular tales, Andersen fans will find the nostalgia and mournfulness that characterize this author in such stories as *La tetera* (The Teapot), *El bisabuelo* (Great-Grandfather), and *El cometa* (The Comet). Children will enjoy Auladell's sensitive dark-toned watercolors, which are scattered throughout the book. Adults will appreciate the well-written prologue and appendix.

Andrea, Leona. *El club de las siete gatas. (The Seven Cats Club)* Barcelona: Umbriel/Urano, 2004. 174p. ISBN: 84-95618-73-7. $15.95. Gr. 6–8.

Twelve-year-old Ana and her younger brother Daniel are eager to keep a litter of seven Siamese kittens that suddenly appeared on their doorstep. Their mother absolutely disagrees, but she is too busy in their new home—an old, semideserted mansion in total disrepair—to notice. Thus unfolds a mystery set in Spain that engulfs the whole town where black magic and inscrutable witches seem to prevail. Ana and Daniel are neither convincing detectives nor developed characters, yet adolescents interested in an easy read with lots of dialogue may be interested in following the clues that solve the mystery of *el club de las siete gatas*. Some Spanish speakers from the Americas may be confused by the use of Peninsular Spanish pronouns and conjugations—e.g., *os, prometed, iros, queréis*.

Andruetto, María Teresa. *El árbol de lilas. (The Lilac Tree)* Illus: Liliana Menéndez. Córdoba, Argentina: Comunicarte, 2006. 24p. ISBN: 978-987-602-015-2. $15.95. Gr. 3–6.

A simple poetic text in the third-person point of view highlights the thoughts of a young man sitting under a lilac tree, who instead of rushing to make money, or to pursue pretty girls, or to play ball, or to be happy, always replies: *Espero.* (I wait.) Conversely, a beautiful young woman travels the world searching: *¿Sos el que busco?* (Are you the one I am looking for?) Upon her return to her hometown, they find each other. Fanciful colorful illustrations provide the right tone to this imaginative depiction of love. Young Spanish speakers will note two Argentinean Spanish conjugations—*sos, hacés*—which are perfectly understood in context.

Auster, Paul. *El cuento de Navidad de Auggie Wren. (Auggie Wren's Christmas Story)* Illus: Isol. Translated by Mariana Vera. Buenos Aires: Sudamericana, 2003. 32p. ISBN: 950-07-2450-2. pap. $12.95. Gr. 2–5.

Vera's fable-like Spanish rendition about a lost wallet, a blind lonely old woman and an unexpected Christmas dinner is as affecting as the English original. Isol's fantastically imaginative color illustrations add a contemporary tone to the shop owner's tale of a young, pitiful shoplifter whose story may or may not be true.

Barrera, Norma. *Diario de Bernardo (1519–1521). (Bernardo's Diary [1519–1521])* 181p. ISBN: 970-37-0025-X.
Saucedo Zarco, Carmen. *Diario de Mariana (1692–1695). (Mariana's Diary [1692–1695])* 173p. ISBN: 970-37-0159-0.

Ea. vol.: (Diarios Mexicanos) Mexico: Planeta, 2004. pap $8.95. Gr. 7–9.

Important episodes in the history of Mexico are recreated through the fictional diaries of fourteen-year-old protagonists. Despite numerous authorial asides as well as awkward narrations and expositions in which the authors expound on important people, events and values, historical fiction fans, especially from Mexico, will welcome these *Diarios mexicanos* (Mexican Diaries). Until more engaging historical fiction is available, adolescents will have to be satisfied with these (mostly bland) renditions of specific times, places and people of the history of Mexico. Unfortunately, these lack the particulars of life and candid discussions that would add insight to the journals. Bernardo, a young soldier who traveled with the Spanish conqueror Hernan Cortés, experiences the conquest of Mexico (1519–1521) in *Diario de Bernardo (1519-1521)*. Mariana, who was born in Mexico City in 1678, tells about life in the capital of the country, including her admiration for the great poet, Sor Juana Inés de la Cruz in *Diario de Mariana (1692–1695)* Other titles in this series are:

Diario de Aurora (1910–13) by Alejandro Rosas
Diario de Clara Eugenia (1864–67) by José Manuel Villalpando

Diario de Cristina (1857–51) by Paola Morán Leyva
Diario de Elodia (1914–16) by Silvia L. Cuesy
Diario de Fernando (1912–14) by Carlos Silva Cázares
Diario de Lucía (1939) by Kathryn S. Blair
Diario de Lupita (1821–24) by Rafael Estrada Michel
Diario de Mercedes (1844–48) by Silvia L. Cuesy
Diario de Sofia (1862) by Silvia Molina
Diario de Tlauhquéchol (1518) by Norma Barrera

Barrie, James. *Peter Pan. (Peter, Pan and Wendy)* Illus: Fernando Vicente. Translated by Gabriela Bustelo. México: Santillana, 2006. 231p. ISBN: 970-770-677-5. pap. $13.95. Gr. 5–7.

Bustelo's serviceable Mexican Spanish rendition will appeal to longtime Peter Pan devotees from the Americas. Despite Vicente's prosaic black-and-white illustrations, which are corny detractors, Barrie's classic fantasy to *el País de Nunca Jamás* (Never Land) where Peter, Wendy, John and Michael meet fairy *Campanita* and defeat the terrible *Capitán Garfio* and his dangerous pirates is as engaging as always.

Barrie, James. *Peter Pan y Wendy. (Peter Pan and Wendy)* Illus: Robert Ingpen. Translated by Carmen Gómez Aragón. Barcelona: Blume, 2004. 216p. ISBN: 84-89396-04-3. $17.95. Gr. 5–7.

This stunning edition of J.M. Barrie's classic fantasy is enhanced by Ingpen's detailed full-page, pastel illustrations depicting Wendy, Michael and John as they accompany Peter to *el país de Nunca Jamás* (Never Land). With a prologue by David Barrie, Gómez Aragón's fluid Spanish rendition presents this timeless flight of imagination with Peter and his friends in *La Laguna de las Sirenas* (Mermaids' Lagoon) with the fairy *Campanilla* against their archenemy *Capitán Garfio* and his pirates. Peter Pan's numerous Spanish-speaking fans in the Americas will not mind the occasional Peninsular Spanish pronouns and conjugations *(podéis, os tomáis)*.

Blume, Judy. *Doble Fudge. (Double Fudge)* Translated by Laura Emilia Pacheco Romo. Miami: Santillana USA, 2004. 222p. ISBN: 1-59437-814-2. $9.95. Gr. 4–6.

Twelve-year-old Peter, who is constantly embarrassed by his younger brother's obsession with money, now has to put up with his long-lost cousins, Flora and Fauna, nicknamed *las Bellezas Naturales*. Pacheco Romo's Spanish rendition, which cheerfully maintains

Blume's playful and teasing conversations and jocular observations, is just right for Spanish speakers in the Americas.

Brennan, Herbie. *El portal de los elfos. (Faerie Wars)* Translated by Raquel Vázquez Ramil. Barcelona: Salamandra, 2004. 317p. ISBN: 84-7888-923-X. $16.95. Gr. 6–9.

From a realistic family breakfast in which Henry finds out that his parent's marriage is having serious problems to a fantasy world where Henry and his friend *señor* Fogarty have to save the life of Pyrgus Malvae, *el Príncipe Heredero del Reino de los Elfos* (the heir of the King of the Fairies), this fast-paced Spanish rendition has enough action to appeal to lovers of strange and imaginary worlds. Some adolescents may be confused by the complex plot where terrible night fairies, evil demons and greedy owners are ready to cause serious danger, yet there is enough humor and engaging characters that readers will cheer Henry through family troubles and mean fairies.

Buckley, Michael. *Las hermanas Grimm. (The Sisters Grimm: The Fairy-Tale Detectives).* Translated by Lucía Lijtmaer and Hara Kraan. Barcelona: Roca Editorial, 2005. 234p. ISBN: 84-96284-78-6. Gr. 5–7.

Set in rural New York, this humorous mystery intermingles magic, fairy tale characters, two courageous sisters, Sabrina and Daphne, and their highly suspicious *abuela* Grimm (Grammy Grimm). Despite several Peninsular Spanish conjugations (e.g., *molestéis, imaginaos, permaneced),* Spanish speakers from the Americas will delight when their favorite fairy tale characters—*Blancanieves* (Snow White), *Jack y la planta de habichuelas* (Jack and the Beanstalk), *Príncipe Azul* (Prince Charming), *Cenicienta* (Cinderella), *Espejo Mágico* (Magic Mirror)—help the orphaned sisters rescue their missing *abuela.* Fantasy fans will appreciate this smooth Spanish rendition where emerald-green meatballs become *albóndigas con una salsa de color violeta.* In contrast to the original English edition, this edition does not include any black-and-white illustrations or vintage silhouettes.

Calderón, Emilio. *Continúan los crímenes en Roma. (The Crimes in Rome Continue)* Madrid: Grupo Anaya, 2004. 183p. ISBN: 84-667-3670-0. pap. $10.95. Gr. 9–12.

Set in ancient Rome where murderers, kidnappers and thieves prevail, this fast-paced novel features eighteen-year-old Manio Manlio Escévola who is falsely accused of the murder of his father, a renowned senator. Fortunately, his beautiful girlfriend, Claudia, has the power and connections to save him and, ultimately, finds a way to prove his innocence. Amid the intrigue, readers are exposed to the cruel abuses of Emperor Tiberius as well as such notorious distractions as gladiator fights in which men were trained to entertain the public by engaging in mortal combat in well-attended arenas. Despite a few coincidences, historical fiction fans will empathize with the protagonist and his brave, resourceful girlfriend.

Calderón, Emilio. *El misterio de la habitación cerrada. (The Mystery of the Locked Room)* Madrid: Anaya, 2006. 129p. ISBN: 84-667-5354-0. pap. $10.95. Gr. 9–12.

While studying psychology in London, Bruno meets Heaven, who needs his help in solving the mystery of a serial killer, *Jack el Limpio* (Jack the Clean One), whose crimes are strikingly similar to the famous Jack the Ripper. Although some readers may be turned off by the heavy psychological jargon—e.g., *personalidad dominante* (domineering personality), *personalidad subyugada* (submissive personality), *test de Rorschach*—mystery devotees will applaud the amateur detective as he studies the clues, proceeds with the investigation, solves the case and beautiful Heaven joyfully embraces shy Bruno.

Cameron, Ann. *Colibrí. (Colibri)* Translated by Alberto Jiménez Rioja. New York: Scholastic, 2005. 236p. ISBN: 0-439-68314-9. $14.99; Zaragoza: Edelvives, 2004. 214p. ISBN: 84-263-5499-8. pap. $10.95. Gr. 5–8.

Nicknamed *Colibrí* by her mother, but renamed *Rosa* by the con man who kidnapped her at age four, a twelve-year-old Mayan girl endures life as a beggar and swindler to please the abusive scoundrel. Set in rural Guatemala and surrounded by traditional Mayan beliefs, customs and contemporary issues where people still remember "the big war" when many people died, Jiménez Rioja's fluid Spanish rendition touchingly conveys the anxious freshness of Colibrí's first-person (very mature) voice as she deals with her own doubts, fears and insecurities. Spanish speakers from the Americas might enjoy comparing Scholastic's Spanish edition with Edelvives's, both by Jiménez Rioja. Of course, *jugo de naranja* (orange juice) (Scholastic) is a more recognizable Latin American usage than *zumo de naranja* (Edelvives), but some will question, why: *Tío me pinchó con el bastón para que siguiera andando.* (Uncle poked me to keep me walking.) (Scholastic, p. 9) is better than *Tío me empujó con el bastón para que no me detuviera.* (Edel-vives, p. 14) and, incredibly, *Los musgos* [sic] (moss) (Scholastic, p. 1) instead of *El musgo* (Edelvives, p. 7). Because translation is an act of interpretation as well of rendering, the individual reader's personal taste is the best arbiter to judge the appropriateness and freshness of these two versions. Nonetheless, both versions movingly depict *Colibrí*'s search for identity amid the magic and miracles of her native Guatemala.

Carman, Patrick. *El límite de los montes negros. (The Dark Hills Divide)* (La Tierra de Elyon) Translated by Iñigo Javaloyes. New York: Scholastic, 2005. 273p. ISBN: 0-439-79175-8. pap. $6.99. Gr. 5–7.

Despite warnings, twelve-year-old Alexa is eager to explore the world outside the forbidden walls that surround her town. Armed with magical powers, including the ability of speaking with animals, inquis-itive Alexa discovers the danger that could destroy *la Tierra de Elyon* (the Land of Elyon). Spanish-speaking fantasy fans from the Americas will especially enjoy this fast-paced rendition with Latin American Spanish usages.

Carroll, Lewis. *Alicia a través del espejo. (Through the Looking Glass)* Il-lus: John Tenniel. Translated by Marià Manent. Barcelona: Juventud, 2006. 143p. ISBN: 84-261-3540-4. pap. $11.95. Gr. 5–7.

In this sequel to *Alicia en el país de las maravillas* (Alice in Won-derland), Alicia goes through the mirror to find a strange world where irrational situations, absurd characters and senselessness prevail. Ma-nent's delightfully satisfying Spanish rendition maintains the topsy-turvy world, including, of course, the famous poem *Jabberwocky*, which in her luminous Spanish version is *El Dragobán* and the mar-velous nonsense words, *hervín* ("brillig"), *Blendes casquines* ("slithy toves"), and *cibines* ("borogoves"). Tenniel's timeless black-and-white drawings are as charming as the originals, first published in the English edition.

Carroll, Lewis; and Robert Sabuda. *Alicia en el país de las maravillas. (Al-ice's Adventures in Wonderland: A Pop-up Adaptation)* Illus: by Robert Sabuda. Translated by Marta and Beatriz Ansón Balmaseda. Madrid: Kókinos, 2007. 14p. ISBN: 978-84-88342-98-0. $31.95. Gr. K–6.

Just as ingenious, fanciful and imaginative as the original, Sabuda's exquisitvely engineering pop-ups, three-dimensional movable images and flaps provide the perfect introduction to young Spanish speakers and their parents to *Alicia's* fantastic world, including *el Conejo B, el gato de Cheshire,* and *el Rey y la Reina de Corazones.* The smooth Spanish edition which does justice to the abridged text, appears in minibooks on each spread bringing to life some of *Alicia's* best-known adventures. Whether for display or enjoyable reading/viewing, this is the right version to truly appreciate this classic of the English-speaking world.

Cervantes, Miguel de. *La fuerza de la sangre; El celoso extremeño. (The Power of the Blood; The Jealous Husband)* Madrid: Catédra/Anaya, 2004. 95p. ISBN: 84-376-2149-6. pap. $10.95. Gr. 9–adult.

Especially designed for high school students, this edition includes two *novelas ejemplares* (exemplary novels) to introduce adolescents to Cervantes's genius as the creator of this genre. Although both novels are set in closed houses, in *La fuerza de la sangre* a dark house is the setting of a rape and an accident that results in redemption and happiness. In *El celoso extremeño* a locked house is like a convent with many luxuries where women are deprived of their freedom. Some adults may object to the themes discussed—rape and implied adultery—yet these short novels continue to appeal to generations of Spanish speakers as they reflect, with wit and ingenuity, life in Spain in the 1600s. A simple yet thought-provoking introduction to his life and work, approachable suggestions for discussion and informative footnotes add to the readers' understanding and enjoyment. Also noteworthy, this edition includes updated punctuation and spelling, which make these short novels even more accessible to contemporary Spanish speakers.

Cuentos hispanoamericanos del siglo XX. (Latin America Short Stories from the 20th Century) Madrid: Grupo Anaya, 2004. 157p. ISBN: 84-667-3666-2. pap. $9.95. Gr. 8–12.

The purpose of this collection is to introduce adolescents to a representative sample of the best short stories from Latin America of the 20th century. Hence, it includes stories by eleven of the most revered Latin American authors—Quiroga, Borges, Onetti, Piñera, Cortázar, Rulfo, Arreola, Monterroso, Benedetti, García Márquez and Byce Echenique—as well as brief informative introductions to the authors and the times. Numerous sidebars and footnotes on almost every page explain specific concepts and words. Readers will surely want to skip the dull didactic exercises and activities at the end.

Dahl, Roald. *Charlie y la fábrica de chocolate. (Charlie and the Chocolate Factory)* Illus: Quentin Blake. Translated by Verónica Head. Miami: Santillana, 2005. 198p. ISBN: 1-59820-059-3. pap. $6.95. Gr 5–8.

Dahl's always popular story about five lucky children who win an entry ticket into *señor* Wonka's mysterious chocolate factory is now even more captivating, with Quentin Blake's witty black-and-white cartoons. Head's delightful Spanish rendition, originally published by Alfaguara, Spain in 1978, joyfully maintains the story's excitement, whimsy and moral intentions. Despite the Peninsular Spanish pronouns and conjugations (e.g., *os imagináis, escuchad*), young Spanish speakers from the Americas will celebrate Charlie Bucket's *Billete Dorado* (Golden Ticket) that allows him into the unforgettable candy factory.

Desnoëttes, Caroline. *Tam-tam colores. (Tam-Tam Colors)* Illus: Isabelle Hartmann. Translated by P. Rozarena. Zaragoza: Edelvives, 2007. 40p. ISBN: 978-84-263-6405-0. $22.95. Gr. 3–5.

Simply and evocatively, Mussa, a grandfather, writes a letter to his granddaughter, Fatu, describing his bus trip from his native Senegal, a country of West Africa, to Ethiopia in Northeast Africa, through the Central African Republic, to his last stop in South Africa. He highlights beautiful sights and details such as the exquisite ceramic pots and woven textiles from Burkina Faso, the dense jungle in Guinea, and the colorful marketplace in Congo. Especially noteworthy are the cut-paper, photos and watercolor illustrations, in bright shades of green and tan, and the facing clear color photos of African art objects. Originally published by Réunion des Musées Nationaux, Paris, this large-format publication is an enticing overview of the people, sights and culture of Africa.

Doyle, Arthur Conan. *El archivo de Sherlock Holmes. (The Case-Book of Sherlock Holmes)* 329p. Translated by Juan Manuel Ibeas. ISBN: 84-667-4527-0.

Twain, Mark. *Las aventuras de Tom Sawyer. (The Adventures of Tom Sawyer)* 296p. Translated by Doris Rolfe. ISBN: 84-667-4528-9.
Ea. vol.: (Tus Libros Selección). Madrid: Anaya, 2005. pap. $11.95. Gr. 9–adult.

Delightful Spanish renditions characterize this series, especially prepared for adolescents, which includes numerous sidebars and footnotes on almost every page explaining particular words and concepts and brief introductions to each author. The last twelve stories written by Doyle about Sherlock Holmes, including *El problema del puente Thor*

(The Problem of Thor Bridge), one of the favorites of his numerous admirers, are included in *El archivo de Sherlock Holmes*. Set in the 1830s in a small Mississippi River town, *Las aventuras de Tom Sawyer* highlights the adventures of Tom, an orphan mischievous boy, who is as irresponsible as he is goodhearted. Generations of Spanish-speakers continue to enjoy these longtime classics of the English language.

Doyle, Arthur Conan. *El último saludo de Sherlock Holmes. (His Last Bow)* 284p. Translated by Juan Manuel Ibeas. ISBN: 84-667-3669-7.
Stevenson, Robert L. *Noches en la isla. (Island Night's Entertainment)* 195p. Translated by María Eugenia Santidrián. ISBN: 84-667-3668-9. Ea. vol. (Tus Libros Selección) Madrid: Grupo Anaya, 2004. pap. $11.95. Gr. 9–adult.

Like previous titles in this series prepared especially for adolescents, these exquisite Spanish renditions include brief introductions to each author as well as numerous sidebars and footnotes on almost every page explaining particular concepts and words. Eight of Conan Doyle's last stories in which mystery, murder, and honor predominate are included in *El ultimo saludo de Sherlock Holmes*. Set in the South Seas, *Noches en la isla* includes three stories that depict Stevenson's attachment to the people of the islands. Spanish-speaking adolescents in search of engrossing short stories will not be disappointed.

Ellis, Deborah. *El pan de la guerra. (The Breadwinner)* Translated by Herminia Bevia and Elena Iribarren. Toronto: Groundwood/Distributed by Publishers Group, 2004. 179p. ISBN: 0-88899-592-X. pap. $8.95. Gr. 5–8.

Eleven-year-old Parvana lives in Kabul, the capital of Afghanistan, during the Taliban regime. When her father is arrested, the family faces starvation and the brutality and beatings of Taliban soldiers. Through Parvana's courage and determination, readers are exposed to life in an abusive and intolerant society. In contrast to the original translation published in Spain, this Spanish rendition has substituted Peninsular usages for more recognizable Latin American Spanish usages (e.g. *permanecieran* instead of *permaneciesen*, *vuelvan* instead of *volved, tendrán* for *tendréis*).

Ellis, Deborah. *El viaje de Parvana. (Parvana's Journey)* Translated by Herminia Bevia. Zaragoza: Luis Vives, 2004. 174p. ISBN: 84-263-5218-9. pap. $10.95. Gr. 5–8.

Just as affecting as its predecessor—*El pan de la guerra (The Breadwinner)*—Bevia's clear Spanish rendition is a heartrending depiction of the effects on the lives of children in war-torn Afghanistan. Amid the malevolence of the Taliban, 13-year-old Parvana sets off alone from Kabul in search of her mother and siblings. Along the way, she saves three other abused children who together face bombings, starvation, land mines and despair until they arrive at a refugee camp. Originally published by Groundwood, Toronto, this realistic novel is an honest cry for assistance.

Ensenyat, Antoni Oliver. *Al-Razi, el médico de la atalaya. (Al-Razi, the Doctor of the Watchtower)* Translated from the Catalán by Joan Antoni Cebrian i Molina. Madrid: Anaya, 2005. 203p. ISBN: 84-667-4567-X. pap. $11.95. Gr. 9–12.

When nine-year-old Marc, a boy from Majorca, Spain, is captured by pirates, he is taken to Algiers and sold as a slave. Fortunately, his owner is an old doctor who teaches him about the medical sciences and instructs him about the Muslim religion. Upon the death of his tutor, Marc continues his studies and helps a beautiful female prisoner from Majorca to escape. Amid a series of quick getaways and mean traitors, this well-paced novel deftly depicts religious conflicts and stereotypes with important Muslim achievements in medicine as well as in the building of hospitals.

Farmer, Nancy. *El mar de los trolls. (The Sea of Trolls)* Translated by Gemma Gallart. Barcelona: Destino, 2006. 476p. ISBN: 84-08-06565-3. pap. $19.45. Gr. 6–9.

Set in England in 793 where fierce Viking warriors and large trolls pillage innocent villagers, Farmer's hugely successful fantasy is now available in Gallart's richly satisfying Spanish rendition that maintains the tension, magic, cruelty and bravery of the original. When Jack, an apprentice to *El Bardo* (the local bard), and his little sister Lucy are captured and taken to the court of *Ivar el Sin Hueso* (Ivar the Boneless) and his evil wife Queen *Frith la Semitroll*, they must embark on a dangerous journey through regions filled with dragons, giant spiders, trolls and talking crows to get back home. Despite the almost 500 pages of text, Spanish-speaking fantasy lovers will delight in Jack's coming-of-age tale with engrossing details of Norse and Celtic mythology. Serious readers also will appreciate the well-done appendix including interesting facts comparing Icelandic and Spanish pronunciations.

Friedman, Laurie. *Mallory se muda. (Mallory on the Move)* Illus: Tamara Schmitz. Translated by Josefina Anaya. Minneapolis: Lerner, 2008. 160p. ISBN: 978-0-8225-7493-4. pap. $5.95. Gr. 2–4.

Despite Mallory's numerous objections, her parents have decided they are moving to a new town. Dejectedly, she knows that she will especially miss her *Mejor Amiga* (Best Friend), Mariana. Although she keeps throwing stones in the *Estanque de los Deseos* (Wishing Pond), things do not go back to the way they were. Nevertheless, her new friend Joey helps her balance her old friend and the new one. Marred by a few Anglicisms, Anaya's serviceable Spanish rendition maintains the short, descriptive sentences of the original, including the prosaic cartoony illustrations. Of particular interest to Spanish-speaking readers is the honest depiction of the difficulties and differences with siblings.

Gavin, James. *Deep in a Dream: La larga noche de Chet Baker. (The Long Night of Chet Baker)* Translated by Juan Manuel Ibeas. Barcelona: Mondadori, 2004. 574p. ISBN: 84-397-1058-5. pap. $27.95. Gr. 10–adult.

With the polished style of the original, Ibeas's Spanish rendition chronicling the life and times of the acclaimed trumpet player and vocalist, Chet Baker, is certainly not for the fainthearted. Jazz enthusiasts, however, will not be dissuaded with the intensity of this well-researched biography that delineates numerous details of Baker's personal and professional life in which heroin addiction, violence and abusive personal relationships ultimately destroy his talent and lead to his death in a drug-infested street in Amsterdam. Despite the almost 600 pages of text, which also include notes, a bibliography and candid black-and-white photos, mature Spanish-speaking adolescents around the world have been fascinated by the life of this tragic musical legend whose many flaws are here painfully depicted.

Grahame, Kenneth. *El viento en los sauces. (The Wind in the Willows)* Illus: Elena Odriozola. Translated by Lourdes Huanqui. Madrid: Anaya, 2006. 213p. ISBN: 84-667-5213-7. $15.95. Gr. 4–6.

Kenneth Grahame's classic series of animal tales, originally published in 1908, is now available in this joyful Spanish rendition with Odriozola's sensitive black line and pastel watercolor illustrations. Like their English-speaking counterparts, Spanish speakers will delight in the adventures of four animal friends—*la Rata* (Rat), *el Topo* (Mole), *el Sapo* (Toad) and *el Tejón* (Badger)—along a river in the English countryside. Well-done notes at the end of the book clarify English terms and expressions.

Greder, Armin. *La isla: Una historia cotidiana. (The Island: An Everyday Story)*. Salamanca: Lóguez Ediciones, 2003. 32p. ISBN: 84-89804-66-4. $19.95. Gr. 3–5.

When an unknown, lonely man arrives on a raft on an island, the angry inhabitants reject him immediately. But a fisherman, who knows the dangers at sea, speaks on the man's behalf and convinces the mob to let him stay. Destitute, hungry, and willing to work, the man is nevertheless shunned by everyone and only succeeds in raising the worst fears of outsiders. As terror spreads, the inflamed mob, apprehends him, pushes him out to sea, burns the fisherman's boat for supporting him, builds a huge wall around the island, and even kills all the sea gulls that fly over so that no one knows about their island. Strong and powerful realistic full-page illustrations, mostly black and white, of a tiny nude man angrily rejected by big fat, hate-filled men armed with pitchforks, rakes, and hoes heighten the somber tone of this "everyday" story. Originally published by Sauerländer Verlag, Düsseldorf, this large-format publication is indeed a compelling depiction of fear and prejudice that many adults might consider inappropriate for children. Others will applaud the honesty and will welcome the undisguised intent.

Grégoire, Fabian. *Los niños de la mina. (Children of the Mine)* Translated by Carlos Fanlo Malagarriga. Barcelona: Corimbo, 2006. 45p. ISBN: 84-8470-234-0. $19.95. Gr. 3–5.

The horror and abuses suffered by young miners in the early 1900s in coal mines in Spain are depicted through appropriately somber watercolor illustrations and a brief text, which appears as captions and accompanies each illustration—from two to four panels per page. Despite the almost melodramatic tone and plot, the fictional lives of young Luis and Toni, who had to quit school to work in a coal mine to help support their families, depict the appalling conditions, hard work, lung diseases, explosions and premature deaths that certainly existed in numerous countries. A nine-page afterword with black-and-white photos provides further information about coal, Spanish miners and child labor in mines around the world. Neither uplifting nor cheerful, this indictment against child labor was originally published by L'école des loisirs, Paris.

Grindley, Sally. *Querido Max (Dear Max)* Illus: Tony Ross. Translated by
Josefina Anaya. Mexico: Castillo, 2006. 143p. ISBN: 970-20-0854-9.
pap. $11.95. Gr. 2–5.

   Nine-year-old Max, an only child who lives with his widowed
mother, writes to his favorite author, D. J. Lucas, and confides that he
wants to become an author. Through brief, humorous letters and post-
cards, the two express their personal likes and adversities. Max tells
about his difficult medical condition and his problems with a school
bully. D. J. not only coaches him as he writes his story, she also tells
about her school visits and personal fears. Anaya's pleasing Spanish
rendition and Ross's witty line illustrations are sure to engage Spanish
speakers, especially budding writers-to-be.

Gudule. *Cuentos y leyendas del amor. (Stories and Legends about Love)*
139p. Illus: Raúl Allén. ISBN: 978-84-667-6244-1.
Joly, Dominique. *Alejandro Magno. (Alexander the Great)* 158p. Illus: Max
Hierro. ISBN: 978-84-667-5387-6.
Ea. vol.: Translated by Ana Conejo. (Tus Libros Cuentos y Leyendas)
Madrid: Anaya, 2007. pap. $11.95. Gr. 5–8.

   Thirteen well-known love stories and legends from Greece, Italy,
Tibet, Ghana, China and Germany featuring such couples as *Romeo y
Julieta, Tristán e Isolda, Orfeo y Eurídice, Adán y Eva* recount, briefly
and succinctly, their passion, happiness and misfortunes in *Cuentos y
leyendas del amor*. With a great deal of drama and adventure, Joly's
readable recreation of the life of the warrior king of Macedonia as he
conquered and united the world from Greece to India is portrayed in
Alejandro Magno. Serious history students might disapprove of some of
the fictionalized characters; nonetheless, Alexander the Great's ambition and desire for conquest and glory that make him one of the most
fascinating conquerors of ancient times are certainly here. Both titles
include simply written historical notes and informative footnotes.

Gutiérrez Nájera, Manuel. *Cuentos. (Stories)* Madrid: Anaya, 2006. 405p.
ISBN: 84-376-2315-4. pap. $11.95. Gr. 9–adult.

   This collection by Manuel Gutiérrez Nájera (1859–1895), who is
considered as one of the best Mexican writers of the 19th-century and
a prime mover of Mexican Modernism, includes 34 short stories that
resonate with his elegant and sensitive vision of reality. He writes about
fantasies unfulfilled, his concern with the unprotected and the inequal-
ities of life in Mexico. Set in Mexico City, his stories depict with good-

natured humor his admiration for European culture. The brevity of many of these stories—from four to fifteen pages each—are just right to introduce Spanish-speaking adolescents to this well-known author and journalist. Serious readers will appreciate the scholarly 84-page introduction and the most complete bibliography.

Hassan, Yaël. *El profesor de música. (The Music Teacher)* Translated by Ana Mª Navarrete. Zaragoza: Edelvives, 2004. 119p. ISBN: 84-263-5210-3. $10.95 Gr. 6–8.

Eleven-year-old Malik is eager to learn to play the violin, but, as the youngest of ten children, his Muslim parents can not afford music lessons. When he meets Simón, his Jewish music teacher at school, both student and teacher must confront their own tragic memories. Originally published by Casterman, Belgium, this novel, which received the 2001 Saint-Exupéry Award, combines the dreams and passions of music lovers with the personal travails of a Holocaust survivor and the prejudices against Muslims in France. Despite some far-fetched plot twists that sometimes come dangerously close to the didactic, music lovers will be moved by the longings of an aspiring violinist and his conflicted teacher.

Henkes, Kevin. *El océano de Olivia. (Olive's Ocean)* Translated by Lourdes Huanqui. León: Everest, 2005. 195p. ISBN: 84-241-1655-0. pap. $9.95. Gr 5–8.

Henkes's compelling novel about twelve-year-old Marta who, on a summer vacation at her grandmother's house by the sea, begins to understand her feelings about the death of a classmate, her aging grandmother, an older boy and her desire to become a writer is as satisfying in this smooth Spanish rendition. Spanish-speaking middle readers will especially appreciate Marta's honest emotions of those difficult growing-up years in which falling in love and feeling disappointed, confused and guilty are as universal as the protagonist experienced in Cape Cod.

Horvath, Polly. *Una vaca ocasional. (An Occasional Cow)* Illus: Ximena Pineda. Translated by Magdalena Holguín. Bogotá: Norma, 2004. 173p. ISBN: 958-04-8191-1. pap. $7.25. Gr. 4–6.

Ifigenia, a New York City girl, is terribly worried as she thinks of her parents' decision to send her to her cousin's home in Iowa for the summer. In a witty and almost slapstick tone, she imagines life with her wild, extravagant cousins where mosquito bites lead to terrible diseases.

Holguín's fresh Spanish rendition is as humorously exaggerated as the original, first published in 1989. Unfortunately, however, Pineda's black-and-white illustrations are uninspired caricatures. They certainly lack Fiammenghi's comic charm, which accompanied the English edition. Nonetheless, Spanish speakers will enjoy this sprightly comedy where Iowan secret societies, laundry chutes, pig talent shows and gum wrappers turn out to be great fun.

Horvath, Polly. *Un verano en La Cañada de los osos. (The Canning Season)* Translated by Juan Manuel Pombo. Bogotá: Grupo Editorial Norma, 2004. 283p. ISBN: 958-04-7669-1. pap. $10.95. Gr. 7–10.

With the lively and at times salty language of the original, this snappy Spanish rendition of two unwanted girls who learn to love a pair of eccentric old ladies will enthrall Spanish-speaking adolescents. When thirteen-year-old Trinqueta is sent by her callous mother to spend the summer with her elderly relatives in a remote area of Maine, she didn't expect to find a life where peaceful isolation, gardening, fending off bears and reminiscing about the old days could be so satisfying. Especially when Harper, another lonely girl, joins the group. Sophisticated readers will appreciate the fantastic elements interwoven amid the sad, realistic circumstances in the girls' lives.

Ibbotson, Eva. *¡Menuda bruja! (Not Just a Witch)* Translated by Patricia Antón de Vez. Barcelona: Salamandra, 2004. 185p. ISBN: 84-7888-881-0. pap. $10.95. Gr 5–8.

Heckie and Dora, her best friend, are determined to be good witches. Following their school motto, *Brujas contra la maldad* (Witches Against Wickedness), Heckie, with the help of local supporters and a little boy, finds a way to get rid of *Los Vengadores Blancos* and to use her power for good causes. Unfortunately, and in contrast to the original English edition, this fluid Spanish rendition with a few Peninsular Spanish conjunctions (*queréis, podáis*) does not include Hawkes's humorous black-ink drawings. Nonetheless, Spanish speakers from the Americas will enjoy the fast pace of this humorous fantasy.

Ihimaera, Witi. *La leyenda de las ballenas. (The Whale Rider)* Translated by Raquel Solà. Barcelona: Juventud, 2004. 175p. ISBN: 84-261-3394-0. $15.95. Gr. 8–12.

The excitement and warmth of the original story about eight-year-old Kahu, a female member of the Maori tribe of New Zealand who has to prove her leadership abilities to her stern great-grandfather, is available in this spirited Spanish rendition. Perhaps some Spanish-speaking adolescents will find the mingling of strict cultural traditions with creation myths and religious reflections somewhat confusing and difficult to read. But the success of the film's adaptation is certain to add interest to Kahu's passion to save her tribe by facing the whales. A Maori-Spanish glossary is appended.

Ivanier, Federico. *Lo que aprendí acerca de novias y fútbol. (What I Learned about Girlfriends and Soccer)* Illus: Daniel Pereyra. Montevideo: Alfaguara/Santillana, 2007. 184p. ISBN: 9974-95-105-4. pap. $10.95. Gr. 6–8.

Sebastián's problems start when he turns thirteen. He is not doing very well in soccer; he can't get beautiful Paula's attention; the pimples on his face keep getting bigger and his mother insists he needs to get braces. In a most engaging first-person point of view and written in a humorous and limber style, this novel is sure to appeal to Spanish-speaking teens who will concur with Sebastian's *lista de Dudas Fundamentales* (list of Fundamental Doubts); such as *¿Cómo es que se hace para poder besar a una chica?* (What do you do to kiss a girl?). A few Uruguayan Spanish expressions and colloquialisms add to Sebastian's charm and candor, especially when he concludes that with girls, as in soccer, *Hay que 'poner huevo' y después se ve* (You've got to have guts and then you wait).

Jones, Terry. *El rey atolondrado y otros cuentos estrafalarios. (Fairy Tales and Fantastic Stories)* Illus: Michael Foreman. Translated by Carlos Mayor. Barcelona: Juventud, 2005. 256p. ISBN: 84-261-3493-9. $25.99. Gr. 3–5.

Collection of fifty-one stories set in fantastic countries where exotic characters defy conventional wisdom and popular beliefs. Originally published by Chrysalis, London, this attractive publication includes Foreman's fanciful watercolor and black-and-white illustrations. Despite the Peninsular Spanish pronouns and conjugations (*vais, vos*), Spanish-speaking fantasy lovers from the Americas (and Spanish learners) will appreciate the brevity of each story (from two to six pages) and the refreshing Spanish rendition that resonates with exquisite Spanish locutions (e.g.. *recontracórcholis, monigote*).

Jones, Terry. *La dama y el escudero. (The Lady and the Squire)* Illus: Michael Foreman. Translated by Daniel Cortés. Barcelona: Destino/Planeta, 2004. 383p. ISBN: 84-08-05165-2. $19.95. Gr. 6–9.

In this sequel to *El caballero y su escudero (The Knight and the Squire)* (2003), Tom meets beautiful Emilia de Valois, who helps him escape from *el Hombre de Negro* (Man in Black). Set in France amid peasant revolts, torture chambers, and the Pope's luxurious residence at Avignon, Tom, his friend Ann who often poses as Alan, and sometimes-difficult Emilia are involved in a series of exciting adventures where they manage to emerge victorious. Maintaining the fast-paced and lighthearted tone of the original, this fluid Spanish rendition is further enlivened with Foreman's black-and-white pen-and-ink illustrations.

Kafka, Franz. *La metamorfosis. (The Metamorphosis)* Translated by Imma Baldocchi. Barcelona: Edebé, 2004. 93p. ISBN: 84-236-7006-6. pap. $9.95. Gr. 9–adult.

Kafka's powerful brief novel in which Gregor Samsa wakes up and realizes he has been changed into a gigantic bug preserves its nightmarish quality in this fluid Spanish rendition. Serious Spanish-speaking readers will appreciate Ana Díaz-Plaja's appendix that discusses the life of the author as well as an accessible analysis of the work addressed especially to contemporary adolescents.

Kipling, Rudyard. *Los libros de la selva (The Jungle Books)* Illus: Ana Juan. Translated by Gabriela Bustelo. Madrid: Grupo Anaya, 2004. 437p. ISBN: 84-667-3678-6. $18.95. Gr. 7–10.

Bustelo's smooth Spanish rendition of Rudyard Kipling's classic tales—*The Jungle Book* (1894) and *The Second Jungle Book* (1895)—is as enthralling as the originals. Presented here in the author's preferred order are all of Kipling's stories about Mowgli, the Indian boy who is raised by wolves from infancy and who learns self-sufficiency and wisdom from the jungle animals, including the wise old bear, Baloo, and the great black panther Bagheera. Numerous full-page color illustrations depict idealized views of Mowgli and the animals. Also included are a well-written prologue and appendices with biographical information about the author and his works.

Lawrence, Caroline. *Los delfines de Laurentum. (The Dolphins of Laurentum)* ISBN: 84-7888-838-1.
———. *Los doce trabajos de Flavia Gémina. (Twelve Tasks of Flavia Gémina)* ISBN: 84-7888-918-3.
Ea. vol.: 187p. Translated by Raquel Vázquez Ramil. (Misterios Romanos) Barcelona: Salamandra, 2004. pap. $10.95. Gr. 6–8.

With the same excitement as its predecessors, set in Ancient Rome, these mysteries feature the four brave sleuths—Flavia Gémina, Lupo, Nubia and Jonatán. In the fifth title, *Los delfines de Laurentum,* the young detectives find a way to save Flavia Gémina's family from ruin. As they take refuge in the *villa de Laurentum,* they learn of a sunken treasure that could solve all their problems. When Lupo accidentally sees Venalicio, the slave trader who killed his father and cut out his tongue, Lupo knows he must act despite the dangers involved. In *Los doce trabajos de Flavia Gémina,* the sixth title in the series, Flavia Gémina is concerned about her father's extraordinary interest in a young widow, Cartilia Poplícola. Determined to discover Cartilia's motives, Flavia Gémina convinces her friends to help her investigate and performs twelve difficult tasks, just like the Greek hero Hércules. A few Peninsular Spanish pronouns and conjugations (e.g., *vosotros, enseñaros, podríais*) will certainly not deter Spanish-speaking mystery fans from the Americas from enjoying these lively Spanish renditions with intriguing historical settings.

Lawrence, Caroline. *Los enemigos de Júpiter. (The Enemies of Jupiter)* Translated by Raquel Vázquez Ramil. Barcelona: Salamandra, 2005. 189p. ISBN: 84-7888-946-9. pap. $11.95. Gr. 6–8.

In this seventh installment of the engaging series set in ancient Rome, the young sleuths—Jonatán, Flavia, Nubia and Lupo—and *doctor* Mardoqueo are called by *emperador* Tito to investigate the mysterious enemy that is threatening to destroy Rome. Although Rome is a dangerous place, the four friends bravely explore the imperial palace and Jonatán makes a frightening decision. Like the other titles, this smooth Spanish rendition uses Peninsular Spanish conjugations (e.g., *os ocupáis, dejadnos*) amid the excitement of Roman political intrigue, medical practices and the destruction of the temple in Jerusalem.

Lawrence, Caroline. *Los gladiadores de Capua. (The Gladiators from Capua)* Translated by Raquel Vázquez Ramil. Barcelona: Salamandra, 2005. 191p. ISBN: 84-7888-974-4. pap. $11.95. Gr. 6–8.

Set in 80 AD in Rome when Emperor Tito announced the 100 days of games to open the new Flavian amphitheater, this eighth volume of this well-translated series presents Flavia, Nubia and Lupo in search of their friend Jonatán amid the horror of gladiator fights, executions and animal sacrifices. Despite the gore and cruelty of the *espectáculos* (spectacles), Spanish-speaking adolescents will enjoy the courage of the intrepid friends who find a way to save their companion.

Limb, Sue. *Chica de 15: Encantadora pero loca. (Girl, 15, Charming but Insane)* Translated by Alejandra Pérez del Real. ISBN: 84-667-4736-2.
——. *Chica (de casi) 16: Una auténtica tortura. (Girl, (Nearly) 16: Absolute Torture)* Translated by Borja García Bercero. ISBN: 84-667-4737-0.
Ea. vol.: 286p. Madrid: Anaya, 2005. pap. $12.95. Gr. 7–10.

With the same risqué humor of the English originals, these delightful Spanish renditions will especially captivate Spanish-speaking teens who have a limited selection of easy reads that deal with topics that particularly interest them. In *Chica de 15: Encantadora pero loca*, Jess, the protagonist, compares her *tetas y culo* (boobs and bum) with Flora's, her best friend and the school beauty, who is as popular as she is wealthy. Although Jess prefers handsome Ben Jones, she happily concludes that her friend Fred, who urgently needs a haircut, is just right for her. In the second installment, *Chica (de casi) 16: Una auténtica tortura*, Jess has to postpone her splendid summer plans with Fred to go with her mother and grandmother on a historical literary trip that ends in a most surprising visit to her father, whom she hasn't seen in several years. With great honesty, the author depicts adolescents' concerns—insecurity, acceptance, body image, gay parents—through characters that are not only candid, they are appealing and most convincing.

Lindgren, Astrid. *Pippi Calzaslargas. (Do You Know Pippi Longstocking?)* Illus: Richard Kennedy. Translated by Blanca Ríos. Barcelona: Editorial Juventud, 2007. 137p. ISBN: 978-84-261-3192-8 pap. $9.95. Gr. 4–6.

Nine-year-old Pippi Calzaslargas, who is incredibly strong and lives alone in Villa Villekula with her horse and her devoted monkey, *Míster* Nelson, enjoys impressing her conventional neighbors, Tommy and Annika. First published in Sweden in 1947, this lively Spanish rendition has maintained Pippi's indomitable vitality as she bakes cookies on the floor, takes on two burglars single-handedly, saves two children from a house on fire, and works other extravagant wonders. Despite the Peninsular Spanish conjugations (*habríais, hubieseis, escuchad*, et al.), Spanish speakers from the Americas will applaud Pippi's independent spirit. The amusing, almost cartoony, black-and-white illustrations are appropriately whimsical.

Martin, Ann M. *Un rincón del Universo.* *(A Corner of the Universe)* Translated by Alberto Jiménez Rioja. León: Everest, 2005. 195p. ISBN: 84-241-8722-9. pap. $9.95. Gr. 6–9.

Hattie turns twelve the summer of 1960 when she meets her extroverted *tío* Adam. Her mother explains that he has *problemas mentales* (mental problems)—schizophrenia, autism. Whereas others reject him and laugh at him, Hattie, though bewildered by his unconventional behavior, enjoys his company and wants to help him. Jiménez Riojas's affecting Spanish rendition is as heartbreaking as the original.

McDonald, Megan. *Doctora Judy Moody.* *(Judy Moody M.D. The Doctor Is In!)* 175p. ISBN: 1-59820-034-8.
——. *Judy Moody.* *(Judy Moody)* 166p. ISBN: 1-59437-816-9.
——. *Judy Moody adivina el futuro.* *(Judy Moody Predicts the Future)* 162p. ISBN: 1-59437-837-1.
——. *Judy Moody salva el planeta.* *(Judy Moody Saves the World)* 167p. ISBN: 1-59437-838-X.
——. *¡Judy Moody se vuelve famosa!* *(Judy Moody Gets Famous!)* 142p. ISBN: 1-59437-817-7.
Ea. vol.: Illus: Peter H. Reynolds. Translated by Atalaire, adapted by Isabel Mendoza. Miami: Santillana USA, 2004–2005. pap. $7.95. Gr. 3–5.

With the easy-to-read engaging style of the originals, these jovial Spanish renditions highlight Judy Moody, a zestfully enthusiastic third grader, whose adventures and ideas are as universal as children everywhere. It is important to note that the scarcity of books in Spanish that depict life's frustrations and challenges from a child's perspective make these books even more appealing to Spanish-speaking children. And, of course, Reynolds's witty, black-and-white watercolor, pen-and-ink illustrations further enhance the humorous prose, snappy dialogues and brief chapters that make this series irresistible. When Judy's third grade class starts to study *Nuestro Fabuloso Cuerpo* (Our Amazing Human Body), she is ready to work on a most unusual class project and to share a truly unexpected show-and-tell in *Doctora Judy Moody.* *Judy Moody* introduces the spirited protagonist who happens to be in a bad mood the first day of school until she gets an intriguing assignment: *preparar un collage sobre sí mismos* (to create a "me" collage). Although Judy obtains a mood ring that describes her *De un humor insoportable* (in a grouchy, impossible mood) she still tries to convince her classmates that she can predict the future in *Judy Moody adivina el futuro.* After

Judy fails to win *un concurso de curitas* (an adhesive bandage design contest), she inspires her class to become involved in a major environment-saving project in *Judy Moody salva el planeta.* Because Judy can't even spell *Berenjena,* she can't win a spelling bee, yet she is still determined to find a way to become famous in *¡Judy Moody se vuelve famosa!*

Mechtel, Angelika. *Enganchado. (Cold Turkey)* Translated by Elsa Alfonso Mori. México: Everest, 2005. 139p. ISBN: 968-893-094-6. pap. $9.95. Gr. 7–12.

As sixteen-year-old Andy becomes involved in the world of alcohol and drugs, his twelve-year-old sister, Simone, persists in her attempts to help him. Although his use of all types of drugs leads to his suspension from school, burglary, drug dealing and junkies, his parents appear not to notice the seriousness of the situation. Originally published by Ravensburger, Germany, this realistic novel reads more like a case study of drug addiction among teens—from marijuana to hashish opium, cocaine and heroin. Some adults may object to the somber drug scenes intermingled with profanity; some adolescents will question the too-good-to-be-true sister and therapist, yet all will approve of the optimistic ending.

Meyer, Stephanie. *Crepúsculo: Un amor peligroso. (Twilight)* 506p. ISBN: 978-970-770-994-2.
———. *Luna nueva. (New Moon)* 574p. ISBN: 978-970-58-0023-8.
———. *Eclipse. (Eclipse)* 636p. ISBN: 978-1-60396-022-9.
Ea. vol.: Translated by José Miguel Pallarés. Miami: Santillana, 2007–2008. pap. $15.99. Gr. 9–12.

The popular vampire love novels for young adults, where romance, danger and malicious vampires coexist, are sure to attract Spanish-speaking adolescents in search of constant adventure and potential gore. Fortunately, Pallarés's fluid Spanish renditions maintain the suspense and quick pace of the English originals. In *Crepúsculo: Un amor peligroso*, the first one of the saga, 17-year-old Bella leaves Phoenix to live with her father in Forks, Washington. At school, she meets and falls in love with Edward, a handsome boy who happens to be a vampire. *Luna nueva* continues the romance and anticipation especially when Bella is injured at her birthday party and causes Edward and his vampire family to leave as the sight of her blood puts her in imminent danger. In *Eclipse* the struggle for survival is deepened as Bella must choose between her friend Jacob, a werewolf, and Edward, the vampire and the object of her affection. As graduation approaches, Bella must decide between life or death. Spanish-speaking fans of the supernatural will be as entranced as their English-speaking counterparts.

Molina, María Isabel. *El vuelo de las cigüeñas. (The Flight of the Storks)* Zaragoza: Edelvives, 2007. 135p. ISBN: 978-84-263-6207-0. pap. $11.95. Gr. 7–10.

Set in 9th-century Spain in the court of King Alfonso III, el Magno, amid the political intrigues between Christians and Muslims, this fast-paced novel intermingles the lives of two teens: Gonzalo, a Christian scribe, and Meriem, a beautiful Muslim girl. For lovers of action there is risk, adventure and ever-present dangers. History buffs will appreciate the depiction of life in Muslim Spain where educated Christians and Muslims studied Latin, Greek and Arabic and excelled in mathematics, music and poetry. And, of course, romance aficionados will cheer the courage of Gonzalo and Meriem, who choose love over arranged marriages.

Monreal, Violeta. *Las espadas del Cid. (The Swords of the Cid)* Illus: the author. Madrid: Bruño, 2006. 45p. ISBN: 84-216-9760-9. $22.95. Gr. 3–5.

Based on the adventures of Rodrigo Díaz de Vivar, (1043–1099), better known as *el Cid*, this fast-paced retelling highlights aspects of the life of the Spanish soldier and national hero whose military exploits, including the capture of Valencia and other battles, are widely admired in the Spanish-speaking world. Colorfully detailed, computer-generated, almost cartoonish illustrations depict life in feudal Spain with a great sense of humor and ingenuity. Beginning with the Cid's childhood in Vivar, a small village in Spain, up to his daughters' marriages to Spanish royalty, this appealing large-format publication is a lively introduction to Spain's long cherished epic poem.

Morpurgo, Michael. *La espada dormida. (The Sleeping Sword)* Illus: Michael Foreman. Translated by Isabel Llasat. Barcelona: RBA, 2005. 124p. ISBN: 84-7871-258-5. $13.95. Gr. 5–7.

Ten-year-old Bun Bundle, who lives with his parents on the island of Scilly, off southwest England, a former haven for pirates and smugglers, loses his eyesight in a tragic accident. Despite difficult times in which he is even ready to commit suicide, he finds the strength to overcome his handicap with the help and understanding of his friends, especially fourteen-year-old Anna. In a fantastic twist, he stumbles upon the Excalibur sword, which, in Arthurian legend, belonged to King Arthur. He now has the energy that changes his life forever. Originally published in the United Kingdom, this fluid Spanish rendition will appeal to lovers of fantasy.

Muñoz Puelles, Vicente. *La foto de Portobello. (The Photo from Portobello)* Zaragoza: Edelvives, 2004. 181p. ISBN: 84-263-5618-4. pap. $10.95. Gr. 8–12.

Although sixteen-year-old Sonia feels she can deal with her weight loss, her parents know that she is anorexic. Despite her objections, she is taken to a hospital that specializes in eating disorders where she meets many women with the same condition. In contrast to the other patients, Sonia, with the help of an understanding doctor and her patient father, finally finds a way to overcome her abnormal fear of becoming obese. Notwithstanding the obvious message to adolescent girls (and their parents), some readers will empathize with Sonia's tribulations and anxieties. And, even though Sonia is not a convincing character, she experiences many teen challenges: parents, social skills, selecting and preparing for an occupation. Perhaps such asides as the U.S. invasion of Iraq and the burial site of an American Indian in Barcelona are more outlandish than necessary, yet some teens will find this to be a hopeful novel about this disorder.

Muñoz Puelles, Vicente. *¡Polizón a bordo! El secreto de Colón. (Stowaway on Board! The Secret of Columbus)* Illus: Federico Delicado. Madrid: Anaya, 2005. 158p. ISBN: 84-667-4749-4. pap. $11.95. Gr. 5–8.

In a most engaging first-person point of view, Gonzalo, a brave and intrepid teen, relates his experiences in Spain in the 1490s, just before the expulsion of the Jews from Spain and as a confidant of Columbus and witness to Columbus's arrival to the New World on October 12, 1492. Perhaps there are too many coincidences as young Gonzalo overcomes ruffians in the slums of Sevilla, meets beautiful and wealthy Simonetta Berardi who teaches him how to read and write, and, seemingly, without too much difficulty, finds a place to hide in one of Columbus's ships. Nonetheless, this fast-paced, historical novel is an accessible introduction to a controversial time in the history of Spain as well as an unconventional view of Christopher Columbus. Unfortunately, Delicado's bland watercolor illustrations lack the excitement of the well-written narrative.

Pardo Bazán, Emilia. *Un destripador de antaño y otros cuentos. (The Ripper of Long Ago & Other Stories)* Madrid: Alianza Editorial, 2003. 197p. ISBN: 84-206-5506-6. Gr. 9–adult.

Fifteen stories about rural Spain that tell about the cruelty of family relationships, the backwardness of jealousy and the transitory nature of feelings are included in this collection by one of Spain's most read authors.

Pescetti, Luis M. *Frin. (Frin)* Illus: O'Kif. Madrid: Alfaguara/Santillana, 2003. 191p. ISBN: 84-204-6574-7. pap. $10.95. Gr. 5–7.

Twelve-year-old Frin hates his physical education class, especially when his teacher wants to make all the students Olympic stars. Because he doesn't excel, his teacher insists on punishing him by making him do extra laps. Fortunately, a new student, Lynko, understands him, and, even more important, he falls in love with Alma. Despite numerous intrusive adult sounding comments about life's injustices, parents who watch too much TV, the books of Italo Calvino and a farfetched trip to visit Alma, the likeable characters and fresh dialogue will appeal to middle readers in search of a story with an authentic Argentine setting, though amazingly, written in Peninsular Spanish. O'Kif's black-and-white cartoons are definitely a plus.

Philbrick, Rodman. *El joven y el mar. (The Young Man and the Sea)* Translated by Iñigo Javaloyes. New York: Scholastic, 2005. 193p. ISBN: 0-439-76958-2. pap. $4.99. Gr. 5–8.

Spanish-speaking readers, especially from the Americas, will not be able to put down this gripping Spanish rendition of Philbrick's exciting survival story in which twelve-year-old Skiff Beaman overcomes his mother's death, a depressed, alcoholic father, mean bullies and a most challenging solo fishing trip. There are very few novels for middle school Spanish-speaking students that depict with such honesty and candor the feelings of a teen boy who can't stand his father's beer drinking— *¡Cómo odio ese olor!* (How I hate that smell!)—and yet manages to catch a valuable blue fin tuna to pay for the repairs of the family boat.

Pilkey, Dav. *El Capitán Calzoncillos y la feroz batalla contra el Niño Mocobiónico, 1a. parte: La noche de los Mocos Vivientes. (Captain Underpants and the Big Bad Battle of the Bionic Booger Boy, Part I: The Night of the Nasty Nostril Nuggets)* ISBN: 0-439-66204-4.

————. *El Capitán Calzoncillos y la feroz batalla contra el Niño Moco-biónico, 2a. parte: La venganza de los ridículos mocorobots. (Captain Underpants and the Big, Bad Battle of the Bionic Booger Boy, Part 2: The Revenge of the Ridiculous Robo-Boogers)* ISBN: 0-439-66205-2. Ea. vol.: 175p. Illus: the author. Translated by Miguel Azaola. 2004. New York: Scholastic. paper, $4.99. Gr. 4–6.

Just as creative and entertaining as the previous adventures of the superhero principal, *Capitán Calzoncillos*, also known as Captain Underpants, these hilarious Spanish renditions with Pilkey's jocular black-and-white cartoon illustrations, action-filled fliporamas and introductory comics are exactly what Spanish-speaking reluctant readers need. Although Jorge and Beto are very bad spellers and not especially good students, they still can save the planet from *las tres tremebundas masas mucosas* (the three humongous Robotic Booger Chunks) in *El Capitán Calzoncillos y la feroz batalla contra el Niño Mocobiónico, 1a parte.* Jorge and Beto must now face the *Ridículos Mocorobots* (Ridiculous Robo-Boogers) in outer space before they return to school in *El Capitán y la feroz batalla contra el Niño Mocobiónico, 2a. parte: La venganza de los ridículos mocorobots.*

Pilkey, Dav. *El Capitán Calzoncillos y la furia de la Supermujer Macroelástica. (Captain Underpants and the Wrath of the Wicked Wedgie Woman)* Illus: the author. Translated by Miguel Azaola. Madrid: Ediciones SM, 2002. 175p. ISBN: 84-348-9109-3. pap. $9.95 Gr. 4–6.

This celebrated title of the popular *Capitán Calzoncillos,* also known as Captain Underpants, features the superheroes, Jorge and Beto, who now turn their attention to their evil teacher *señora Pichote.* With the same tongue-in-cheek adventures, action-filled fliporama and introductory comic strips, full of deplorably misspelled words (e.g., *hodioso, habenturas, conzidencia*) as the original, this title is sure to appeal to devoted fans. Spanish speakers from the Americas, especially reluctant readers, may be confused by the numerous Peninsular Spanish conjugations—*os habéis, empezad, estáis.* Nonetheless, the rowdy black-and-white illustrations and imaginative superheroes who manage to transform mean *señora Pichote* into a kind-hearted teacher will win many more followers.

Plaza, José María. *¡Tierra a la vista!: La historia de Cristóbal Colón. (Land Ho!: The History of Christopher Columbus)* Illus: Julio Carabias

Aranda. Madrid: Espasa Calpe, 2005. 202p. ISBN: 84-670-1957-3. pap. $11.95. Gr. 5–8.

Written in a carefree, almost colloquial style, this fictional biography is based on the life of the Italian explorer who, in the service of Spain, discovered the New World. Reluctant history readers will not mind Plaza's dramatized or invented parts that show how Columbus might have thought regarding his predicaments at sea, popular acclaim and ultimate repudiation. The computer-generated, color cartoon illustrations and such title chapters as *Un rey tramposo* (A tricky king) and *¿Qué se propone este loco?* (What does this madman propose?), as well as a humorous color cartoon book cover, may encourage the heretofore unenthusiastic Spanish-speaking readers to read more about Columbus. Serious readers will appreciate the appended detailed chronology and list of important historical people and notes.

Poe, Edgar Allan. *El gato negro y otras narraciones extraordinarias. (The Black Cat and Other Stories of the Supernatural)* Translated by Mariano Orta Manzano. Barcelona; Juventud, 2005. 183p. ISBN: 84-261-3454-8. pap. $10.95. Gr. 8–adult.

An excellent introduction to the life and work of Edgar Allan Poe, written by the French literary critic, Charles Baudelaire, first published in 1852, provides a distinctly European and laudatory view of the American author's imaginative and powerful stories. Beginning with the classic story *El gato negro (The Black Cat)*, in which a man's obsession with his black cat escalates into disaster and murder, this collection is followed by eight stories of the supernatural. The brevity of these well-rendered, horror stories—from nine to thirty pages—is certain to appeal to Spanish-speaking fans of this genre. A timeline is also included.

Pullman, Philip. *La princesa de hojalata. (The Tin Princess)* Translated by Isabel de Miquel. Barcelona: Umbriel, 2004. 351p. ISBN: 84-95618-52-4. $15.95. Gr. 9–12.

Set in 1882 in London and in the imaginary kingdom of Razkavia in Central Europe, this action-packed third novel of the series maintains the political intrigue, adventure and romance in this fluid Spanish rendition. Especially appealing are the main characters—Becky, a sixteen-year-old language tutor; Jim, a young detective; and Adelaide, a beautiful and illiterate young woman, who suddenly becomes queen. Despite the intricate plot, numerous characters, and

labyrinthine location, Spanish-speaking teens in search of bloody hap-
penings will applaud the heroes as they overcome bombs, poison, dag-
gers and street fights. They will also enjoy the previous titles, *Sally y
la sombra del norte (Shadow in the North)* and *Sally y el tigre en el
pozo (Tiger in the Well)*. In contrast to the more subdued covers of the
English editions, this cover features two swashbuckling, comic-book-
style heroines ready for a fight.

Rayó, Miguel. *El cementerio del capitán Nemo. (Captain Nemo's Ceme-
tery)* Illus: Pablo Auladell. Translated by Angelina Gatell. Zaragoza:
Edelvives, 2004. 126p. ISBN: 84-263-5448-X. pap. $8.95. Gr. 5–8.

In an almost poetic evocative voice, an unseen narrator relates
Miguel's summer experiences, from age seven to thirteen, with his
grandfather in a small town in the coast of Spain. In brief chapters he
tells about Miguel's experiences collecting fossils, getting in trouble,
fishing, swimming and meeting María, his first love. Especially emo-
tive is his relationship with his always-understanding, nature-loving
grandfather, who knew the needs of a maturing teen. Spanish speakers
from the Americas may be perplexed by the use of Peninsular Spanish
conjugations (e.g., *compartíais, barríais, quitabais*), yet they will be
touched by a wonderful grandfather. Auladell's softly shaded pencil and
watercolor illustrations maintain the reverie tone of Miguel's reminis-
cences.

Reiche, Dietlof. *Freddy, un hámster en peligro. (Freddy, a Hamster in Danger)* Translated from the German by María Falcón Quintana. Barcelona:
Salamandra, 2003. 158p. ISBN: 84-7888-825-X. pap. $10.95. Gr. 4–6.

In a lively first-person point of view Freddy, a golden hamster
with large cheek pouches and a short tail, narrates his experiences with
evil *profesor* Dittrich. Although Freddy promises his master John that
he would never reveal his extraordinary abilities—he learned how to
read and write by sitting alongside his previous master—he posts his
autobiography on the Web with almost terrible consequences. With the
help of his friends, however, he manages to elude the danger. The simple fluid Spanish text maintains the humor and fast pace of the highly
successful original German edition.

Repún, Graciela. *El mago y el escritor: Biografía de J. R. R. Tolkien. (The Magician and the Writer: Biography of J. R. R. Tolkien)* Bogotá: Grupo Editorial Norma, 2006. 106p. ISBN: 958-04-9309-X. pap. $11.95. Gr. 5–8.

Repún intermingles a story "in the manner of Tolkien" about Gandalf, an old magician and revered storyteller, and his avid listener-elves with the life and work of J. R. R. Tolkien (1892–1973), the British writer of the well-known fantasies, *El Hobbit (The Hobbit)* and *El Señor de los Anillos (The Lord of the Rings)*. Admirers of the South African-born author will want to skip Repún's contrived storyline and her plodding recitation of Gandalf's narrative, but will enjoy the simply told life of the popular author that has captivated readers around the world. An appendix explaining Tolkien's perception of myths and folklore including such classics as *El Beowulf (Beowulf)*, *El Kalevala (Kalevala)* and *El Rey Arturo (King Arthur)* as well as a chronology are also included.

Rosen, Michael. *El libro triste. (Michael Rosen's Sad Book)* Illus: Quentin Blake. Translated by Esther Rubio. Barcelona: Serres, 2004. 34p. ISBN: 84-8488-151-2. $15.95. Gr. 3–6.

In this touching, personal memoir, Rosen tells about his intense sadness upon the sudden death of his eighteen-year-old son Eddie. With absolute honesty, poignantly maintained in this affecting Spanish rendition, he explains that when his feelings of dejection, anger, loss, rage make him sad: *hago cosas malas. Son cosas que no puedo contarte. Son demasiado malas* (I do bad things. I can't tell you what they are. They're too bad). Yet he also surprises himself by remembering his late mother walking in the rain and happier times with Eddie. Blake's expressive watercolor-and-ink illustrations in shades of grey and occasionally bright colors featuring a cheerful Eddie add to the heartbreaking simplicity that only great loss and grief can evoke.

Rowling, J. K. *Harry Potter y el misterio del príncipe. (Harry Potter and the Half-Blood Prince)* Translated by Gema Rovira Ortega. Barcelona: Salamandra/Distributed by Lectorum, 2006. 602p. ISBN: 84-7888-996-5. pap. $15.99. Gr. 5–10.

Spanish speakers from the Americas will be especially delighted with this vigorous Spanish rendition of the sixth title of Harry Potter's saga. Now sixteen, Harry must confront the difficult challenges posed by the forces of evil including untrustworthy *Príncipe Mestizo* (Half-Blood Prince) and the always-feared *El-que-no-debe-ser-nombrado* (He-who-must-not-be-named). With the dark and somber mood of the original as well as the trials and tribulations of Harry's teen friends, this engrossing tale has the action, drama and philosophical implications that readers universally contemplate in their own *Bosque Prohibido* (Forbidden Forest).

Rowling, J. K. *Harry Potter y la Orden del Fénix. (Harry Potter and the Order of the Phoenix)* Translated by Gemma Rovira Ortega. Barcelona: Salamandra, 2004. 893p. ISBN: 84-7888-742-3. $25.95. Gr. 5–10.

Despite the 893 pages of small print, Spanish-speaking fans are just as enthusiastic with this fifth installment of Harry Potter's magical adventures. Now a 15-year-old, angry teenager, Harry finds himself upset at the *Ministerio de Magia,* the mean *profesora* Dolores Umbridge and other hypocritical adults who neither understand nor care for the students at the school. The occasional Peninsular Spanish pronouns and conjugations (*os turnáis, vosotros habéis*) will not deter Spanish-speaking fans from the Americas to applaud a maturing Harry as he confronts his own at times awkward emotions in this long and imaginative coming-of-age story.

Ruiz Zafón, Carlos. *El Príncipe de la Niebla. (The Prince of Fog)* New York: Rayo/HarperCollins, 2006. 230p. ISBN: 978-0-06-128438-0. $21.95. Gr. 8–12.

Originally published in 1993 in Spain with great success, this is the first of a series of novels for adolescents—*El Palacio de la medianoche* (The Midnight Palace), *Las luces de septiembre* (September Lights) and *Marina* (Marina)—of the popular Spanish author. Ruiz Zafón states that he wrote *El Príncipe de la Niebla* because this is the novel that he would have liked to read when he was in his teens. Featuring thirteen-year-old Max, his sister Alicia and their new friend, Roland, who together uncover the strange circumstances that led to the death of young Jacob. In a fast pace, full of mystery, death, magic and romance, and set in Spain during the Civil War, this gothic novel will not disappoint lovers of the fantastic eager to solve the machinations of the diabolic *Príncipe de la Niebla.*

Seidler, Tor. *Hermanos bajo cero. (Brothers Below Zero)* Translated by Liwayway Alonso. León: Everest, 2004. 118p. ISBN: 84-241-8076-3. pap. $8.95. Gr. 6–8

With the brisk clear tone and breezy dialogues of the original, Alonso's readable Spanish rendition makes this almost sensational novel about sibling rivalry slightly more believable. Although seventh-grader Tim Tuttle tries to measure up to his popular and successful younger brother John Henry, he finds he can not compete. Intuitively, his kind and eccentric *tía abuela* Winifred encourages him to paint and avoid comparing himself to his younger brother. John Henry, however, cannot accept his brother's talent and parents' attention. After almost causing his brother's death, John Henry is suddenly repentant, acknowledges his misdeeds, and realizes how much he really cares for him. Despite the quick conversion, the fast-paced plot and honest details about family life will appeal to Spanish-speaking teens.

Sepúlveda, Luis. *Historia de una gaviota y del gato que le enseñó a volar. (The Story of a Seagull and the Cat Who Taught Her to Fly)* Illus: Chris Sheban. New York: Levine/Scholastic, 2003. 126p. ISBN: 0-439-56026-8. $15.95. Gr. 4–6.

When Zorbas, *un gato grande, negro y gordo* (a big, black cat) promises a dying seagull that he would care for the egg she leaves behind, raise the chick and teach it to fly, he didn't know how much help he would need. Fortunately, his wise feline friends—*Sabelotodo, Secretario, Colonello*—and a human poet find a way to teach *Afortunada* to fly, and to have the strength to leave and to realize her true nature. Originally written in a simple, almost lyrical Spanish and later gracefully rendered into English, Zorbas's story embraces such difficult topics as respect for the environment, compassion, and acceptance through humorous situations and engaging characters. Sheban's delicate black-and-white illustrations are as expressive as Sepúlveda's tender thought-provoking story. It is indeed difficult to find such a beautifully written fantasy with artfully chosen words in a fresh natural style as well as the humor, dramatic events and intelligent themes that young Spanish speakers deserve.

Sierra i Fabra, Jordi. *Buscando a Bob. (Searching for Bob)* Madrid: Grupo Anaya, 2005. 203p. ISBN: 84-667-4565-3. pap. $10.95. Gr. 8–12.

Seventeen-year-old Héctor, who lives in a small city in Spain, is having a hard time at home. As an avid fan of Bob Dylan, his dream is to go to Barcelona to attend a concert of his idol. Perhaps there are too many coincidences as the confused teen hitchhikes his way to Barcelona and the numerous adult-sounding "friends" he encounters along the way are too obvious in helping Héctor discover himself; nevertheless, Spanish-speaking adolescents will enjoy Héctor's brief escapade. It is important to note that there are more than sixty quotes from Bob Dylan's songs interspersed throughout, which may sound too dated for most teens.

Sierra i Fabra, Jordi. *La guerra de mi hermano.* *(My Brother's War)*
Madrid: SM, 2004. 169p. ISBN: 84-675-0178-2. pap. $11.95. Gr. 9–12.
  Set in Spain shortly after 9/11/2001, this novel highlights the
strong reactions about the *misión humanitaria* (humanitarian mission)
in the Middle East as experienced by a Spanish family: Seventeen-year-
old Gabriel, a committed pacifist and severe critic of the Bush administration's policies in Iraq, introduces each chapter with *El día que mi
hermano se marchó a la guerra . . .* (The day my brother went to war . . .);
Marcos, who is eager to serve in a peaceful mission; Father, who knows
terrorism should be defeated; Mother, who loves her son and can't stand
the idea of his going to war; and other siblings, who can't understand.
Some readers will certainly disagree with the frequent authorial asides
expressing anti-American ideas; others will question the political dia-
tribes; others will object to the stereotypical characters—pro-war, anti-
war, loving mother, materialistic sister. Nonetheless, this novel has been
eagerly read by Spanish-speaking adolescents.

Sierra i Fabra, Jordi. *Las mil y una noches . . . [o casi].* *(A Thousand and
One Nights . . . [or Almost])* Illus: Francesc Rovira. Barcelona: Edebé,
2006. 174p. ISBN: 84-236-8210-2. $29.95. Gr. 3–6.
  Based on the always-popular Scheherazade's Arabian Nights,
Sierra i Fabra's exquisitely readable adaptation of 15 tales definitely
capture the flavor, excitement and wisdom of the original stories with
an added contemporary twist. Rovira's humorously expressive, full-
page ink-and-watercolor illustrations are a most amusing complement to this beautifully designed large-format publication. It includes such well-known favorites as *La historia de Aladino o el
cuento de la lámpara maravillosa* (The Tale of Aladdin and the Wonderful Lamp), *La historia de Alí Babá o el cuento de los cuarenta
ladrones* (The Tale of the Forty Thieves) and *La historia de Simbad
o el cuento del cementerio de los elefantes* (Sinbad the Marine) as
well as others that tell about good and bad deeds, righteous men,
clever embezzlers and wise enchanters. A few Peninsular Spanish
pronouns and conjugations (e.g., *dictamináis, narráoslo, os digo),*
which are easily understood in context, do not detract from their
magic and allure.

Simon, Francesca. *Pablo Diablo y la bomba fétida.* *(Horrid Henry's
Stinkbomb)* Illus: Tony Ross. Translated by Miguel Azaola. Madrid:
SM, 2003. 93p. ISBN: 84-348-9684-2. pap. $10.95. Gr. 3–5.

Pablo Diablo, known in the original English as Horrid Henry, is a pest, both at home and at school. In this humorous collection of four stories he manages to annoy his teacher, *señorita Guillotina* and his brainy classmates, *Clarisa la Monalisa* and *Benito el Cerebrito* when he ties in the *Mundolibro* contest; to surprise club members *Marga Caralarga* and *Susana Tarambana;* to embarrass his teacher in front of the principal; and to be asked to leave from his friend's house. Despite the Peninsular Spanish pronouns and conjugations (e.g., *os estáis, formad vuestros*), reluctant Spanish-speaking readers from the Americas will enjoy the brisk accessible Spanish rendition and witty black-and-white cartoons highlighting Pablo's incessant pranks.

Singer, Isaac Bashevis. *Cuentos para niños. (Stories for Children)* Illus: Javier Sáez Castán. Translated by Andrea Morales. Madrid: Anaya, 2004. 351p. ISBN: 84-667-3986-6. $15.95. Gr. 4–9.

To commemorate the 100th anniversary of the birth of Isaac Bashevis Singer (1904–1991), this refreshing Spanish rendition of his collection of 36 stories, first published by Farrar, Strauss and Giroux in 1984, includes some of his most famous, such as *Mazel y Shlimazel, o la leche de leona* ("Mazel and Shlimazel") and *Los tontos de Chelm y la carpa estúpida* ("The Fools of Chelm and the Stupid Carp") as well as other lesser known tales. Fans of the 1978 Nobel-Prize-winning author will also appreciate the evocative prologue, which highlights the author's personal life and achievements and the informative appendices that include notes, a glossary and facts about the author and his times. Readers, however, will note an interesting inconsistency: Although Singer states in the author's note that he is delighted that this collection is not illustrated (which is true in the original edition), it is unfortunate that this otherwise splendid collection is marred by pedestrian and at times corny full-page watercolors that neither clarify nor simplify the text. What a shame.

Sortland, Bjorn. *Mamá vale 10 camellos. (Mother Is Worth 10 Camels)* Illus: Eulogia Merle. Translated by Cristina Gómez Baggethun. Zaragoza: Edelvives, 2005. 102p. ISBN: 84-263-5612-5. pap. $11.95. Gr. 3–5.

Nine-year-old Arve knows that his mother is upset since his father left them. For a change of scenery, mother decides to take Arve, his older brother Frederick and an aunt to a vacation in Jordan. Meantime, Frederick is dealing with his own teen problems at school, where he is ignored by all his classmates and, especially, by the pretty girl he likes. In Jordan, mother meets a Saudi prince who is willing to pay her 10 camels if she marries him. The first-person point of view adds a believable tone to this humorous novel about the relationship between mother and sons, teenage love and Arab customs. In addition, the fast-paced smooth Spanish rendition and witty two-tone illustrations increase the appeal of this chapter book, originally published in Norway.

Soto, Gary. *Béisbol en abril y otros cuentos. (Baseball in April and Other Stories)* Translated by Enrique Mercado. Miami: Santillana USA, 2007. 140p. ISBN: 978-0-59820-519-0. pap. $9.95. Gr. 5–9.

    Mercado's joyous Spanish rendition of Gary Soto's popular collection of eleven short stories about the trials and tribulations of growing up should not be missed. The everyday worries and anxieties of preteen Latino boys and girls in Fresno, California, are sensitively depicted as they deal with such concerns as lack of money, embarrassing moments at school, obstinate parents and other difficult situations. Of special interest because of their universal themes are *Séptimo grado* (Seventh Grade), *Madre e hija* (Mother and Daughter) and *La bamba* (La Bamba).

Soto, Gary. *Cebollas enterradas. (Buried Onions)* Illus: Patricia Madrigal. Translated by Ilán Adler. Mexico: Fondo de Cultura Económica, 2002. 151p. ISBN: 968-16-6669-0. pap. $12.95. Gr. 8–12.

    Nineteen-year-old Eddy, a college dropout, is struggling to find a job in his violent barrio in Fresno, California. Despite numerous murders, including his best friend and cousin, Eddy does not want revenge. But finding a way out for a young Mexican American is not easy. Violence pervades and young men are the victims. Adler's smooth Spanish rendition maintains Soto's spare, poignant descriptions depicting the harsh reality of life in the *barrio*, where random bloodshed triumphs amid vengeance and distrust. In contrast to the original English edition, which is not illustrated, this paperback edition is marred by numerous pedestrian black-and-white illustrations that neither enhance the text nor extend the mood. The story is real and sad; the illustrations are unexciting and trite.

Soto, Gary. *Cruzando el Pacífico. (Pacific Crossing)* Translated by Enrique Mercado. Miami: Santillana USA, 2007. 161p. ISBN: 978-1-59820-521-3. pap. $9.95. Gr. 6–9.

Soto's delightful contemporary American slang and Japanese terms are just as enticing in Mercado's gracious Spanish rendition that will especially appeal to travel fans interested in the martial art of *kempou*. Despite the slight story and uneventful narrative, Spanish-speaking teens will appreciate the cultural collisions experienced by Lincoln and Tony, two fourteen-year-old Mexican Americans from California who are chosen as exchange students for a summer in Japan. Well-placed footnotes assist readers with Japanese terms.

Soto, Gary. *Tomando partido. (Taking Sides)* Translated by Enrique Mercado. Miami: Santillana USA, 2007. 144p. ISBN: 978-1-59820-520-6. pap. $9.95. Gr. 6–9.

Spanish-speaking adolescent boys will identify with Lincoln Mendoza, the fourteen-year-old protagonist who has problems both on and off the basketball court in Mercado's flowing Spanish rendition of Soto's realistic novel. Lincoln's fears and hopes as well as his worries about his new school in the suburbs, a misunderstanding with his best friend, a bad knee, and, most disturbingly, a prejudiced coach who obviously doesn't like Mexicans are genuine and universal.

Spinelli, Jerry. *Misha. (Milkweed)* Translated by Alberto Jiménez Rioja. Barcelona: Entre Libros, 2004. 223p. ISBN: 84-9338831-9. $16.95. Gr. 6–9.

Set in the streets of Nazi-occupied Warsaw during World War II, Spinelli's powerful first-person novel is fortunately now available in Jiménez Rioja's cogent Spanish rendition. As seen through the eyes of *Aladrón* (Stopthief), a gentle inquisitive and incredibly trusting orphan whose greatest ability is stealing food to survive, readers are exposed to the brutalities of the Nazi *Botas* (Jackboots) and the horrific life inside the ghetto. Despite a few Peninsular Spanish pronouns and conjugations (e.g., *traed, os queréis),* Spanish speakers from the Americas will be moved by this realistically tragic Holocaust tale.

Steinbeck, John. *El poni rojo. (The Red Pony)* Translated by Jaime Zulaika. Madrid: Alianza, 2004. 127p. ISBN: 84-206-5819-7. pap. $9.95. Gr. 5–10.

Steinbeck's memorable four related stories that chronicle a young boy's maturation through his contacts with nature and his relationship with his stern father are now available in this smooth Spanish rendition. From *El regalo*, the first and best-known story where ten-year-old Jody is given a red pony by his rancher father but despite Jody's care, the pony dies, to *Las grandes montañas, La promesa,* and *El jefe,* Jody experiences the joys and sorrows of affection, loss, and the adult world.

Strich, Christian, ed. *El libro de los 101 cuentos. (The Book of 101 Stories)* Illus: Tatiana Hauptmann. Translated by Enrique Bernárdez and others. Madrid: Anaya, 2005. 672p. ISBN: 84-667-5169-6. $25.95. Gr. 3–7.

This collection of 101 of the most popular European traditional tales, legends and classic stories is sure to appeal to readers/listeners of all ages. Strich's fast-paced retellings, which are just as enticing in these refreshing Spanish renditions, are beautifully complemented by Hauptmann's lively and engaging black-and-white and watercolor illustrations. It includes such long-time favorites as *La Bella Durmiente* (Sleeping Beauty) and Andersen's *La pequeña cerillera* (The Little Match Girl) as well as lesser known Norwegian, Irish and Croatian tales. Originally published by Verlag, Zurich, this revised second Spanish edition offers Spanish speakers an incredible selection of brief tales in a most attractive large format. A few Peninsular Spanish pronouns and conjugations (e.g., *tenéis, vosotros queréis)* will definitely not deter Spanish speakers from the Americas.

Thal, Lilli. *Mimus. (Mimus)* Translated by Moka Seco Reeg. Madrid: Anaya, 2007. 507p. ISBN: 978-84-667-6291-5. $22.95. Gr. 8–11.

After many years of cruel wars, the medieval kingdom of Vinland seems to be ready to sign a peace treaty with the kingdom of Monfiel. Sadly, twelve-year-old *príncipe Florín* finds out that his father *el rey Teodor* has been tricked and is now imprisoned in the castle's dungeons. Young Florín is now obligated to serve as an apprentice to Mimus, Teodor's enigmatic and unpredictable court jester. Originally written in German, and hugely successful in English-speaking countries, Seco Reeg's exquisitively flowing Spanish rendition will enthrall Spanish speakers in search of a thought-provoking fantasy, with strong historical fiction elements. It is important to note that Spanish speakers from the Americas will not mind a few Peninsular Spanish conjugations (e.g., *esperad, créais).*

Thomas, María José. *¡Bravo, Rosina! (Bravo, Rosina!)* Illus: Claudio Muñoz. Caracas: Ekaré, 2005. 38p. ISBN: 980-257-242-X. $15.95. Gr. 3–5.

Set in the 1930s in Chile, this tender story recounts the life of young Rosina whose grandfather's gramophone influenced her long-lasting love of music and opera. Perhaps Rosina's encounter and singing with the well-known Italian tenor, Dino Borgioli, a Rudolph Valentino look-alike, are a little far-fetched. Nonetheless, opera fans will enjoy the reverie, which is appropriately portrayed in Muñoz's dreamy ink-and-watercolor pastel illustrations. An author's note and the text in Italian of the song *Se il mio nome saper voi bramate* (If You Wonder What My Name Is) from *The Barber of Seville* are appended.

Thomson, Sarah L. *Imagina un día. (Imagine a Day)* Illus: Rob Gonsalves. Translated by Élodie Bourgeois Bertín. Barcelona: Juventud, 2006. 34p. ISBN: 84-261-3543-9. Gr. 3–6.

With the same arresting double-page spreads of the original English edition, this companion to *Imagina una noche* (Imagine a Night) encourages Spanish-speaking readers/viewers to delight in everyday activities as they let loose their imaginations. Most appropriately, rather than presenting a literal translation of the English text Bourgeois's expressive Spanish rendition states, as an example: *Imagina que un día un soplo de viento/lleva tus deseos/para que el cielo/vuelva a pintarse de azul*, which in the original English is: "Imagine a day/when you release a handful of blue balloons/into a cloudy, gray sky/to create a postcard-perfect day." Both are beautiful and opportune. Artists-to-be especially will appreciate Gonsalves's surreal acrylic paintings that make this large-format book a unique view.

Thomson, Sarah L. *Imagina una noche. (Imagine a Night)* Illus: Rob Gonsalves. Translated by Élodie Bourgeois Bertín. Barcelona: Juventud, 2007. 34p. ISBN: 978-84-261-3626-5. $19.95. Gr. 4–7.

Like its companion *Imagina un día* (Imagine a Day) Gonsalves's magical double-page spreads invite readers/viewers to imagine a night when the ordinary becomes almost mythical: *Descubres que la gravedad no funciona como te lo esperabas* (You find that gravity doesn't work quite as you expected) or *Resuena un silbido en un pasillo vacío, y una voz llama '¡Todos al tren!'* (Your toy train rumbles on its tracks out of your room and roars back in). Rather than a literal translation, Bourgeois's eloquent Spanish rendition reflects the fantastic imagery of the illustrations.

Tsukiyama, Gail. *El jardín del samurai (The Samurai's Garden)*. Translated by J.M. Pomares. Barcelona: Obelisco, 2006. 237p. ISBN: 89-9777-248-2. $27.95. Gr. 10–adult.

Maintaining the fluid smooth dignity of the original, Pomares's refined Spanish rendition tenderly depicts the mixed emotions of seventeen-year-old Stephen just before World War II when he was sent to a small coastal village in Japan to recuperate from tuberculosis. Under the care and guidance of Matsu, a quiet housekeeper and a master gardener, he meets young beautiful Keiko and kind Sachi, a woman afflicted with leprosy. Through their kindnesses, he recovers his physical strength and a renewed perspective on life. Despite the complicated story, sensitive young adults will be moved.

Vallbona, Rafael. *Recambios Luna. (Moon Spare Parts)* Translated by Raimon Artis. León: Everest, 2003. 110p. ISBN: 84-241-8559-5. pap. $12.95. Gr. 8–10.

Sixteen-year-old Alex and his three friends—Miguel, Javi, and Salva—are disgusted with their bad grades at school and their problems at home. With no money, no jobs, and no prospects for a better future, they decide to spend their summer vacation stealing motorcycles for resale. Written in Alex's first-person voice and peppered with the vernacular and interests of Spanish-speaking adolescents, including references to drugs and the human body, this is an insightful depiction of the lives of adolescents whose uncertain future often leads to violence and tragedy. At times, an intrusive adult voice discussing such issues as abusive employers and racism may seem unnecessary. Nonetheless, this is a fast-paced easy read that many adolescents will recognize.

Veciana-Suárez, Ana. *Vuelo a la libertad. (Flight to Freedom)* New York: Scholastic, 2004. 228p. ISBN: 0-439-66358-X. pap. $4.99. Gr. 6–9.

Thirteen-year-old Yara writes in her diary about life in Havana in 1967 followed by her family's experiences in Miami as Cuban exiles. As in the original English edition, this fluid Spanish rendition depicts Yara's (and her family's) strong feelings against Fidel, the Communist Party, and Che Guevara: *Uno de los líderes comunistas de Cuba, lo mataron en Bolivia donde intentaba iniciar una revolución. Abuela María dijo que se lo merecía por ir a un país pacífico a tratar de crear problemas* (p. 72). (One of Cuba's Communist leaders was killed in Bolivia where he was trying to start a revolution. Abuela María said it served him right for going to a peaceful country and trying to make trouble.) Yara also describes her pain in adjusting to her new life in Miami where she has problems with the English language, new classmates and social/cultural differences. More revealing are her father's *macho* attitudes regarding his wife and daughters while he participates in a militant anti-Castro organization in his eagerness to return to Cuba. This first-person account will be particularly touching to readers who share the author's political views. Most readers, however, will want to ignore the suggested reading guide at the end.

Verne, Jules. *Cinco semanas en globo. (Five Weeks in a Balloon)* 303p. Illus: Gabriel Hernández. Translated by Juana Salabert. ISBN: 84-667-4702-8.

———. *Miguel Strogoff. (Michael Strogoff)* 367p. Illus: Raúl R. Allén. Translated by Iñigo Valverde Mordt. ISBN: 84-667-4704-4.

———. *Viaje al centro de la Tierra. (Journey to the Center of the Earth)* 292p. Illus: Pere Ginard. Translated by María del Rosario Arocena. ISBN: 84-667-4701-X.

———. *La vuelta al mundo en 80 días. (Around the World in 80 Days)* 284p. Illus: Pablo Torrecilla. Translated by Javier Torrente Malvido. ISBN: 84-667-4703-6.

Ea. vol.: Madrid: Anaya, 2005. $18.95. Gr. 7–adult.

Novels by Jules Verne are perennial favorites of Spanish-speaking adolescents. Hence, these splendid Spanish renditions with appealing covers, full color illustrations, notes, brief introductions and stimulating afterwords are sure to continue their long-standing allure. The intrepid adventures of *doctor* Samuel Fergusson, his friend Dick and his servant Joe in a balloon across Africa are narrated in *Cinco semanas en globo.* (This title is also known in English as *Journeys and Discoveries in Africa by Three Englishmen.*) Set in Russia in 1876, *Miguel Strogoff* includes a sinister plot, political intrigues, dangerous missions and a satisfying conclusion. The travels of Axel and his uncle *profesor* Lidenbrock to explore the Earth's interior by way of a secret passage through an Icelandic volcano are imaginatively told in *Viaje al centro de la Tierra.* In 1872, an English gentleman Phineas Fogg has pledged his fortune to win a bet that he can travel around the world in eighty days, thrillingly depicted in *La vuelta al mundo en 80 días.*

Verne, Jules. *La esfinge de los hielos.* (*The Sphinx of the Ice Fields*) (Tus Libros Selección) Translated by Javier Torrente. Madrid: Anaya, 2005. 431p. ISBN: 84-667-4725-7. pap. $11.95. Gr. 8–adult.

Published in English as *An Antarctic Mystery*, this novel includes a summary of Edgar Allan Poe's *The Narrative of Arthur Gordon Pym*, which Verne always admired. With a brief introduction about the author, extensive footnotes and sidebars and an appendix, this polished Spanish rendition tells about *capitán* Len Guy's voyage to the South Pole in search of his missing brother. Spanish-speaking adolescents never tire of Len Guy's exciting adventures in the Antarctic Ocean and his discovery of the frozen secret of the sphinx.

Verne, Jules. *Miguel Strogoff. (Michael Strogoff)* 416p. Translated by Iñigo Valverde Mordt. ISBN: 84-206-5922-3.
———. *Los quinientos millones de la Begun. (The Begum's Millions)* 207p. Translated by Miguel Salabert. ISBN: 84-206-5923-1.
Ea. vol.: Illus: Ángel Uriarte. (Biblioteca Juvenil) Madrid: Alianza, 2005. pap. $10.95. Gr. 9–adult.

Jules Verne's novels, which are some of the most widely read and longtime favorites of Spanish-speaking adolescents, continue to be included in series, especially for teens. In handy paperback formats with numerous black-and-white illustrations, these are indeed fluid Spanish renditions. Set in Russia during the reign of the Czar Alexander II, *Miguel Strogoff* is the classic adventure story in which a brave, intrepid, courteous and steadfast courier is able to accomplish his mission in Siberia and defeat the treacherous Ogareff. The contrasts between good and evil and the uses of technology for potential destruction are powerfully depicted through two scientists, kindhearted French doctor Sarrasin and strong-willed German professor, Herr Schultze, in *Los quinientos millones de la Begun*.

Verne, Jules. *Miguel Strogoff. (Michael Strogoff)* 366p. Translated by Iñigo Valverde Mordt. ISBN: 84-667-3981-5.
Wells, Herbert George. *La guerra de los mundos. (The War of the Worlds)* 248p. Translated by Ramiro de Maeztu. ISBN: 84-667-3980-7.
Ea. vol.: Illus: Enrique Flores. (Tus Libros Selección) Madrid: Grupo Anaya, 2004. pap. $12.95. Gr. 9–adult.

Like the previous twenty titles of this series, especially prepared for adolescents, these are exquisite Spanish renditions of two well-known works. Set in Russia in 1876, Jules Verne's *Miguel Strogoff* is a fascinating tale of intrigue in which only one of the Czar's couriers is qualified to handle an arduous and perilous mission to warn the Siberian Governor of an impending invasion. Wells's acclaimed science-fiction novel, *La guerra de los mundos*, first published in 1898, details twelve days in which invaders from Mars and their terrifying machines invade the Earth. Each title includes a brief introduction about the author, extensive footnotes and sidebars and an appendix noting special characteristics of the novel.

Villar Liébana, Luisa. *Su-Lin, la niña abandonada. (Su-Lin, the Abandoned Girl)* Illus: Jesús Gabán. Madrid: Pearson/Alhambra, 2003. 63p. ISBN: 84-205-4021-8. pap. $6.95. Gr. 4–7.
    Set in China where parents are only allowed to have one child, this simply written story intermingles fantasy with reality to depict the cruel fate of girls. When Suo-Mo gives birth to beautiful Su-Lin, her husband forces her to abandon the child. But Suo-Mo finds a way to raise her daughter away from home. Perhaps the appearance of *Orejitas Blancas*, a gentle white panda bear, is too coincidental, yet readers will identify with the injustices suffered by girls (and women) in many countries around the world. Gabán's ink-and-watercolor illustrations, though melodramatic at times, beautifully depict Chinese customs and celebrations.

White, E. B. *La telaraña de Carlota. (Charlotte's Web)* Illus: Garth Williams. Translated by Guillermo Solana Alonso and Omar Amador. New York: HarperCollins, 2005. 207p. ISBN: 0-06-075739-6. $16.99. Gr. 4–7.
    E. B. White's classic story about the special friendship between a kind and gentle spider, Carlota, and a lovable pig, Wilbur, is now available in this revised, fluid Spanish rendition that Spanish speakers from the Americas will especially enjoy. Garth Williams's original, black-and-white illustrations accompany this 1953 Newbery Honor Book.

White, E. B. *Stuart Little. (Stuart Little)* Illus: Garth Williams. Translated by Héctor Silva Míguez. Miami: Santillana USA, 2004. 142p. ISBN: 1-59437-554-2. pap. $9.95. Gr. 4–6.
    White's beloved tale, first published in 1945, about a two-inch tall boy mouse with a big heart and a love for adventure is now available in the United States in this fluid Spanish rendition that resonates with its original wit, whimsy and intermingling of fantasy and real family life. Especially engaging to Spanish speakers is Míguez's joyous translation, which appropriately maintaines White's rhyming play on words by such substitutes as *gorrión, dragón, ratón* instead of the

English rhyme, "louse," "grouse," "souse." A few Peninsular Spanish pronouns and conjugations (*vuestras, podéis, sabréis*) should not deter Spanish speakers from the Americas from enjoying Stuart Little's delightful escapades as he sets out to search for his dear friend Margalo, a little bird who is scared away by the family's mean cat.

Winter, Jeanette. *La bibliotecaria de Basora: Una historia real de Iraq. (The Librarian of Basra: A True Story from Iraq)* Illus: the author. Translated by Elodie Bourgeois and Teresa Farran. Barcelona: Juventud, 2007. ISBN: 978-84-261-3582-7. $19.99. Gr. 3–5.

With the power and immediacy of the original English edition, this spare Spanish rendition tells about Alia Muhammad Baker, the librarian of Basra who feels that books *son más valiosos que todo el oro del mundo* (are more precious than mountains of gold) and her struggle to save most of the library books from *la bestia de la guerra* (the beast of the war). Winter's radiant folk-art style illustrations present the tragedy of the destruction in Basra with sensitivity and great subtlety. Spanish speakers will note that neither in the Author's Note nor in the text is the United States mentioned; only Iraqi people discuss their fears about *la guerra* (the war).

Woolf, Virginia. *La señora Dalloway. (Mrs. Dalloway)* Translated by José Luis López Muñoz. Madrid: Alianza, 2003. 218p. ISBN: 84-206-5528-7. pap. $11.95. Gr. 9–adult.

Maintaining the vividness and directness of Woolf's account of one day in the life of Clarissa Dalloway, this smooth Spanish rendition is as intricate and moving as the original. Sophisticated Spanish-speaking adolescents will enjoy the details of Clarissa's preparations for an evening party as these mingle with her hidden thoughts, friends from the past and her feelings regarding society's overwhelming demands.

Graphic Novels

Abel, Jessica. *La perdida. (La Perdida)* Translated by Ernesto Priego. Barcelona: Astiberri/Distributed by Public Square Books, 2006. 270p. ISBN: 978-1-59497-367-3. $34.95. Gr. 10–adult.

When young Carla Olivares, a half Mexican American, goes to Mexico City to find her roots, she expects to find herself, learn Spanish and get to see the "real" Mexico. Her misadventures and naiveté lead her to an American ex-boyfriend and from there to a group of pseudo-intellectual malefactors involved in drugs, petty crimes and kidnapping who don't hesitate to beat her and slap her around. It is interesting to note that Priego's fluid Spanish rendition, full of Mexican vulgarities and obscene expressions, uses Peninsular Spanish pronouns and conjugations, which sound strange in a graphic novel set in Mexico City. Especially well realized, and much more authentic, is Abel's powerful artwork that depicts the ambience and people of Mexico City with a strong sense of realism rarely portrayed in graphic novels published outside of Mexico. Mature Spanish-speaking adolescents will enjoy the suspense and Spanish learners unfamiliar with Mexico City will appreciate the extensive glossary.

Atangan, Patrick. *El jarrón amarillo: Dos relatos de la tradición japonesa. Vol. I. (The Yellow Jar: Two Tales from Japanese Tradition. Vol. I)* Translated by Carles M. Miralles. ISBN: 84-8431-748-X.

———. *El tapiz de seda y otras leyendas chinas: Canciones de nuestros ancestros. Vol. 2. (The Silk Tapestry and Other Chinese Folktales. Vol. 2).* Translated by Carles Muñoz. ISBN: 84-96415-51-1.

Ea. vol.: 48p. Illus: the author. Barcelona: Norma Editorial/Distributed by Public Square Books, 2003–2004. $22.95. Gr. 4–7.

In an appealing comic-book format, these vigorous Spanish renditions depict the magic, culture and ancient beliefs of Asian traditions. With the striking earth-tone colors and Japanese-style woodblock art, *El jarrón amarillo: Dos relatos de la tradición japonesa. Vol. I* tells about a simple fisherman who finds a beautiful maiden, in a big yellow pot, followed by a tale about a meticulous monk who is surprised to find two chrysanthemums in his spectacular garden. Three Chinese tales about the struggle of artists to save the world are included in *El tapiz de seda y otras leyendas chinas: Canciones de nuestros ancestros. Vol. 2.* A few Peninsular Spanish conjugations (*habéis, os hayáis, perdonadnos*) should not deter Spanish speakers from the Americas from enjoying Atangan's well-conceived graphic adaptations of Japanese and Chinese time-honored accounts.

Delisle, Guy. *Pyongyang. (Pyongyang: A Journey in North Korea)* Illus: the author. Translated by Laureano Domínguez. Bilbao: Astiberri/Distributed by Public Square Books, 2006. 176p. ISBN: 1-59497-296-6. pap. $29.95. Gr. 9–adult.

Delisle's simple and revealing cartoons in various shades of gray combined with Domínguez's fresh Spanish rendition provide an inside view of the incongruous, totalitarian regime in North Korea. Intermingling facts, irony and deadpan anecdotes, this graphic novel depicts the paranoia, absolute control, propaganda and ubiquitous indoctrination that permeate this closed society. Despite a few expletives, Spanish-speaking adolescents will realize how this highly regimented society has affected its children and resulted in *pequeños monos amaestrados* (young trained monkeys).

Eisner, Will. *La conspiración: La historia secreta de los protocolos de los sabios de Sión. (The Plot: The Secret Story of the Protocols of the Elders of Zion)* Barcelona: Norma Editorial/Distributed by Public Square, 2005. 150p. ISBN: 1-59497-145-5. pap. $24.95. Gr. 10–adult.

Using the power and simplicity of the graphic-novel format, Eisner presents, through expressive ink-wash drawings, the plagiarisms and fabrications behind *Los protocolos de los sabios de Sión (The Protocols of the Elders of Zion)*, a widely circulated anti-semitic 19th-century essay. Accepted as a Jewish political conspiracy by Czar Nicolas II, Henry Ford, Adolf Hitler and other hate groups, this vigorous Spanish rendition confronts the baseless propaganda behind the unfounded Jewish international plot. Despite long, detailed passages and comparisons, Eisner's last work may appeal to Spanish-speaking adolescents as an example of bigoted political propaganda and opinionated disinformation.

Eisner, Will. *Fagin el judío (Fagin, the Jew)* Illus: the author. Translated by Enrique S. Abulí. Barcelona: Norma Editorial/Distributed by Public Square Books, 2004. 128p. ISBN: 1-59497-090-4. pap. $23.95. Gr. 9–adult.

Eisner's graphic novel interpretation of Fagin, the trainer of young thieves from Dickens's Oliver Twist, is available in this accessible Spanish rendition with the original sepia tone drawings. Reluctant readers will be attracted by the powerful depictions of life in 19th-century London, where street crime, fights and constant abuse predominate. Mature readers will be interested in the prologue and afterword in which Eisner explains his views on ethnic stereotypes as well as Dickens's perspectives on Jewish people. Despite a few risqué scenes and innuendos and a heavy dose of melodrama with well-timed coincidences, mature Spanish-speaking adolescents will be intrigued by this view of Fagin, the mean troublemaker, who is now portrayed as a product of prejudice and poverty and a most unjust fate.

Fontes, Justine, and Ron Fontes. *El caballo de Troya: La caída de Troya: Un mito griego. (The Trojan Horse: The Fall of Troy: A Greek Myth)* Illus: Gordon Purcell and Barbara Schulz. ISBN: 978-0-8225-7970-0.

Limke, Jeff. *Isis y Osiris, hasta el fin del mundo: Un mito egipcio. (Isis and Osiris, to the Ends of the Earth: An Egyptian Myth)* Illus: David Witt. ISBN: 978-0-8225-7971-7.

――――. *El Rey Arturo: La espada Excalibur desenvainada: Una leyenda inglesa. (King Arthur, Excalibur Unsheathed: An English Legend)* Illus: Thomas Yeates. ISBN: 978-0-8225-7968-7.

――――. *Thor y Loki en la tierra de los gigantes: Un mito escandinavo. (Thor and Loki in the Land of the Giants: A Norse Myth)* Illus: Ron Randall. ISBN: 978-0-8225-7969-4.

Storrie, Paul D. *Hércules, los doce trabajos: Un mito griego. (Hércules, the Twelve Labors: A Greek Myth)* Illus: Steve Kurth and Barbara Schulz. ISBN: 978-0-8225-7967-0.

Ea. vol.: 48p. Translated by translations.com. (Mitos y Leyendas en Viñetas) Minneapolis: Lerner, 2008. pap. $8.95. Gr. 4–8.

With fast-action, colorful cartoon graphics and the look of comic books, this Mitos y Leyendas en Viñetas series, now available in a fluid most accessible Spanish rendition, introduces some of the world's best known myths and legends. These are not for purists nor for serious students of ancient tales; rather, these may appeal to reluctant Spanish-speaking readers who will prefer the contemporary language, cartoon-like embellishments and supernatural feats. Each title includes a glossary, additional English-language readings and Web sites. The ancient Greek legend about the hollow wooden horse in which the Greeks hid and gained entrance to Troy, later opening the gates to their army, is retold in *El caballo de Troya: La caída de Troya: Un mito griego*. The ancient Egyptian goddess Isis's efforts to save the throne of her husband, Osiris, from his jealous brother are depicted in *Isis y Osiris, hasta el fin del mundo: Un mito egipcio*. Although England is in trouble, young Arthur pulls the mysterious sword in the stone and wins the loyalty of *los Caballeros de la Mesa Redonda* (the Knights of the Round Table) in *El Rey Arturo: La espada Excalibur desenvainada: Una leyenda inglesa*. Thor, powerful god of thunder, and his brother Loki travel to *la tierra de los gigantes* (land of giants) to determine whether strength or brains win in the Norse myth as narrated in *Thor y Loki en la tierra de los gigantes: Un mito escandinavo.* Hercules, the son of Zeus and a mortal mother, is a hero of extraordinary strength who won immortality by performing twelve seemingly impossible labors as retold in *Hércules, los doce trabajos: Un mito griego.*

Gaiman, Neil. *El día que cambié a mi padre por dos peces de colores. (The Day I Swapped My Dad for Two Goldfish)* Illus: Dave McKean. Translated by Ernest Riera. Barcelona: Norma Editorial/Distributed by Public Square Books, 2003. 54p. ISBN: 1-59497-076-9. $34.95. Gr. 2–4.

In an understated and matter-of-fact manner, a young narrator tells what happened the day he swapped his dad for his friend's two goldfish. He is delighted with his fish until mama comes home and threatens him to get his father back and not to return without him. Thus begins a hilarious search in which these boys swap the dad for an electric guitar, a gorilla mask and a white rabbit. And, of course, papa is still reading the newspaper, oblivious to all the excitement. Upon returning home, mama has the boy promise he would never swap dad again . . . although he never promises anything about his pesky younger sister. McKean's expressive cartoons and colorful collage artwork maintain the avant-garde bittersweet tone of the original. Despite a few Peninsular Spanish pronouns and conjugations, Spanish speakers from the Americas will certainly smile and enjoy.

Jaraba, Fran. *Campos de Cuba. (Cuba's Countryside)* Illus: the author. Vigo: Xerais, 2004. 55p. ISBN: 84-9782-184-X. pap. $14.95. Gr. 9–adult.

Set in rural Cuba in 1897 during the struggle for Cuba's independence against the powerful Spanish army, Jaraba's graphic novel rendition highlights the exploits of Maxi Torres, a fictional self-described dropout, poet and fool who deserts from the Spanish forces. After capture by his former *compañeros,* he is assisted by his courageous girlfriend, Marina, who suffers the abuse of violent ruffians. The attention-grabbing, full-color visuals (with some mature scenes) make this wildly romantic war story about dashing heroes and cruel villains just right for reluctant readers of historical fiction. A simply written four-page introduction with black-and-white photos provides an overview to Cuba's war of independence from Spain, the United States's intervention and the role of the *mambises* (Cuban guerrilla fighters) in harassing and undermining the Spanish army. Some adults will object to the sexual violence; others to a few extravagant, nonstandard Spanish expressions.

Nonetheless, this may be the only way to engage some Spanish-speaking adolescents to read a book with one continuous plot, albeit with dialogue in bubbles and narrative captions.

Juan, Ana and others. . . . *De ellas.* (. . . *About Her)* Murcia, Spain: Instituto de la Mujer, 2006. 110p. ISBN: 84-89929-84-X. $25.95. Gr. 10–adult.

With a great sense of irony and candor, thirteen female graphic artists, mostly from the Spanish-speaking world, depict their own vision of human relationships, injustice and daily life to celebrate women and girls. Striking dramatic black-and-white visuals and forceful texts make this large-format collection of comic-style vignettes a profoundly moving experience. Although some adults will object to the risqué content and illustrations of several selections—such as María Alcobre's (Argentina) depiction of the *innombrable* (unspeakable) alluding to girls' discussing menstruation; Victoria Martos's (Spain) tribute to Yoko Ono's talents and strength; Cintia Bolio's (Mexico) scathing view of the role of mothers and women and Nicole Schulman's (United States) personal experiences with breast cancer—mature Spanish-speaking adolescents will appreciate their outspokenness and will not mind the at times provocative themes, laced with extravagant words and expressions.

Kaufman, Ruth. *Gritar los goles. (Shouting Goals)* Illus: Pablo Sapia. Buenos Aires: Pequeño Editor, 2003. 20p. ISBN: 987-20847-1-8. pap. $6.95. Gr. 3–6.

Graphic novels and the thrill and excitement of a soccer match are a good combination, especially when a thin, almost wimpy uncle invites his two young nephews to a soccer game. In the first story, as the uncle tries to teach his nephews to shout *¡GOOOOL!,* a big bully decides he can do a better job. After repeated instructions, the boys are ready to shout *¡GOOOL!,* which they do at exactly the wrong time. In the second story, one of the boys needs to urinate. To avoid missing the game, the uncle hands him a beer can to use. As they all celebrate a *¡GOOOOOOL!,* the big bully takes away the beer can, drinks most of its contents, questions the "warm beer" and commands the scared uncle to finish it. Written in the vernacular of Argentina, these witty stories accurately depict the ambiance of Latin American soccer matches that soccer fans enjoy. Sapia's expressive computer-generated cartoons are as exaggerated as the passion of soccer fans. Young soccer fans will not mind the small size—6" × 6½"—of this graphic novel.

Kubert, Joe. *Yossel: 19 de abril de 1943: Historia de la sublevación del gueto de Varsovia. (Yossel: April 19, 1943: A Story of the Warsaw Ghetto Uprising)* Translated by Enrique S. Abulí. Barcelona: Norma Editorial/Public Square Books, 2004. ISBN: 1594970912. $25.95. Gr. 9–adult.

Kubert's dramatic black pencil sketches depict the poignancy and horror of life in the Warsaw ghetto and the increasingly barbaric treatment that led to the uprising through the life of fifteen-year-old Yossel and his family. Abulí's stirring Spanish rendition, which accompanies the powerful artwork in well-placed captions, maintains the immediacy and significance of the tragic events that occurred in Nazi-occupied Poland during World War II. Some adults may be repelled by the shocking vividness and escalating barbarism portrayed, but the graphic novel format is sure to compel Spanish-speaking adolescents to question and reflect.

Sacco, Joe. *El rock y yo. (Rock and Me)* Illus: the author. Translated by Joe Sacco. Barcelona: La Cúpula, 2006. 88p. ISBN: 84-7833-700-8/ Distributed by Public Square Books. ISBN: 978-1-59497-298-0. pap. $17.95. Gr. 10–adult.

Cartoonist Joe Sacco describes his passion for the world of rock-'n'roll in this compilation that includes some of his early works as well as examples of his powerful rock posters. In addition to his biting depiction of punk bands, groupies, triumphant stars and sexy women, Spanish-speaking rock fans will enjoy his brief introductions and sarcastic notes, which, he explains, are a result of his *atentas e inteligentes investigaciones* (thorough and intelligent research). Some Spanish speakers from the Americas will object to the Peninsular Spanish pronouns and conjugations (e.g., *vuestras, acordáis*), others will object to numerous slang terms and vulgar expressions, others to the risqué cartoons, yet Sacco's humor and irrevence toward popular musicians and the music industry are most appealing in this fluid Spanish rendition.

Sacco, Joe. *Palestina en la Franja de Gaza. (Palestine: In the Gaza Strip)* Translated by Roberto Rodríguez. Barcelona: Planeta DeAgostini/ Distributed by Public Square Books, 2004. 286p. ISBN: 1-59497-182-X. $28.95. Gr. 9–adult.

With a thoughtful and most informative introduction by the eminent historian and scholar Edward Said about the Palestinian people, Rodriguez's compelling Spanish rendition is as insightful and perceptive as the original. Sacco's detailed black-and-white graphics, full of imagery and action, provide a firsthand view into the lives of Palestinian refugees, prisoners, children and farmers as well as the Israeli soldiers who control the West Bank and Gaza strip. Serious Spanish-speaking students interested in understanding the complexities of the Israeli/Palestinian conflict will find much to ponder.

Satrapi, Marjane. *Persépolis 1 (Persepolis: The Story of a Childhood, Part I)* 76p. ISBN: 1-59497-035-1.
———. *Persépolis 2. (Persepolis: The Story of a Childhood, Part II)* 84p. ISBN: 1-59497-036-X.
———. *Persépolis 3. (Persepolis: The Story of a Return, Part I)* 84p. ISBN: 1-59497-037-8.
———. *Persépolis 4. (Persepolis: The Story of a Return, Part II)* 100p. ISBN: 1-59497-096-3.
Ea. vol: Illus: the author. Translated by Albert Agut. Barcelona: Norma Editorial/Distributed by Public Square Books, 2004. pap. $22.95. Gr. 9–adult.

Just as successful in Spanish-speaking countries as in the rest of the world, Agut's Spanish rendition of Satrapi's powerful graphic autobiography resonates with the spirit of Teheran in this candid portrait of Iran's recent political turmoil. As opposed to U.S. editions, which were published in two volumes, these are available in four volumes. Despite a few Peninsular Spanish pronouns and conjugations, Spanish speakers from the Americas will be engrossed by Satrapi's compelling black-and-white bold artwork and poignant honesty. *Persépolis 1* depicts her life in Iran in 1980 from the perspective of a ten-year-old girl who tries to make sense of *la revolución islámica* (the Islamic revolution) up to the outbreak of the Iran-Iraq War. *Persépolis 2* relates the feelings of a rebellious adolescent who questions the totalitarianism of the Ayatollah Khomeini's regime up to her parents' decision to send her to Austria. *Persépolis 3* details her difficult life in Vienna from age 14 where she experienced sexual relationships, prejudice, drugs and homelessness up to age 18 when she decides to return home to Iran. *Persépolis 4* narrates her life in a repressive Teheran where she eventually marries a selfish art student, divorces and, with her parents' support, prepares to go to France. This graphic memoir is certainly not for purists, but Spanish-speaking adolescents will not be able to put down or forget Satrapi's provocative, personal, and, at times humorous, depiction of life before and after the Islamic revolution.

Satrapi, Marjane. *Pollo con ciruelas. (Chicken with Plums)* Translated by
Manel Domínguez. Barcelona: Norma Editorial/Distributed by Public
Square Books, 2006. 86p. ISBN: 978-1-59497-181-5. pap. $22.95. Gr.
10–adult.

Like her much-lauded *Persépolis 1–4*, Spanish-speaking fans of
the graphic novelist Satrapi will be engrossed with this poignant Spanish rendition that tells about the last eight days in the life of her great-
uncle Nasser Ali Khan, one of Iran's most celebrated musicians. Although some adults will find many reasons to object—vulgar
expressions, opium smoking, eroticized images of Sophia Loren—and
others will note the Peninsular Spanish conjugations, Satrapi's always-
expressive boxy black-and-white artwork brings to life Iran in the
1950s through the troubled family relationships of a great musician.
Mature adolescents will certainly understand.

Sauré, Jean-François. *Un bus en Alabama. (A Bus in Alabama)* Illus: Sandra García Ruíz. Madrid: Saure, 2006. 32p. ISBN: 84-95225-01-8.
$20.95. Gr. 8–adult.

Bold, bright and often somber and dark color graphics provide a
compelling background to the fight for civil rights of African Americans in the United States. Beginning with the inhumane treatment of
Africans in slave ships, to discrimination in schools and the military, to
the Ku Klux Klan, Rosa Parks, Martin Luther King Jr. and President
Kennedy, this large-format publication was awarded the III Fernando
Buesa Peace Prize in Spain. This is not a detailed historical overview;
rather, it is an emotional appeal in support of fundamental individual
rights and equality between black and white people. The concise simple text and visual story-telling format make its message even more
convincing.

Smith, Jeff. *Bone, Lejos de Boneville. (Bone, Vol. I: Out from Boneville).*
Translated by Enrique S. Abulí. Bilbao: Astiberri/Distributed by Public
Square Books, 2006. 142p. ISBN: 978-1-59497-297-3. $24.95. Gr. 5–12.

This first volume of the popular graphic novel fantasy featuring
the three Bone cousins—spunky Fone, greedy Phoney, and carefree
Smiley—in their struggle against power and evil is as humorous and as
adventure-filled as the original. Abulí's engaging Spanish rendition is a
perfect complement to the classic comic art depicting three blobby creatures who end up in a valley full of magic, monsters, a sweet princess,
an amazingly handy *abuela* and a colossal, dependable *dragón*. Despite

the Peninsular Spanish conjugations (*haced, queráis*), Spanish speakers from the Americas certainly enjoy graphic novels, especially those that are as action-packed, witty and satisfying as this one.

Spiegelman, Art. *Sin la sombra de las torres. (In the Shadow of No Towers)* Translated by María Ferrer. New York: Norma/Public Square Books, 2004. 42p. ISBN: 84-96370-38-0. $36.95. Gr. 9–adult.

Spiegelman's powerfully fervent depiction of the events of 9/11 are just as compelling in this cogent Spanish rendition with his original comic strips that have mesmerized Spanish speakers worldwide. Although some readers may disagree with his strongly felt political beliefs and his negative portrayal of the Bush administration who *los trágicos acontecimientos . . . mientras me distraéis con esa guerra vuestra del petróleo* (have since hijacked the tragic events . . . while distracting me with your damn oil war), Spiegelman's artistry is definitely conveyed in this oversize cardboard book that also includes political comic strips of the early 20th century. Despite the Peninsular Spanish pronouns and conjugations, Spanish speakers around the world have empathized with this *cosmopolita "arraigado"* ("rooted" cosmopolitan).

Appendix

Dealers of Books in Spanish
for Children and Young Adults

ARGENTINA
 Librería García Cambeiro
 LatBook
 Cochabamba 244
 C1150AAB Buenos Aires, Argentina
 Tel.: (54-11) 4300-2797
 Fax: (54-11) 4307-2735
     U.S. Address:
     P.O. Box 591286
     Miami, FL 33159-1286
 Website: www.latbook.com
 E-mail: cambeiro@latbook.com.ar

CENTRAL AMERICA
 Vientos Tropicales
 4823 Meadow Dr., Ste. 114
 Durham, NC 27713-9208
 Tel.: (919) 361-0997; (800) 334-4993
 Fax: (919) 361-2597
 Website: www.vientos.com
 E-mail: vientos@vnet.net

CHILE
 Herta Berenguer L. Publicaciones
 Correo 9, Casilla 16598
 Santiago, Chile
 Tel./Fax: (562) 231-7145

U.S. Address:
EXP#1106
P.O. Box 025285
Miami, FL 33102-5285

COLOMBIA
Libros de Colombia
Apartado Aereo, 12053
Bogotá, Colombia
Tel.: (571) 612-9430
Fax: (571) 619-3897
E-mail: libcojnh@colomsat.net.co

Editorial Norma
P.O. Box 195040
San Juan, Puerto Rico 00919-5040
Tel.: (787) 788-5050
Fax: (787) 788-7161
Website: www.norma.com
E-mail: ulises.roldan@normausa.com

COSTA RICA
Editorial Costa Rica
Edificio Central Apartado 10010
1000 San José, Costa Rica
Tel.: (506) 253-5354
Fax: (506) 253-5091
Website: editorialcostarica.com
E-mail: ventas@editorialcostarica.com

MEXICO
Librerías Gandhi para Niños y Jóvenes
Miguel Ángel de Quevedo, 134
Col. Chimalistac
01050 México D.F., México
Tel.: 011 (555) 095-2540
Fax: 011 (555) 095-2542
Website: www.ghandi.com.mx
E-mail: gandhi@mail.internet.com.mx

PERU
   E Iturriaga y Cia. S.A.C.
   Libros y Revistas Recientes Editadas en el Peru
   Casilla, 180721
   Lima 18, Perú
   Tel.: (511) 428-1979
   Fax: (511) 426-2642
   E-mail: perubooks@computextos.com.pe

SPAIN
   Tiendas Crisol
   Juan Bravo, 38
   28006 Madrid, Spain
   Tel.: (3491) 423-8283
   Fax: (3491) 423-8288
   Website: www.crisol.es
   E-mail: menendez@crisol.es

UNITED STATES
   Brodart
   500 Arch Street
   Williamsport, PA 17701
   Tel.: (800) 233-8467
   Fax: (570)-326-1479
   Website: www.brodart.com
   E-mail: support@brodart.com

   Lectorum Publications, Inc.
   524 Broadway
   New York, NY 10012
   Tel.: (800) 345-5946; (212) 929-2833
   Fax: (877) 532-8676 (toll free)
   Website: www.lectorum.com
   E-mail: lectorum@scholastic.com

URUGUAY
   Librería Linardi y Risso
   Juan Carlos Gómez, 1435
   11.000 Montevideo, Uruguay
   Tel.: 011 (598-2) 915-7129; 011 (598-2) 915-7328

Fax: 011 (598-2) 915-7431
   U.S. Address:
   8424 NW 56th St.
   Suite MVD 82830
   Miami, FL 33166
Website: www.chasque.apc.org/lyrbooks
E-mail: libros@linardiyrisso.com

VENEZUELA
   Ediciones Ekaré
   Av. Luis Roche, Edif. Banco del Libro
   Altamira Sur
   1062 Caracas, Venezuela
   Tel.: 58-212 264 7615/58-212-264-1421
   Fax: 58-212 263 3291
   Website: www.ekare.com
   E-mail: books@ekare.com.ve

Author Index

(including coauthors and editors)

Title Index

Subject Index

About the Author

Dr. Isabel Schon was born in Mexico City. She came to the United States in 1972, where she obtained a doctorate in philosophy from the University of Colorado in 1974.

She has received several national and international awards, including the 2006 Distinguished Alumni Achievement Award from Minnesota State University, Mankato, for "professional success and the positive impact made to the profession and the community"; the 2005 Dorothy C. McKenzie Award for Distinguished Contribution to the Field of Children's Literature presented by the Children's Literature Council of Southern California; the 1992 U.S. Role Model in Education Award presented by the U.S.–México Foundation; the 1992 Denali Press Award from the Reference and Adult Services Division of the American Library Association for "achievement in creating reference works that are outstanding in quality and significance and provide information specifically about ethnic and minority groups in the U.S."; the 1987 Women's National Book Award, "One of 70 women who have made a difference in the world of books"; the 1986 American Library Association's Grolier Foundation Award for "unique and invaluable contributions to the stimulation and guidance of reading by children and young people"; and the 1979 Herbert W. Putnam Honor Award presented by the American Library Association, "to study the effects of books on students' perceptions of Mexican American people."

She is the author of twenty-four books and more than four hundred research and literary articles in the areas of biliteracy/multicultural education and literature for Latino children and adolescents.

Dr. Schon has been a consultant on bilingual/bicultural educational materials to schools, libraries, and ministries of education in Mexico, Colombia,

Guatemala, Argentina, Venezuela, Chile, Spain, Italy, Ecuador, and the United States.

From 1989 to 2008 she was founding director of the Barahona Center for the Study of Books in Spanish for Children and Adolescents and a professor and founding faculty at California State University San Marcos.

Currently, she is director of the Isabel Schon International Center for Spanish Books for Youth, San Diego Public Library, San Diego, California.